The Nazi Mind

The Nazi Mind

Twelve Warnings from History

LAURENCE REES

PENGUIN
VIKING

VIKING

UK | USA | Canada | Ireland | Australia
India | New Zealand | South Africa

Viking is part of the Penguin Random House group of companies
whose addresses can be found at global.penguinrandomhouse.com

Penguin Random House UK,
One Embassy Gardens, 8 Viaduct Gardens, London SW11 7BW

penguin.co.uk

First published 2025

003

Set in 12/14.75 pt Bembo Book MT Pro
Typeset by Jouve (UK), Milton Keynes

Printed and bound in Great Britain by Clays Ltd, Elcograf S.p.A.

The authorized representative in the EEA is Penguin Random House Ireland,
Morrison Chambers, 32 Nassau Street, Dublin D02 YH68

A CIP catalogue record for this book is available from the British Library

ISBN: 978-0-241-74081-1

To Oliver

Contents

Prologue   I

Introduction   3

1. Spreading Conspiracy Theories   11
2. Using Them and Us   37
3. Leading as a Hero   61
4. Corrupting Youth   85
5. Conniving with the Elite   101
6. Attacking Human Rights   127
7. Exploiting Faith   154
8. Valuing Enemies   181
9. Eliminating Resistance   209
10. Escalating Racism   234
11. Killing at a Distance   254
12. Stoking Fear   283

Postscript   315

Twelve Warnings   331

Acknowledgements   341

Notes   343

Index   405

List of Illustrations

1. A crowd in Munich celebrates Germany's entry into the First World War
2. German soldiers killed during the First Battle of the Marne
3. Adolf Hitler as a soldier
4. Hermann Göring
5. An artillery shell lands on a German gun crew
6. Ernst Röhm
7. Paul von Hindenburg with Erich Ludendorff
8. German revolutionaries drive past the Brandenburg Gate
9. The Freikorps Werdenfels march in Munich
10. Heinrich Himmler
11. Joseph Goebbels
12. Adolf Hitler in Landsberg prison
13. Hitler's comfortable prison conditions
14. A motley crew of Nazis in the early 1920s
15. Hitler addresses a meeting of Nazis in 1925
16. Members of the Hitler Youth on the back of a lorry
17. Members of the BDM
18. High jinks at a gymnastics and sports festival
19. Election posters in Berlin
20. The aristocratic German elite
21. Hitler gives an election speech
22. Hitler shakes hands with President Hindenburg
23. A poster of Hindenburg and Hitler
24. The burning of the Reichstag
25. Inmates forced to work at Dachau concentration camp
26. A mass protest meeting against Nazi atrocities
27. The Nazi boycott of Jewish businesses
28. Cover of a Nazi calendar showing an idealized family
29. The Nazis criticize the cost of caring for the disabled
30. Hitler drives past cheering crowds in Vienna
31. A group of Jews are forced to scrub the streets clean

32. Hitler visits German troops in Poland

33. The Nazi occupation of Poland

34. General Johannes Blaskowitz

35. Georg Elser

36. Hitler promotes his leading generals

37. Horst Schumann

38. Irmfried Eberl

39. A group of civilians murdered by a mobile killing squad

40. Nazi propaganda film *Jud Süss*

41. *Münchhausen*, a Nazi entertainment film

42. Clemens von Galen, Bishop of Münster

43. Hitler's reaction to Galen's protest

44. Göring, Goebbels, Himmler and Martin Bormann

45. Jewish arrivals at Auschwitz Birkenau

46. A group of Nazi personnel from Auschwitz

47. Two elderly German men in the rubble of Berlin

48. A mass grave at Bergen-Belsen concentration camp

Prologue

Until 1933 it was a very nice comfortable life. But once Hitler came to power, the children that lived in the same building no longer spoke to us; they threw stones at us and called us names. And we couldn't understand what we had done to deserve this. So the question was always – why?[1]

Lucille Eichengreen, a member of a Jewish family in Hamburg – transported to Auschwitz in 1944

I had a very Catholic upbringing, and it did not enter my head that something evil [like this] could happen . . . It was beyond our life experience . . . After the experiences I had in the camp there are no values . . . This tormented me desperately, to the brink of suicide.[2]

Mieczysław Brożek, an assistant professor at Jagiellonian University in Kraków, transported to Dachau concentration camp in 1940

We had dogs at our house, but we never were as cruel to them as the fascists were to us . . . I was thinking all the time, 'What makes these people so cruel?'[3]

Vasyl Valdeman, a Ukrainian Jew, who in 1941 witnessed the Nazis taking his fellow villagers to be murdered

Why did the Nazis commit the crimes they did? How was it possible that people from a cultured nation perpetrated the worst atrocities in history?[4] What relevance does this terrible past have for us today? These are the questions this book strives to answer.

But while the focus of this work is on the mentalities of the Nazis, we must never forget the suffering of those they sought to destroy.

Introduction

I first met a former member of the Waffen SS, the Nazis' elite fighting force,[1] while researching a television documentary in Austria in 1990. It was an extraordinary experience.

Not only was he intelligent and amiable – it was easy to understand how, after the war, he had forged a career as a senior executive with a German car company – but I soon discovered over our lunch that while he managed to function extremely successfully in the present, his view of the past was a fantasy: an alternative history in which the Third Reich had been a 'golden era', the war had not been Germany's fault and the Jews had been a 'problem' that had to be dealt with 'one way or another'. His eight years of imprisonment in Stalin's Gulag immediately after the war had made him even more convinced that the Nazis deserved praise for trying to protect Europe from the 'scourge of Bolshevism'. Over coffee he said he had agreed to see me because he admired the British, although he criticized Churchill for making the 'terrible mistake' of not pursuing an alliance with Nazi Germany, because then 'we could have both ruled the world'.

Ever since that lunch I've sought to understand how it was possible for this sophisticated individual to think, long after the end of the war, in the way he did. And in pursuit of that goal, over the intervening years I've met hundreds of other people who experienced the Third Reich.

While I recognize, of course, that it is vital for historians to study archival material, it was the chance to meet those who experienced this history first hand that has most transformed my understanding.[2] This is a privilege that is no longer available to anyone else, since virtually all the people we researched and interviewed over the last thirty years are now dead.[3]

In the 1990s I spent several years working on a television documentary series and book which I called *The Nazis: A Warning from History*. The 'warning' I intended was a general one, inspired by the words of Karl Jaspers, the German philosopher: 'That which has happened is a warning. To forget it is guilt. It must be continually remembered.'[4]

Now, after further study into the mentalities of the Nazis, I believe I can be more specific about the warnings we should take from this history. Consequently, the following twelve chapters don't just examine the reasons why the Nazis developed the mentalities they did, they also each illustrate a particular warning that I think is of value to us today. I then discuss the specific relevance of these different warnings at the end of the book.

I focus on warnings because I don't believe that history has any precise lessons. How often, for instance, do we read on social media that a lesson politicians should take from Nazism is that you shouldn't 'appease' a foreign power? Remember, they say, Winston Churchill warned against appeasing Hitler, and so appeasement is wrong. But history doesn't work like that. While it's true that Churchill didn't appease Hitler, he appeased Stalin a great deal.[5] So what's the lesson here? You can appease some people in some circumstances, but don't appease others in different circumstances?

However, unlike a lesson which is a fixed rule, a warning is only a tendency. Doctors can't say it's a medical lesson that if you smoke you will die early – after all, some smokers live to be a hundred – but they can warn of the dangers of smoking. That is still valuable advice, if not as prescriptive as a lesson.

This history matters. Many democracies are currently under threat and it is useful to be aware of the techniques that would-be tyrants are likely to use to subvert our freedoms. But I'm conscious that this remains a history book, not a piece of political commentary. And that without knowing the history, the warnings can't be fully grasped.

One of the first things I learnt in my studies was that in order to understand why the Nazis possessed the mentalities they did, we must embrace the reality of a fundamental truth: we are all creatures of a particular time and a particular place. That might seem self-evident, but my experience is that many people don't fully appreciate the extent to which they are shaped by time and place.

A film I commissioned and executive-produced back in the early 1990s called *The Stolen Child* dramatically made this point.[6] It was about a Polish child named Alojzy who was snatched from his mother in 1942 when he was four years old. Heinrich Himmler, head of the SS, wanted to kidnap any Polish children who were considered 'racially desirable' and send them to Germany. Alojzy, as part of this inhuman policy, was taken from Poland and adopted by a German couple who were both committed Nazis. He was blissfully happy in his new home and loved his adopted German mother. He had no memory of his early years in Poland.

Alojzy was seven when the war ended, and 'wept' when he heard that Germany had been defeated. A few years later his real mother found him, and he discovered the shocking truth – he was not German but Polish. Alojzy refused to accept it at first – not surprisingly, as he had been brought up to believe that Poles were 'subhuman'. But he was eventually forced to acknowledge that he was not who he thought he was.

Can there be a clearer example of the power of the situation to influence our beliefs? Alojzy's story is all the more salutary given that the majority of the Polish children snatched by the Nazis were never returned to their original homes. How many lived and died believing that they were Germans, and were disappointed that Hitler lost the war?

Alojzy's story also demonstrates the extent to which it's not just the particular time we live in that helps determine our mentality, but the particular place. This reality came home to me most powerfully when I visited two of the most significant places in the world – Jerusalem and Varanasi – and looked at the influence these cities had on Jesus and the Buddha. It soon became clear that the words and actions of these two giants of religion reflected in large part the places in which they happened to live and die. Jesus could not have railed against the money changers in the temple of Jerusalem had this place not been of such significance to him, nor would the Buddha have preached his first sermon at Sarnath, just outside the holy city of Varanasi in India on the River Ganges, had he not understood the spiritual importance of that particular place. I believe it's important to emphasize this kind of linkage because – especially in popular culture – historical figures are frequently ripped from their context.

Occasionally in history the context changes dramatically during one person's lifetime. That was the case with many of the Nazi believers I met. The certainties they were taught in Nazi Germany in the 1930s were destroyed in the aftermath of defeat in 1945. This often caused a fundamental disconnect in their minds. They understood after the war that the world thought Nazism was appalling, but they couldn't accept that they had done anything wrong while the Third Reich flourished.

'If only you'd been there,' they would say, 'you'd understand.' This feeling also led to a few of them peddling the 'we were hypnotized' myth – the idea that they had fallen under Hitler's spell only to awaken when their Führer put a bullet through his head on 30 April 1945.

It was nonsense, of course. No one was mesmerized into becoming a Nazi. Instead, what I think they were struggling to express was the duality within them – the 'me' that was a Nazi and the 'me' that now recognized that the Nazis did terrible things. In that context we need to remember that it was only Germany's defeat that caused this dichotomy. If the Nazis had won the war they would almost certainly still have been believers in the cause.

As our own culture has changed, I've witnessed something similar – albeit on a much smaller scale. Growing up in the 1960s I used to see a lot of my favourite Uncle, who had been born in Scotland in the early 1900s. He was a lovely man, kind and generous, but with a passionate dislike of homosexuality. He often made deeply homophobic comments – words that would rightly see him condemned today. But when he made the remarks homosexual acts were illegal and he was reflecting what many others thought. So, looking back, should I forgive or condemn him? In Cape Town, on a lecture tour, I told this story to one of South Africa's leading historians, and I remember him commenting, 'Since the fall of Apartheid, we've all got an uncle like that here . . .'

In this book, for the first time in my work, I explore how psychology as a discipline can help us understand the mentalities of the Nazis, and aspects of neuropsychology and behavioural and social psychology have all offered me valuable insights. Before talking to academic psychologists and studying relevant scientific papers, I had not been aware of the immense advances that have been made in these areas in recent years.

In particular, the relatively new field of evolutionary psychology has been of considerable value. We sometimes forget that our brains evolved while our ancient predecessors were hunting on the savannah, and insufficient time in evolutionary terms has passed since then to allow much change. Professors Leda Cosmides and John Tooby, two of the pioneers of evolutionary psychology, believe that 'the key to understanding how the modern mind works' is to understand that the circuits of the mind 'were designed to solve the day-to-day problems of our hunter-gatherer ancestors'. If you doubt this, ask yourself why so many people are frightened of snakes when, in most places in the developed world, 'electric sockets pose a larger threat than snakes do'. Yet virtually no one has a phobia about electric sockets.[7]

Recent psychological research into various cognitive biases – such as the 'just world' hypothesis and negative bias – has also been helpful. While circumstances have changed since the time of the Nazis, cognitive biases existed then just as much as they do now.

However, I've approached the use of this material sparingly and with care, always remembering that this is a history book informed on occasion by psychology and not a psychology book informed by history. I don't believe it helps, for example, to try and psychoanalyse leading Nazis at a distance. Anyone tempted to pursue that course should read the lengthy analysis of Hitler written during the war by an American psychoanalyst called Walter Langer for the OSS, the forerunner of the CIA. It was speculation piled on speculation and contained much outright absurdity. Perhaps the most ludicrous suggestion was that Hitler was prompted to build the Eagle's Nest – a tea house high on the Kehlstein, a mountain in Bavaria, reached by a tunnel and lift – by a desire to retreat to the safety of his mother's amniotic fluid. 'If one were asked to plan something which represented a return to the womb,' wrote Langer, 'one could not possibly surpass the Kehlstein.'[8] It was all drivel. The tea house on the Kehlstein wasn't even Hitler's idea. It was the initiative of Martin Bormann, his secretary, and Hitler wasn't fond of the place.[9] He much preferred the Berghof, his home lower down the Obersalzberg, which not even a Freudian psychiatrist could claim resembled a womb.

At least Langer was a contemporary of Hitler's – even though he never met him. Any attempt to psychoanalyse infamous Nazis now, long after their death, is bound to be still more fraught. Such speculation often merely reframes questions about them and can even come close to exonerating them for their crimes. Not just that, but attempts since the war to define a particular Nazi 'type' have been staggeringly unsuccessful.[10]

The idea that there was a specific 'Nazi personality' is exactly the kind of categorical thinking we need to avoid. Just as it was a mistake for behaviourists like John Watson to believe that human beings are infinitely malleable and can be utterly changed by the environment, or for the neurologist Egas Moniz to think that frontal lobotomies were the way to cure 'mental disorders',[11] so it is a mistake to approach this history in a similarly prescriptive way. We need to be careful not to generalize with psychology just as much as we should beware of generalizing in history. It's understandable that many people want to think there is a single explanation for human behaviour – particularly one that explains horrendous crimes – but there never is.

It follows that just as one should approach the study of history with a sense of humility, one should approach the application of psychological research to history in the same spirit. I always keep in mind the words of one of the world's leading neuroscientists, who remarked that 'It's a huge messy process trying to make sense of the biology of human social behaviour.'[12] Myriad factors influence who we are – including our genetic inheritance, our prenatal environment, the socio-economic circumstances of our parents, how much we learnt certain types of behaviour as children, our education and so on. We are all a jumbled mix of our environment and biology.

A few words on the title and content of the book. By 'Nazi Mind' I mean various different Nazi mentalities – not just the beliefs of card-carrying Nazis, but also those of others who supported the regime. Equally, the fact that the focus of this book is on the perpetrators of these terrible crimes should not be misunderstood as an attempt to exonerate them. To understand is not to excuse. Everyone in this book had a choice whether to commit atrocities or not. The scandal is that many of them – after the war was over – were never held properly to account.

The book is largely chronological in structure, which allows us to see how these mentalities developed over time. I feature the experiences of a number of eyewitnesses – chosen because they represent archetypes within the Third Reich – with much of this testimony published here for the first time. This material is interwoven with the story of infamous Nazis such as Himmler, Röhm, Heydrich, Streicher, Göring and, of course, Hitler. I don't attempt to tell the full biographies of these familiar figures but focus instead on the way their mentalities formed.[13] The Nazi propagandist Joseph Goebbels also plays an important part in this history. He was responsible to a large extent for what he called the 'mobilization of mind and spirit' in the 1930s – the attempt to convince all those he considered 'true' Germans to embrace Nazism.[14]

Goebbels has interested me ever since I wrote and produced a film about him more than thirty years ago. I vividly remember interviewing the famous German actress Margot Hielscher about Goebbels in her dressing room before she went on stage in Berlin. Then in her early seventies, she talked about the extent to which he had dominated the German film industry. But it was an almost throwaway remark she made that has stayed with me the most. She said she had never met a 'politician' who was as 'charming' as he was, and she compared him favourably to 'some of the big movie stars'.[15] Goebbels was a 'politician' who had 'charm'? How was this possible? Goebbels was one of the worst Nazi war criminals, glorying in the destruction of the Jews in the early 1940s.

Just as meeting the Waffen SS officer who thought the Third Reich was a 'golden era' had a profound effect on me, so did meeting Margot Hielscher. They each made me question how I would have behaved had I lived through that period in German history. But because we are each the product of an intricate relationship between our biology and the circumstances we inhabit, I can't be sure what I would have done.

Then I asked myself a related question. If my own life altered dramatically today, how would I behave?

Sometimes, in the lectures I give about the mentalities of people during the war, I ask the audience what they would do if their circumstances suddenly changed. I ask them to imagine that terrorists have locked all the doors to the lecture hall and that a couple of hundred of us are forced to stay in the room for forty-eight hours without food or water. Then, at the end of those forty-eight hours, six bottles of water are chucked into the room, and we're told we will get nothing more for another forty-eight hours. Can you predict how you will react when that water comes in? Will you fight for it at all costs? Will you share it? Will you let the most deserving people have it first? And if you can't predict what you would do, how well do you know yourself?

As the history examined in this book demonstrates, people's behaviour changed as the situation changed. The challenge is to understand why it changed as it did and what we can take from their experience for today.

1. Spreading Conspiracy Theories

The Nazis thrived on conspiracy theories. And they used the same mental processes to convince themselves they were right as conspiracy theorists do today. The only difference is that the Nazis' conspiracy theories underpinned the most horrific crime in history – the Holocaust.

It was the First World War that gave birth to many of the conspiracy theories the Nazis employed. Indeed, without the First World War and the long shadow it cast, there would have been no Nazi Party and no Adolf Hitler as Chancellor of Germany. So it is vital, if we want to penetrate the mentalities of the Nazis, that we understand how this First War – the Great War – became the prism through which many of them saw the world and Germany's place within it.

Part of the reason this war had such an effect, not just on the Nazis but on the whole German psyche, was because of the enormous swings in emotion it engendered. The ultimate humiliation of 1918 was made all the harder to bear by the joyous anticipation many Germans had felt when war had been declared just four years before. The conspiracy theories that emerged towards the end of the war could not have had the power they did had it not been for this initial euphoria.

'At last life had regained an ideal significance,' wrote the left-wing writer Ernst Glaeser, describing the mood in August 1914. 'The great virtues of humanity, fidelity, patriotism, readiness to die for an ideal . . . were triumphing over the trading and shopkeeping spirit . . . The war would cleanse mankind from all its impurities.'[1] It was a sentiment that the historian Friedrich Meinecke, from the opposite side of the political spectrum, heartily agreed with when he wrote after the war, 'All the rifts which had hitherto existed among the German people, both among the bourgeoisie themselves and between the bourgeoisie and the working class, were suddenly healed in the face of the common danger.'[2]

While the extent to which Germans embraced the war in the summer of 1914 has been challenged and contextualized by scholars in recent years,[3] the fact remains that many people felt in the outbreak of hostilities that August a sense of unification. This togetherness was encapsulated by the famous phrase uttered by Kaiser Wilhelm II that same month: 'I no longer recognize [political] parties; I recognize only Germans.'[4] These words may have little effect on us today, but they were electrifying at the time. Germany had only been unified in 1871 – less than fifty years before the outbreak of the war – and even after unification the country still contained twenty-five separate states. While each of them acknowledged the primacy of the Kaiser, they jealously guarded their own independence within the German federation. Bavaria still retained its own army and monarch.

What the Kaiser was proclaiming in August 1914 was a nationalistic sense of 'Germanness'. This was especially appealing given how much the country had changed as it modernized during the nineteenth century, not just politically but economically and culturally as well. All this change left in its wake one overarching question – what exactly did it mean to be a German, rather than a Bavarian, a Prussian or a Hessian? The Kaiser sought to provide an answer. It didn't matter what political party or federal state you came from, above all else you were a German, and being a German meant you should fight for Germany's honour.

Emil Klein was a schoolboy at the time – later he would become a devoted Nazi – and he remembered that 'there was always great jubilation when a special train full of soldiers in field grey set off from the station. And I was often there and watched them go off, especially when my own father went to war . . . We were raised as nationalists.' When he and his fellow pupils were marched off to gym class they sang 'patriotic songs' like 'O Germany highly honoured!'[5]

Ernst Jünger, a writer much admired by the Nazi movement, joined the army in August 1914 at the age of nineteen. 'Grown up in an age of security,' he wrote, 'we shared a yearning for danger, for the experience of the extraordinary. We were enraptured by war. We had set out in a rain of flowers, in a drunken atmosphere of blood and roses. Surely the war had to supply us with what we wanted; the great, the overwhelming, the hallowed experience.'[6]

Similar feelings were shared by a twenty-five-year-old painter of pictures for tourists living in Munich that August – Adolf Hitler. Born in Austria, he had immediately joined a Bavarian regiment because he considered himself German. 'To me those hours seemed like a release from the painful feelings of my youth,' he would write ten years later.

'Even today I am not ashamed to say that, overpowered by stormy enthusiasm, I fell down on my knees and thanked Heaven from an over-flowing heart for granting me the good fortune of being permitted to live at this time. A fight for freedom had begun, mightier than the earth had ever seen.' The epic question, as Hitler saw it, was 'whether the German nation was to be or not to be'.[7]

At the War Office in Berlin, just before the conflict began, the pre-vailing mood was one of optimism. The Bavarian military attaché saw 'everywhere beaming faces, shaking of hands in the corridors; one congratulates oneself for having taken the hurdle [of deciding to go to war]'.[8]

All this seems incredible to us now, but only because we know what was to come – four years of warfare that would cost the lives of around ten million soldiers, two million of them Germans. This was, of course, far from the outcome the German leadership had intended. The High Command had planned for a swift campaign, following Frederick the Great's dictum that Prussia should fight 'short and lively' wars. The enemy was to be overwhelmed in a matter of weeks if possible, months if necessary, but certainly not in a debilitating conflict over four years. Under Frederick the Great, Prussia had never had the resources to con-duct such a war, and, still sandwiched between enemies to the east and west, neither did Germany under Kaiser Wilhelm II.[9]

At first, German optimism seemed merited when the German Army won the Battle of the Frontiers, the first major engagement on the west-ern front. But this collection of battles, fought in the south of Belgium and the north-east of France in August and early September, also dem-onstrated with shocking immediacy that this was to be a different kind of war. At Morhange the French Army went into battle still wearing their traditional uniform of blue coats and red trousers. Easy targets for the Germans, they were mowed down. It was a bloody lesson in the need for camouflage in a modern conflict.

Ernst Röhm, who would later become leader of the Nazi Stormtroop-ers, fought in the Battle of the Frontiers as a twenty-six-year-old lieutenant. He wrote after the war that, before they went into action, 'joy and enthusiasm for battle reigned throughout the regiment.'[10] But then Röhm witnessed first hand how the initial 'joy and enthusiasm' of his soldiers were tested by the devastating power of modern weap-onry. He remembered the 'overwhelming infantry, machine-gun and artillery fire' that pinned them down in a 'dreadful' fight.[11] And even though the Germans won the battle, his regiment suffered 'terrible losses'.[12]

Nonetheless, the Germans were able to press on, pushing the Allies back into France. On 27 August 1914 a report from German Supreme Headquarters claimed that the enemy was 'in full retreat [and] incapable of offering serious resistance to the German advance'.[13] By 1 September, soldiers of the German Army were around 30 miles from Paris. This marked the high point of their success. A few days later the whole course of the war changed.

French and British forces managed to mount a powerful counter-attack against a German Army that was overextended, at what became known as the First Battle of the Marne. In little more than a few days they forced the Germans to retreat to more defensible lines. Paris had been saved, and a new type of conflict began to develop on the western front – trench warfare.

This signalled the start of a war the Germans and their allies were all but incapable of winning. This wasn't the 'short and lively' war they wanted, but a long and static fight that demanded a depth of resources they did not possess. But this was not how the German media explained what was happening. The shattering events of the First Battle of the Marne were portrayed as a minor setback – merely a positional change, a tactical alteration.[14] It was one of the first examples of a dishonesty that would pervade the official German coverage of the war – a dishonesty that would have enormous psychological consequences. The true culprits for the difficulties the German Army now faced – the military leaders who had made a fundamental miscalculation – hid behind a barrage of falsehoods: lies that subsequently helped conspiracy theorists peddle whatever fantasies they chose.

It is ironic, given that the First World War lives on in the public consciousness as a deadening, unimaginative conflict, that these first months of the war also represented a revolution in warfare. A series of modern developments had come together to alter forever the way battles were fought. The first change, as Ernst Röhm witnessed at the Battle of the Frontiers, was the terrifying power of modern weaponry – most notably advanced artillery and the machine gun. Added to that was the use of barbed wire to protect defensive emplacements and telephones and wireless to aid communication. Finally, the availability of tinned food meant that millions of soldiers could stay fighting in one place for years at a time.[15]

Each of these innovations favoured the defender rather than the attacker. The cumulative effect of all of them on the soldier who was ordered to advance was horrendous. Adolf Hitler, in a letter he sent from the front line to an acquaintance in Munich, tried to convey a flavour of this new kind of war: 'At last the command rang out: "Forward!" We swarmed out and chased across the fields to a little farm. To left and right the shrapnel were bursting, and in between the English bullets sang. But we paid no attention. For ten minutes we lay there, and then we were again ordered forward . . . We crawled on our bellies to the edge of the woods. Over us the shells were howling and whistling, splintered tree trunks and branches flew around us. And then again grenades crashed into the wood, hurling up clouds of stones, earth, and roots, and stifling everything in a yellowish-green, stink-ing, sickening vapour.'[16]

In 1941, Hitler spoke in private of the lesson he had taken from this experience: 'It was with feelings of pure idealism that I set out for the front in 1914. Then I saw men falling around me in thousands. Thus I learnt that life is a cruel struggle, and has no other object but the preser-vation of the species. The individual can disappear, provided there are other men to replace him.'[17]

Ernst Röhm shared with Hitler this understanding of the true horror of war on the western front. Indeed, Röhm's experience was worse. Shortly after the Battle of the Frontiers, as he was sleeping, he suddenly 'received a heavy blow in the face . . . When I felt my bleeding head, it turned out that a splinter from a shell had torn off the upper part of my nose. A deep wound opened in my face; the blood gushed inces-santly . . .'[18] Doctors would save Röhm's life, but could do little to repair his looks. Until the day he died he would bear a reminder of this night on his disfigured face.

The manner of Röhm's injury symbolized a new and disturbing dimension to modern warfare – one with lasting psychological effects. Röhm had been wounded by an assailant who was likely miles away. This made the battlefield a bloodier place than ever before. As Dave Grossman wrote in his influential work *On Killing: The Psychological Cost of Learning to Kill in War and Society*, it is difficult for most human beings to kill another person face to face. A survey even claimed that many American soldiers during the Second World War had been unable to kill with their rifles when they could see their victims.[19] Only radical changes in combat training in the post-war years managed to increase the close kill rate. That is why artillery is such a powerful and effective weapon. Not only do you kill from a distance but you work as part of a gun crew. The responsibility for killing is thus shared. It is significant, as Grossman points out, that Napoleon was an artilleryman and always wanted to have more artillery on the battlefield than the enemy.[20]

Many of those who would go on to gain positions of significance within the Nazi movement were, by now, fighting in these deadly conditions. Alongside Hitler and Röhm were Hermann Göring, who towards the end of the war became the highly decorated commander of Baron von Richthofen's squadron; Rudolf Hess, who fought at the Battle of Verdun and after the war would become the Deputy Führer; Julius Streicher, who displayed bravery under fire on the western front and was later one of the most infamous Nazi anti-Semites;[21] and Rudolf Höss, who was the youngest non-commissioned officer in the German Army, and just over twenty years later was appointed commandant of Auschwitz.

All these people, like everyone who served at the front, witnessed the most appalling carnage – so much so that it's hard for us today to fully grasp what they must have experienced. Consider, for example, the giant monument at Thiepval dedicated to the British and South African soldiers who fought at the Somme. This memorial commemorates the more than 70,000 'missing' – soldiers who have no known resting place. How, one might ask, could over 70,000 people go 'missing'? The answer is because most people who died fighting on the western front were killed by artillery, and recent technological advances meant that artillery was more deadly than ever before. Suffering a direct hit from a high-explosive shell was akin to standing in front of a speeding train. You went 'missing' because you disintegrated into small pieces.

It wasn't just future Nazis who witnessed all this during the First World War; so did future pacifists, communists and socialists. Just as not every German joyously welcomed the war, not everyone who served in the German Army subsequently became a Nazi – far from it. Erich Maria Remarque, for instance, served only a few weeks on the front line in the summer of 1917 before suffering a war-ending shrapnel wound, but the experience was life changing. The novel he wrote years later about the conflict, *All Quiet on the Western Front*, became a worldwide bestseller. As Remarque saw it, he was part of a generation that had been broken by the war.[22] The novel detailed the experiences of a character called Paul Bäumer, who described how life on the western front turned him and his comrades into creatures who had lost their humanity.[23] The horror of the field hospital, with dead and dying all around, made Bäumer conclude that life was without meaning.[24] Ultimately, he despaired for the future and questioned, after this devastating experience, what the post-war world could possibly offer.[25]

The Nazis loathed *All Quiet on the Western Front* when it was published in 1929. They despised Remarque's vision of the pointlessness of suffering. It was as far as one can imagine from the way that the Nazi Party would later demand that Germans view the war. Though Hitler saw life as a 'cruel struggle' he still felt there was nobility in dying for your nation, and Remarque's nihilistic vision was anathema to him.

The Nazis' preferred view of the conflict was presented by another soldier, Ernst Jünger. While serving on the western front, he had an altogether different emotional experience from Remarque's. In his literary account, *Storm of Steel*, Jünger projected himself as a courageous, steadfast leader, a warrior who was able to inspire his men to stay at their posts by demonstrating his own bravery. 'What helped me make my case', he wrote, 'was the fact that I myself was in the place of greatest danger.'[26]

As a hail of artillery raged around him, Jünger had an almost spiritual awakening. He watched as his men stood 'stony and motionless' and 'then, by the light of a flare, I saw steel helmet by steel helmet, blade by glinting blade, and I was overcome by a feeling of invulnerability. We might be crushed, but surely we could not be conquered.'[27]

Stirring stuff, and the opposite of Remarque's vision of savages grappling with each other in the mud. And yet what's fascinating is that much of their descriptive writing is similar, as both Jünger and Remarque each vividly portray the nightmare world of trench warfare. So how can one writer take nihilistic despair from the experience of this war and another dignity and courage?

The first answer, obviously, is that they came from very different backgrounds. From a young age Jünger was imbued with a spirit of adventure – he ran away to join the Foreign Legion in his teens, before realizing he had made a mistake and escaping. In contrast, Remarque was a bookish youngster with a gloomy side to him. He later confided that he had 'spent a disconsolate youth interspersed with thoughts of suicide'.[28] They also had dissimilar backgrounds. While Remarque came from humble circumstances, Jünger was from a wealthy family and was a member of the Wandervogel, a romantic youth movement.

There is also the question of timing. Jünger joined the German Army in the initial moment of enthusiasm for the war in the summer of 1914. Remarque, three years younger, was conscripted in 1917. As the German dramatist Carl Zuckmayer, who also served in the First World War, later recalled, 'It is remarkable how swiftly in such times a difference between generations develops and how deep a gulf [exists] between groups only a year or two apart in age.' By the time Remarque was recruited, the 'degeneration of the initial advance into a war of attrition, into a universal, systematic mass slaughter',[29] was all too apparent.

More than ten years after the end of the war the Nazi propagandist Joseph Goebbels would generate enormous publicity by trumpeting his hatred of *All Quiet on the Western Front* and contrasting it with his admiration for Jünger's wartime writing. It was a battle for the cultural memory of the nation, and it was a fight the Nazis were determined to win. Future German soldiers needed to be imbued with Jünger's vision of the First World War, not Remarque's.[30]

The challenge Nazi propagandists would face, however, was that as the First World War progressed the reality of the conflict increasingly resembled Remarque's novel. Bread rationing was imposed in Germany as early as January 1915, and soon the search for scapegoats began. Since German newspapers followed the line laid down by the military – that no mistakes had been made by the General Staff – someone else had to be blamed for what was happening.

Hitler, in a letter written in 1915, gave a hint of the opinion he was forming: 'we hope that those of us who have the good fortune to see their homeland again will find it purer and more purified of foreign influence.'[31] Exactly what Hitler meant by 'foreign influence' or 'foreignness' – the German word he used was *Fremdländerei* – is unclear. It's been suggested that he was referring to Czech influence in Vienna or Linz, but the world expert on Hitler maintains that it's improbable that the word did not also encompass the Jews. Whatever Hitler meant, in common with many of his comrades at the front he was searching for a scapegoat.[32]

The Jews, of course, have been scapegoats for more than 2,000 years. And now, once again, there would be an attempt to blame them for the mistakes of others. In 1916 the Prussian Minister of War claimed that members of the 'population at large' were 'continually' writing to him claiming that Jews were dodging the fighting at the front. So a census was organized to find out exactly how many Jews were serving in the armed forces. The result of this count was never made public – almost certainly because the findings showed that Jews were not avoiding military service at all. The truth was that German Jews were more than doing their bit.[33]

The latest psychological research demonstrates that this attempt at scapegoating fits into a typical pattern. The social psychologist Professor Karen Douglas believes that as most conspiracy theorists are 'looking for someone to blame', the idea that 'there are these people pulling the strings behind the scenes' helps deal with their 'feelings of powerlessness and disillusionment'. Research suggests that 'people sometimes believe conspiracy theories about other groups as a way of protecting or enhancing their own group. People who are especially narcissistic about groups they belong to tend to be more likely to believe conspiracy theories about other groups.'[34] The 'narcissism' of the German High Command was considerable. They considered themselves the best soldiers in the world. So how could they be losing this war? It must be someone else's fault.

There's also a possible link between conspiracy theories and the evolution of language. Professor Robin Dunbar, an evolutionary psychologist, believes that language may have evolved so that human beings could gossip.[35] Rather as our ape ancestors used grooming to establish and maintain social connections, so human beings evolved language to bond by discussing topics such as who is dating whom, who is cheating on their wife and what the real story is behind the leader's recent actions.[36] With this insight as a starting point, though Professor Dunbar does not make this link himself, one might see conspiracy theories as the ultimate gossip – secrets others try to hide. Thus it's possible we have an evolutionary tendency towards finding conspiracy theories enticing.

The timing of the 1916 census also revealed an aspect of anti-Semitism that is often forgotten. It can lie dormant for years, only to surface with renewed intensity during a crisis. Jews had previously benefited from the unification of Germany in 1871. Having been restricted within Germany in a variety of ways − they were prohibited, for example, from entering certain professions − the Jews were now living with fewer restraints.

Before the First World War, though anti-Semitism still existed within Germany, it was far from universal. The majority of Germans did not vote for political parties that espoused overtly anti-Semitic policies. Indeed, many eastern European Jews fled to the relative safety of Germany to escape persecution elsewhere.[37] But there were groups within Germany − particularly many of those who called themselves *völkisch* − who blamed the Jews, at least in part, for the immense changes that had occurred as the country modernized during the nineteenth and early years of the twentieth century. These *völkisch* groups rhapsodized about the beauty of the forests and the almost spiritual qualities of the peasant farmer and considered Jews the antithesis of this bucolic ideal.[38] Rather than living the rural life, Jews tended to settle in cities and work in commerce − a legacy of the previous restrictions on the professions they could pursue.

This meant that when some Jews didn't conform to this anti-Semitic urban stereotype the anti-Semites could be confused. Eugene Leviné, a German Jew, remembered travelling back from a hiking trip in the countryside with his Jewish friends after the First World War and listening as a man sitting in the same railway compartment was 'swearing about the Jews, and so we said, "Well look, we are all Jews." And he roared with laughter, and he said, "You must think that we country people are daft. You are obviously nice clean-living, sporting German boys. You're not going to tell me you're Jews." And he meant it.'[39]

In February 1917, dramatic events in St Petersburg started a chain of causation that reinforced the anti-Semites' warped idea that the Jews were behind Germany's ills. There was an uprising in St Petersburg as workers protested about the shortage of food. The crisis soon escalated and, supported by Russian soldiers, the revolutionaries forced the Tsar to abdicate in early March. The swiftness with which the House of Romanov had been toppled was a warning to all the monarchies of Europe.

The Provisional Government, which replaced the Tsar, carried on fighting the war against the Germans and their allies. This was a huge mistake. Not only was the new Russian offensive in Galicia in the summer of 1917 a failure, but Vladimir Lenin and the Bolsheviks were fomenting revolution on the home front and mutiny in the army. A few months later, in November 1917, the Bolsheviks managed to seize power from the Provisional Government.

A conspiracy theory subsequently developed that the Jews were behind Bolshevism. Some leading Bolsheviks – notably Leon Trotsky – were indeed of Jewish origin, and the claim was that Karl Marx, the theorist behind the revolution, was as well. But the idea that the November 1917 revolution was driven or controlled by 'the Jews' was nonsense. Jews were actually in a minority among leading Bolsheviks, and Karl Marx, while he had Jewish ancestry, was baptized a Lutheran. But, just as today, facts did not matter to the conspiracy theorists, and the lie that the Jews controlled Bolshevism was subsequently to become a central part of Nazi thinking.

Desperate to secure the revolution, Lenin wanted to bring an immediate end to Russia's involvement in the war. By December 1917 the new Russian regime had agreed an armistice with Germany and its allies – collectively known as the Central Powers – and opened peace negotiations at the city of Brest-Litovsk, little more than a hundred miles east of Warsaw.

Simultaneously, there was a reminder to the Central Powers that their own support on the home front was fracturing. In the winter of 1917–18 there was a series of strikes, first in Vienna and Budapest, and then in Berlin. It seemed as if the demand for 'peace and bread' which had helped spark the Russian Revolution was spreading west. Subsequently, leading Nazis would remember how hunger had sapped the will of Germans during the First World War, and they were determined that it wouldn't happen again in the Second.[40]

Leon Trotsky saw the January 1918 strikes as evidence that the revolution was spreading across Europe. He claimed that the 'international proletariat' would rise up if 'German imperialism attempts to break us on the wheel of its military machine'.[41] He was wrong.

German security forces managed to suppress the January 1918 strike in Berlin and on 9 February the Central Powers signed a peace treaty with Ukraine. In return for a million tons of bread a year, the Germans and their allies would now recognize Ukrainian independence. This was a clear provocation to the new Bolshevik regime in Russia, since Ukraine had previously been part of the Russian Empire.

The war in the east, which had paused while negotiations took place, once again erupted into life as around a million soldiers of the Central Powers advanced into Latvia, Estonia, Belarus and Ukraine. Russian forces lacked the power and motivation to stop them, and by March the Central Powers had captured Kiev.

Lenin was now more anxious than ever to exit the war. He knew that one of the reasons the Tsar had been overthrown was the presence in St Petersburg of conscript soldiers who did not want to be sent to the front. The message Lenin took from this was simple. Do whatever is necessary to stop the fighting. Even a humiliating peace would be better than no peace at all. The desperation of the Bolsheviks to sign a deal did not go unnoticed, with Lieutenant Colonel Pokorny of the Austro-Hungarian General Staff remarking that 'a peace treaty is seemingly a matter of life and death for Lenin's government.'[42]

But the treaty the Bolsheviks agreed with the Central Powers was much worse than merely humiliating. It was one of the most draconian, one-sided deals in history. Under the terms of the Brest-Litovsk treaty, signed on 3 March 1918, the Russians forfeited a third of their pre-war population and nearly 90 per cent of their coal. 'Independence' was granted to a host of territories that had been under Russian control, including Finland, Lithuania and Ukraine. But for many of these places this 'independence' meant German soldiers stationed on their land.[43]

Even though the whole deal was dismantled by the Allies after the First World War and all these German gains were lost, one fact remained. The treaty of Brest-Litovsk had demonstrated that it was possible to force the Russians to accept an agreement that stripped them of precious resources. When Hitler decided to invade this same territory during the Second World War, the Germans would remember this crucial piece of history. As the historian Golo Mann wrote, 'Brest-Litovsk has been called the forgotten peace, but the Germans have not forgotten it. They know that they defeated Russia and sometimes they look upon this proudly as the real, if unrewarded European achievement of the war.'[44]

But while the Central Powers had made spectacular gains in the east, in the west the situation was deteriorating. The United States had declared war on Germany in April 1917, and six months later American

soldiers were taking part in the fighting. On the home front Germans
were suffering worse shortages than ever, and the mood was fractious.
In May 1918, in Ingolstadt in Bavaria, protests erupted when an invalid
complained loudly in the street about the war and was assaulted by the
police.

Alois Pfaller took part in the Ingolstadt demonstration while still a
boy. 'There was a big crowd,' he remembered. 'I came from the countryside, [and] had never experienced anything like it . . . by the Town
Hall . . . there were thousands of citizens and soldiers in front of the
police station, demanding that the officer who was supposed to have
beaten up the war invalid [come out] . . . They shouted, more and
more, but he didn't stir, he didn't come out. Then a soldier picked up a
stone and said to me: "Come on, let's smash a window, then maybe
he'll come out." Well, he didn't have to tell me twice . . . it was fun to
be allowed to smash a window. So I did it, oh Lord! Then it started! As
soon as one pane was broken, they all looked for stones and broke
windows.'[45]

The crowd eventually managed to enter the Town Hall and trash the
contents. 'I had already left by then,' recalled Pfaller. 'It was too much
for me. I was frightened, I scarpered . . . I'd had enough for a first time.
I thought it was too risky.' But he always remembered how the soldiers
garrisoned in the city 'wanted to stop the war' and 'were all shouting:
"We want peace, we want peace!"' As Pfaller saw it, this was an example
of how ordinary people could stand up against oppression. Inspired by
this protest, Pfaller later became a member of the German Communist
Party.

As the demonstration in Ingolstadt raged, a last-ditch German attack
was under way on the western front. The German High Command
recognized that something radical had to be done to bring the war to
a conclusion – and that something was the Ludendorff offensive, an
attempt to push the Allies back towards the English Channel. The focus
was on all-out attack as specially trained units of Stormtroopers charged
the Allied line, protected by a rolling artillery barrage that fell just in
front of them.

Initially, the Germans made considerable gains. At the end of March
1918, Alfred Hugenberg, chairman of the gigantic conglomerate Krupp
Steel and later a member of Hitler's cabinet, sent an effusive message to
Field Marshal Hindenburg: 'Those who timidly doubted the German

victory and those who never believed in it now see it as an attainable possibility before them . . .'[46]

By the end of May, it seemed as if Paris might be under threat once again. 'It's wonderful to see the present look on the faces of our valiant regiments as they advance in an assault,' wrote Herbert Sulzbach, a German lieutenant; 'they are almost laughing for joy, and all they can see is victory. If you people at home could only see it!'[47] Captain Fritz Matthaei, a battalion commander in the 36th Division, was similarly ecstatic. 'Everywhere was battle joy, battle enthusiasm,' he wrote in a letter back home. 'Victory called from every corner, prisoners and booty were brought past, and the shining May sun smiled success. The days of 1914 seemed to have returned.'[48] In a sense he was correct. For just as the initial victories in 1914 had proved to be a false dawn, so did the Ludendorff offensive. Just six months later Germany lost the war.

Given the optimism of May 1918, many Germans sought an explanation for this catastrophic change in fortune in a whole series of conspiracy theories – frequently involving the fantasy of a betrayal engineered by Jews and socialist politicians. But the actual reason for the Germans' defeat was more prosaic. Yes, the German Army had made great headway in the spring of 1918, but it had been at enormous cost – in excess of 680,000 soldiers killed, injured, captured or missing.[49]

Herbert Richter, a German soldier who took part in the offensive at the Marne in 1918, confirmed that while his unit 'made good progress' and 'took many prisoners', nonetheless 'we suffered severe casualties.' Once all the other officers in his unit had been killed he – a lowly ensign – had to command an artillery battery: 'Luckily I got through it, and then we were pulled back behind the front so that we could recuperate.' Richter noticed something else during the fighting that summer. The Allies 'were better equipped. They had waterproof boots,' while Richter and his comrades 'had to wade through the mud' in their leaking footwear.[50]

Though the Allies had also suffered losses, the difference was that the arrival of a stream of American troops allowed them to be replaced. This massive imbalance in resources was one reason why Ferdinand Foch, the Supreme Commander of Allied Forces, felt able to tell other Allied military leaders on 24 July 1918 – via a memo read to them by

Maxime Weygand, his chief of staff – that a 'turning point' had arrived. 'The moment has come', said Weygand, echoing Foch's view, 'to abandon the general defensive attitude forced upon us until now by numerical inferiority and to pass to the offensive.'[51]

The Germans were battered into submission. Using tanks and planes in coordination with precise artillery bombardment, the Allies broke through the enemy's defensive lines and over the next few months pushed the exhausted Germans back. By the end of September 1918, both Field Marshal Hindenburg and General Ludendorff – effectively the most powerful people in Germany – had decided that the situation was untenable. The knowledge of what had happened the year before in Russia, when disheartened troops had helped overturn the established order, weighed heavily upon them. At all costs they wanted to avoid Germany suffering a similar fate. They told the Kaiser that not only was an armistice needed at once, but the Allies – in particular the Americans – urgently had to be reassured that they were dealing with a more democratic Germany.

It was a strategy that had an added benefit as far as Ludendorff and Hindenburg were concerned – it distanced them from defeat. They could blame hapless politicians for this debacle, rather than accept responsibility themselves. That is the background to the famous statement Ludendorff made to his military staff at the end of September: 'I have advised his Majesty to bring those groups into the government whom we have in the main to thank for the fact that matters have reached this pass . . . Let them now conclude the peace that has to be negotiated. Let them eat the broth they have cooked for us.'[52]

A key part of the plan to make the politicians eat this broth was to continue to withhold information about the impending disaster from the German public and ensure that army propaganda carried on pumping out optimistic lies.[53] This ruse – obviously designed to calm the mood at home and protect the reputations of the German commanders – had a devastating long-term effect. It meant that when the armistice did come in November, with the actual fighting still taking place far from the centres of German power, there was widespread astonishment. 'We did wonder,' recalled Herbert Richter, 'because we didn't feel beaten at all. The front-line troops didn't feel themselves beaten, and we were wondering why the armistice was happening so quickly, and why we had to vacate all our positions in such a hurry, because we were still standing on enemy territory and we thought all this was strange.'[54]

In late October and early November 1918, events moved at speed. Sailors mutinied at Wilhelmshaven when ordered to leave port for what they perceived to be a pointless attack on the British Navy, and the protests soon spread to Kiel and elsewhere. Echoing the words of the Russian revolutionaries the previous year, many of the German protesters demanded the abdication of the Kaiser.

From German military headquarters in Spa in Belgium, the Kaiser declared that if there was a Bolshevik revolution, 'I will take my place at the head of a few divisions, advance on Berlin and string up anyone who commits treason.'[55] But he was dissuaded from taking such dramatic action by those around him, not least because some generals doubted whether the army would be prepared to follow him.

General Wilhelm Groener had another idea. He proposed that 'the Kaiser must immediately make his way to the battlefield in order to seek his death there.'[56] This self-sacrifice, thought Groener, would have a dramatic effect on the way the Germans perceived the war. But the Kaiser was not keen to lose his own life, and so he abdicated on the evening of 9 November and fled to exile in the Netherlands.

Predictably, many were outraged by the ousting of the Kaiser. Ludwig Beck, later Chief of the General Staff of the German Army, wrote to his sister, 'Never in my life have I been so upset about something I personally witnessed as I was on 9 and 10 November. Such an abyss of meanness, cowardice, lack of character, all of which I had until then considered impossible. In a few hours 500 years of history have been shattered; like a thief the emperor was deported to Dutch territory. It could not happen fast enough – this to a noble and morally upstanding man.' Significantly, Beck also wrote, 'we have been stabbed in the back.'[57] It was a phrase that would resonate for years.

But this wasn't the only response. Some younger officers, like Ernst Jünger, felt that the Kaiser had betrayed his high office by not sacrificing himself in battle. In 1922 Jünger wrote that the death of the Kaiser 'may be demanded by those countless figures who went to their deaths before him'.[58]

Fridolin von Spaun, eighteen years old and yet to join the German Army, also felt let down by the Kaiser's decision to flee: 'I had to watch the German ruling classes, that is the aristocracy, emperor, kings, princes, deserting without being forced to by a coup. I found this incomprehensible. That not one of them tried to put up any resistance. Why did the crown prince not march into Berlin with an army – even though the war was lost? And instead [they] left chaos behind.' Spaun, who would later join the Nazi Party, 'learnt from this that the ruling classes of the old era were no longer fit to govern. This was a painful realization, but for me a very important one.'[59]

The image of the Kaiser scurrying away and saving his own skin would live on – a permanent stain on the reputation of the monarchy. The contrast was later obvious between the Kaiser, safe behind the lines during the war and afterwards living in opulence in exile, and Hitler's own service as an ordinary soldier at the front who had won an Iron Cross for bravery.

Yet, despite their defeat, when the German soldiers returned home they were not treated as part of a humiliated army. A journalist from *The Times* witnessed an 'enormous crowd' greet the soldiers in Berlin with a 'hearty reception'. On 10 December 1918, the new Chancellor, Friedrich Ebert, told troops parading at the Brandenburg Gate, 'No enemy has overcome you. Only when the preponderance of our opponents in men and material grew ever heavier did we give up the struggle, and just because of your heroic courage was it our duty not to demand further useless sacrifices of you.'[60]

It is not hard to imagine why Ebert preached the falsehood that the German Army hadn't been defeated. There was a danger of revolution, and if bending the truth could keep the soldiers loyal then so be it. But in taking this course of action he fuelled the more pernicious lie voiced by Ludwig Beck and others – that the army at the front had been 'stabbed in the back' by enemies behind the lines in Germany.

It was a conspiracy theory embraced the following year by one of the most respected men in the country – Field Marshal Paul von Hindenburg. He had done everything he could to escape the blame he deserved for the disastrous course the war had taken. Army propaganda had been careful to paint him as the 'Hero of Tannenberg' – a victory he had masterminded on the eastern front in 1914. The later defeats were scarcely mentioned alongside this early triumph.

At a public hearing in 1919, Hindenburg seized the chance to distance himself still further from Germany's humiliation the previous year. He asserted that he had 'wanted forceful and cheerful cooperation' from German political parties during the war but had instead 'encountered failure and weakness'. He quoted with approval the words of an 'English general' who had allegedly said, 'the German army was stabbed in the back.' Consequently, he claimed, the army could not be blamed for what had happened.[61]

By these words Hindenburg did enormous damage to the psyche of many Germans. In the chaos that existed in the aftermath of the war, the longing for one trusted figure to tell millions of nationalistic Germans the truth was immense. And who could be more trusted than the all-conquering Hero of Tannenberg? Given his supposedly honourable background, Hindenburg's role in the propagation of the lie of the 'stab in the back' can scarcely be overestimated. As the journalist Theodor Wolff wrote perceptively in November 1919, 'The unfortunate scapegoat theory could not emerge if the infallibility theory [that Hindenburg and Ludendorff had done nothing wrong] had not risen on the other side.'[62]

Worse still, as Professor Douglas points out, psychological research shows that 'It's very difficult once someone holds a belief very strongly to change those beliefs.' Moreover, 'If someone believes one conspiracy theory, they are more likely to believe in or look for others. People can go down the rabbit hole and you can get a bit lost.'[63]

In January 1919, amid this febrile atmosphere, it even seemed that there might be a successful German revolution. There were riots on the streets of Berlin, encouraged by two key figures on the left – Karl Liebknecht and Rosa Luxemburg – with Liebknecht openly calling for world revolution. Fridolin von Spaun listened to Liebknecht speak and was appalled. 'They wanted to plunge Germany into chaos,' he remembered. 'They wanted to topple Ebert's government. I came to the conclusion that this should be resisted. And from then on I did just that, to the best of my ability.'[64]

Shortly afterwards, Spaun joined one of the Freikorps. These were groups of right-wing paramilitaries, often in the pay of the government, that formed in the wake of the lost war. Many of them hoped that in the future a 'Third Reich' would be created. (The 'First Reich' was considered to be the Holy Roman Empire and the 'Second Reich' the empire formed by German unification, which lasted up to the end of the

First World War.) But for many the idea of the Third Reich amounted to little more than a belief in a nebulous concept of a Germany reborn. 'Nothing is more characteristic of the associative spirit of the *Oberländer* than their Idea of the Third Reich . . .' wrote one supporter of the Frei-korps Oberland. 'The men dreamed deep dreams of this Mystery – a mystery which would have been debased into a concrete political program[me] as soon as one attempted to define it precisely.'[65] The men of each Freikorps gave their commander absolute loyalty – an act which symbolized 'the subordination of the individual . . . to the needs of the whole nation'.[66]

Freikorps units played a crucial role in suppressing the uprising in Berlin, and on 15 January 1919 both Luxemburg and Liebknecht were captured and murdered. Ebert, together with Gustav Noske, who had helped quash the revolution in Kiel just weeks before, was happy to use these freelance toughs alongside government troops. It is notable that Ebert and Noske were not politicians of the right but members of the Social Democratic Party (SPD). In these desperate times even those on the centre-left were prepared to make use of right-wing paramilitaries.

Four days after the deaths of Luxemburg and Liebknecht, German voters went to the polls to elect representatives for the new National Assembly. This was an historic moment in German political history – the first election in which women were able to vote. The results demonstrated the unequivocal desire of the German people for a fresh start, with a large majority voting for parties committed to both dem-ocracy and the new Germany.

But none of this meant that the political situation had stabilized. In Munich, for instance, the situation was fraught. A socialist journalist called Kurt Eisner had managed to use a demonstration on 7 November 1918 to incite soldiers to revolt. Events moved astonishingly swiftly, and in the early hours of the next day Bavaria was declared a republic. The Bavarian royal family – including the King – hurriedly left the city.

Ernst Röhm, who travelled through Munich that November, was appalled by what had happened. He thought it 'the most shameful over-throw of the system'. In his autobiography, published in 1928, he quoted from a series of leaflets which he 'drew up and distributed' in February 1919 and which expressed 'my views at the time'. Röhm admonished the soldiers who had taken part in the revolution and told them that 'In the Fatherland's hour of the most terrible need, you have betrayed your

Emperor and King and violated the oath sworn to God.' The 'spirit' of
the soldiers had been poisoned by 'bribable Jews and scoundrels'. These
'Jews and foreigners now rule over you', said Röhm, and together with
other 'traitors to our country' they had stabbed 'our brave forces in the
back'. He called on the soldiers to 'save your honour, restore it after you
violated the oath you formally swore to God!'[67]

These are the early stirrings of an approach that the Nazis would
employ in the years ahead. Hitler would subsequently welcome into the
party many soldiers who had previously supported the socialists – or
even the communists – as long as they renounced their 'betrayal'. So
much so that Hitler would later stretch reality and claim that in the
early 1920s '90 per cent' of the Nazi Party had been composed of 'left-
wing elements'.[68] Vital, of course, to permitting this change of allegiance
was maintaining the conspiracy theory that those on the left had been
misled by a core group of 'Jews' and 'traitors' – the instigators of the
mayhem, who could never be forgiven.

Many other different groups on the right also blamed the Jews for
what was happening in Germany. The day after Kurt Eisner declared
the 'People's State of Bavaria', a *völkisch* organization called the Thule
Society held a meeting in Munich that was addressed by its founder,
Rudolf von Sebottendorff. 'Brothers and sisters!' began Sebottendorff.
'Yesterday, we experienced the collapse of everything that was familiar,
dear and worthy to us. Instead of our princes of the blood, our mortal
enemy rules: Judah. We don't know yet what will arise from this chaos.
We can guess. The time of fight will come, of bitter hardships, a time of
danger! We who are in this fight are all in danger, for the enemy hates
us with the infinite hatred of the Jewish race. It is now an eye for an eye,
a tooth for a tooth . . .'[69]

The fact that Kurt Eisner had recently served time in prison accused
of inciting a strike, and was born Jewish, played perfectly into the story
that Sebottendorff wanted to tell. To Sebottendorff, Eisner was unquestionably someone who possessed the 'infinite hatred of the Jewish race'.
But, like all prejudice, Sebottendorff's argument – if we can dignify his
rantings as such – relied on selectively picking the facts. The fundamental cause of the Munich revolution in November 1918 was not a figure
like Eisner, extraordinary as he was, but the fallout from a lost war. All
Eisner did was give voice to the resentment and anger that already
existed.

It should not be forgotten that Eisner only succeeded in bringing down the Bavarian monarchy because thousands supported him, including the feminists Anita Augspurg and Lida Gustava Heymann. 'Anita Augspurg and I went to see Kurt Eisner,' wrote Heymann years later. 'What this man wanted coincided with our aspirations, which our life's work was directed at; we were united by the same yearning for liberation from slavery, for freedom and justice . . . Thinking back, the following months seem like a wonderful dream, that's how incredibly marvellous they were. The heavy weight of the war years had disappeared; you strode with a spring in your step, optimistic. The time of the day lost its significance, meal hours were forgotten, night turned into day, you didn't need any sleep; there was only one living flame burning: to be active, helping to build up a better community . . . Finally, women could create something out of plenty . . . Those were winter weeks full of work, hope and happiness.'[70]

However, Eisner was always at risk from an attack by a counter-revolutionary, and on 21 February 1919 he was the victim of a brutal assault. Count Anton von Arco auf Valley shot Eisner and killed him as he made his way to parliament. 'Eisner aims for anarchy,' Arco had written before he attacked him, 'he is a Bolshevik, he is a Jew, he's not German, he doesn't feel German, he is undermining every kind of German feeling, he is a traitor to his country.'[71]

Eisner's death was bitterly ironic. First, because he had already experienced a major political setback having lost ground in a recent election, and second because Arco was likely motivated in part by his own Jewish ancestry and the refusal of Sebottendorff to admit him to the Thule Society. Sebottendorff wrote that Arco 'had Jewish blood in his veins on the side of his mother (née Oppenheim), he is a Yid'.[72] It didn't matter that many of the Oppenheims had converted to Christianity and were on the political right – they were still Jews to Sebottendorff. As a fanatical racist, he believed all that mattered was the 'blood' that flowed in your veins; the very motto of the Thule Society was 'Remember that you are a German! Keep your blood clean!'[73]

Amid continuing economic problems – made worse by the prevalence of a Spanish flu epidemic that killed more than a quarter of a million Germans – a socialist 'Räterepublik' or 'councils' republic' was formed in Munich in April. The radical proponents of this new regime had originally planned that the Communist Party would take part in the government, but the communists withdrew their support at the last minute. Meanwhile the Social Democrats, under the leadership of Johannes Hoffmann, fled to Bamberg in northern Bavaria and denounced the revolutionaries in Munich.

This initial Räterepublik existed for less than a week. But it was still long enough to become a lasting joke. In response to a message from Lenin asking how the 'revolution' was going, the Deputy Foreign Minister Dr Franz Lipp replied that the good news was that 'the proletariat of Upper Bavaria [is] happily united' but the bad news was that 'the fugitive Hoffmann . . . has taken with him the key to my ministry toilet.'[74] Lipp also declared war on Switzerland for refusing to 'lend' the new government sixty railway locomotives. It later transpired that he had recently been discharged from a mental hospital.[75]

The regime that followed this first Räterepublik could hardly have been more different in attitude. This second Räterepublik, a hard-line Soviet republic, was run by tough revolutionaries, and the catalyst for their seizure of power was Hoffmann's plan to regain control of Munich. In order to stabilize the situation within the city, Eugen Leviné, a German communist born in Russia, removed the dilettantes from the original Räterepublik and took control himself. When Alois Pfaller heard the news, he felt 'it was a ray of hope that socialism would be coming, that unemployment would be vanquished, that you would have a right to a job, and that you would be paid more . . . there was hope of course, that's clear . . .'[76]

Many of the leaders of this new regime had been born Jewish. This precipitated yet more anti-Semitic propaganda from their opponents, once again falsely claiming an inextricable link between Judaism and Bolshevism.

By the end of April, government forces supported by Freikorps were ready to attack. They first took Dachau, 12 miles north-west of Munich, and then entered the Bavarian capital on 1 May. Their assault was fuelled by the knowledge that, the day before, the leaders of the Bavarian Soviet Republic had ordered the murder of ten hostages – killings that would live on in the propaganda of the nationalists for years to come. Several factors combined to make the murders especially notable. The first was that a woman was shot – and not just any woman, but an aristocrat, Countess Heila von Westarp. Another was that the killings took place in the playground of a school, at the Luitpold gymnasium.

Emil Klein, a teenager in Munich who was 'slowly becoming political', was appalled at the news of the killings. 'That was the first time I ever heard of hostage shootings,' he remembered. 'And that was the measure of the horror for me . . . And that's a powerful memory that I have never forgotten, the Reds shooting the hostages in the grammar school in Munich, that's something I have a very clear memory of.'

Klein witnessed the arrival of the right-wing Freikorps units in the city and saw how 'the people greeted them with flowers . . . and shouted "Hurrah!" At that point people hadn't started to shout "Heil!", they shouted "Hurrah" . . . And the Reds were gone! That was the best thing that could have happened . . . Of course, we young ones were very enthusiastic about it.' He remembered how the Freikorps let him and his friends sit on top of their armoured cars, 'and they took us part of the way with them and then let us off . . . naturally, it was a great day when they marched in.'[77]

Ernst Röhm, who entered Munich as part of a Freikorps led by Franz von Epp, was involved in the 'cleansing' of the city that followed. This was a bloody affair – up to a thousand people were killed.[78] Yet it was the death of ten hostages at the Luitpold gymnasium, perpetrated by the communists, that lived on in Klein's mind as a 'clear memory'. This wasn't surprising, as the Nazis would subsequently emphasize the 'threat' that had been posed by the brief existence of this Soviet Republic in Bavaria.

Just a week after the Freikorps and other troops entered Munich, an event of even greater importance took place 420 miles to the west, on the outskirts of Paris. A German delegation journeyed to the palace of Versailles to be handed details of the treaty which would formally end the war. The Germans, as the losers in the conflict, had not been involved in the Allies' discussions about this document, despite the fact that it would fundamentally alter all their lives.

While it is common knowledge how much Hitler and the Nazis would subsequently use the treaty of Versailles as justification for many of their acts of aggression, one important aspect of the history is often forgotten. The Nazis – together with many other Germans – claimed the Allies had broken their promise about the nature of the peace settlement. Specifically, they felt the American President had lied to them.

In January 1918, President Woodrow Wilson had spoken to the

United States Congress about 'Fourteen Points' that should be used as principles to create peace after the war. They were progressive ideas, with talk of self-determination, disarmament and free trade. Wilson's words seemed to offer a way of healing Europe after the war.

Fridolin von Spaun spoke for many Germans when he said that 'some of these points appeared to us quite acceptable. There were two points in particular: the right to national self-determination, wonderful. And the second point was: Germany must disarm. But that's only the start of general disarmament.' However, instead of a peace agreement based on Wilson's Fourteen Points, Spaun learnt – to his 'great disappointment' – that the Versailles treaty imposed a series of measures which would punish their country. 'They call it a treaty,' he said; 'it wasn't a treaty, I can only call it a diktat.'[79]

Under the terms of the Versailles treaty Germany would lose 13 per cent of its territory, including Alsace and Lorraine and large portions of West Prussia. But – and again this point is often missed – in terms of scale this was nothing like as much territory as the Germans and their allies had forced the Russians to relinquish under Brest-Litovsk, or the Hungarians would shortly be made to give up in the treaty of Trianon.

For the Germans it wasn't just loss of territory that was the issue. Not only were the 'reparations' they had to pay predicted to be crippling, but there was also a clause in the treaty which forbade Germany to unite with Austria – even if the Austrians wanted it to happen. In addition, more than a million ethnic Germans lived in territories that were to be taken from Germany and incorporated into a reconstituted Poland. What was all this if not a betrayal of the Wilsonian dream of self-determination?

Emotionally at least, there was an even worse provision. Under the so-called 'war guilt' clause, Germany was forced to accept blame for the war. This felt especially unjust to many Germans. After all, they argued, hadn't a Bosnian Serb lit the spark for the conflict when he assassinated the Austrian Archduke? And what about the mobilization by the Russians of their armed forces, hadn't that played a part in causing the war?

It had been possible for Germans to hope, in the troubled days and months following the armistice, that a happier future might beckon. They had faith that President Wilson's Fourteen Points offered a new start, and they had been told by no less a figure than their new

Chancellor that their army hadn't been defeated. Now, in a catastrophic reversal of fortune, they were ordered to accept the blame for starting the war.

Count Ulrich von Brockdorff-Rantzau, Foreign Minister and leader of the German delegation at Versailles, was outraged when he read the terms of the settlement. On 7 May 1919, he delivered a devastating response to the Allies, reminding them of the suffering imposed on Germany after the armistice by the continuation of an Allied blockade, which had prevented food and other supplies reaching the country. 'The hundreds of thousands of non-combatants who have perished [in Germany] since 11 November [1918]', he said, 'were destroyed coolly and deliberately after our opponents had won a certain and assured victory. Remember that, when you speak of guilt and atonement.' Moreover, he emphasized, the Allies had reneged on their promise that the 'basis of peace' was to be the principles outlined by Woodrow Wilson.[80]

In Berlin, Philipp Scheidemann, who had replaced Ebert as Chancellor following Ebert's elevation to President, was just as incensed. He told the Reichstag: 'Today it seems as if the bloody battlefield from the North Sea to the Swiss border has come alive once more in Versailles, as if ghosts are fighting one last battle of hatred and despair on top of the heaps of corpses ... I ask you: What honest man – I will not say German – what honest, loyal man would accept such conditions? What hand would not wither rather than bind us in these chains?'[81]

Heinz Guderian, a German officer who had fought in the trenches and would later become one of the most famous tank commanders of the Second World War, was in despair: 'If we accept this peace we are finished,' he said, 'and if we don't, we're probably finished anyway.' He believed that signing the treaty would be dishonourable, even if the price was that the Allies would restart the war. At least then, thought Guderian, 'They can do no more than destroy us.'[82]

Scheidemann could not bear to implement the terms of the treaty and resigned as Chancellor on 20 June. Germany was now at a crossroads. The Allies were poised to make good on their threat to invade unless the Germans signed the treaty, and the German generals had made it plain that there was little chance of resisting them. In this desperate situation, President Ebert bent to the inevitable. His new cabinet under Gustav Bauer agreed that the treaty had to be signed, even in the face of public outrage.[83] Those Germans who did put their names to the treaty, in a ceremony in the Hall of Mirrors in Versailles on 28 June 1919, were to be forever vilified by the nationalist right.

Opposition to Versailles was one of the reasons why a former soldier called Adolf Hitler came into politics. In his book *Mein Kampf,* he wrote that he had decided to pursue a political career in November 1918, disgusted at the way the war had ended.[84] But that was a lie. For the entire period discussed in this chapter – right up until the signing of Versailles – he had drifted along, seemingly uncertain what the future held for him.

That was about to change.

2. Using Them and Us

Before 1919, Adolf Hitler was something of a misfit. He was a pro-foundly bitter man, full of passionate vitriol and uninterested in the opinions of others. 'Wherever he looked, he saw injustice, hate and enmity,' said his flatmate from before the First World War. 'Choking with his catalogue of hates, he would pour his fury over everything . . .'[1] But now, in part for psychological reasons, these very qualities were about to ease his entry into politics.

His public life began on 12 September 1919, when he was thirty years old and walked into the Sterneckerbräu beer hall in Munich to observe a meeting of the German Workers' Party, a Bavarian political group with just a handful of members.

His journey to this point had been haphazard and unplanned – although he would later claim the opposite. He was keen afterwards to emphasize how his previous existence had been ideal preparation for his new life as a politician. Everything, he said, fitted into a pattern. He claimed, for instance, that he had been an active anti-Semite in his years in Vienna before the First World War.[2] But this claim, like many others he would subsequently make about his past, was false.[3] It was important for Hitler to invent these fictions because the reality – that he had been a vacillating and inconsequential nobody – was far too devastating to reveal, especially for a leader who thought it essential to project an image of certainty and strength.

The truth was that when the war ended in November 1918 Hitler had been consumed by one overreaching desire – to stay in the army, the only home and family he possessed. For a man unable to make lasting friendships, often uncertain where the next meal was coming from, living frugally in flats and rooming houses, the army in 1914 had been his saviour. And to Hitler, in the days immediately following the end of the war, what did politics matter compared to having food in his stom-ach and a roof over his head? 'When I first met him,' said Captain Karl Mayr, Hitler's superior officer in 1919, 'he was like a tired stray dog looking for a master.'[4]

In June 1919, Mayr sent Hitler on a propaganda course designed to educate soldiers about the dangers of Bolshevism. And it was only now, around the time of the signing of the Versailles treaty, that Hitler's political beliefs appear to have crystallized.[5]

In the weeks that followed, Hitler relished the chance to lecture other soldiers about the political situation in general and the insidiousness of Bolshevism in particular. Anti-Semitism pervaded his speeches, and he held the Jews responsible for a variety of the problems Germany faced. Since many of the leaders of the brief Soviet Republic established in Munich a few months before had been Jewish, it was common at the time to make the unjustified leap and say that the Jews were behind Bolshevism as a whole.

Later that summer, when Hitler was talking at a military camp in Lechfeld in southern Bavaria, reports started to emerge praising the power of his rhetoric. One soldier who heard him talk called Hitler a 'brilliant and spirited speaker who compels the whole audience to follow his exposition'.[6]

Psychological research offers us an explanation for Hitler's immediate success. He was, without knowing the scientific reasons, tapping into a profound truth about the way the brain works. By stirring up hatred against Jews and Bolsheviks he was targeting the amygdala – the part of the brain that immediately processes feelings of anxiety, fear and anger. These powerful emotions are produced almost instantly, because it's the amygdala that helps us avoid sudden danger.

We are descended from human beings who needed to respond instantaneously to threats in order to survive. Are these new people approaching friends or foes? Should I be happy to see them or ready to fight them? It's a decision that we shouldn't think about for long. Consequently, we possess the ability to process people at once into one of two categories – Them or Us.

According to the neuroscientist Professor Robert Sapolsky, 'Them and Us' is 'hard-wired into us via the amygdala and we'll never get rid of it'. He points out that 'it is a neurobiological tendency that is way older than humans. So the most pessimistic thing I can say is that it is virtually inevitable that your average human is wired up so that very quickly they have a strong pull towards Them/Us dichotomizing with a propensity towards thinking that the Thems are not such great people. That said, it is incredibly easy to manipulate people as to who counts as a Them and who counts as an Us. Germany and Hitler is mostly a lesson in how powerful pseudo-speciation is [that is, deciding that someone belongs to a type of 'Them' that is almost a different species from 'Us'].[7]

As we progress through this history, we will encounter many examples of how central this 'Them/Us dichotomizing' was to Nazism. Indeed, it isn't going too far to say that this was the very core of the ideology. Hitler, without studying neuroscience or psychology, intuitively knew the power of this approach. He seemed to confirm as much at a private speech to the Hamburger Nationalklub in 1926, when he remarked that 'the only stable emotion is hate.'[8]

Several weeks after lecturing at Lechfeld, and by now working as a propagandist for Captain Mayr's unit in the army, Hitler attended the 12 September meeting of the German Workers' Party at the Sterneckerbräu in Munich. It wasn't an impressive gathering. Just a few dozen people sitting around talking and drinking. The leader of the party, a locksmith called Anton Drexler, asked Hitler to join, but he agreed only after his army superiors had approved the idea.[9]

Hitler later claimed that he had been the seventh member of the party. This was another lie. Anton Drexler was subsequently so outraged by Hitler's attempt to portray himself as one of the earliest members that years later he wrote him a letter of complaint. 'Nobody knows better than yourself, my Führer,' said Drexler, 'that you were never the seventh member of the party, but at best the seventh member of the committee when I asked you to step in as propaganda representative.' Drexler went on to state that he had been 'forced to complain' because Hitler's membership card had been 'falsified' and the 'number 555 had been deleted and the number seven inserted'.[10]

At first sight this spat seems odd, because Hitler was undoubtedly a relatively early member since the party started numbering from 501 to make it look as though it was larger than it was. So why did it matter so much to Hitler to be member number 7?

Hitler gave a clue to the answer in *Mein Kampf*, the rambling account of his actions and views that he wrote in prison in 1924. 'I had no intention of joining a ready-made party,' he wrote, 'but wanted to found one of my own.'[11] The idea of this virtually penniless ordinary soldier founding his 'own party' at this point is fanciful, but it was a myth that Hitler was anxious to propagate. A 'great man' in his eyes was never a follower, always a leader. And the only sure way of being the leader of a political party was to start it yourself.

It was impossible for Hitler to claim that he had founded the German Workers' Party, but he could do the next best thing and pretend that he was one of the earliest members. He longed to tell the world that he had been part of the original group – that together with a mere handful of men he had decided to change the course of history.

In *Mein Kampf*, Hitler devoted space to ridiculing the state of the party he joined in 1919, emphasizing the small membership numbers and the general hopelessness of the organization. 'Terrible, terrible!' he wrote about the German Workers' Party. 'This was club life of the worst manner and sort.'[12] He then attempted to justify joining such a 'terrible' group by saying that though it was an 'absurd little organization', it nonetheless offered the right individual a chance 'to put [it] into the proper form'.[13] So by this bizarre logic Hitler did his best to convince his readers that he had, in effect, created a party that already existed.

Given the space he devoted in *Mein Kampf* to this question, it is obvious the matter troubled him. His decision, years later, to award a Golden Party Badge to the first 100,000 people to join the Nazi Party was part of this attempt to show he had effectively been the creator of the movement. It's an interpretation that's confirmed by his insistence that his own Gold Party Badge – one of the few decorations, along with his Iron Cross, that he wore – should be inscribed with the number 1. He couldn't get a party membership card that called him the number one Nazi, but he could award himself a badge that did.

Having joined the German Workers' Party, Hitler quickly became its star speaker and the dominant figure in the movement, channelling his anger at the state of Germany into a series of uncompromising speeches. This first phase of his involvement in politics culminated with the unveiling of the party programme at the Hofbräuhaus beer hall in Munich.

By February 1920, when the programme was launched, Hitler possessed a handful of political beliefs that would never leave him. When he formed them, we can't know exactly. Some, such as his pan-Germanism – the view that all Germans belonged together – he had held for many years.

As we've seen, even though Hitler had been born in Austria he considered himself German, and Germans, he believed, should keep themselves pure and live only with other Germans. It had been his furious verbal attack on a speaker who called for Bavarian separatism that had initially drawn Drexler's attention to Hitler during the first meeting of the German Workers' Party that he attended. 'Goodness, he's got a gob,' Drexler is supposed to have said. 'We could use him.'[14]

Hitler wasn't alone in proselytizing pan-German beliefs. The pan-German movement had been influential for years and had received a boost with the unification of Germany during the nineteenth century. But there was scarcely a more passionate pan-Germanist than Adolf Hitler. It was thus no accident that the very first point in the party programme announced in February 1920 called for all Germans to be united within a greater Germany.

The second belief that Hitler already held by this point was anti-Semitism. In a letter to another soldier, Adolf Gemlich, dated 16 September 1919, he explained the nature of his hatred.[15] In the Gemlich letter he blamed the problems Germany faced on the Jews, but significantly he did not say that his hatred was founded on 'traditional' Christian-based anti-Semitism. Instead, he asserted that the Jews were a 'race' and not a 'religious association' and he used the terminology of disease to claim that they 'produce a racial tuberculosis among nations'.

This pseudo-scientific anti-Semitism was not something that Hitler had thought up himself. During the nineteenth century a number of other writers – often twisting new discoveries in biology – had attempted to 'prove' that some races were 'superior' to others. The German scholar Eugen Dühring, for instance, had decided by 1880 that the Jewish question was a racial question.[16]

Where and when Hitler first developed his anti-Semitic beliefs has been debated by scholars for years. But one thing is certain – we can't rely on his own explanation. Hitler's claim in *Mein Kampf* that he lectured Jews in Vienna about their shortcomings is almost certainly a lie – in fact, research has shown that he had amicable dealings with Jews in the Austrian capital.[17] It is more plausible to suggest that while he was exposed to anti-Semitic rhetoric in Vienna, and may well have held some anti-Semitic views at the time, his radical anti-Semitism did not fully develop until he both subscribed to the fantasy that Jews had been responsible for the loss of the war and had witnessed first hand the establishment of the Soviet Republic in Munich – one which, as we have seen, was perceived to have been created by Jews.

Despite its lack of originality, Hitler's statement in the Gemlich letter that the Jews were a race not a religious association was an important assertion. The basis of responsibility in any state that subscribes to the rule of law is individual culpability. If, for instance, individual German Jews had been found to have broken the criminal law during the First World War and acted, as was claimed, as 'profiteers' then they could have been prosecuted. They would have been held responsible for their behaviour, not for their heritage. Hitler's assertion that the Jews were a race led to a different approach. It 'blamed' the Jews en masse and thus helped make the Holocaust possible more than twenty years later. That is because there was no possibility of those with a Jewish heritage subsequently escaping death by demonstrating either that they were willing to renounce their religion or that they had broken no law. The mere fact they were categorized as Jews was enough to condemn them.

None of that is to say that Hitler was contemplating the Holocaust when he wrote to Adolf Gemlich in 1919. He did however demand, towards the end of the letter, 'the uncompromising removal of Jews altogether'. While we can't know what intentions lurked deep within his mind, it's extremely unlikely that by this he meant the extermination of the Jews. The policy of his government until the outbreak of the Second World War was to persecute the Jews, take away their citizenship, rob them and force them out of the country. Though Jews did die at the hands of Nazis in the 1930s there was no attempt at mass extermination.

Significantly, the party programme of February 1920 didn't go as far as Hitler's statement in the Gemlich letter. Although point 4 announced that only those of German 'blood' could be citizens, and so German Jews would be denied citizenship, there was no explicit call to expel them from the country. Though Hitler was by now a rabid anti-Semite, he was also a politician, dealing in what was practicable. He knew that not all his supporters felt as radically about the issue as he did.

Emil Klein, for instance, a member of the party in the early 1920s, was not as extreme an anti-Semite as Hitler. He had formed his anti-Semitism as a schoolboy and saw nothing radical about it: 'Where I went to school, they [Jews] were all sons of businessmen, and there were

Jews in the school, in the B class. Even then, there was already friction between us in class A and the B class where the Jews were. But if they'd been Arabs or Turks, there would probably have been the same brawling, that's how it is at school. It just happens with schoolboys, if someone doesn't like your face you get jibes, it happens everywhere.'[18] After he joined the Nazi Party, Klein added a new element to his anti-Semitism – the belief, proselytized by Hitler and others, that the Jews controlled world finance: 'So, [we were] not against the Jews as individuals, but against capitalism, which stems from Jewry, from Wall Street that is. Wall Street was always being mentioned.'[19]

Bruno Hähnel, who also became a party member in the 1920s, had a similar mindset. He didn't support the idea of killing German Jews, but wanted to see them 'removed from public life, from the media-controlling posts which they might have held'. Like Emil Klein, he also subscribed to the conspiracy theory that the Jews plotted together across national borders: 'I have to come back to global Jewry, because we looked at it in terms of the global Jewry which wanted to gain power, which wanted to rule the world, [and] because of this propaganda the demand to remove them from public life was understandable.'[20]

Two young men who would later go on to become infamous as Nazis – Heinrich Himmler, future head of the SS, and Joseph Goebbels, who became Propaganda Minister – were also shaping their own anti-Semitic views around this time. Himmler, at the age of twenty-one and before he had even met Adolf Hitler, took a Hitlerian line when he described a Jewish lawyer in his diary as 'extremely amiable and kind' but added that 'he cannot hide his Jewishness. After all, he can be a very good person, but that kind of thing is in those people's blood.'[21]

The young Joseph Goebbels' anti-Semitism was more confused. On the one hand he could write in his diary in 1923, when he was twenty-six, that 'the Jews are the poison that is killing the body of Europe' and that 'one would like to punch' the Jews 'in the face'.[22] While at the same time he was going out with a young woman called Else who had a Jewish mother. He described Else as 'good and beautiful',[23] although he also referred to her as a 'half-breed'.[24]

At first sight all of these different approaches to anti-Semitism among Nazi supporters in the 1920s seem confusing. Nonetheless, they offer an insight into the appeal of the party in these early days. As long as you accepted that the Jews – in one form or another – were a danger, then the kind of anti-Semitism you believed in was to a large degree up to you.

By the time Hitler wrote his letter to Adolf Gemlich the Jews had, for many German nationalists, become the scapegoat for almost everything that had gone wrong for the country: the lost war; the Versailles treaty; the socialist revolutions; the destruction of the old regime; the financial difficulties ordinary people now endured, and more. Believing in anti-Semitic conspiracy theories wasn't unusual in those immediate post-war years. So the fact that Hitler voiced his prejudice in such an extreme pseudo-scientific way didn't seem remarkable.[25]

Understandably, given the horrors to come, much of the focus today on the motivations of Nazi Party members is on the nature and cause of their anti-Semitism. But it would be a mistake to conclude that hatred of the Jews was the main reason that Germans came to support the movement. The evidence shows that large numbers – almost certainly the majority – joined the party in the 1920s and early 1930s for another reason altogether. Their hope was that Hitler would deliver a *Volksgemeinschaft* – a 'people's community'.

Peter Merkl in his seminal analysis of Theodore Abel's study of several hundred Nazi supporters who became involved with the party before 1933 concluded that the most common ideological theme binding them together was not anti-Semitism but their belief in the *Volksgemeinschaft*.[26] However, as we will see, the two concepts were often linked in many people's minds.

The *Volksgemeinschaft* is an idea rich in meaning and resonance in German, but its essence is impossible to convey in English in just one or two words. A straightforward translation might be 'people's (or national) community', but that ignores much of the complexity. The word *Volk* meant more than just 'people' and suggested a whole series of shared ethnic and cultural beliefs. *Volksgemeinschaft* went further still and implied that all Germans should be bound together in a particular kind of community, and that this community ought to matter more than the individual. Many political parties at the time proclaimed that their aim was to create a *Volksgemeinschaft*, but by concentrating on the racial purity of those who belonged to that community the Nazis focused on the idea in a more intense and racist way.

The concept of the *Volksgemeinschaft* pervaded the programme of the

German Workers' Party. It didn't just lurk behind the measure to deny Jews citizenship, it was also the inspiration for many of the social policies that were included in the programme, such as the plan for gifted children of poor parents to be educated at the expense of the state (point 20) and the demand that the activities of the individual should not conflict with the needs of the community as a whole (point 10).

It is also important to recognize that the idea of the *Volksgemeinschaft* was a profound statement of the Nazis' categorizing of people into 'Them and Us'. Only those they judged 'pure' Germans in racial terms could be part of the *Volksgemeinschaft*. There was nothing you could do as an individual to join this club; the Nazi view was that your 'blood' was your destiny. Thus, since the Jews were considered an 'alien race', they were automatically excluded from the 'people's community'.

The *Volksgemeinschaft* simplified enormously the task of working out who was friend or who was foe. No longer did you have to spend time getting to know someone to see if they were welcoming or not. You only had to ask one question – are you a member of the German 'race' or not? The desire to categorize people, as Gordon Allport pointed out in his pioneering work *The Nature of Prejudice*, can often lead to biased thinking.[27] The *Volksgemeinschaft* made that biased thinking easier than ever.

However, the concept of the *Volksgemeinschaft* is sometimes misunderstood. It is easy to fall into the trap of thinking that it meant the Nazis were a socialist movement. After all, calling for gifted poor children to be educated at the expense of the state certainly sounds socialist. It is also the case that the German Workers' Party changed its name to the National Socialist German Workers' Party (or Nazis for short) after the launch of the party programme in February 1920 at the Hofbräuhaus beer hall in Munich. But none of this meant that the Nazis were a genuine socialist movement – most obviously because many large capitalist enterprises thrived under Nazi rule. Instead, their seemingly socialist policies need to be understood within the concept of the *Volksgemeinschaft*.

In a revealing speech in April 1922, Hitler explained what he meant by 'National Socialist'. ' "National" and "social" are two identical conceptions,' said Hitler. 'It was only the Jew who succeeded, through falsifying the social idea and turning it into Marxism, not only in divorcing the social idea from the national, but in actually representing

them as utterly contradictory.' Hitler then went on to explain why the
Nazis believed the two ideas were identical: 'We said to ourselves that to
be "national" means above everything to act with a boundless and all-
embracing love for the people [*Volk*] and, if necessary, even to die for it.
And similarly to be "social" means so to build up the State and the community of the people [*Volk*] that every individual acts in the interest of
the community of the people [*Volk*] . . .'[28]

The notion of the *Volksgemeinschaft* thus knitted everything together
for the Nazis: fanatical nationalism allied to a desire to fight for the
common good of all 'racially pure' Germans. It meant that Hitler could
even assert that 'there are no such things as classes: they cannot be. Class
means caste and caste means race.'[29]

It was a seductive idea for Nazi supporters like Emil Klein: 'This
party wanted to eradicate class differences, with the working class here,
the bourgeoisie here and the middle classes here. These were deeply
ingrained concepts that split the nation into two parts. That was an
important point for me, one that I liked . . . the nation has to be united.'[30]
His fellow Nazi Bruno Hähnel was also enormously attracted by the
Nazi desire to form a 'national community' in order to 'ensure that both
the intellectuals and the workers would join forces'. As he understood it,
the idea 'was expressed in the catchphrase, which I think most of us used
again and again, "The public interest comes first" '.[31]

All this had a special meaning because of the timing of the emergence
of the Nazi Party. Everyone knew of the previous attempt to create a
sense of community in 1914 when war was declared. While not every
German had been enthusiastic about the conflict, there was still a powerful sense that the nation as a whole had to come together – no political
parties, 'only Germans', as the Kaiser had said. Understandably, the contrast with the political upheaval at the end of the war was stark. What
had happened to the *Volksgemeinschaft* of just six years before? Could it
ever be recovered?

It was a question brought into even sharper focus by the belief many
people held of a *Frontgemeinschaft* – the conviction that soldiers in the
trenches had bonded together in a brotherly community. This, as outlined in the previous chapter, was a flawed way of looking at what had
happened, but nonetheless it attained a mythic quality. Many Nazi
supporters believed the fantasy that both the *Frontgemeinschaft* and the
Volksgemeinschaft had been subverted by the Jews and socialist politicians

who had plotted against the brave soldiers at the front and the loyal Germans at home. Consequently, there was a strong desire to recover both the mystical *Volksgemeinschaft* of 1914 and the alleged *Frontgemein-schaft* of the trenches.

In the circumstances of the moment, Hitler was the ideal leader to pursue this quest. The fact that he had been a 'simple soldier' worked to his advantage, given that the leadership class of officers and aristocrats was perceived to have failed Germany. Dietrich Eckart, Hitler's mentor in the early 1920s, remarked that what was needed was a 'fellow who can stand the rattle of a machine gun. The rabble has to be scared shit-less. I can't use an officer; the people no longer have any respect for them. Best of all would be a worker who's got his mouth in the right place . . . He doesn't need much intelligence; politics is the stupidest business in the world.'[32] Eckart was an important influence on Hitler during this period. An alcoholic playwright in his fifties, he was tren-chant in his views, remarking that if people 'saw through' what the Jew 'is and what he wants, screaming in horror they would strangle him the very next minute'.[33]

From the moment he announced the party programme, Hitler was adamant that it was inviolate.[34] Understandably, this inflexibility was to cause problems, because so much of the content was ambiguous. For instance, what exactly did 'the activities of the individual must not clash with the general interest' really mean (point 10)? Inevitably, various factions quarrelled over the correct interpretation.

But any discord caused by the lack of detail in the party programme was a price Hitler was willing to pay. That's because the imprecision of the content allowed him to interpret it how he liked. And the inher-ent vagueness of the concept of *Volksgemeinschaft* – how, for instance, does one begin to define in practical terms 'the common interest before self-interest' (point 24) – only added to the ease with which the Nazi leader could avoid detailed policy discussions and speak in visions instead.

In the early 1920s Hitler also relied on the power of ambiguity to deal with the sensitive question of the relationship between Christianity and Nazism. The problem he faced was not just that there was a vast spread of belief within the party – some were committed Christians while others were passionate atheists – but he also had to conceal his own feel-ings. He attempted to reconcile this by stating in point 24 of the Nazis'

programme that the movement was committed to 'positive Christianity'. Typically, he never defined exactly what he meant by this phrase.
Many took it to mean an acceptance of Jesus as a religious figure, coupled with a belief in a version of Christianity that was suffused with
racial anti-Semitism.

But even this supposed commitment to 'positive Christianity' was
almost certainly just pragmatic. Not only is it highly improbable that
Hitler in 1920 believed in the fundamental precepts of the Christian
faith, but he subsequently remarked in private during the war that he
thought Christianity 'has crippled all that is noble in humanity'[35] and
that 'Christianity is an invention of sick brains.'[36] Nonetheless, from the
moment of the announcement of the party programme in February
1920 until Hitler's death twenty-five years later, the party's stated policy
remained one of 'positive Christianity'.

It's easy to understand why this was so. As Hitler remarked to General Ludendorff before he came to power, 'I need Bavarian Catholics as
well as Prussian Protestants to build up a great political movement. The
rest comes later.'[37] In pursuit of this goal Hitler even praised Jesus in a
speech in 1922 as a 'fighter' who recognized the 'Jews for what they
were'.[38]

In the years to come it would prove to be a tricky balancing act,
because Hitler had to ensure not only that Christian Nazis like the
brutal district leader Erich Koch were happy within the party, but that
passionately anti-religious figures like Martin Bormann, who would
come to dominate the party organization, were content as well. By
keeping to a vague commitment for 'positive Christianity' while
simultaneously – once he was secure in power – attacking in private the
whole basis of Christianity, Hitler hoped to keep them all on board.

By emphasizing these few broad concepts – 'positive Christianity',
pan-Germanism, anti-Semitism, hatred of Versailles and the pursuit of
Volksgemeinschaft – Hitler kept the appeal of the Nazi Party simple.

But none of that would have been sufficient to grow the party without Hitler's rhetorical gifts. His laser-like focus on 'Them and Us'
combined with his vision of the *Volksgemeinschaft* soon allowed the Nazis
to book ever bigger venues for their gatherings.

Kurt Lüdecke, an ardent German nationalist, memorably described
seeing Hitler speak in 1922. Initially, Lüdecke 'critically . . . studied this
slight, pale man, his brown hair parted on one side and falling again

and again over his sweating brow'. But soon his 'critical faculty was swept away' by the power of Hitler's rhetoric as 'He urged the revival of German honour and manhood with a blast of words that seemed to cleanse . . . I experienced an exaltation that could be likened only to religious conversion.'[39]

However, we must treat Lüdecke's recollections carefully. Even though he claimed he fell 'under a hypnotic spell' because of the force of Hitler's 'conviction', that was not quite what was going on. What he actually felt was an intense emotional and intellectual connection.

The crucial precondition for Lüdecke's conversion to the Nazi cause was that he was predisposed to find Hitler entrancing. He admitted as much, writing that he was already 'looking for the German soul, or rather for the leader who would know how to reanimate it', and he conceded that he was 'ripe for this experience'. But he was wrong in his judgement that 'no one who heard Hitler that afternoon could doubt that he was the man of destiny, the vitalizing force in the future of Germany.'[40] On the contrary, plenty of people who heard Hitler speak did doubt exactly that, and came away thinking that he was a crank, or worse.[41] Why else would Hitler need to be protected at meetings by members of the euphemistically named 'Gymnastic and Sports' section of the party – later called the Nazi Stormtroopers?

When he heard Hitler speak in January 1920, Hans Frank, a nineteen-year-old student – and later an infamous Nazi war criminal – experienced a similar awakening to Lüdecke's. 'Everything came from the heart,' he wrote years later, 'and he struck a chord with all of us . . . He uttered what was in the consciousness of all those present.'[42] Unlike Lüdecke, Frank thus understood that Hitler was connecting with members of the audience because of what was already in their own minds.

In the wake of a lost war, revolution and a peace treaty that millions considered unjust, Hitler didn't just legitimize the anger felt by many of those who listened to him, he also offered hope. As Konrad Heiden, an opponent of Hitler's who studied his speaking style, wrote: 'His speeches are day-dreams of this mass soul . . . The speeches begin always with deep pessimism and end in overjoyed redemption, a triumphant happy ending; often they can be refuted by reason, but they follow the far mightier logic of the subconscious, which no refutation can touch. Hitler has given speech to the speechless terror of the modern mass . . .'[43]

This is part of the solution to a seeming conundrum. How could Hitler, an ordinary soldier during the war, convince distinguished veterans like Hermann Göring – a former commander of the Richthofen Squadron and a charismatic figure himself – to join the Nazi Party in the early 1920s? The answer is primarily because Göring connected with what Hitler was saying. 'Hitler spoke . . . about Versailles,' remembered Göring years later. 'He said that . . . a protest is successful only if backed by power to give it weight . . . This conviction was spoken word for word as if from my own soul.' When he met Hitler subsequently, Göring recalled, 'We spoke at once about the things which were close to our hearts – the defeat of our Fatherland . . . Versailles. I told him that I myself to the fullest extent, and all I was and possessed, were completely at his disposal for this, in my opinion, most essential and decisive matter: the fight against the Treaty of Versailles.'[44]

Not only did Hitler like to talk in broad concepts in his speeches – such as 'the fight against the Treaty of Versailles' – but he was also content, as long as the party machinery still functioned, to allow those beneath him to quarrel among themselves about what the details of Nazi policy should be. This also maximized his chances of growing the party, as prospective members couldn't feel excluded by opposition to the details of the party programme. They soon realized there *were* no detailed policies proposed by the Nazis, only a vision of a wonderful future based on simple ideas.

It would be a mistake, however, to portray Hitler as a weak or laissez-faire leader. When it came to any possible challenge to his own authority he acted decisively. An early example of this phenomenon occurred in July 1921, when Anton Drexler became interested in the work of an academic at Augsburg University called Professor Otto Dickel, who had not only written a book on nationalistic political ideas but founded his own party, the Deutsche Werkgemeinschaft.

Drexler, and others within the Nazi party leadership, believed that the best way for the movement to grow was to merge with other, similar political groups like Dickel's. Previously Drexler had been keen on a merger with the Deutschsozialistische Partei (German Socialist Party) and had even managed to drag Hitler along to a meeting to discuss a potential union – only for Hitler's intransigence to torpedo the idea.

When he first heard of the planned merger with Dickel's group, Hitler had been in Berlin with Dietrich Eckart, trying to raise money for party funds. He was outraged at the news. Even though officially he was merely propaganda chief of the Nazi Party, he believed that as the star performer he had the right to decide the future of the movement. He hurried back to Bavaria to attend a meeting about the proposed merger, and listened as Dickel made a series of proposals – all of which Hitler angrily rejected. After three hours he could take no more and flounced out of the room.[45] Despite Hitler's fierce opposition, Drexler and his allies announced that they would consult a larger group within the party on whether they wanted to move forward with Dickel. For Hitler, that was the breaking point. On 11 July 1921 he resigned from the Nazi Party.

Throughout his political career Hitler was emotionally attached to either/or actions and arguments. His speeches were full of false but dramatic dichotomies – in the context of the Jews, for instance, he often asserted that if they were not defeated then Germany would be destroyed. 'There can be no compromise,' he said in a speech in April 1922, 'there are only two possibilities: either victory of the Aryan or annihilation of the Aryan and the victory of the Jew.'[46]

Hitler was also fond of either/or choices in the context of the policies of the Nazi Party. The announcement of the party programme in February 1920 ended with the words 'the leaders of the Party promise to work ruthlessly – if need be to sacrifice their very lives – to translate this programme into action.'[47] So it should have come as no surprise when Hitler walked out of the meeting with Dickel and resigned. As Hitler saw it, either the party stopped dealings with Dickel or he quit. He wasn't about to share the limelight with anyone. It was another simple either/or, and more evidence of Hitler's devotion to the power of 'Them and Us' thinking.

Obviously, this placed Drexler and his comrades in a difficult position, especially since Hitler told them that he would rejoin the party only if he was given absolute power over the movement. Drexler floundered around for a few days, but it was plain that the Nazi Party risked a return to the wilderness without Hitler. Desperate to avoid that fate, they succumbed and gave Hitler everything he wanted. On 29 July 1921 he was appointed chairman of the party with dictatorial powers.

It is vital to understand that this radical development was not a calculated move on Hitler's part. He had reacted instinctively – and to a large degree emotionally – to a new situation. He wasn't the type of

---

politician who calmly weighed up alternatives and chose from a number of strategic options. Ultimately, he did what came naturally to him.

Spontaneous as Hitler's choice had been, it is still possible to identify two basic reasons for his actions. The first is that he was incapable of engaging in an intellectual debate with Dickel – his mind simply didn't function that way. The second is that any proposed 'merger' was anathema to him. Sharing the key position in the party with anyone went against his core belief in the way the world ought to be. His political – and life – philosophy was simple. 'Always before God and the world the stronger has the right to carry through what he wills,' he said in a speech in 1923. 'The whole world of Nature is a mighty struggle between strength and weakness – an eternal victory of the strong over the weak. There would be nothing but decay in the whole of Nature if this were not so.'[48]

With all idea of a 'merger' with Dickel's party dismissed, Hitler proceeded to demonstrate his preferred method of expansion by convincing a thirty-seven-year-old teacher called Julius Streicher and his followers to join the party. Years later Streicher spoke in mystical terms about his reaction to Hitler's oratory: 'I saw this man shortly before midnight, after he had spoken for 3 hours, drenched in perspiration, radiant. My neighbour said he thought he saw a halo around his head; and I . . . experienced something which transcended the commonplace.'[49]

However, this was not the whole story. After having fought in the war, Streicher had moved between several anti-Semitic parties searching for his political home. The problem he faced was not that the parties he sampled were too radical, but that they weren't radical enough. In 1919 Streicher had read Theodor Fritsch's *Handbuch der Judenfrage* (Handbook on the Jewish Question) and this compendium of delusional conspiracy theories about the Jews had led to him developing his own brand of all-consuming anti-Semitism.[50] Three years later, in 1922, he was convicted by the district court in Schweinfurt for claiming that Jews ritually murdered German children.[51]

Streicher was a belligerent, aggressive man. But he was also capable of inspiring others. Prior to meeting Hitler, Kurt Lüdecke had encountered Streicher on his own quest to find the 'leader' who could rescue Germany. Streicher was 'an entirely new type to me', wrote Lüdecke, 'and soon I found his enthusiasm infectious.'

Streicher's warped theories were not just focused on the Jews; he also had bizarre ideas about how Germans should ready themselves for the fight to save their country. He told Lüdecke that it was important to fast in preparation for the ordeal ahead. And since Streicher maintained that 'Jesus Christ had given cherries to his disciples' he persuaded Lüdecke that they too should try and survive on nothing but cherries.

Lüdecke and Streicher lived together in one room in a village as they tried their new diet regime, with Lüdecke buying cherries from a local farmer. But while Streicher's enthusiasm was 'infectious' his willpower was lacking, and on the third day the plan fell apart when Lüdecke caught him in a restaurant eating a 'huge' omelette.[52]

In November 1921, during his journey around various Bavarian *völkisch* parties, Streicher had led his followers into the Deutsche Werkgemeinschaft, the organization founded by Hitler's hated rival Professor Dickel. Once ensconced within Dickel's new party, Streicher retitled his own propaganda newspaper the *Deutscher Volkswille* – Will of the German People – and published anti-Semitic material of the vilest sort. This offended Dickel, who did not approve of the extreme content.

Hitler saw an opportunity and approached Streicher with a compelling offer. The Nazis would pay off the newspaper's debts and Streicher could become Gauleiter (Nazi district leader) of his native Franconia, the area of Bavaria containing Nuremberg. Swapping Dickel for Hitler while simultaneously clearing his debts was an offer Streicher felt he couldn't refuse, and so he not only joined the Nazi Party himself in October 1922 but persuaded many of his followers to do likewise.[53]

This is a much more complex reason for Streicher's hero worship of Hitler than the one he later gave, and while it's still possible that Streicher was entranced by Hitler's oratory, his conversion to Nazism only happened after this advantageous deal had already been struck. As for Hitler, Streicher's defection from Dickel's party must have been doubly pleasing. Not only had the Nazi Party expanded by his preferred method – absorption – but a hated rival had been thwarted.

Hitler understood that Streicher was radical, unpredictable, almost unbalanced. Years later he recalled that Dietrich Eckart had remarked to him that Streicher was a 'lunatic' but had added that the Nazis could never be successful without welcoming such people into the movement.[54] Not surprisingly, keeping extreme people like Streicher on board – especially when they were quick to quarrel with their comrades – was a challenge. And internal rivalries and shifting alliances were to be a characteristic of the party until the final days. What is important to note at this point is that this infighting was prevalent from the very beginning – inevitably so given that 'lunatics' such as Streicher were encouraged to join.

What Hitler sought to create, as he wrote in January 1922, was a party of 'struggle and action',[55] and he did not just welcome proven warriors such as Streicher, Hermann Göring and Ernst Röhm, but deliberately targeted others who sought excitement and danger. As he said in a speech in the summer of 1922, 'He who today fights on our side cannot win great laurels, far less can he win great material goods – it is more likely that he will end up in jail . . .' What mattered, said Hitler, was that the Nazis were driven by what he claimed were honourable motives: 'The conviction that our Movement is not sustained by money or the lust for gold, but only by our love for the people, that must ever give us fresh heart, that must ever fill us with courage for the fray.'[56] Inevitably, such words appealed especially to young Germans, and as we shall see in a later chapter, this focus on youth offered the Nazis valuable psychological benefits.[57]

These were violent times. But the fledgling Nazi Party was emerging as one of the most uncompromisingly violent groups of all. In particular the party's SA (Sturmabteilung – Storm Section) attracted a number of young toughs – including former Freikorps members.

Ernst Röhm played a crucial role in building up the Stormtroopers, using his contacts across right-wing groups to help develop and equip these Nazi paramilitaries. That the Stormtroopers might become an organization that was difficult to control was obvious, but for Hitler this was an issue he was prepared to accept. He could not have a party of 'struggle and action' without them.

Hitler tried his best to epitomize this need to fight. As well as employing his bruisers to keep order during his speeches, he also led them in battles against rival political speakers. In September 1921 they burst into the Löwenbräukeller in Munich and broke up a meeting of the pro-monarchist Bayernbund. Initially the Nazi supporters just shouted out the word 'Hitler' over and over so that the speaker could not be heard, but this soon escalated into an all-out fight. Hitler was subsequently prosecuted for his part in the violence and served a month in prison.[58]

Nazi Stormtroopers didn't only break up other people's meetings, they also provoked the communists by crossing into their part of the city. Emil Klein joined the Stormtroopers in the early 1920s and he claimed that he and his comrades 'preferred to march through the Red districts' because 'we wanted to have the communists on our side.' But, to no one's surprise, this act of obvious provocation often resulted in fights between the two groups.[59]

Hitler provoked the communists further by deciding that the colour most associated with their movement – red – should be the predominant colour on Nazi Party banners and armbands. It was a decision that, in those early days, could cause confusion. 'I remember the first time my [nationalist] father saw my red armband with the swastika,' said Emil Klein. 'He said, "Tell me, aren't you embarrassed walking about wearing a red armband?" So I said, "You don't seem to see that there's a swastika on it." "Yes, but it's red!" '[60]

Despite these headline-making actions, the Nazi Party remained on the periphery of Bavarian political life. By the summer of 1921 only a few thousand people had joined – less than 1 per cent of the population of Munich. Eighteen months later, at the end of 1922, party membership was still only 22,000 – rapid growth, but still an almost insignificant figure compared to established parties.[61] Hitler's response to this challenge – then and later – was to try and exploit opportunities as they happened. The Nazi Party thrived on turmoil and despair, and in 1923 Germany was to be filled with plenty of both.

It was apparent by the end of 1922 that the Germans could not make their reparation payments to the Allies. The burden, as many had predicted, was just too onerous. So, to enforce reparations, in January 1923 Belgian and French soldiers marched into the Ruhr – the industrial heartland of Germany that had been demilitarized in the wake of Versailles.

Werner Best, a university student who later rose to a high position in the SS, saw this as a moment of colossal danger for Germany. Too young to fight in the First World War, Best believed that the occupation of the Ruhr heralded the start of another epic conflict – one in which, this time, he could participate. 'We are now confronted by an ambitious French plan of extermination,' he wrote in 1923. 'We need now to clarify for our people the consequences and the ruthless nature of the French extermination plan. Resistance and combat, or annihilation without mercy! For us, more than ever, one thing alone counts: to be ready.'62

The German government disagreed. Given the weakness of the German Army, they decided not to confront the French on the battlefield. Instead, Wilhelm Cuno, the Chancellor, called for workers in the Ruhr to resist the occupiers by withdrawing their labour. But his government still carried on paying civil service employees who were no longer working as a consequence of the strike. This was one of the reasons that German inflation – already high – rose to stratospheric levels.

Bernd Linn grew up in Bavaria during this period, and he remembered witnessing customers in his father's shop who were unable to afford basic foodstuffs: 'First and foremost [it was] worst for the old people, because in the inflation period they could not manage with their money at all.' Inflation soon turned into hyperinflation, and when Linn took the shop's daily takings to the bank across the street he found he needed a 'basket' to hold the bundles of paper money.63

Emil Klein also recalled the 'plight of the people as the famine grew terribly. It ended up with the inflation, that was the worst thing, when I think about how I once paid four billion [Marks] for a sausage-meat roll! That's stuck in my memory, that it cost four billion.'64

It's hard for us today to appreciate the sense of crisis provoked by this combination of hyperinflation and the occupation of the Ruhr – the humiliation millions felt as their money became worthless, and their erstwhile enemy walked into a vital part of their country. For German nationalists it was yet another demonstration of the impotence of the state, another sign of dishonour.

The Nazis had never accepted the legitimacy of the Weimar Republic and claimed that the Versailles treaty and the current economic hardship represented just two of the manifest failures of the regime. Moreover, they saw themselves as revolutionaries and believed the occupation of the Ruhr was yet another example of why a revolution was necessary. So it was not surprising, amid this frenzied atmosphere, that some Nazi supporters decided it was time to take the law into their own hands.

That is the background to a bloody murder that took place in northern Germany in May 1923. It's a crime of particular significance as it offers us an insight into the mentality of two Nazis who would later become infamous – Martin Bormann, who served as a powerful adviser to Hitler during the Second World War, and Rudolf Höss, who helped establish Auschwitz concentration camp in 1940, and as commandant oversaw the site of the largest mass murder in history.

Born in 1900, Bormann had joined the German Army during the First World War but hadn't seen action. By 1923, and already a confirmed anti-Semite, he was managing an agricultural estate in Mecklenburg in the north of Germany. Near the estate lived Rudolf Höss, also in his twenties. Unlike Bormann, he had fought both in the trenches and later as a member of a Freikorps in a bloody conflict in the Baltic. Höss, who had joined the Nazi Party the previous year, was living in a hostel with other agricultural workers, many of whom held nationalist beliefs – so much so that they were known collectively as the 'swastika people' or the 'Rossbach people', after the name of the commander of the Freikorps they had belonged to, Gerhard Rossbach.[65]

At the start of 1923 a young worker called Walther Kadow joined their group. He soon became unpopular. Not only did he borrow money from his new comrades, but they suspected he might be a spy. As a result, he was forced out of town. Höss and his friends let it be known that if Kadow turned up again he would be in trouble. But turn up he did on 31 May when he was spotted drinking in a local pub. Bormann, who had been instrumental in sacking Kadow from the agricultural estate, lent his car to Höss and his comrades and suggested they beat him up. They leapt at the idea, travelled to the pub and bundled a drunken Kadow into the car.

Having taken Kadow to a nearby field, they beat him with a baton and a walking stick. Höss, according to the court judgment, 'coshed Kadow with full force'. The unconscious Kadow was then dragged to the car and put on a luggage rack at the back. As they drove away the group discussed what they should do with him – take him to hospital or finish him off and dispose of the body. Eventually they agreed with Höss' suggestion that Kadow should be murdered and dumped in the woods.

Once in the woods, one of the assailants cut Kadow's throat and two bullets were fired into his head – who exactly pulled the trigger was later disputed. Kadow was buried in a shallow grave, his belongings burned, and the group then drove off to clean up the car prior to returning it to Bormann.

The next day, having heard rumours that Kadow had been murdered, Bormann advised Höss that he and his friends should disappear for a bit if they had 'done something wrong'. But none of the killers heeded this advice. They thought running away would just draw more attention to themselves.

The true facts about the killing were only discovered weeks later because one of the conspirators confessed the crime to a journalist. He claimed he was frightened his colleagues might turn on him and gave the impression, said the newspaper editor who listened to his story, of being 'an animal hunted to death'. At a trial the following year every member of the group was found guilty and sentenced to time in prison – Höss to ten years and Bormann, as an 'accessory', to one year.

Superficially, this was a tawdry tale of brutal murder. But it also laid bare the attitudes of Bormann and Höss as young men, and revealed how they were perceived by others. One journalist wrote shortly after the crime was discovered that Höss and his comrades were 'bandits' and that they had formed 'a state within a state' in Mecklenburg. It was also thought 'certain' that 'these armed Rossbach gangs work hand in hand with the landowners.'[66] It is a plausible accusation. Not only was Bormann an estate manager but, as the German currency collapsed, agricultural foodstuffs were an attractive target for thieves. A gang of Freikorps toughs would have provided useful protection to the landowners.

In the memoirs he wrote in prison, after he had been convicted of war crimes, Höss attempted to defend the killing by claiming that Kadow had betrayed another of their comrades – Albert Schlageter – to the French authorities in the Ruhr. He also wrote that the 'Freikorps and their successor organizations . . . administered justice themselves' in the manner of the 'ancient Germanic pattern'. He further argued that since 'in all probability' a German court wouldn't have convicted Kadow 'it was left to us to pass sentence . . .'[67] But no evidence that Kadow had been connected to the Schlageter betrayal was presented at the trial. Almost certainly years later Höss was merely trying to justify the killing. Better to be thought a principled murderer than a drunk thug with a grudge.

The defendants were described at the time as 'militarily trained without exception', and Höss was singled out in a newspaper report as a 'so-called educated man. He attended grammar school and was considered possible officer material. But you can already tell by his face, the hard mouth and the nasty chin that he is capable of any brutality.'[68]

Also noteworthy is the reaction of both Höss and Bormann to their convictions. Just days after he was sentenced, Höss wrote defiantly to a friend, 'According to everyone's opinion, except for that of our comrades and of those who know us, we are the scum of mankind, that's just how it is. I'm not bothered. I have never cared for the majority's opinion. I have faith in the triumph of our cause and in my leaders and my comrades. Come what may, we remain the same, even in jail. This doesn't dishonour me.'[69] Höss also believed that the existing regime didn't have long left. As he wrote later, 'the political crisis in the Reich was so acute that the overthrow of the government by one side or the other seemed inevitable.'[70]

In August 1929, four years before the Nazis came to power, Bormann wrote an article for the Nazi newspaper the *Völkischer Beobachter*, entitled 'In the Dungeons of the Republic', in which he emphasized that he and the others who had been found guilty 'were firmly convinced, and still are today, that we were not wrong but right, and that we didn't deserve punishment, but praise'. Imprisonment had 'hardened us, it didn't teach us to love this so-called republic and its bearers, but has deepened and strengthened our love for our *Volk* and at the same time the hate for all those who think they can play fast and loose with this *Volk*'.

The realization, said Bormann, that 'constant fraud' was being committed against 'our national comrades' by 'the Marxists as well as by the so-called bourgeois parties . . . drives us to an unremitting fight against vermin and the enemies of our *Volk*'. He concluded by asserting that 'we stand loyally until death by the man who by virtue of his outstanding talents and leadership qualities is capable on his own of leading our *Volk* to the sun, to freedom again – our Adolf Hitler.'[71]

Höss and Bormann claimed this was a story of revolutionaries fighting against a corrupt system, even though the crime for which they were convicted – the brutal killing of a drunken man – would be an offence in any civilized legal system. But they recognized only their own 'laws' and felt excused by them.

Significantly, Höss was not only habituated to violence, he was used to giving himself over to a charismatic leader. When he served in the Freikorps, he believed the leader of each unit possessed an almost god-like authority. In his memoirs he wrote that every member of the

Freikorps was 'bound by a personal oath of loyalty to their Corps leader. The Corps stood or fell with him. As a result, there developed a feeling of solidarity and an *esprit de corps* which nothing could destroy . . . Woe to anyone who attempted to divide us – or betray us!'[72] They were words that Höss and many other Nazi supporters could just as easily have written to describe their relationship with Adolf Hitler.

It was also profoundly 'Them and Us' thinking. Exactly the sort Hitler encouraged.

3. Leading as a Hero

Hitler's failure to initiate a widespread revolution in Germany in November 1923 ought to have led to the end of his career and to the emasculation of the Nazis as a political force. Yet both survived – Hitler with his leadership credentials enhanced. The reasons behind this extraordinary outcome offer us vital insights not only into the nature of his appeal, but also into the peculiar characteristics of the Nazi movement. Above all, they reveal how psychologically valuable it was for Hitler that he came to be perceived as a 'hero' by his followers.

At the start of 1923 Hitler demonstrated more than ever before that he was far from a 'normal' political leader. His tendency towards impulsiveness – verging on hysteria – was on show in January when the Bavarian authorities prohibited a Nazi Party rally. Hitler's response was to threaten to push on regardless and he proclaimed that he was prepared to risk his life to do so.[1] Ironically it was left to Ernst Röhm, no stranger to impetuosity himself, to manoeuvre a way through the situation by negotiating with the Bavarian security forces, and reassuring them that there would be no attempt at a putsch if the rally was allowed to go ahead.

At both the subsequent rally on the Marsfeld in Munich on 28 January – in the presence of several thousand Nazi Stormtroopers – and at the various meetings at which he spoke the night before, Hitler was cheered on by his supporters. But his position was less secure than they believed – a fact that was exemplified by his relationship with Ernst Röhm.

Not only was Röhm not exclusively committed to the Nazis during this period – he was also a member of many other right-wing groups – but he didn't necessarily see himself as Hitler's disciple. He considered himself almost in a partnership. He was the military brains of the movement and Hitler the politician who roused the masses. Röhm knew that Hitler needed him because he controlled weapons that had been secreted away for use by right-wing paramilitaries.

As winter turned to spring in 1923 the political and economic situation in Munich grew still more unstable, and the Bavarian authorities feared that the Nazis might make a concerted effort to incite violence on 1 May. This was traditionally a day of celebration for the left, but Hitler wanted to subvert the occasion. He knew that 1 May was also the fourth anniversary of the battle for Munich in 1919, when armed members of the Freikorps had helped free the city from communist rule.

It was a moment that symbolized the almost impossible line that the Bavarian authorities had to tread – they were simultaneously worried about a socialist uprising and about a right-wing putsch. In his attempt to defuse the situation, General Otto von Lossow, the regional army commander, ordered that the Nazis should not be allowed access to weapons. Röhm didn't obey Lossow's order, and the night before the planned demonstration he arranged the delivery of an armoured car to 'a car rental company' in the city.[2] But this was an isolated show of defiance. Ultimately, the Nazis just didn't make the detailed preparations necessary to confront the state, and the 1 May demonstrations went off peacefully.

Nonetheless the incident demonstrated the tensions in Bavaria, not just between left and right, but within the government and the armed forces. Röhm was not the only army officer who supported armed insurrection, and what hadn't yet been tested was how many of his comrades were ready to back a revolution of the right. Hitler knew this was the decisive question, because any uprising the Nazis attempted would be doomed if soldiers didn't come over to their side.

But this was not the only unknown that Hitler had to manage. He also had to force himself to cooperate with other right-wing groups. The Dickel incident two years before had shown just how much he loathed any form of collaboration, but now he had little choice. The Nazis on their own just weren't powerful enough to foment revolution.

In September 1923, after the Nazis had taken part in a rally of nationalist groups in Nuremberg, Hitler agreed to join the new Deutscher Kampfbund – the German Combat League. This umbrella organization also contained the toughs of the Oberland Freikorps and the Reichskriegsflagge – a group of paramilitaries formed by Röhm earlier in the year. And while Hitler was recognized as the best speaker in the group and was accepted as the political leader, that didn't mean that he was in overall control. Not with the iconic figure of General Ludendorff lurking in the background. Ludendorff was the former Quartermaster

General of the German Army during the First World War and had previously taken part in the Kapp Putsch in 1920, a failed attempt to overthrow the government in Berlin. Now, three years later, he wanted to try once again to destroy the Weimar Republic.

The exact relationship between Ludendorff and Hitler – the General and the ordinary soldier – was never defined. Who was the actual leader? Who would be in overall control if the revolution succeeded? This vagueness was especially problematic because Ludendorff had a history of undermining the person who was in nominal charge, as he and Hindenburg had demonstrated during the First World War when they had taken effective control of the army away from the Kaiser. Would he now do the same to Hitler? On top of all these uncertainties rested one giant unknown – how would the overall political and economic situation in Germany develop during 1923? Crucially, would the current crisis escalate still further? Revolution is all but unheard of during days of calm, and the Nazis needed tempestuous times to succeed.

In September it looked as if they might get their wish when the Bavarian government protested at the decision of the new German Chancellor, Gustav Stresemann, to end the passive resistance in the Ruhr and reach an accommodation with the French. It was a deal that made many Bavarians angry, and in response Gustav von Kahr was appointed as Bavarian State Commissioner and loaded with the powers of a dictator. He was supported by Otto von Lossow, commander of the army in Bavaria, and Colonel Hans von Seisser of the state police. On the one hand this presented Hitler with an opportunity, since the stand-off between the national government in Berlin and the state government in Munich was serious, but on the other the new ruler of Bavaria, Kahr, was acting as if he was the tough figure that many had longed for.

'Hitler wasn't the only strong man,' remembered one Nazi Stormtrooper. 'Kahr was given dictatorial powers in order to counter the goings-on that could no longer be tolerated . . . And Kahr, an administrative official, was a blank page and actually on a par with Hitler, on the same level . . .'[3]

Meanwhile, Germany remained in economic crisis. The hyperinflation reached such a point that October that Röhm paid a thousand million marks for his lunch.[4] But who knew how long these problems would continue? Hitler understood that if he didn't take action soon he might miss the best moment for revolution. Examples from elsewhere offered the Nazis hope. The previous year the Fascist leader Benito Mussolini had gained power in Italy after a much publicized 'March on Rome'. Could the Nazis accomplish something similar?

By November 1923 Hitler was trying to reconcile a whole host of competing pressures: his Stormtroopers were demanding action; he had to manage a constellation of difficult personalities around him, including the 'hero' of the First World War, General Ludendorff; he feared that Kahr and his associates would establish their own 'strong' rule over Bavaria; and the response of the police and army in Munich to an attempted coup remained hard to predict. Above all, Hitler had to gain the cooperation of the three most powerful figures in Bavaria – Kahr, Lossow and Seisser. He knew that action by the Nazis could only be the catalyst for revolution. They couldn't sustain a revolution on their own.

It was against this background that Hitler decided to mount one of the most bizarre attempts at a takeover in history. His plan was to co-opt the three people currently in power in Bavaria in a coup against those in power in Berlin. As he later said: 'that was the rashest decision of my life. When I think back on it today, I grow dizzy.'[5] Not for the first time, and certainly not for the last, Hitler had relied on his instinct to guide his actions.

On 8 November 1923 all three of these key figures were due to attend a public meeting at the Bürgerbräukeller in Munich. Around half past eight in the evening, as Kahr was speaking to the crowd, Hitler and his Stormtroopers entered the building with their guns drawn. After firing a shot into the ceiling and announcing that this was the start of the revolution, Hitler took Kahr, Seisser and Lossow away from the hall into a back room. Here, still holding his pistol, he announced his plan for the government of Germany. He would be in charge, with subordinate roles for the three in the room plus Ludendorff. Would they support him? They dithered for a while but eventually accepted an offer that they could hardly refuse. Ludendorff, meanwhile, had turned up and expressed his support for the coup while claiming that the events of the evening had come as a surprise to him.

It was at this point that the whole affair began to unravel. Hitler left to check on the progress of the coup elsewhere in the city, leaving Ludendorff in charge of Kahr, Seisser and Lossow. He promptly released them. They had promised, he later said, to continue to support the uprising. But since they had been forced into voicing their cooperation at gunpoint, they quickly said they were opposed to the whole ill-planned scheme.

Next morning, in an attempt to revive a plan that had gone badly wrong, Hitler and the Stormtroopers marched through Munich. 'We didn't imagine that this would be an armed march aiming to take over Berlin by force,' recalled Emil Klein, a Nazi Stormtrooper present that day. 'It was to be a propaganda march, a demonstration.' But the Nazis' 'demonstration', in the style of Mussolini's March on Rome, managed to progress only a couple of miles. At the war memorial at the Feldherrnhalle they were confronted by armed units of the Bavarian security forces. Contrary to their hopes, the Nazis had failed to achieve the most vital precondition for their success – convincing significant numbers of the Bavarian police and army to support them. Who fired the first shot is unknown. But in the subsequent firefight at the Feldherrnhalle fourteen Nazis and four policemen died.[6]

It was hard to know what the putschists had died for. All that seemed certain was that the Nazis had shown themselves to be utterly incompetent revolutionaries. Yet incredibly – in one of the most successful propaganda actions in history – the death of these men in this harebrained scheme was subsequently portrayed as heroic, and they were declared martyrs to the Nazi cause. They were thus a great deal more effective as revolutionaries when they were dead than when they had been alive.

This is all the more remarkable because Hitler had made a series of catastrophic decisions during the putsch. Most notably, he had let circumstances dictate his actions. Once Kahr and the rest had escaped from the Bürgerbräukeller, he had been at a loss what to do. The march through Munich had been hurriedly organized only because no one could think of a better option. Hitler's leadership had been weak and ineffectual.

Everyone who participated in the putsch had committed high treason. But, incredibly, in the aftermath of the failed coup the Bavarian authorities were exceptionally lenient towards the perpetrators. Consider, for instance, what happened to the twenty-three-year-old Heinrich Himmler. He had taken part in the uprising as a member of Ernst Röhm's Reichskriegsflagge group – a photo survives of the bespectacled Himmler standing behind barbed wire during the putsch, holding the unit's standard. Himmler had joined in Röhm's occupation of the army headquarters in Munich, and on the morning of 9 November had been involved in a confrontation with soldiers loyal to the existing Bavarian regime.[7] After an exchange of fire in which two of the revolutionaries died, there had been a stand-off with the Bavarian units surrounding the paramilitaries. After discussions between the two sides, Himmler and his Reichskriegsflagge comrades were allowed simply to walk free.[8] It was one of the first signs of how sympathetic the Bavarian authorities were to the aims of these paramilitaries, if not their methods.

Ernst Röhm, like Himmler, had spent the night of 8/9 November occupying the army headquarters. But unlike his young comrade he was not able to stroll to safety after the putsch failed. The terms he was offered had been very different – his men could go free if he was arrested. The Bavarian authorities didn't feel able to let one of the highest-profile leaders of the putsch escape all censure. Even so, Röhm was treated with every consideration after he arrived at Stadelheim prison in the south of Munich. According to prison reports he even felt secure enough to act 'very arrogantly'.[9]

As for Ludendorff, his fate was symptomatic of the stance of the Bavarian authorities. He had taken part in the march through Munich, and once the marchers were fired upon the legend is that he walked bolt upright towards the Bavarian security forces and straight through their ranks. It was supposedly an example of courage in the great tradition of the imperial officers of Frederick the Great. But several eyewitnesses – including an American diplomat – said that Ludendorff 'fell flat to escape the hail of bullets'.[10] Arrested by the police, he was later permitted to return home under house arrest. The Bavarian authorities didn't want to imprison one of the most famous figures of the First World War – even if he had just attempted an armed uprising.

Julius Streicher was not treated as leniently – although still a great deal more leniently than he deserved. He had travelled around Munich on the morning of 9 November giving a series of bloodthirsty speeches to rally support for the putsch. 'Revolution races through the country,' he proclaimed to an audience of passers-by. 'Profiteers, whether Christians or Jews, will be hanged . . . The time of shame is over. The time of freedom has arrived. After this there will be but two parties, one of the poor, free and loyal German people, the other of the usurious Jew. To which party do you want to belong? . . . He who does not obey the National Government will be hanged, but he who does will be happy.'[11]

After these impromptu exhortations, Streicher took part in the march to the Feldherrnhalle and was subsequently arrested, only to be released from prison in February 1924. Although he was sacked from his job as a teacher, he escaped lightly, especially given the incendiary nature of the speeches he gave on the morning of 9 November.

Hermann Göring suffered a more lasting reminder of the Nazi revolution. He had been in the forefront of the attack on the Bürgerbräukeller and marched with Hitler and Ludendorff the next day, only to be shot in the leg by the police during the firefight. In agonizing pain, he was spirited away by his comrades, eventually surfacing in a hospital in Austria. It was here that he was introduced to morphine for pain relief and subsequently became addicted to the drug.

Adolf Hitler had also managed to flee the scene of the crime. When the shooting started he had fallen to the ground – whether he was pushed or fell on his own initiative was never conclusively established. Not surprisingly, his supporters preferred the former explanation and his detractors the latter, since it suggested cowardice. With his shoulder dislocated by his fall, Hitler was driven away to a supporter's house where he was found by the police two days later. He was then taken to prison to await trial. This should have been the end of Adolf Hitler.

Just before he was seized by the police, Hitler named the person he wished to lead the Nazi Party in his absence.[12] His choice came as a shock. It was the editor of the *Völkischer Beobachter*, a thirty-year-old ethnic German from Estonia called Alfred Rosenberg. Not even Rosenberg's most fervent supporters – and there were not many of them – would have called him a man with first-rate leadership skills. Indeed, it is doubtful if he even saw himself that way. Rather, he considered himself an intellectual. While Hitler, Göring and Röhm had been fighting at the front during the First World War, Rosenberg had been completing his PhD. On leaving Estonia, he made a new life in Munich where he joined the nationalist and radically anti-Semitic Thule Society.

Though unquestionably loyal to Hitler, Rosenberg was widely disliked by his fellow Nazis. One reason was that he was tremendously dull – the opposite in temperament to passionate and combative figures like Goebbels and Streicher. A flavour of Rosenberg's character can be gained from his diaries, which though of historical significance could scarcely be drearier to read: 'The conference of the Nordic Society in Lübeck was satisfactory in every respect. The speeches intermeshed admirably,' is a typical entry.[13]

All of which makes the question of why Hitler would appoint such a man to lead the Nazi Party still more intriguing. One theory is that he was just short of candidates for the job as so many of the contenders were now in prison or on the run. Another is that he deliberately wanted to place the party in the hands of a loyal but anti-charismatic figure – someone who could never be a threat. This latter explanation is sometimes quoted as an example Hitler's Machiavellian cleverness, and it may indeed have been the impression he later wanted the world to have. But it presupposes that Hitler was thinking strategically at the time, whereas the evidence is that he was feeling both desperate and despondent. As the police were on their way to arrest him he had allegedly reached for his gun in a dramatic attempt to kill himself – only to be prevented by the wife of Nazi supporter Putzi Hanfstaengl.[14]

Hitler, not just in this moment but in the days to come, was severely depressed by the failure of the putsch. He was unlikely to be thinking through the implications of appointing a bore such as Rosenberg to lead the Nazi Party. What, after all, was the point in worrying about the new leader of an organization that seemed to be falling apart and which was about to be banned? Instead, he was concerned that he would be blamed for the debacle and that his political career was over. 'I've had enough,' he told Alois Maria Ott, the prison psychologist ten days after the putsch. 'If I had a pistol, I would take it.'[15]

Hitler's despondency is significant. Not only does it go against the popular image from propaganda, such as the 1935 documentary *Triumph of the Will*, of a man who could remain strong under pressure, but it also demonstrated how successful an alternative course could have been. If the Bavarian authorities had wished it, Hitler could have vanished from the political scene from this moment onwards. He wasn't in control of events – they were.

It's thus something of a misnomer to call the attempted revolution of November 1923 the 'Hitler Putsch' – as so many do. It was more a 'Bavarian Putsch', and Hitler was just one of the players. He and his supporters had attempted the uprising only because they believed it was likely that the Bavarian authorities would support them, since Kahr and his colleagues were already in dispute with the national government in Berlin; indeed, they also wanted the Berlin government overthrown.

Paradoxically, it was the fact that Hitler was not the sole leader of the putsch that now helped save him. He had done his best to convince Lossow and Seisser, who respectively controlled the army and police in Bavaria, to fall in with him. Although he had not succeeded, these discussions did still amount to collusion between Hitler and the Bavarian authorities. Kahr, Lossow and Seisser were thus in a vulnerable position – their unconvincing position being that while they had not been in favour of an armed insurrection involving Hitler, they still might have been in favour of overthrowing the national government on their own. It was this knowledge that helped pull Hitler out of his depression and made a mockery of his trial.

By the time he and the rest of the putschists entered the Munich courtroom on 26 February 1924 the situation in Bavaria had changed. Kahr had been removed from office and the economy had been stabilized with the introduction of the Rentenmark, which would shortly be converted into the Reichsmark. Since it was obvious that Hitler and his motley crew of revolutionaries relied on a political crisis to succeed, they now seemed less of a threat.

None of that meant, however, that Hitler didn't still have the capacity to embarrass the Bavarian state. So the decision was taken to deal leniently with him and the other putschists – a decision epitomized by the appointment of Georg Neithardt as the presiding judge. Neithardt had already demonstrated his sympathetic attitude towards the Nazis by his treatment of Hitler at a trial two years before. Having led his supporters in breaking up a rival meeting in the Löwenbräu cellar, Hitler had been charged with the most minor offence possible – breach of the peace. Neithardt had even lobbied for Hitler's eventual sentence of three months to be commuted to just one month in jail and a period on probation.[16]

Though the trial of the putschists was supposed to be held in public, sections were still conducted in secret. This was because of the embarrassing nature of Hitler's defence – which was not only that he and his supporters had expected the police and army to support them, but that armed revolution had been planned by the Bavarian state itself.

Given all this, Hitler must have known that he would almost certainly be treated leniently. He could thus appear defiant and intransigent without his behaviour risking the wrath of the judges.

He could pose as a man of courage and principle, prepared to take whatever punishment the state chose to throw at him rather than compromise his honour. Consequently, the German and international press covering the trial prominently reported Hitler's unyielding commitment to his cause.

Hitler's speeches from the court became famous. 'The army which we have formed grows from day to day,' he said; 'it grows more rapidly from hour to hour . . . You may pronounce us guilty a thousand times, but the Goddess who presides over the Eternal Court of History will with a smile tear in pieces the charge of the Public Prosecutor and the verdict of this court. For she acquits us.'[17] Defiant words, and hugely beneficial to Hitler's reputation as a leader.

Often perceived only as a dictatorial egotist, Hitler was instead conscious of the need to inspire his followers and keep them with him. It is a common misconception, believes Professor Alex Haslam, an expert on the psychology of leadership, that leadership is about 'the great "I" '. 'Leadership', he says, 'is always all about "us".'[18] You don't become a good leader by possessing a checklist of personal qualities, he argues, but by understanding the aspirations of the group you lead and pressing on towards a common goal. This was something Hitler understood, announcing during the trial that he had 'resolved to be the destroyer of Marxism' – a common goal his followers shared.[19] Moreover, the fact that Hitler had been a 'simple soldier' during the war meant that he could position himself as one of the millions of ordinary Germans who had felt betrayed by the traditional leadership class. What could be more a demonstration of 'Us-ness' than that?

Emil Klein was one of the many Nazis who thought that Hitler's conduct at the trial had enhanced his reputation: 'I said to myself that he's come out of it well and behaved decently before the court.'[20] Importantly, Hitler had fulfilled another of Professor Alex Haslam's desirable leadership qualities, since what matters if you are a leader is whether 'you're perceived by people in your group to have attributes which are relevant and good for us'.[21]

From Hitler's perspective, what could be more 'relevant and good' than a demonstration of his heroism? His followers already knew that he had won an Iron Cross for bravery during the war, but now he appeared to have defied the traditional elite who had charged him with high treason. During the trial he had specifically referred to himself as the 'hero' who was called by 'the whole of German youth' to lead the 'political struggle'.[22]

As the anthropologist Ernest Becker wrote, 'the hero has been the centre of human honour and acclaim since probably the beginning of specifically human evolution. But even before that our primate ances-tors deferred to others who were extra powerful and courageous and ignored those who were cowardly.'[23]

In Germany there was a cultural background to all this, one that made many people – particularly those from a *völkisch* background – especially keen for a 'hero' to appear on the scene to rescue the country from despair. The head of the Pan-German League, Heinrich Class, had written just before the First World War that 'the need still lives on today in the best of our people to follow a strong, able leader; all who have remained unseduced by the teachings of un-German democracy yearn for it . . .'[24]

In the previous century Bismarck, credited with uniting Germany, had been widely perceived as just such a strong leader, and much further back in time Hermann, chieftain of the Cherusci, had been hailed as one of the great Teutonic leaders for defeating the Romans. There were monuments to Bismarck throughout Germany and a giant statue of Hermann in the Teutoburg Forest. Finished in 1875 it was one of Ger-many's most popular tourist attractions. Germans, therefore, knew all about the importance of heroes, and their presence in popular culture helped define a sense of 'Germanness' in a country that had been united for little more than fifty years.[25]

For Hitler, there was also a personal dimension. According to his flat-mate in pre-First World War Vienna, Hitler's favourite book had been *Die Deutschen Heldensagen* (The Sagas of German Heroes) and he had been obsessed with the heroic operas of Wagner – *Lohengrin* in particu-lar, which featured the heroics of a Knight of the Holy Grail. For Hitler, wrote his flatmate, 'nothing appeared more worthy of the struggle than a life like theirs, full of brave acts of great consequence, the most heroic life possible . . .'[26]

It is not hard to see why Hitler – brought up by an authoritarian father who drank and beat him, filled with love for his mother who died tragically young of cancer in 1907, the same year he was rejected by the Vienna Academy of Fine Arts – might as an adolescent have fantasized about becoming a hero and righting the wrongs of his life.

This was the moment, in the courtroom in Munich in spring 1924, when Hitler was finally able to project the image of the hero he had longed to be. Prior to the trial he had never explicitly said that he saw himself as the hero who would rescue Germany, rather than being merely the 'drummer' preparing the way for that hero to appear. Now he was clear. He was that man.

He was en route to becoming the archetypal 'charismatic leader' – a term used to define a type of leadership that relies heavily on the personal qualities of the leader rather than the support of a bureaucratic structure. 'Charisma' in this sense is morally neutral. There can be charismatic leaders who use their power to create havoc and destruction as well as those who promote peace and fellowship.

Psychological research points to the importance of charismatic leadership in our evolutionary development, as our ancestors moved from a hunter-gatherer existence to living in larger villages and cities where the presence of charismatic leaders helped unite the population.[27] Scholarly work has also shown that different types of leaders tend to be preferred at different times: 'People prefer leaders with dominant, masculine-looking faces in times of war and conflict, yet they prefer leaders with more trustworthy, feminine faces in peacetime. In addition, leaders with older-looking faces are preferred in traditional knowledge domains, whereas younger-looking leaders are preferred for new challenges.'[28] This, remember, is only a tendency; there are examples in history that run contrary to this analysis. Nonetheless, during the violent, unstable years immediately after the First World War, it is easy to understand why the relatively youthful Adolf Hitler might have possessed an additional advantage over many of his rivals.

In his theory of charismatic authority, developed before Hitler came to power, the German sociologist Max Weber argued that evidence of 'personal heroism' was also one of the signs that a leader possessed 'genuine charisma'.[29] And we've already seen how a combination of his wartime record and his behaviour at the 1924 trial allowed Hitler to claim to be just such a hero. Another hugely advantageous trait for charismatic leaders is rhetorical ability – something, as previously discussed, Hitler possessed above all else.

But Hitler's flowery rhetoric didn't convince everyone. General Otto von Lossow, for instance, told the court about his own discussions with the Nazi leader during 1923. 'In the beginning, Hitler's well-known enchanting and suggestive eloquence made a great impression,' he said. 'It is readily apparent that Hitler was right in many ways, but the more I listened to Hitler, the weaker this first impression became . . . I noticed that his long talks almost always contained the same points. One part of his remarks is obvious to every nationally thinking German, and another part of them bore witness that Hitler had departed from a sense of reality and proportion for what is possible and achievable.' The lesson Lossow took from all this was blunt – Hitler was merely 'a swashbuckling little ward politician'.[30]

Lossow's testimony is a reminder of the insight that we encountered earlier: Hitler convinced you, proved himself charismatic, only if you were predisposed to be attracted by him. Lossow, a hardbitten, aristocratic officer, easily saw through him. But, equally, this sophisticated judgement of Hitler – that he was a common rabble-rouser who could excite the ordinary people but lacked mature political gifts – would also prove problematic. It's the same judgement that several other intelligent, well-bred Germans would form about Hitler during the early 1930s, with catastrophic consequences.

Though Hitler was found guilty of high treason, the sentence passed on him was predictably lenient – five years in prison. But even that was not what it seemed, as everyone knew he was likely to be freed on probation in just a few months. Others were treated even more lightly. Röhm was released on probation and walked straight out on to the streets of Munich. Ludendorff was acquitted on all charges. The court's verdict – ludicrously – was that the war hero hadn't understood that he was part of an attempted coup. As if this wasn't madcap enough, a further note of farce was struck when Ludendorff refused to accept his own acquittal, calling it 'a disgrace which this uniform and these decorations do not deserve'. Unable to convince the court to change its verdict and convict him, he stomped out of the building.[31]

The *New York Times* reported that 'Ludendorff was acquitted' and 'Adolf Hitler was practically acquitted' amid 'the wild joy of German reactionaries and utter dismay of the partisans of the German Republic'. The paper railed against 'the Munich court's idea of [the] punishment which a traitor to the German Republic should suffer'.[32]

The Bavarian authorities, typified during the trial by Judge Neithardt, were responsible for not eliminating Hitler as a future threat. This was widely recognized at the time, not just in the American papers but in European ones as well. The London *Times*, for instance, reported that 'Munich is chuckling over the verdict' because it demonstrated 'that to plot against the constitution of the Reich is not considered a serious crime in Bavaria'.[33]

Hitler was sentenced to 'fortress imprisonment', serving his time in the most comfortable conditions the German penal system could provide. At Landsberg prison, west of Munich, he received presents of food from friends and well-wishers, and plenty of visitors. Many of the guards sympathized with the Nazis and he was treated as something of a celebrity.

He also used the time to work on a book – *Mein Kampf* (My Struggle). Hitler, as anyone who has tried to read *Mein Kampf* will know, was not much of a writer. But he made up for his lack of technique with the vehemence of his views. The muddled structure of the book is held together by one overarching theme – his hatred of the Jews. Having falsely claimed that he was a vociferous anti-Semite during his time in pre-war Vienna, he proceeded to blame the Jews for virtually all of Germany's problems. *Mein Kampf* was yet more proof of Hitler's view that 'the only stable emotion is hate'.[34]

A particular focus of the work was the false link Hitler made once again between the Jews and Bolshevism, the political system he most despised. As he saw it, the purpose of Nazism was straightforward – to destroy the perceived power of the Jews, right the 'wrongs' of Versailles, defeat the Bolsheviks and create a racially pure Germany in which all Aryan citizens pulled together as one. Hitler also asserted that Germany needed to grow larger and declared that Germans should create an empire in the western part of the Soviet Union. Years later he would try and make this vision a reality.

As Hitler worked on this hate-filled tract, the Nazi movement faced a struggle to survive. After the party had been banned by the Bavarian authorities, Alfred Rosenberg, acting in Hitler's place, had founded a replacement organization called the Greater German People's Community. Not surprisingly, without Hitler's presence the new group struggled to make an impact.

The fortunes of Rosenberg's ersatz Nazi Party weren't helped by the continuing economic recovery within Germany. The Dawes Plan, a new financial agreement brokered by Britain and America, was signed in Paris in August 1924. The deal gave financial hope to Germany by providing the country with loans, chiefly from the United States. The benefits of the plan were at once short term – the hated occupation of the Ruhr was soon to be over – and long term – the industrial base of the country, particularly the steel industry, had the necessary financial backing to rebuild. Consequently, for large numbers of Germans the instability that had fuelled dissent was melting away.

Nonetheless, the supporters of the banned Nazi Party did not disappear. There remained a core group of believers – one that by 1924 included an unemployed young man from the Rhineland called Joseph Goebbels. He was twenty-six years old at the time of the Beer-Hall Putsch and disillusioned about his life. He had been unable to fight in the First World War because of a disability – his right leg was shorter than his left and the foot twisted inwards – and although he had gained a PhD in German literature, he had still not found an outlet for his talents.

In a revealing entry in his diary, dated 27 October 1923, Goebbels mused: 'This is the only thing I still believe in: the truth being stronger than the lie in the end, in the final victory of the truth and in myself. This belief shall live on in me strongly and firmly. This is what I will derive all my strength and all my kindness from. After all, it is trivial what we believe in, if only we believe at all. The nation that loses its belief loses itself. We can take everything from the people, but not what they want to believe in, whether Christ or Rome or race or nation or goodness knows what.'[35]

Goebbels developed this same idea three months later, writing: 'Any thought is right; you must only be able to prove it convincingly. Every time has its own ideas, and in any time, its ideas are right. It's not the times that are changing, but man. The thought that has the strongest advocate gains acceptance. The idea of all existence and events being relative is the only absolute thing in the empire of the mind.'[36]

Given Goebbels' centrality in what was to come, these are important insights into his mentality. It would be superficial, however, to think that he was simply saying that it doesn't matter what we believe in, as long as we believe, given that he qualified his relativism by placing tremendous emphasis on 'the truth'. He understood that this 'truth' could shift from epoch to epoch, but nonetheless there was a 'truth' present in every period. The task was to find it.

In the spring of 1924, he believed he had achieved his goal. Nazism

was his 'truth'. He and a small group of like-minded people founded a
Nazi branch in Rheydt, his hometown in the Rhineland. The fact that
the Nazi Party was banned did not put them off; most likely it only
added to their sense of adventure.

Despite going out with a girlfriend who had a Jewish background,
Goebbels was now a vehement anti-Semite.[37] 'What we are lacking in
Germany is a strong hand,' he wrote in his diary on 4 July 1924. 'Send
the Jewish rabble, which doesn't want to bow to the responsible idea of
the people's community [*Volksgemeinschaft*], packing.' He coupled this
prejudice with a desire for a strong personality to take control of the
country: 'Germany is longing for the one, the man, like the soil is longing for rain in summer . . . Lord, show the German *Volk* a miracle!
A miracle! A man!!!'[38]

It was clear who the 'man' was that Goebbels had in mind to perform
this 'miracle'. Three months before, he had written that 'Hitler is an
enthusiastic idealist. A man who brings new faith to the German people.
I'm reading his speech, inspired, and carried to the stars. The path runs
from the brain to the heart . . .'[39]

Steeped in the *völkisch* longing for a strong man to save Germany,
Goebbels was predisposed to find Hitler attractive – especially after his
'heroic' performance at the putsch trial. Nazism thus filled a gap in
Goebbels' personality. It gave him more than something to believe in,
it utterly transformed his life. His disability had prevented him from
fighting in the war, but he threw himself into this new struggle with the
enthusiasm of a fanatic.

Around the same time as Goebbels discovered his love of Hitler and
Nazism, a twenty-three-year-old Heinrich Himmler also decided to
devote himself to the cause. As we have seen, Himmler took part in the
putsch not as a Nazi but as a member of Röhm's Reichskriegsflagge. It
was only in 1924 that he became a Nazi activist and devotee of Adolf
Hitler. 'He is a truly great man and above all a genuine and pure one,' he
wrote in early 1924 in the log he kept of the books he read. 'His speeches
are marvellous examples of Germanness and Aryanness.'[40]

Just as Goebbels' personality was already visible through his diary
entries – sarcastic, passionate and longing for a hero – so Himmler's was
also revealed through his activism in the party – pedantic and stiff-
necked. 'I got to know Himmler before the takeover of power,' said
Emil Klein, a member of the Nazi Party in Bavaria. 'I couldn't have

made a friend of him. There are simply people, even today, when I see someone on the street, I say to myself, well that's not someone I'd want to have a beer with, I'll look for someone else instead.'[41]

Released from prison on 1 April 1924, Ernst Röhm hurried to shore up the Stormtroopers, the paramilitary side of the Nazis. Hermann Göring was still nominally the head of the group, but he was wanted by police for his part in the putsch and couldn't return to Germany, so he gave Röhm his blessing to act in his place.[42]

The Stormtroopers were supposed to disperse as part of the ban on the Nazi Party, so Röhm created a new organization known as the Frontbann. He wanted to offer a home not just for the Stormtroopers but for paramilitaries from other right-wing groups. Inevitably, this put him on course for conflict with Hitler, who continued to be suspicious of an alliance with any organization that did not owe its allegiance to him.

On 20 December 1924, Hitler was released from Landsberg prison. The Bavarian supreme court had overruled the wishes of the state prosecutor, who had wanted him to stay behind bars. It was less than nine months after Hitler had been sentenced to five years for high treason. But the judges knew that Hitler was re-entering a calmer Germany than the one he had left. The twin crises of hyperinflation and the French occupation of the Ruhr were both resolved.

Hitler had spent time in his cell musing over the failure of the putsch and had now decided on a new way forward. The Nazis would use democracy as a means of destroying democracy. 'Instead of working to achieve power by an armed *coup*,' he said, 'we shall have to hold our noses and enter the Reichstag against the Catholic and Marxist deputies. If out-voting them takes longer than out-shooting them, at least the results will be guaranteed by their own Constitution!'[43]

By promising the Bavarian Minister-President, Heinrich Held, that he would not engage in another putsch and that the Nazis would be a bastion against communism, Hitler managed to get the ban on the Nazi Party lifted. He re-formed the movement on 27 February 1925 at an emotional meeting at the Bürgerbräukeller, the very place he had launched his attempted putsch sixteen months before.

It was a gathering that represented a paradox. *Völkisch* parties had declined in support – the Reichstag election of 7 December 1924 had been disastrous for them – and Nazi Party members had proved that they couldn't work together in his absence. But while all this had been happening, Hitler's star had risen higher. The publicity he had received because of his behaviour at the putsch trial had propelled him to the forefront of the whole *völkisch* movement.

The climactic moment of this refounding of the party came when Hitler ordered his supporters to put their past arguments behind them. Individuals who disliked, even despised, each other now came up on to the stage and pledged to work together. It demonstrated a skill of Hitler's that is often overlooked – his ability to convince his followers to unite around a shared ideological mission. It also illustrated in dramatic terms his power over the Nazi Party. To Kurt Lüdecke, who was present that night, Hitler resembled a 'revivalist' preacher calling on 'sinners' to repent.[44]

Above all, Hitler reminded his followers that they were all part of the same 'Us-ness'. They were a family. While you could dislike a family member, the family still stuck together through good times and bad times. And just as children should obey their fathers, so party members should obey him.

The meeting of 27 February was a powerful reinforcement of a reality that everyone in the Nazi Party now knew – Hitler was vital to any chance of success. In that respect the debacle of the putsch, and his absence from the political scene during 1924, had been beneficial for him.

Ernst Röhm certainly recognized that Hitler was politically essential to the *völkisch* movement. But he hadn't yet grasped how their relationship had changed since the putsch. Hitler wanted him to return to the recreated Nazi Party as leader of the Stormtroopers, but Röhm had a different idea. Although he was prepared to merge the Frontbann, the organization he had recently helped form, with the Stormtroopers, he sought the exclusive leadership of the new group. Once again it implied a kind of partnership – Hitler as political leader of the movement and Röhm as military supremo. Hitler, when he met Röhm in his flat in Munich on 16 April 1925 to discuss matters, acted true to form. He said he wasn't going to partner – let alone share leadership – with anyone.[45]

Röhm wrote to Hitler after the meeting resigning from the Stormtroopers, adding that he thought he should also resign from the Frontbann. Hitler didn't reply. Röhm wrote again. Still no reply. So Röhm just resigned from the Frontbann and walked away.

It had been a cold-hearted demonstration of Hitler's authority. Not only had Röhm underestimated how much Hitler had grown in status since the putsch, but by not replying to Röhm's letters Hitler had revealed how much he understood about the nature of power. Röhm had always considered himself a close comrade of Hitler's – he was one of a small number of people that Hitler talked to using *du*, the familiar form of 'you' in German. But given the infighting among his subordinates in the higher reaches of the Nazi Party, Hitler realized that there was no benefit in putting anything on paper to Röhm. In keeping quiet, he demonstrated that the most effective reply can sometimes be no reply at all.[46]

This incident wasn't about Hitler trying to alter Röhm's character and force him to become less of a swashbuckling adventurer. He was merely – once again – acting to protect his own prestige. Indeed, one of the attractions of the Nazi Party for any new member was the knowledge that the leader was not looking to 'mould' those who joined. There was space for Julius Streicher, a rabid populist, just as there was space for Alfred Rosenberg, a bookish intellectual.

'I do not consider it the duty of a political leader to attempt to improve, let alone unify, the human material which he has at his disposal,' wrote Hitler in a revealing article in the *Völkischer Beobachter* on 26 February 1925, the day before he refounded the Nazi Party. 'The temperaments, characters and abilities of individual people are so various that it is impossible to merge together a large number of similar people. It is also not the duty of a political leader to try and remove these shortcomings by "educating" people to be united. All such attempts are doomed to failure. Human nature is pre-existing – a phenomenon which cannot be changed in the individual, but can only be transformed through a process of development lasting for centuries . . . If a political leader deviates from this insight and instead only wants to seek people who come up to his ideal, he will not only fail, but also very quickly leave behind him chaos instead of an organization.'[47]

But while Hitler was not about to force anyone to conform to his ideal, his relaxed approach to the 'temperaments, characters and abilities' of those who joined the movement had at least one significant downside. What happened when these diverse characters started to express different opinions about Nazi policy? Given the vagueness of the original twenty-five points of 1920, there was a lot of scope for that to happen – as Hitler was about to discover.

★

During 1925, the controversy focused on one key question – just how 'socialist' were the members of the National Socialist German Workers' Party? From Hitler's perspective, it was a question so potentially explosive that he preferred not to answer it in any detail. But one of his old party comrades, Gregor Strasser, disagreed with this cautious approach.

Strasser was a Nazi with impeccable credentials. Having volunteered as a twenty-two-year-old student to fight in the First World War, he had been commissioned as an officer and subsequently won the Iron Cross. After the war ended, he joined a Freikorps and then in 1922 became a member of the Nazi Party, taking part in the Beer-Hall Putsch the following year. Convicted by the Munich court, he was released from prison because he had been elected to the Bavarian State Parliament and so gained an amnesty.

Strasser wanted his life after the war to make an impact. Though he had settled down in the immediate post-war years, qualifying as a pharmacist and having children, he demanded much more.[48] He claimed that he had become not just a nationalist in the trenches of the First World War, but a socialist as well – he had realized how vital it was that all Germans looked after and cared for each other.[49] This, in essence, wasn't so very different from Hitler's vague concept of the *Volksgemeinschaft*. But it turned out that Strasser wanted to define the precise socialist policies that should underpin the nebulous 'people's community' of their dreams. And this was something Hitler would never do.

Asked by Hitler to grow the Nazi Party in the north of Germany, Strasser discussed with his colleagues a more overtly 'socialist' agenda. Joseph Goebbels was one of Strasser's supporters, and he wrote in his diary on 15 June 1925 that 'Socialism is the final objective of our fight' and that he was 'full of suspense' as he waited to read Hitler's latest speech to see if it answered the crucial question, 'will he be a nationalist or a socialist?'[50]

But a month later, when Goebbels saw and heard Hitler speak at a meeting in Weimar, he was overcome primarily on an emotional level. 'Weimar was [a] resurrection in the entire sense of the word,' he wrote on 14 July. 'A day that I will never forget. I still feel like I'm in a dream. Hitler has answered all, all questions, and in a way that I expected. Now everything is clear . . . Hitler begins to speak. What a voice. What gestures, what passion. Just like I wanted him to be. I can barely control myself. I await every word. And every word proves me right. I hadn't expected that much . . . Everyone stands up and shouts, cheers, claps, waves, screams. I am standing outside at the window and cry like a toddler . . . I am a different man. Now I know that the one who leads is born to be a leader. I am ready to sacrifice everything for this man.'[51]

This was a strange reaction to Hitler's speech, because had Goebbels studied the content he would have seen that Hitler was not supporting his idea of socialism at all. Goebbels' longing for a 'great man' to lead Germany had caused him to hear what he wanted to hear, rather than what was actually said.

That's the background to a surprising article in the *Völkischer Beobachter* that Goebbels wrote that November outlining his views. He focused his attention on the Soviet Union and found much to praise in Lenin's actions in breaking down the class structures within the country. The challenge, as he saw it, was to separate out the negative 'Jewish influence' within Bolshevism from the positive aspects of the Russian Revolution. This was radical thinking indeed. So radical that Alfred Rosenberg, the editor of the *Völkischer Beobachter*, wrote an article attacking Goebbels' argument which was printed in the same edition.[52]

It was a bizarre situation. Goebbels was simultaneously connected to Hitler on an emotional level while advocating policies that could only be anathema to the author of *Mein Kampf* – a book that portrayed the Bolsheviks as evil incarnate. Such a disconnect could not be sustained for long, and the conflict between these two sides of Goebbels' psyche – emotional and intellectual – would be exposed the following year.

Other Nazis were also voicing their objections to the ideas of Strasser, Goebbels and the remaining members of their 'working group'. In December, Franz Pfeffer von Salomon wrote a diatribe against them in a provocative document called 'Breeding: A Demand for Our Programme'.[53] Salomon was another of those Nazi supporters who had fought not just in the First World War but with the Freikorps immediately afterwards. Though a supporter for years of the *völkisch* cause, he didn't join the Nazi Party until 1925. But such were his obvious leadership qualities and *völkisch* connections that Hitler soon confirmed him as district leader – Gauleiter in Nazi parlance – of Westphalia.

Salomon proclaimed at the start of his article that his opinions were 'diametrically opposed' to Strasser's. He accused Strasser and his colleagues of believing that all Germans were equal, whereas he took as his starting point the 'iron law of inequality'. Since 'there are higher-value Germans and lower-value Germans' it followed that there must be 'unequal treatment, unequal share of state power, property, culture'. In addition, 'The higher-value [people] must be increased and further raised, and the lower-value [people] must be reduced.' Salomon saw this as a 'breeding challenge' and believed that 'there are no differences between the principles of noble animal breeding and those of the breeding of humans . . . The breeder cares for the highest-valued animals and tries to grow their descendants, among whom the highest-valued are selected. The spread of inferior animals is prevented; the worst are continually sifted and repelled. Our German national state must act upon similar principles.'

Salomon argued that there must be 'No mercy for the last levels within the inferior group: cripples, epileptics, the blind, lunatics, deaf-mutes . . . criminals, prostitutes, sexually disordered etc'. In conclusion, he wrote that it was necessary to 'hoe out fruitless trees and throw them into the fire'. Notwithstanding the radical – and potentially murderous – nature of Salomon's aspirations, they matched Hitler's ultimate aims for Germany more closely than Goebbels' vision of socialism ever did.

As Salomon worked on his 'breeding' document, Gregor Strasser set himself the ambitious task of reworking the twenty-five points of the original Nazi programme. The results, however, were almost as incoherent as the existing document, though the working group did agree on one issue they wanted to pursue – the 'socialist' idea of requisitioning, without compensation, land owned by the German princes.

So far Hitler had allowed his fellow Nazis to work on their ideas without much interference. But the suggestion that land should be expropriated from German aristocrats was going too far, so he convened a conference at Bamberg in February 1926 to clarify matters. Here in the north of Bavaria, the 'socialist' thinkers were outnumbered. Hitler, as usual, did not deign to debate policy with Strasser and his working group. He just spoke for two hours, and this time there was no ambiguity. He emphasized that there was no possibility of extracting the 'positive' bits of Bolshevism from the 'negative' as Goebbels had suggested, and no question of taking land without compensation in the way proposed.

Given that Strasser and his colleagues had never intended to challenge Hitler's authority, merely to debate party policy, there was little else they could do but accept defeat. After this debacle, no one would try and rework the party programme again without Hitler's approval. The one clarification that would be made in the future was authorized by Hitler himself. In April 1928 he wanted it made plain that point 17, the call for 'land reform', only meant stopping 'Jewish' land speculation – again a rejection of Strasser's radical 'socialist' ideas.[54]

Goebbels was devastated by the events of Bamberg. 'I'm shattered,' he wrote on 15 February 1926. Hitler, he thought, was 'completely wrong' on the 'Russian question' and it was a mistake for him to say that private property was sacrosanct. There was nothing for Goebbels to do but to leave for a 'sad journey home'. He concluded, 'I do not entirely believe in Hitler any more. That is the terrible thing.'[55]

Yet, less than two months later, there was a turnaround in Goebbels' thinking. Hitler asked him to speak in Munich and made a considerable effort to win him over during his visit. Not that this was a difficult task. Goebbels was charmed from the start when Hitler sent his car to meet him at the station. After Goebbels had made a speech – during which he stayed clear of the topics that had caused problems at Bamberg – Hitler embraced him 'with tears in his eyes'. Afterwards they had dinner together and, wrote Goebbels, Hitler 'calmed me in all respects . . . I bow to the great, the political genius.' Goebbels even confessed, 'I love him.'[56]

It would be easy to misunderstand what was happening here and think this was either an example of Hitler's charisma and that Goebbels had simply succumbed, or alternatively that Goebbels was just a pragmatic opportunist. But it was more complex than that. Many elements were in the mix – Goebbels' longing for a 'great man' to lead Germany, the fact that he had been unable to convince Hitler that his views on socialism were correct, and the knowledge that if he didn't support Hitler there was no future for him in the party. Above all it was the certainty with which Hitler expressed his vision that was the basis of the successful subjugation of Goebbels. Rudolf Hess, a leading Nazi, realized how important this quality was for the leader of the Nazi movement. He recognized that Hitler 'must not weigh up the pros and cons like an academic, he must never leave his listeners the freedom to think something else is right . . . The great popular leader is similar to the great founder of a religion: he must communicate to his listeners an apodictic faith.'[57]

If Hitler had been prepared to debate issues of policy and to amend the party programme at the request of his supporters, it would have done more than show he was willing to listen – it would have made him look weak. He was thus the very opposite of a consensus politician, and yet paradoxically he allowed his followers enormous latitude in the way they went about trying to fulfil his vision. It was this combination that helped make him so effective as a leader, and preserved the sense that he was acting not as the 'great I' but as 'one of us'.

In the wake of the Bamberg conference Hitler tried to smooth over relationships with those who had been unhappy with the result, including Gregor Strasser, but it was Goebbels who was his most valuable convert. Seven months after his visit to Munich, Goebbels was given a new position of considerable importance to the Nazi Party – Gauleiter of Berlin. The German capital had a large working-class population and a significant liberal sector. It was the antithesis of conservative, Catholic Bavaria. Goebbels knew that his work in Berlin would not be easy, but it was a chance to make an impact.

Despite all these internal machinations, however, the Nazis had not succeeded in breaking through to the mainstream of German politics. By 1928, with the economy further stabilized and hyperinflation just a bad memory, it appeared that their time might have passed. The results of the German general election that year seemed to confirm this. On 20 May 1928 the Nazi Party received just 2.6 per cent of the vote.

In the three and a half years since he had been released from Landsberg prison, Hitler had established himself as the undisputed leader of the Nazi movement – the 'hero' to whom every party member deferred. But what did that matter if the Nazis remained an irrelevance?

4. Corrupting Youth

Without the ability Hitler and the Nazis possessed to convince millions of Germans to support their racist utopian dream, they could never have come to power. It was a dream, as we shall see, that many young people found attractive. And this was partly because of a psychological truth about the way the brain develops.

Not that it appeared obvious, after their pitiful share of the vote in May 1928, that the Nazis had much of a future. Indeed, many of their opponents now dismissed them as a political force. But on closer inspection there were hints that this could mark a new beginning. The Nazis had reached the bottom, and the way might be up.

Unemployment in Germany was growing, and the agricultural sector was experiencing economic difficulties. Such bleak news could only help the Nazis. It was almost axiomatic: as unemployment increased and people became more disillusioned with conventional political parties, so did the Nazi vote and party membership. So much so that by the end of 1928 over 100,000 people were card-carrying Nazis. One of them was a young man called Wolfgang Teubert, who became a Stormtrooper around this time. 'I was happy to join,' he said, 'because I said to myself this is the only thing, the only solution.' Teubert was excited by the Nazis' revolutionary nature, even though his own family didn't want him 'marching around in a brown shirt and carrying out hall supervision' because of the potential danger from opposition parties – the communists in particular.[1]

Teubert believed in what he called a 'superficial' anti-Semitism. He disliked Jews because, he claimed, his relatives had suffered business losses as a result of Jewish influence. But, more than anything, he was attracted to the movement by 'the core of the [Nazi] programme, to set up a *Volksgemeinschaft*'. His commitment to the *Volksgemeinschaft* also had an anti-Semitic element to it since, as we've seen, Jews were excluded from the Nazis' racist vision of a 'people's community'.

Teubert took part in fights against the communists as each group tried to disrupt the other's meetings. But he had one major advantage in the struggle – the police, many of whom held authoritarian political views – were almost always on his side. 'I was a bike messenger,' he recalled, and 'I had to go to a [political] meeting which was being surrounded [by political opponents], in the next-door town, in Freiburg. I thought that I wouldn't be conspicuous in my biker's gear, but I was noticed, and the cry of "Nazi!" rang out, and the people turned on me and threw me to the ground. I just managed to grab hold of a policeman with one hand, with my left hand, and I hung on to him, and he helped me fight my way out. But I was still injured, especially my abdomen and stomach, but only through punches.'[2]

Alois Pfaller, a young communist activist, confirmed that the police 'were on the side of the right wing. They [the Nazis] always got protection. But nobody gave us protection, we could be beaten up, they just looked on. They didn't do a thing.' In Bavaria, he and his communist comrades found it almost impossible to get permission to hold a demonstration: 'We always had to do it illegally. I used to walk the streets in the working-class areas, check the entrance doors [to blocks of flats], find out when the doors were open and when they were locked, and then [check] with the officers of the youth organization. I told them to go into such and such a building, [saying] "you can wait there until I whistle." And the people would hide in there, and when it was time I would whistle and they would come out, and we would stand four abreast and start singing a song, and we would march.'[3]

Many young Bavarians who wanted to join a radical party simply chose between the Nazis and the communists. Pfaller even considered becoming a Stormtrooper himself: 'But well, we discussed it in the group [of friends] and they convinced me that "It gets us nowhere, they only support business and not the workers, it's just rubbish! You're not so stupid as to join them."' Pfaller also objected to the Nazis' anti-Semitism. He believed that 'we were all Germans' and 'why should you hate them [the Jews], someone can't do anything about his birth.'[4]

As he observed the Stormtroopers at close quarters, Pfaller became certain that he had made the right decision: 'Even when they marched, you didn't notice anything about representing the interests of the workers, they only spoke in support of their Führer, and about what a great Reich that they wanted to build and the treaty of Versailles. Well, we were opposed to the treaty of Versailles too, that was clear. But theirs wasn't a programme that would help people in general, it helped certain forces, that was soon evident.'[5]

While the May 1928 election had been disappointing for the Nazi movement as a whole, there was at least one member of the party who had gained from the result – Joseph Goebbels. He had been elected a Reichstag deputy, something which was to be of immediate benefit to him.

As Nazi Gauleiter of Berlin, he had been trying to incite unrest through the newspaper he had founded – *Der Angriff* (The Attack). The paper soon became infamous for the viciousness of its anti-Semitic articles, with Goebbels specially targeting Dr Bernhard Weiss, the deputy commissioner of police. Weiss – a German Jew – was vilified in almost every edition during the late 1920s.

In parallel with maligning his enemies in print, Goebbels also encouraged attacks in the streets and beer halls. To provoke his opponents, he organized Nazi meetings in areas of Berlin that contained large numbers of communist supporters.[6] In February 1928, after he had been held responsible for the violent actions of Stormtroopers during one such meeting, he was sentenced to six weeks in prison.[7] But his election as a Reichstag deputy now allowed him to escape punishment, as every Reichstag member received not just a free first-class rail pass but immunity from prosecution.[8]

Goebbels, who portrayed himself as a revolutionary, was defensive about his participation in the democratic process. 'We're an anti-parliamentary party,' he wrote in a revealing article in *Der Angriff* just before the May election, 'for good reasons opposed to the Weimar constitution and the republican institutions it introduced.' But despite this anti-parliamentary stance, he claimed, it was still necessary to participate in elections so that they could 'paralyse the Weimar sentiment'. It was a complex, apparently contradictory message – especially to the Stormtroopers, many of whom wanted to seize power by revolutionary means.

Stretching this self-justification still further, Goebbels argued that 'Mussolini went into parliament as well. However, not long afterwards he marched to Rome with his Blackshirts. The communists also sit in parliament. Nobody will be so naive as to believe that they would make a sober and positive contribution.'

This paradoxical stance meant that even though Goebbels demanded 'belief, dedication, [and] passion!' he was not prepared to 'beg for votes'. He summed up his attitude to the Reichstag this way: 'We flout coop- erating in a stinking dung heap. We come to clear away the dung . . . We do not come as friends, nor even as neutrals. We come as enemies! As the wolf bursts into the flock, so we come.'[9]

This notion that the Nazis were 'wolves' was just one example of Goebbels' commitment to the pseudo-Darwinian philosophy that per- vaded the Nazi movement. When he saw a film about Africa three years later, he wrote: 'A marvellously captivating wild drama . . . That is what nature is like. Fight, fight, is what the creature shouts. Peace nowhere, only murder, only manslaughter . . . For the lion as well as for man. We only lack the courage to openly admit what is real. The sav- ages are better humans in this respect. Rather ruffian than intellectual.'[10] It's easy to detect a level of fantasy projection in this commitment to violent struggle, given that Goebbels was both an intellectual and dis- abled. In a fight against 'savages' he would have had little chance.

Goebbels also spent time musing about the difficulty of producing effective propaganda when the Nazis were not yet in power. In August 1929 he revealed how he thought people formed their views, claiming that individual 'opinions are mostly only the gramophone record of public opinion. Public opinion, in turn, is made by the press, billboards, radio, cinema, school, university and the general education of the people.' It followed that the problem the Nazis faced was that 'the government owns these methods [of persuasion].'

Consequently, thought Goebbels, the current government was responsible for the passivity of large sections of the public. The govern- ment did not have the right to call the Germans a 'cowardly people' as 'the government has made the people cowardly in the first place.' More- over 'it makes the people cowardly in order to be able to conduct cowardly politics in accordance with its inner nature.' The problem was that 'since 1919, the German government has been pacifist' and 'tolerates treason'.[11]

It is an insightful article for anyone seeking to understand how Goebbels approached the task of shifting mentalities. It revealed his commitment to the belief that people could 'mostly' be made to hold whatever views the government wanted as long as the government controlled the means of communication. Bombarded with govern- ment propaganda they would respond like sheep. The article also demonstrated his hatred of democracy and his longing for dictatorial powers. How could propagandists be expected to succeed unless they controlled not just the press and cinema, but the theatre and the education system as well?

His short-term solution to the problem – given that the Nazis were not yet in power – was a good deal less convincing than his statement of future intent. The 'first duty' of 'National Socialist propaganda', said Goebbels, had to be 'wresting the manipulation of the national psyche from the government's hands'. Quite how that task was to be achieved was left unspoken – almost certainly because Goebbels hadn't yet worked out how to do it.

It still didn't seem, as he voiced these views in the summer of 1929, that the Nazis had much hope of gaining power, even though membership of the party had increased to around 150,000 by that September. The fact that in three years' time they would be the biggest political party in Germany, and in less than four years Hitler would be Chancellor, was largely due to a crisis in the German state.

Many of the preconditions for this collapse were already present in the summer of 1929 – the fragility of Weimar democracy, the fragmentation of political parties, the polarization of debate and the fear of communism. But the most important catalyst of all didn't occur until the autumn – to be precise, on 24 October.

The American stock market crashed on 'Black Thursday'. Previously buoyed up by a wave of speculative buying, the market endured first a correction and then a full-scale panic as people sold their shares in droves. Because the German economy relied on American loans to keep functioning, this was a catastrophe for Germany. Once those American loans were called in, a German economic collapse was all but inevitable.

The timing of the Wall Street Crash was especially devastating because just two months earlier the Young Plan had been agreed. This renegotiation of reparation payments had seemed like financial salvation for Germany. Chaired by the American banker Owen Young, an Allied committee had agreed to a massive reduction in reparations.

However, the Nazis and other nationalists had vociferously objected to the idea of paying any reparations at all, and the sudden Wall Street Crash made their voices louder. Amid a worldwide economic crisis, they shouted, how could the talk still be of paying anything for a war that had ended more than ten years ago? Even though their demand for a plebiscite on the reparations was rejected, the issue remained a running sore.

Merely because it was an improvement on the previous reparation arrangements, Field Marshal Hindenburg, who became Germany's President in 1925, approved the Young Plan. This made many nationalists even more furious – the fact that Hindenburg engaged with reparations payments at all was anathema to them. It was a bizarre situation, because Hindenburg empathized not just with the nationalists' hatred of the Versailles treaty but more generally with their distrust of democracy. As an aristocrat, a landowner and a former military commander, he had been listening sympathetically to those around him who claimed the Weimar system was unstable.

German unemployment grew rapidly. In August 1929 there were fewer than 1.3 million unemployed, but by February 1930 that figure had leapt to nearly 3.4 million. 'You had to sign on every day at the dole office,' remembered Alois Pfaller, 'and then you would meet [others], and then the discussions would start, the fights, the SA [Stormtroopers] were there too, the SPD [Social Democrats] were there, the communists were there, everybody met at the dole office . . . There were fights, yes, but I only liked the discussions, I just wanted to learn something from the others who knew more . . . But it was a hopeless business, [with] people walking around with spoons in their pockets, because they got a meal for one Mark [from the soup kitchen] . . . I had 30 Marks' assistance a month . . . from the 30 Marks I paid 15 Marks in rent and the other 15 Marks were supposed to be enough for the whole month. That was awful, it was impossible.'[12]

Predictably, all this suffering was helpful for the Nazis, and on 8 December 1929 they achieved a breakthrough in Thuringia in the centre of Germany. At the state elections they gained more than 10 per cent of the vote – a hurdle they had not passed before.[13] Their 11.3 per cent share meant that they could participate for the first time in the region's coalition government. It was a victory that demonstrated once again the intractable link between Nazi success and crisis in the German state. And even though the Nazis subsequently demonstrated that they couldn't govern competently in Thuringia, this did not prevent them making electoral progress.

Alois Pfaller believed he knew the reason why: 'Everywhere there are people who are able to mislead people, let's say, tempt them towards something which they would never reasonably do, but in need, in their unhappy circumstances, in this despair, they will do things which normally they wouldn't.'[14]

During this decisive period of the early 1930s, the people who were disproportionately 'tempted' to join the Nazi Party were those in their twenties.[15] The pseudo-Darwinian nature of the party had obvious appeal to the young and healthy, as did the notion of 'righting the wrongs' of a war in which almost all of them had been too young to fight, but which had cast a shadow over their childhood.

Many universities had for years been bastions of the *völkisch* movement and the pain of the loss of German territory in the post-war settlement was still keenly felt. Students – large numbers of whom would later fight for the Nazi cause – were even told that it was their duty to recover what had been taken from Germany by the Versailles settlement. At the University of Tübingen, the rector declared in 1929 that 'nobody should have the right to sing *Deutschland über alles* unless he is determined to reconquer what has been lost, and this can be accomplished only by force of arms . . . Never will diplomats grant us freedom.'[16]

Although the Hitler Youth wasn't formally established until 1926, Nazi youth groups had existed for years before that. They had piggy-backed off the widespread success of previous *völkisch* groups such as the Wandervogel, the popular pre-First World War club that emphasized the value of spending time in the German countryside. 'I went into the mountains with lots of Hitler youths,' said Emil Klein, one of the earliest members of the party. 'The youth movement had been around a long time previously, perhaps we were just more enthusiastic about the whole thing. Everyone came freely and did not come just because their parents wanted them to. Many came precisely because their parents were against it, because their father was a Social Democrat perhaps. They came in spite of it.'[17]

The Hitler Youth had considerable impact on the psyche of many of these youngsters – especially on those from families who were suffering in the depression. 'I shall never forget one person telling me that he was the son of a communist,' recalled another Nazi youth leader. 'The whole family was unemployed, and he had spent his whole life in the big city of Essen. Then he was sent to a youth camp by the Hitler Youth and he saw a forest for the very first time. It was a real experience for that boy. I was deeply touched that the forest had made such an impression on him.'[18]

The Nazis' commitment to violence could also prove seductive. One teenager in Bernburg in central Germany revealed that he was attracted to the movement by the fact that 'dashing Stormtroopers . . . fought meeting-hall battles against communists'. He 'hated nothing more than the communists because I always pictured them as these unemployed people looking like bandits, wearing peaked caps, hands in their pockets, standing at the corners sluggardly and swearing. And these SA men [Stormtroopers], in my eyes, were the opposite to this rabble.'[19]

As the economic depression intensified, the young Stormtrooper Wolfgang Teubert was one of many who fought against the communists in the streets: 'Of course, one can't understand it looking at it from today's perspective, but in those days we were literally pushed to the limit. The people were unemployed and just obeyed the slogans, one lot following the Marxist slogans and we followed the others. And that resulted in these conflicts. And the fact that these conflicts weren't always dealt with verbally, well, that was obvious.'[20]

An article in May 1932 in the local socialist newspaper in Bernburg bemoaned the fact that 'These young people, from mostly sheltered families, who now cannot find a livelihood . . . have, with their anger about this [situation] and with their political ignorance (school and parents have failed completely here), become easy prey for political adventurers. The Nazis have promised these youths everything and anything conceivable: the less specific these promises, the stronger they are.'[21]

Psychological research helps us to understand why so many young people were susceptible to the extreme, passionate message of the Nazis, and demonstrates why the Nazis' focus on youth was such an astute strategy. The key reason is because the frontal cortex, the part of the brain responsible for regulating emotional impulses and analysing problems, is not fully formed until around twenty-five years old. 'We were selected for delayed maturation of the frontal cortex,' says Professor Robert Sapolsky, 'because it takes a long time to learn your culture's hypocrisies and learn your culture's exceptions and to learn the difference between laws that should be followed and laws that shouldn't be followed and can be ignored, and laws that you can die for and laws that you would die for opposing.'

While young people's critical faculties are not yet completely developed before their mid-twenties, the parts of the brain which long for novelty and excitement are already shaped. This can lead to thrill seeking of the wildest kind. 'The most interesting thing about adolescence', says Professor Sapolsky, 'is that it's not only the time of life when you're most likely to become a murderer, but it's also the time of your life you're most likely to commit your life to becoming Mother Teresa. If you're going to form a new religion – that's the time. If you're going to stupidly horrify your parents by giving away all your savings to a charity, that's the time. If you're going to join some hateful ideology, that's the time. It's the extremes.'[22]

Hitler instinctively knew this. In a speech in July 1922 he explicitly called on young Germans to join the Stormtroopers and fight for the Nazi cause, and 'if you are reviled and insulted, good luck to you, my boys! You have the good fortune already at 18 or 19 years of age to be hated by the greatest of scoundrels . . . You are the defence of a Movement that is called one day to remodel Germany in revolutionary fashion . . .'[23]

As part of this 'revolutionary' remodelling, Hitler outlined a murderous new idea at the 1929 Nuremberg rally – one that would have appealed to the fit young Stormtroopers more than to mature Germans. Hitler emphasized that it wasn't the number of people in a population that mattered, but their quality. He railed against 'our modern sentimental humanitarianism' which meant that 'we make an effort to maintain the weak at the expense of the healthy.' He extolled the virtues of ancient Sparta, calling it the 'strongest racial state in history', and praised the idea of killing a certain number of babies as soon as they were born: 'If Germany gained a million children a year and eliminated 700,000–800,000 of the weakest, then the final result would probably be an increase in strength. The most dangerous thing is for us to cut ourselves off from the natural process of selection . . .'[24]

When Hitler became Chancellor this idea of murdering most babies born in Germany was not pursued. It was way too radical. But once they were in power the Nazis did continue to focus on German youth and promoted both pseudo-Darwinism and anti-Semitism as they politicized the entire education system. 'Racial science and the Jewish question must run like a red thread through education at every level,' said one instruction booklet for teachers published in 1937. 'There is no subject in our schools from which valuable knowledge of the Jewish

Question cannot be drawn in unexpected fullness.' It should be empha-sized that 'like is drawn to like and produces its own kind.' Thus 'No white who is aware of and proud of his race will mate with a Negress or a Jewess.' It was vital to warn of the dangers of 'racial defilement' because 'racial defilement is racial death. Racial defilement is bloodless murder. A woman defiled by the Jew can never rid her body of the foreign poison she has absorbed.'[25]

Another textbook, entitled *Heredity and Racial Biology for Students*, stressed that children should be taught to pay proper attention to people's racial characteristics. It suggested pupils should cut out photos and pictures from magazines and newspapers of 'great scholars, states-men, artists and others who distinguished themselves' and then work out their 'preponderant race'.

Anti-Semitic content was insidiously worked into these 'assignments' via instructions to 'observe the Jew: his way of walking, his bearing, gestures and movements when talking'. Students should ask themselves 'what strikes you about the way a Jew talks and sings?' The conclusion the author wanted children to reach was most apparent in one of the final assignments, which was to list the 'occupations in which Jews are not to be found' and then 'explain this phenomenon on the basis of the character of the Jew's soul'.[26]

Research published in 2015 demonstrates that much of this Nazi edu-cational propaganda was successful, with one statistical paper concluding that 'Germans who grew up under the Nazi regime are much more anti-Semitic today than those born before or after that period' and 'it was probably Nazi schooling that was most effective [as propaganda] and not radio or cinema propaganda.' Nazi educational propaganda was particularly successful when it could 'tap into existing prejudices', with the authors of the report claiming that 'this suggests confirmation bias [the tendency to favour new information that is consistent with one's prevailing beliefs] may play an important role in intensifying attitudes toward minorities.'[27]

What was particularly insidious about the way children were edu-cated was that the overall thrust of the teaching they received was designed to make them feel good about themselves. For instance, they learnt that 'racial defilement is racial death' only in the context of their own superiority. 'People had the conceit to say that a German is special, that the German people should become a thoroughbred people . . .

[they should] stand above the others,' remembered Erna Krantz, who was a schoolgirl in Bavaria during the 1930s. 'I have to say it was somewhat contagious. You used to say that if you tell a young person every day, "You are something special," then in the end they will believe you.' She admitted that she looked back on her schooldays with enormous pleasure. She liked the fact that 'a certain camaraderie was being nurtured' and an 'elite race was being promoted', even though she maintained that she was 'apolitical' at the time.[28]

Despite her whole education having an anti-Semitic slant, Krantz claimed that she was opposed to the persecution of the Jews – especially the radicalization during the war that led to the Holocaust. 'You said, what can we do?' she recalled. 'If you think about it, that a highly civilized people as the Nazis saw themselves, that an elite group could lower themselves to do something like that – that is something which in retrospect we cannot understand, isn't it?'[29]

Alongside the changes in the educational curriculum, boys were encouraged to join the Hitler Youth and young women the League of German Girls, the BDM (Bund Deutscher Mädel). Neither of these organizations was compulsory until 1939 – Erna Krantz, for instance, didn't join the BDM even though she enjoyed living in Nazi Germany. But for those who did decide to take part, often after pressure from their schoolteachers or parents, a new level of ideological propaganda was on offer.

Jutta Rüdiger, leader of the BDM in the 1930s, revealed in an interview after the war that a major emphasis was placed on indoctrinating girls in the concept of the *Volksgemeinschaft* : 'At first we concentrated on team sports, joint exercises, teamwork so to speak, learning how to pull together in play, trying to teach them comradeship. Then we went on trips and camping where they also learnt to help each other. Later competitive sport was added, but we did not want to create any star-hype, they were always supposed to feel committed to their community . . . That was what I stood for then and I still think it is right today. First, they should learn to live in a community and then there should be some individual education, but again the individual with all their gifts and capabilities should remain committed to the community as a whole.' She claimed that 'Everyone wanted to help rebuild Germany, because in their home and with unemployment they had experienced poverty first hand. And then they were told it was going to work if everybody joined in, we would manage.'

In addition to this focus on the community, there was 'the ideological training. That training was meant as supplementary to school
and was not intended to convey knowledge to the young people, but
rather to convey experience. They were being told about their home
country and its traditions. They were introduced to historical figures
through stories and songs about them. For the girls these were people
like the Empress Maria Theresa and for the boys Frederick the Great
of Prussia.'

Rüdiger met Hitler on several occasions and always found him
inspiring. She remembered that he 'wanted the girls to be beautiful,
graceful girls, a goal which was meant to be achieved by gymnastics
among other things'. And while she claimed that her focus was not on
teaching the girls to be good mothers, she nonetheless believed that 'if a
girl is healthy then she will automatically become a healthy wife and
mother later on.'

She particularly liked the way Hitler could convey ideas clearly to
young people. She remembered hearing him say that only 'very simple
people could be communists. They would all have the same house and
the same garden and the same furniture, but he said that the more
sophisticated a people became the more pronounced the differences will
be. And that if you put in more effort, you should earn more as well.'
She didn't think this conflicted with the idea of the 'national community' as even though Hitler 'favoured private capital' he still wanted
everyone to 'do something for their people'.[30]

For many of the BDM girls, Hitler came to be seen less as a father-
figure and more as a man suffused with sex appeal. One fourteen-
year-old girl confessed that when she and others saw Hitler in Stuttgart,
'Everybody screamed like crazy. Mass suggestiveness! The scream
became a roar . . . Especially the women were fascinated. Their emotions were strongly touched and so were, without a doubt, unfulfilled
sexual wishes and desires.' Another fourteen-year-old girl fell 'totally in
love' with Hitler and wanted to give him a child but didn't yet know
'technically' how 'this was to be done'.[31]

The combination of freedom from parental supervision, proximity
in camps to the adolescents of the Hitler Youth and teaching which
proselytized the importance of mixing only with their 'racial' equals
led to many sexual encounters – some of which had long-term consequences. For example, after a large group of BDM girls camped out

near the Hitler Youth at the Nuremberg rally in 1936, many of them became pregnant.[32]

As for the pervasive anti-Semitism of Nazi ideology, Jutta Rüdiger claimed that 'even though there was some kind of anti-Semitic paragraph in the party manifesto' she 'did not place too much emphasis on it'. And indeed historical research into the BDM confirms that political messages were conveyed almost 'subliminally' – not least by the fact that Jewish girls were refused membership.[33]

Rüdiger was prepared to admit that the Jews were 'perceived as an alien element'. The best way forward for any society, she argued, was for strict racial segregation: 'There is an ancient Indian saying: "The white man is from God and the black man is from God, but the half-caste is from the Devil." Meaning that in the long run nothing creative will come from the multicultural approach.'[34]

But not everyone who experienced either the BDM or the Hitler Youth came away quite so committed to the Nazi cause. Franz Jagemann, for example, had a very different experience. He was born in 1917 in what was then the province of Posen in Prussia, an area which became Poznań in the newly reconstituted country of Poland after the Versailles treaty. And even though Jagemann and his family moved to Germany to escape living under Polish rule, he was still 'very much aware of my Polish heritage and affinity'.

Jagemann's father had Polish ancestry, but he had married a German woman and 'studied at German universities and had joined the Prussian civil service'. So even though, claimed his son, he 'never liked the National Socialists' he tried to assimilate in the new Germany and so joined the Nazi Party. As a further step in demonstrating his commitment to the Nazi regime he signed his son up for the Hitler Youth.

Jagemann was an intelligent and sensitive adolescent, and he quickly discovered that the Hitler Youth was not for him: 'People in the Hitler Youth had a vulgar way of dealing with each other – a very unpleasant and violent manner was customary. The way, for example, we were told: "If your teachers haven't yet grasped the new era, then smack them in the mouth!"' And though 'to start with it was highly interesting, with cross-country manoeuvres during the night, the feeling grew more and more clear that the real attitude that lay behind it was basically a very violent, very brutal, very crude manner. And one had to obey people your own age who played your superiors without question, following the Führer principle. Well, that was something that I didn't like at all.'

He was shocked to discover that the bully-boy tactics of the Hitler Youth even extended to intimidating teachers. 'There was an incident when I was at school,' he remembered. 'A boy in the Hitler Youth, in my class, had written a load of propaganda slogans in his German essay and the German teacher didn't give his work a good mark. Whereupon my fellow student from the class went to the school inspector and initiated an investigation into the teacher.'[35]

Jagemann felt compelled to intervene. He and two of his classmates 'were elected as class representatives to go to the school inspector and make it clear that the teacher had been very objective' and that since he was 'a very calm, sensible, reliable teacher' he could 'only hand out the most appropriate grade'. The response from the school inspector was unexpected. He 'was shocked. He told us off, in fact, for not understanding the new era properly.'

Two years after he joined the Hitler Youth, Jagemann was sent to 'the polling office' on election day, at the time of a referendum, and ordered to offer a 'little sticker' to voters with the word 'yes' on it. They could then label themselves as 'Hitler voters'. He could see that some voters felt 'inner dislike and repulsion' at the idea of wearing the sticker but did so nonetheless. 'I felt sorry for them in a way. I felt somehow cheapened with them. I, as the active one, putting the thing on them, and them for allowing it to be done to them. We were engaged in mutual theatre.'

Jagemann's experience, though revelatory, was unusual. The majority of German boys who joined the Hitler Youth 'loved its program of activities and did feel looked after, knowing that they would graduate to become bearers of the new Reich'.[36] Hubert Lutz, for instance, was a member of the Jungvolk, the pre-Hitler Youth group, and he felt it was an 'honour' to wear the dagger which was offered as part of the uniform. So much so that the punishment meted out 'if you did something really nasty' was to have the dagger taken away from you, along with the distinctive scarf the boys wore. This meant that you were 'like an outcast' from the group.

Lutz and his friends looked back on their childhood in Nazi Germany as 'the most exciting time of our lives . . . We didn't know any better. You see, when the Nazis came to power, I was five years old. I grew up in this, so it was a normal way of life to me.'[37]

A report written in 1935 by members of the underground left-wing opposition group Neu Beginnen confirmed not just that many of the most passionate Nazi supporters were young but concluded disconsolately that it was 'youths who haven't experienced the World War at first hand' who were 'incited and made drunk by National Socialism'. Another of their reports the following year admitted that the regime had succeeded in 'artificially creating the "unity of the nation"' and emphasized that it was important to witness 'these military parades, the tattoos, the rallies and demonstrations . . . to understand what is currently happening'.[38]

The militaristic aspect of the Hitler Youth – the marches, the uniforms, the camping and the rough-housing – offered a taste of what life would be like as a soldier. In 1937 this link was made explicit when Lieutenant Colonel Erwin Rommel, later a famous general during the war, was appointed liaison officer between the Hitler Youth and the German Army.

Without question, the various Nazi youth groups, combined with the racist education they received, had a huge impact on the psyche of young Germans during the 1930s. And by 1938 just over seven million of the nine million German children between the ages of ten and eighteen were participating in a Nazi youth organization.[39]

In the mid-1930s, Emil Klein, by now one of the national organizers of the Hitler Youth, was pleased to discover how much other nations valued their work. When he and his comrades visited England, they were buoyed up by the praise they received. A British historian inscribed his book to them with the words 'England would be delighted and proud to have such a youth as Germany's today.' 'Well,' said Klein, 'should we say we'll creep away in the light of that?' He was still 'delighted', long after the end of the war, 'that this [admiration] was the case'. Consequently, 'I regret nothing of what happened [at the time], even if I have a different view today.'[40]

Other prominent Englishmen praised the way Germans were being moulded by the Nazi regime. 'During the past three months I have watched Young Germany at work and at play in every part of the country,' said Sir Arnold Wilson MP in July 1934, during a speech at Königsberg. 'I admire the intense energy evoked by the National Socialist Movement. I respect the patriotic ardour of German youth. I recognize, I almost envy, the depth and earnestness of the search for national unity which inspires your schools and colleges: because it is wholly unselfish, it is wholly good.'[41]

Wilson had made a monumental misjudgement. The Nazi youth programme was neither 'wholly unselfish' nor 'wholly good'. Quite the contrary. One of the many ways in which it damaged German society was by splitting some families apart as the young were radicalized. One widow worried that her two boys 'spent the whole day in the Hitler Youth, where they were constantly being stirred up, against their own mother, against religion, and against everything'. Another mother was concerned that her son was such an 'enthusiastic Nazi' that 'father and son could not understand each other any more.' Still more parents were anxious that if they criticized the regime in their child's hearing they might be denounced.[42]

All this turmoil was a consequence of the Nazis' successful targeting of young Germans. But this in turn had been made possible only by the appointment of Hitler as Chancellor of Germany. And that would never have happened if powerful people in the German elite hadn't believed that it was in their interests to propel him into office.

It is one of the most disturbing aspects of this history – and something that tells us a great deal about how would-be dictators can gain control of a modern state. And it is the subject of the next chapter.

5. Conniving with the Elite

In the early 1930s it wasn't possible to become Chancellor of Germany merely by leading the most popular political party. It didn't matter how many votes you received, the only way to gain power was for President Hindenburg to offer you the job. And before deciding whether or not he should, he listened to the advice of his friends in the German elite. Like Hitler, many of them also wanted to see democracy destroyed, and so they connived together to make it happen.

Early signs that the Nazis were becoming a force in German politics were clear by the spring of 1930. In May, the Prussian Interior Ministry produced a report that revealed how successful the Nazis were at linking the current 'economic situation' with the 'lost war'.[1] The result was that many Germans now believed that only the Nazis offered the 'radical remedy' the country needed. The voters' desperate 'urge to somehow get out of the catastrophe' prevented people from seeing 'through the deceptive economic and political slogans of National Socialism'.

The report confirmed that it was 'those sections of the population who suffer most from the prevailing economic hardship' who were particularly attracted to the Nazis. These groups included not just 'the middle class' and 'small traders and tradespeople', but 'young academics and college students' as well. The prevalence of these young supporters gave 'the movement a very special impetus'.

Great attention in the report was paid to the power of Nazi propaganda. The scale of the Nazi effort was 'not remotely matched by any other party or movement'. Nazi speakers were given 'systematic training' which allowed them to tailor their speeches directly to individual audiences – helped by the vagueness of the original party programme of 1920 and Hitler's subsequent refusal to clarify exactly what it meant. Farmers were told their land might be taken from them, and shopkeepers that department stores would destroy their business. The only consistent part of the message was that the Jews were behind all these threats.

Against that background, Goebbels realized the value of focusing public attention on what the Nazis opposed rather than on any detailed policies of their own. To that end, in 1929, he had seized on the publication of Erich Maria Remarque's *All Quiet on the Western Front*. Remarque's novel, with its anti-war message, directly contradicted the Nazi propaganda stance that the noble soldiers in the trenches had been 'betrayed' by Jews, profiteers and socialist politicians back home.

In July 1929 Goebbels wrote in his diary that he found the book a 'dreadful tendentious sham' and both 'nasty' and 'subversive'. But he also recognized that 'it has had an effect on millions of hearts.'[2] A few weeks before, the Nazis' newspaper the *Völkischer Beobachter* had attacked the novel, saying the problem was that it 'didn't take the great bloodletting [of the war] as an eternal law of nature'.[3]

On 14 August 1929 the *Völkischer Beobachter* published a critique of the book by a veteran called Hans Zöberlein – 'someone who has lain in the trenches and craters of the west for three years'. He claimed that the book was 'written from the perspective of someone sitting on the latrine'. Consequently, the 'memorial of the unknown soldier becomes a single big pile of faeces'. Remarque – 'such a dirty fellow' – would, in another country, 'be hanging from a streetlamp'.[4]

It was inevitable that the news the following year that Hollywood was making a film of the book would raise the Nazis' attack to a higher level. The *Völkischer Beobachter* was quick to claim that the director of the film, Lewis Milestone, was a Jew who possessed 'all his race's "qualities"'.[5] It was a story that played straight into the Nazis' prejudices. Not only could they push the lie that the Jews had plotted to lose Germany the First World War, but now they could claim that America was controlled by Jews.

In early December 1930, shortly after the film was released in Germany, Goebbels orchestrated a headline-grabbing protest. During a showing of the film at the Mozart Hall in Berlin, the Nazis threw stink bombs into the auditorium and let loose mice. According to the liberal newspaper the *Vossische Zeitung*, they also 'continuously made noise, stridently whistled and physically threatened the rest of the audience'. Goebbels then announced, 'Now we are going to get our money back,' and a group of Nazis clashed with police as they tried to reach the box office.[6] The *Völkischer Beobachter* published a different version of events and alleged that there was 'outrage' from the audience at the 'disgusting scenes' in the film and that some even shouted 'Enough! We don't have to put up with such Jewish impudence!'[7]

Goebbels was ecstatic about the protest, writing that 'after 10 minutes the cinema is like a madhouse. The police are powerless. The enraged crowd takes violent action against the Jews . . . [shouting] "Jews out!" "Hitler is at the gates!" The police sympathize with us. The Jews are small and ugly. Outside storming of the ticket offices. Windowpanes rattle. Thousands of people enjoy this spectacle immensely.'[8]

A few days later, when the film was shown again, Goebbels organized a mass demonstration on Nollendorfplatz in Berlin, where thousands of Nazi supporters clashed with the police. Goebbels was elated once more. He was even happy to see the police use rubber truncheons against the protesters. 'Our people are pale with rage,' he wrote. 'This is the beginning of a revolution. Just keep it up!'[9]

Shortly afterwards, the film was pulled from the cinema. It was impossible for the police to search every cinemagoer for stink bombs or mice and allow a normal evening's entertainment to go ahead. Goebbels boasted that he had won a great victory and wrote disingenuously in *Der Angriff*: 'We claimed the right to freedom of speech in this democracy for ourselves, and above all expectations our appeal was heard . . . In the end, it was a fight for a matter of principle. We were the bearers of the moral idea of the state.' He crowed that by marching 'against the Jewish provocation of the Remarque film . . . all the hungry and freezing people, those abandoned and in despair, the front-line soldiers that were lied to and betrayed, the intellectuals and craftsmen' had together formed an 'army of determined and radical young Germans who don't want to put up with public life in Germany becoming a scandal'. They were not prepared to witness the 'ridiculing of German honour'.[10]

Goebbels was delighted to discover that 'My reputation in Munich [among the Nazi leadership] has grown extremely because of the Remarque matter.'[11] This was hardly surprising. He had successfully used a small, almost trivial, dispute about the content of a film to express the Nazis' supposed core values of self-sacrifice and love of Germany – principles which they said underpinned their promise of a *Volksgemeinschaft*. He also claimed that this was only the beginning: 'Do we still need to explain in detail that the fight totally and completely goes on, and that we have reason to hope to win it once and for all one day? . . . Remarque has been eliminated, but the entire German public is still covered in Jewish filth; it is necessary to clean it up.'[12]

Goebbels, without knowing the psychology, understood the power of referring to 'Jewish filth'. That is because the part of the brain which makes you react to hideous smells is also activated merely by 'thinking about something morally disgusting'.[13] Thinking 'of the neighbouring tribe as loathsome cockroaches', wrote Professor Robert Sapolsky, causes the 'insula and amygdala' to activate and is central to how our brains process 'Us and Them'.[14] The Nazis' description of Jews as 'filthy' or 'vermin' had a similarly powerful effect.

But Goebbels' attack on *All Quiet on the Western Front* and his attempt to link it to Jewish 'filth' did not go entirely his own way. There was a coda to this story, one which demonstrated the monstrous hypocrisy at the heart of Goebbels' propaganda. On 6 May 1931, *Der Angriff* published a long article entitled 'Night at the Front', a vivid description of life in the trenches. This was intended to debunk Remarque's portrayal and tell the 'true' story of the heroism of German soldiers during the war.[15] There was just one problem. The Nazis had been duped by a prankster, as the article submitted was – word for word – an extract from *All Quiet on the Western Front*. The *Sozialistische Bildung* found the affair 'priceless' as it was 'generally known that the Nazis under the leadership of Dr Goebbels are waging war to the death against Remarque's book'.[16]

Der Angriff was forced to print a humiliating admission of the mistake: 'Yesterday, our editorial department fell prey to a Jewish trick. Among the submitted manuscripts, there was an article sent in for free printing by a seeming party comrade: R. Scheinpflug. As it turned out, this little article is an extract from Remarque's Jewish book: *All Quiet on the Western Front*. We regret that we were persuaded by this cunning deception to print a part of a book – in principle innocent – that all German-minded people have rejected . . . This makes clear to everyone what tricks the Jew uses in his fear to harm the NSDAP.'[17]

The fact that there was no evidence that those behind the prank were Jewish didn't stop Goebbels claiming they were. The accusation only served to illustrate yet again the Nazis' knee-jerk reaction to anything they hated: the Jews must be responsible. Indeed, to the Nazis the lack of any evidence merely demonstrated how clever the Jews were at covering up their tracks.

Large numbers of ordinary Germans thought this sort of thinking dishonest. They were also suspicious that the Nazis were still committed to revolution rather than the pursuit of power through democratic means. Consequently, at a trial held in September 1930, Hitler had to tread the most delicate of lines. Three army officers had been accused of trying to convince their comrades to back a Nazi revolution. So, the court wanted to know, was Hitler a politician who respected the verdict of the majority or an insurrectionist?

Hitler testified that, while it was inevitable that the party would contain some 'temperamental members', the truth was that 'we are a purely spiritual movement.' When questioned if he had said, as reported, 'heads will roll in the sand in this struggle, either ours or the others',' he replied that he was committed to a 'legal struggle' but that after the Nazis won and had established a 'German Supreme Court' then 'November 1918 will find its retribution, and heads will also roll.'[18]

While Hitler did his best to equivocate at the trial, he also knew that more control had to be exerted over these 'temperamental members' – many of whom were Stormtroopers. Fortunately for him he was soon able to call on the services of one of his oldest comrades – Ernst Röhm. In 1928 Röhm had accepted an invitation to become an adviser to the Bolivian Army, but he now wanted to come back to Germany, and so he sent a telegram to a colleague in September 1930 which read simply: 'Returning November, notify mother and Hitler.'[19]

In November 1930, the *Völkischer Beobachter* celebrated Röhm's re-emergence and praised him as Hitler's 'loyal fellow fighter from the hardest days of the National Socialist movement'. Röhm was welcomed back at Munich's main station by 'numerous party comrades, companions and friends', including Adolf Hitler himself.[20]

Hitler's celebration of Röhm's homecoming, and his subsequent decision to appoint him Chief of Staff of the Stormtroopers, was a risk. He knew all about Röhm's downside. The issue that had split them apart years ago – the extent to which the paramilitary wing of the Nazis was an independent force or not – still lurked in the background. And Röhm's character had not changed. He was still the rumbustious buccaneer of old. Moreover, he was a practising homosexual at a time when homosexual sex was illegal under section 175 of the Weimar constitution. Not that section 175 had prevented Berlin becoming a centre of gay sex during the Weimar years. And Röhm had participated enthusiastically in all that the gay clubs and bathhouses of the city had to offer.

Many Nazis were outraged by Röhm's sexual orientation. 'Revolting!' wrote Goebbels in his diary in February 1931. 'Hitler not taking enough care again. We can't have this, the Party as the El Dorado of the 175ers.'[21] But Hitler rejected such concerns, declaring that same month that he 'rejected' as an 'impertinence' the 'reports directed against SA leaders'. The Stormtroopers, he wrote, were 'an aggregation of men for a particular political aim'. They were not 'a moral institution for the education of young ladies, but a union of rough fighters'.[22] The Führer had spoken – Röhm's value outweighed any considerations about his personal life.

But just a few months later Röhm became a target for the Nazis' opponents. The *Münchener Post* publicized Röhm's sexual preference in an article on 22 June 1931 called 'Homosexuality in the Brown House' – the Brown House was the Nazis' headquarters, based in Munich. Other media picked up the story, including newspapers in Berlin.

Hitler brushed all this talk aside. He still felt he needed Röhm – and it's easy to see why. The Stormtroopers remained a vital resource. Everyone knew that a dozen years ago there had been gun battles on the streets of Munich, and without the paramilitary forces of the Freikorps the communists might have consolidated their rule over the city. Who was to say that something similar might not happen again? In such circumstances the Stormtroopers would likely be the saviour of the Nazi Party and, in Hitler's eyes, quite possibly the saviour of the nation.

The trouble was that the Stormtroopers also remained a potential liability – something Goebbels discovered first hand in February 1931 when the leader of the Stormtroopers in Berlin, Walter Stennes, wrote a series of articles rejecting the Nazis' constitutional route to power and calling for an armed struggle. The following month he and his Stormtroopers attacked the Nazi Party offices in Berlin and seized the headquarters of *Der Angriff*. This was too much for Hitler, and to Goebbels' satisfaction – and with Röhm's backing – Stennes was expelled from the party.

Given all this, it's clear why Hitler valued the emergence of another paramilitary group within the Nazi movement – the Schutzstaffel (Protection Squad), popularly known as the SS. The SS came into existence in 1925, after the debacle of the Beer-Hall Putsch, at a time when the

Stormtroopers were a banned organization. Heinrich Himmler became deputy head of the SS two years later, and in 1929 was promoted to command the unit as Reichsführer SS. Himmler was likely chosen for the job because in his previous role he had organized party meetings that needed protection.[23]

Few could have predicted that the SS of the late 1920s – with not even 1,500 members – would eventually grow into the most infamous of all Nazi organizations. But, unprepossessing as he was, Himmler was astute enough to recognize that there was a gap in the movement that he and his SS could fill – that of an ultra-loyal, elite paramilitary unit. And even though in those early years the SS was under the overall command of the leader of the Stormtroopers, Himmler wanted to lead men who espoused values that were antithetical to those held by Röhm's ill-educated street thugs.

The very motto of the SS – *Meine Ehre heisst Treue* (My Honour is Called Loyalty) – drew a distinction between the SS and the Stormtroopers. In April 1931, after the SS had tried to protect the party headquarters in Berlin from Stennes' men, Hitler had written that for the SS man 'your honour is loyalty', and Himmler had subsequently adapted the phrase and proclaimed it to be the maxim of the whole organization.

Bernd Linn, who became a member of the SS in the early 1930s, joined the organization because he thought it was something special. 'My gut feeling was that the SS was one level above the SA [Stormtroopers],' he said. He had been impressed that the SS were the last group in any Nazi parade and so 'were always most at risk'. He was so proud to have been an SS man that remnants of loyalty to the group never left him. Long after the war he still refused to say whether his original decision to join the SS was 'right or wrong' – only that it was 'impossible to say now'.[24]

In pursuit of his desire to create an elite unit, Himmler naturally wanted to attract elite recruits. And in the summer of 1931 he thought he had found one of the most impressive of all, a man who, more than any other, would come to epitomize how intelligence and culture are no hindrance to barbarism – Reinhard Heydrich. Yet, surprisingly, up until the moment he joined the party on 1 June 1931 he had shown little interest in the Nazi movement.

Born in 1904, Heydrich had been too young to take part in the First

World War and had grown up in a cultured milieu – his father established the music conservatory in Halle near Leipzig. It was only the unrest at the end of the war that brought home to the teenage Heydrich the reality that Germany could be subsumed in revolution.

Heydrich decided to pursue a career as a naval officer and began training as a cadet at Kiel in 1922. If all had gone to plan, the German Navy is almost certainly where he would have remained. There would have been no lasting infamy as one of the architects of the Holocaust, just Heydrich the sailor.

In December 1930, with his naval career progressing well, Heydrich met a self-assured nineteen-year-old woman called Lina von Osten. Within days they were engaged. The swiftness of his proposal was evidence of one of Heydrich's most notable character traits. 'He always knew exactly what he wanted,' said Osten years later.[25]

After Heydrich had announced his engagement, there was an immediate difficulty – one that would forever alter the course of his life. Another woman came forward and claimed he had made a prior commitment to her. Her father was outraged at the way Heydrich had treated his daughter and complained to senior officers in the navy.

At a 'court of honour' held in January 1931 Heydrich's arrogance counted against him. He didn't deny he knew the woman but said she had attempted to seduce him rather than the other way around. Furthermore, he claimed he had never asked her to marry him.[26]

This lack of gallantry did not endear Heydrich to his superiors, and he was thrown out of the navy in April. 'Discharge from the navy', said Lina von Osten after the war, 'was the heaviest blow of his life . . . It was not the lost earning capacity which weighed on him, but the fact that with every fibre of his being he had clung on to his career as an officer.'[27]

Osten, who stuck by Heydrich throughout his tribulations, encouraged her fiancé to consider another option – the Nazis. She was both a true believer in the Nazi cause and a committed anti-Semite. The only difficulty she faced was that Heydrich didn't share her passion for the Nazis. 'Politically he was clueless,' she said later. 'He regarded all parties, particularly the Nazi Party, with arrogance and considered politics itself to be vulgar. In this connection he acted very much the snob and regarded his naval career as the most important thing. The rest didn't count.'[28]

But with his naval career in ruins and no hope of getting married without a job, Heydrich was open to persuasion. Encouraged by his wife, he joined the Nazi Party, and through family contacts obtained an introduction to Heinrich Himmler. On 14 June 1931, just two weeks after he had joined the party, Heydrich met Himmler for the first time. They formed an immediate connection. Himmler was looking for someone to start up an intelligence unit within the SS and he thought Heydrich looked the part – tall, blond and with an officer's bearing. The fact that Heydrich had no relevant experience – he had been a radio officer in the navy and had never worked in intelligence – was brushed aside.

While hardly a normal recruitment process, the meeting was symptomatic of how Himmler worked in two important ways. First, he was focused on physical appearance. In 1938, for example, he had spotted an ordinary SS man whom he considered a perfect Aryan specimen. He thought a soldier who was such a 'capable, good-blooded German' surely deserved a higher rank, and so, motivated purely by the man's appearance, he ordered him promoted after an examination of his SS file.[29] Second, Himmler was prepared to give someone he valued another chance. Having left the navy under a cloud, Heydrich was at a low point and needed help. Himmler was willing to give it, and in the process gain both Heydrich's gratitude and his loyalty. And, like Hitler, Himmler demanded loyalty above everything else.

More surprising still is the knowledge that Heydrich joined the SS without any burning commitment to the cause. It is one of the most dramatic examples in this history of the swiftness with which an individual's behaviour can change as the situation changes.

The intelligence unit that Himmler tasked Heydrich with creating was subsequently called the Sicherheitsdienst (Security Service), or SD for short, and would grow into one of the most powerful and feared organizations in the state. But its beginnings were modest. With barely an office and a phone, Heydrich attempted to recruit people who could gather intelligence on enemies of the Nazi Party and search out potential spies within the movement itself.

It was also imperative to Himmler that Heydrich do more than just sit behind a desk – members of the SS also had to be men of action. So Heydrich took part in attacks on meetings held by the Nazis' political opponents. He was soon noticed by the press, with the *Münchener Post* in November 1931 calling him Himmler's 'right-hand man' in the 'organization of executioners' of the SS.[30]

The SS was still numerically insignificant compared with the Stormtroopers – about a tenth of the size at the time Heydrich joined. But Himmler had grandiose plans. In June 1931, the same month he met Heydrich, he gave a speech to senior members of the SS in which he claimed that 'We have been given the greatest and most magnificent task that a nation can be faced with.' This 'magnificent task' was the life-and-death struggle against 'Bolshevism' and the need to create a 'nation of 200 million' by settling Germans in 'surrounding territory'.[31]

Himmler didn't imagine that this epic goal could be accomplished quickly. He spoke of preparing the way for this new empire – establishing the 'foundations' – so that it could be achieved by the 'next generation'. Nonetheless, it's significant that even before the Nazis came to power, when the SS was just a few thousand men, Himmler believed that a future armed conflict of gigantic proportions was inevitable, and that the SS would be central to the fight.

Himmler continued to recruit men of intelligence for the epoch-shaking tasks he thought lay ahead – including Werner Best, a lawyer with a doctorate. Best was a twenty-seven-year-old member of the judicial service at the time Himmler gave his speech in June 1931, and would shortly prove that a postgraduate degree in law is no hindrance to the planning of extra-judicial killings.

Best, who was the party's legal head in Hesse in western Germany, helped draw up plans to be implemented by the Nazis in the event of a communist uprising. In November 1931 newspapers got hold of the material, and there was an immediate scandal. 'Death penalty!' said the headline in *Vorwärts*, the newspaper of the Social Democratic Party. 'The National Socialist's government agenda reveals shootings and famine!' The article went on to outline how the Nazis planned to replace 'law' with 'legalized murder . . . This is a revelation of bloody madness, of cruelty, of inhumanity . . . the unleashing of the beast in man, the raging of all against all – the agenda cannot be summarized any other way.'[32]

The liberal paper *Vossische Zeitung* voiced similar concerns: 'In mid-September 1931, a secret meeting of National Socialist leaders was held at the Boxheimer Hof near Lampertheim . . . a restricted circle of them was presented, by the assistant judge Dr Best, with drafts for measures planned in a "case of emergency" . . . The draft breathes the spirit of the most brutal violence. Almost every infringement is threatened by the death penalty . . . even executions by shooting without trial are to be carried out.'[33]

Despite the brutal nature of the Nazis' contingency plans, the affair did no lasting damage to the image of the party. The Nazi leadership claimed this was a local matter – Best and his regional colleagues, they asserted, had merely become overexcited – while the 'unleashing of the beast' and 'legalized murder' were contemplated only if the communists attempted a takeover.[34]

The fact that the scandal was not calamitous for the Nazis despite the extensive press coverage is remarkable. Although against the use of violence themselves, many Germans clearly believed the violence of the Nazis might be necessary to protect them from a communist uprising. In short, their longing for peace and quiet made them embrace a party that promised to use violence to achieve that aim. It is a key reason why millions of law-abiding people felt able to vote for a law-breaking political party. It is also evidence of an important psychological insight. Research demonstrates that, as a species, very few of us are against violence in absolute terms. What we care about is that aggression is used only in appropriate situations. In the right circumstances most of us can be enthusiastic supporters of violence.[35] Almost all of us want the security forces to protect us, for instance, and if they have to kill people who are about to kill us, then so be it.

Both the economic depression and the Nazis' promise of a future 'people's community' were important factors in their electoral success during this period, but so was the belief that the Nazis as a party of violence were best equipped to restore order. It is significant that women – who before 1932 were less inclined to support the Nazis – now voted in increasing numbers for the movement. Previously, women had tended to favour the more centrist parties and had avoided the extremes of either the Nazis or the communists. That was beginning to change.

It was around this time that Jutta Rüdiger, then a student in her early twenties, first turned to the Nazis. Her parents had suffered in the depression and her studies were threatened by her family's financial difficulties. Amid this worrying atmosphere, she found the Nazis' unique combination of 'nationalism' and 'socialism' especially appealing: 'It was explained that if you are a nationalist and you love your home and your fatherland, then you must take responsibility for the simplest man and the simplest woman. And if you are a socialist and you want to help your people then that has to be adapted to the national character, that is to say what is needed is not a Russian socialism but a national German socialism. That made sense to me at the time, and I was really convinced that was the way forward . . . And at that point I pulled myself together and said to myself, now you join and take part, so I joined the National Socialist German Students' Association.'[36]

She recalled that 'communist students' were also 'very active' at the time, and out of curiosity she went along with some friends to one of their meetings: 'They were talking about what a wonderful life women were leading in the Soviet Union – they could go out to work and the children were looked after. And I was told by my friends, "Now you have to say something" even though I had never spoken in public before. And I had not been trained at all. So I just said what I thought, and explained that I did not consider it an ideal situation if the mother does not look after her children, especially in the first formative years, and that children needed love and security if they were to grow up healthy in body and soul.'

She saw Hitler speak at a rally for the first time in 1932. Her recollections of both the context of the times and Hitler's speaking style are typical of many who became Nazi supporters in the early 1930s. 'The [unemployed] people were really hungry and had no proper clothes to wear,' she said. 'The rumours went round that he [Hitler] was the bringer of salvation . . . It was dead quiet, and then he started to speak extremely calmly, he spoke slowly with a sonorous voice and ever so slowly got caught up in his own enthusiasm. He described how the German people could be helped, how they could be led out of this misery. And when the rally was over I had the feeling that here was a man who did not think about himself and his own advantage, but solely about the good of the German people.'[37]

Inspired by this belief, Rüdiger progressed within the Nazi movement, eventually becoming, as we saw in the previous chapter, the leader of the BDM – the Bund Deutscher Mädel, the League of German Girls, the female equivalent of the Hitler Youth. But, like all women in the Nazi Party, she could not hope to hold a significant position of leadership over men in the movement. Indeed, prior to 1932 less than 10 per cent of the membership of the party was female. Hitler believed that a woman's primary role was that of housewife and mother – there was no possibility of a Nazi equivalent of Rosa Luxemburg, one of the communist leaders of the 1919 revolution in Berlin.

This is not to say that there were not a number of forceful women in the Nazi movement. Lina von Osten, for instance, who became Lina Heydrich on 26 December 1931, later confessed that 'I have always had a loose tongue.'[38] She even told jokes about Himmler's wife, mocking her size 'X X X L knickers'[39] and calling her 'a she-goat or something like that'.[40]

Her husband was evidently attracted to his wife because of her lively character. Osten remembered that after they were married she met the woman who had complained that Heydrich had jilted her, and later asked her husband why, since she was so pretty, he had not married her instead. 'She was so boring,' her husband replied.[41]

Nonetheless, when Heydrich and his wife met Hitler for the first time, the Nazi leader's reaction was to call them a 'handsome couple'. It was not Lina Heydrich's animated nature that Hitler appreciated, but her Aryan looks.[42]

Around the same time that Reinhard Heydrich became involved with Lina von Osten, another more prominent Nazi also became enamoured of a woman – one who was to become infamous. Magda Quandt first saw Joseph Goebbels speak in the summer of 1930. She was already a Nazi supporter, having been introduced to the movement by Kurt Lüdecke, with whom she was rumoured to have had an affair. Recently divorced from the vastly rich industrialist Günther Quandt, Magda was captivated not just by Nazism but by Goebbels, one of its chief proponents.[43] A few weeks after hearing him speak, she managed to get close to the man himself, having volunteered to reorganize his 'private papers'.[44]

Goebbels found the twenty-nine-year-old Magda Quandt – a statuesque blonde – immensely attractive. But, worryingly for their relationship, so did Hitler. Goebbels was initially jealous of Hitler's interest, but Magda had already made her choice and embarked on a love affair with Goebbels. According to Goebbels, Hitler was 'resigned' and did not begrudge him his happiness. Moreover, Hitler told Goebbels that she was a 'clever and beautiful woman. She won't hold you back, but help you to make progress.'[45] Hitler even agreed to be a witness at Magda Quandt and Joseph Goebbels' wedding on 19 December 1931, just a week before Heydrich married Lina von Osten.

Both Lina von Osten and Magda Quandt were intelligent women committed to the Nazi movement. Magda's ex-husband later said that 'She became the most fervent advocate of National Socialist ideas and tried to convert my son and me for the party.'[46] Significantly both women had decided to support the movement before meeting their respective partners – they were Nazis first, lovers second. But because of the party's view of women they could not progress far within the Nazi movement.

As the festivities were held for Goebbels' and Heydrich's weddings, the political crisis in Germany was worsening – to a large extent because of a decision President Paul von Hindenburg had taken in March the previous year. He had appointed Heinrich Brüning of the Centre Party as Chancellor, but – because of lack of support in the Reichstag – Brüning had to rely on the help of Hindenburg in a more direct way than any of his predecessors. Increasingly, Brüning was forced to use a clause in the Weimar constitution – Article 48 – which allowed Hindenburg to circumvent the Reichstag and enforce emergency legislation. So, when Brüning couldn't get his financial measures through parliament, Hindenburg had to issue them as an 'emergency decree'. But Article 48 didn't offer Hindenburg and Brüning unfettered power, because a simple majority vote in the Reichstag could force a new election.

Between April 1931 and the end of 1932 Hindenburg authorized an incredible ninety-nine emergency decrees. It was not just a recipe for political instability. It was a sign that democratic government had almost ceased to function. As *Time* magazine observed, it looked like Hindenburg was presiding over a regime that sought to 'out-Hitler Hitler' as Germany descended towards an authoritarian state.[47]

Hindenburg obviously bears a great deal of responsibility for all of this, not least because he was so widely respected. He was seen on the political right as a symbol of loyalty, probity and steadfastness, and his age and experience played into the notion that he was the father of the nation. He had retired from the German Army at the age of sixty-four, three years before the First World War started, only to return when needed.[48] He was still lauded as the Hero of Tannenberg, the German victory over the Russians in 1914, and his stern face, furrowed brow and white moustache stared out of countless newspapers as the physical embodiment of German military power. Eleven years after

Tannenberg, he was elected President. But he would not prove to be a champion of Germany's fledgling democracy. Far from it.

Many of those around Hindenburg had doubts about the democratic process. General Schleicher, for instance, was strongly opposed to the current system of government. Schleicher was one of the most powerful of Hindenburg's circle of advisers and the ultimate behind-the-scenes fixer, liaising between the armed forces and the President. Operating in the shadows, hiding behind the authority of the Minister of Defence, General Wilhelm Groener, he regularly briefed Hindenburg on the mood of the Reichswehr.

But in their search for an authoritarian solution to Germany's problems, these members of Germany's elite faced a difficulty: how to accommodate the unpredictable and potentially violent Nazis, who at the September 1930 election had increased their representation in the Reichstag from 12 seats to 107. To Schleicher it was obvious that the Nazis had to be drawn into government in one way or another. Surely, he felt, there must be a way of taming them.

Hindenburg was uneasy about dealing with the Nazis, but he was not wholeheartedly behind Chancellor Brüning's administration either. Other than by relying endlessly on Article 48, Brüning could stay in power only by asking the socialists in the Reichstag to tolerate his regime – the very group that Hindenburg and those around him disliked.

Hitler, having been briefed by Schleicher, met President Hindenburg for the first time on 10 October 1931. The encounter was not a success. Hindenburg was appalled by how Hitler spoke and acted. Famously, according to the state secretary Otto Meissner, Hindenburg said he considered Hitler suitable for office only at the level of Postmaster General. In that capacity, Hindenburg said, Hitler could 'lick [his] backside' – a vulgar joke, as the stamps bore his image.[49]

Hindenburg was just one of many who were appalled at the prospect of Hitler as Chancellor. Another was the distinguished American journalist Dorothy Thompson, who interviewed him a few weeks after his meeting with the German President. Walking into Hitler's suite at the Kaiserhof Hotel in Berlin she was initially 'convinced that I was meeting the future dictator of Germany. In something less than fifty seconds I was quite sure that I was not.' She found him 'formless, almost faceless, a man whose countenance is a caricature . . . He is the very prototype of the Little Man.'

She tried to analyse his political views, only to discover that every-thing boiled down to his belief that the 'Jews are responsible for everything'. Not surprisingly, she concluded that it didn't 'make sense'.[50]

Consequently, she became the latest in a long line of educated mem-bers of an elite milieu to misjudge Hitler. She thought that since she, as a worldly-wise journalist, could see through the bluster and spot the mindless prejudice that lay beneath, then others would do the same. Hitler, she believed, did not pose an immediate threat.

She was also wrong about Hindenburg. She thought that he 'believes that it is the duty of the President of a Republic to protect the Republic'. That, as we shall see, turned out not to be the case.

As for Hindenburg, he didn't just dislike Hitler as an individual, he loathed the way the Nazis conducted their politics. The previous year he had pursued a libel action against Goebbels, after he had seen a cartoon Goebbels had published mocking his age and inactivity. The cartoon's caption read – 'Hindenburg, are you still alive?'[51] It was one of the first demonstrations of a tactic Goebbels would often employ to attack him. Rather than focus on Hindenburg's character or war record, he concentrated on his age and supposed failure to focus on current events.

The judge in the defamation case accepted Goebbels' argument that he was criticizing contemporary politics and not questioning Hinden-burg's heroic status. As a result, he was fined rather than sent to jail. His admission that he hadn't been attacking Hindenburg's war record seemed to satisfy the President, who refused to cooperate when the prosecution appealed against Goebbels' lenient punishment.[52]

Hindenburg's seven-year term as President was due to expire in spring 1932, and he was loath at the age of eighty-four to stand for elec-tion again. However, he let it be known that if parliamentarians pleaded for him to continue without the need to ask ordinary Germans to vote, then he might think again. But after an inconclusive series of discussions the idea was rejected. Even the mythic figure of Hindenburg couldn't dodge democratic scrutiny.

In response, his supporters organized a public petition imploring Hindenburg to stand for re-election. Eventually, after more than three million Germans had signed the document, Hindenburg agreed to put himself forward. But he still refused to campaign. Let others travel the country talking him up, he wasn't going to demean himself by begging for votes.

Hitler was now in a difficult position. If he stood against Hindenburg – the symbol of German nationalism – he risked humiliation if he lost badly. But this was also a route to power if he succeeded. After several weeks dithering, he decided that he would take a chance and stand in the election, and Goebbels broke the news at a speech in the Sportpalast in Berlin on 22 February 1932.[53]

By challenging Hindenburg, Hitler had created a bizarre situation in German politics – a reversal of the expected. When Hindenburg had been elected in 1925, he had been the candidate of the nationalist right. Yet now, seven years later, he would have to rely on the support of Social Democrats, proponents of an ideology he disliked, to defeat the most rabidly nationalist candidate of all, Adolf Hitler. The irony was not lost on the Social Democrats themselves, with *Vorwärts*, their own newspaper, encouraging readers to vote for Hindenburg with the less than stirring slogan of 'If you don't do it out of love, do it out of hate [of Hitler]'.[54]

Having decided to compete, Hitler threw himself into the campaign, often speaking at several meetings a day. But Hindenburg's campaign outspent the Nazis and focused on the incumbent President's solidity and experience. Who else, they argued, was fit to lead the nation in such unstable times, with unemployment now over six million?

The result was that Hindenburg won comfortably in the first round with nearly – but not quite – the 50 per cent of the vote that would have meant there was no need for a run-off between the top two candidates. The other serious candidates in this first round, the communist Ernst Thälmann and the nationalist Theodor Duesterberg, gained just 20 per cent of the vote between them. It was Hitler who emerged as the undisputed challenger with 30 per cent of the vote.

Hitler and Hindenburg now embarked on another battle to determine which of them would be President. Hitler's 'flying over Germany' campaign – devised by Goebbels – had him journeying between speaking locations by plane. It was more than practical, it was symbolic and modern, offering a dramatic contrast with Hindenburg's stasis. It was obvious how the Nazis were playing this contest between the two candidates: Hitler young and up to date, Hindenburg old and out of touch.

The trouble was that young and up to date didn't play so well in the aftermath of a scandal which had broken during the first Presidential election campaign, involving, almost inevitably, Ernst Röhm. Helmut Klotz – who had been a Nazi but was now critical of the movement – published *Der Fall Röhm*, a booklet containing letters that Röhm had written from Bolivia to a friend called Dr Heimsoth back in Berlin, in which he talked about his sexual proclivities.[55]

The material was explosive, and the press rushed to publish the salacious content. Goebbels was appalled. 'Embarrassing letter by Röhm to Dr. Heimsoth in the *Welt am Montag*,' wrote Goebbels in his diary on 7 March 1932. 'Telephone calls to R [Röhm] in Mü [Munich]. He admits that it's true. Terrible!' Goebbels immediately contacted Hitler, who ordered that the letters – which Röhm had just told Goebbels were genuine – should be declared a 'lie lock, stock and barrel'.[56]

Röhm revealed a great deal about himself in the letters. 'I fancy myself as being homosexual,' he wrote from La Paz to Berlin in February 1929, 'but I really only "discovered" this in 1924. I can remember a number of homosexual feelings and acts before that, going back to my childhood, but I have also had intercourse with many women. Never with particular pleasure though. I also got gonorrhoea three times, which later I considered as a punishment from nature for unnatural intercourse. Today, women are loathsome for me.' He confessed that 'everything would be fine [in Bolivia] if I didn't need love interests . . . According to all of my so far carefully conducted investigations, the kind of activity I prefer seems to be unknown here . . . I sadly think back to wonderful Berlin where one can be so happy.'[57]

In another letter, Röhm reiterated his longing for the 'unique city' of Berlin. 'For God's sake, I am already counting the days until I can be there again. The steam baths there, in my opinion, are really the epitome of all human happiness. In any case, the manner of intercourse there has particularly pleased me.'[58] All of which leads one to suspect that Röhm didn't just return to Germany because he wanted to rejoin the Nazi movement.

Röhm was also open and forthright both about his opposition to section 175, the anti-homosexual law of the Weimar Republic, and about factions within the Nazi Party that condemned homosexuality. 'I am engaged in the fiercest fight with Mr Alfred Rosenberg, the doltish moralizer,' he wrote. 'His articles [in the *Völkischer Beobachter*]

A crowd in Munich celebrates Germany's entry into the First World War on 1 August 1914. The people in the foreground are standing on the Feldeherrnhalle, a military monument close to the spot in November 1923 where security forces would open fire on Nazi insurrectionists during the Beer Hall Putsch.

German soldiers killed during the First Battle of the Marne, in early September 1914. The ability of the Allies to halt the enemy's advance here ended the German dream of a swift victory. The French called this victory the 'Miracle on the Marne'.

3. Adolf Hitler (*middle row, far right*) as a soldier in the First World War. Always somewhat distant from his comrades, it's no accident that in wartime photographs – as here – he's often to be seen on the edge of the group.

4. Hermann Göring as a young and charismatic flyer during the First World War. In this photograph he's almost unrecognizable from the obese, drug-addled figure he would later become.

. An artillery shell lands on a German gun crew. During the First World War
1ore people died on the battlefield from artillery attacks than any other cause.
: was a method of destruction that allowed the perpetrators to maintain distance
both physically and emotionally – from those they killed.

. Ernst Röhm, Chief of Staff of the Nazi
tormtroopers. During the First World
Var he was badly injured by an artillery
arrage, his face permanently disfigured.

7. On the left, Field Marshal Paul von
Hindenburg, the highest-ranking German
military officer during the First World War.
Next to him is General Erich Ludendorff,
the army's Quartermaster General.

8. In the immediate aftermath of the end of the First World War, German Revolutionaries drive past the Brandenburg Gate in the centre of Berlin, holding a red flag.

9. The Freikorps Werdenfels march through Munich in 1919 wearing traditional Bavarian costumes. The majority of the right-wing Freikorps dressed as normal soldiers, but the Werdenfels represented, visually at least, more of the bucolic 'völkisch' ideal.

10. Heinrich Himmler in action during the Beer Hall Putsch in November 1923. A member of Ernst Röhm's Reichskriegs-flagge group, Himmler is in the middle of the picture holding the unit's banner.

11. A young Joseph Goebbels. Unable to fight in the First World War because of a disabled foot, he was unsure what to do with his life until joining the Nazi party in the early 1920s.

12. Adolf Hitler in Landsberg prison in 1924. This was the preferred Nazi propaganda image – a picture of a man of destiny, cruelly incarcerated, gazing through the bars to the future beyond.

13. This was the reality. Hitler in Landsberg prison reading the paper, with a teacup and saucer in front of him, serving his time in the most comfortable conditions the German prison service could provide.

14. A motley crew of Nazis in the early 1920s. The man who took over the leadership of the Nazi party while Hitler was in prison, Alfred Rosenberg, is fourth from the left in the second row down from the top; he's wearing a white hat, and unlike most of the others isn't displaying a swastika on his arm.

15. Hitler addresses a meeting of Nazis in 1925. Seated second from the right, next to Hitler, is Gregor Strasser, a leading light in the movement whom Hitler would order to be murdered nine years later. Next to Strasser is the bespectacled figure of Heinrich Himmler, whose SS men would orchestrate the killing.

6. Members of the Hitler Youth in the back of a lorry in Berlin, during the early
930s, drumming up support for Hitler. The Nazi movement particularly appealed
ɔ those under twenty-five years old.

17. It wasn't just the young men of the Hitler Youth who were entranced by Hitler; so were many young women of the BDM, the Bund Deutscher Mädel, the League of German Girls.

18. High jinks at a gymnastics and sports festival in 1938. The BDM and Hitler Youth often intermingled at events – so much so that a number of BDM young women became pregnant after camping out near the Hitler Youth at the Nuremberg rally in 1936.

are particularly directed towards me, since I make no secret of my attitude.'[59]

Unfortunately for Röhm, it wasn't just the 'doltish moralizer' Alfred Rosenberg who was against homosexuality. In his diary on 17 March 1932, Goebbels revealed how on a 'beautiful night' at the Tegernsee he 'chatted' with Hitler about 'all kinds of things. Especially the question of section 175. I was glad to hear that here, too, Hitler takes the same rigorous view as I do. This is very reassuring to me. Eradicate! . . . Otherwise, it will become a national epidemic.'[60]

Despite his unequivocal rejection of homosexuality, Hitler declared that Röhm would remain as Chief of Staff of the Stormtroopers. But he also recognized the damage the scandal was doing to the party, since a few weeks later he altered the command structure of the Stormtroopers to make the leader of the Hitler Youth report directly to him rather than to Röhm.[61] No one knows for sure how badly this scandal affected the Nazi vote at the Presidential election. Most likely many potential voters dismissed it as gossip – especially given the seriousness of Germany's economic and political problems.

Nonetheless, at the ballot box in the final round of the Presidential election, the German voters expressed their preference for the elderly man who hadn't bothered to campaign, rather than for the young firebrand who had flown around the country, and Hindenburg beat Hitler comfortably by nearly six million votes.

But after their initial disappointment Hitler and his colleagues realized that they had accomplished something important. Hitler, not Hindenburg, was the undisputed champion of the nationalist cause, and the result served to reinforce the intensity of the dilemma Hindenburg faced. He sympathized with those who wanted an authoritarian nationalist government, yet he had won the Presidency with the help of the Social Democrats. Meanwhile the leader of the strongest authoritarian faction in the country had stood against him and come runner-up.

Now confirmed as President for another seven years, Hindenburg took dramatic action. After discussions with Schleicher and others, he decided at the end of May 1932 that the current Chancellor Brüning should go, along with his dealings with the Social Democrats. Even though Brüning had been prepared to discuss working with the Nazis, it wasn't enough to save him.

The new Chancellor was Franz von Papen, a fifty-two-year-old aristocrat. He was a friend of General Schleicher's and his qualifications for the job – as far as Hindenburg was concerned – were excellent. Unlike Hitler, he was unquestionably a member of the German elite. He was urbane, rich, charming and a former officer who dabbled in politics. But, unfortunately for Hindenburg, Papen was also unlike Hitler in a more important respect – he had no support from the public.

Papen's appointment as Chancellor was a watershed moment in German politics. Hindenburg had given the Chancellorship to a man who wasn't even a member of parliament. Hindenburg could hardly have expressed his contempt for the Reichstag more eloquently.

It was obvious that Papen's regime could progress in only one of two ways – either by gaining the support of the Nazis, or by attempting to rule without popular support, perhaps by altering the constitution and claiming that the newly enfranchised Hindenburg represented ordinary voters.

Papen was initially hopeful that the Nazis could be talked into providing democratic legitimacy for his government, especially since he was awash with self-conceit and thought himself superior to Adolf Hitler – just like Dorothy Thompson, he thought him a 'Little Man'.[62] Papen found the Nazi leader 'curiously unimpressive' when he met him for the first time on 9 June 1932. 'I could detect no inner quality which might explain his extraordinary hold on the masses,' he wrote in his self-serving memoirs. 'He was wearing a dark blue suit and seemed the complete *petit-bourgeois*. He had an unhealthy complexion, and with his little moustache and curious hair style had an indefinable bohemian quality. His demeanour was modest and polite, and although I had heard much about the magnetic quality of his eyes, I do not remember being impressed by them.'[63]

It is a patronizing judgement – one that is also reminiscent of the words used by another German aristocrat, General Otto von Lossow, when he described Hitler in 1924 as 'a swashbuckling little ward politician'.[64] It is noteworthy that neither Lossow nor Papen nor many others in the German elite were swayed by Hitler's alleged 'charisma'. They felt the Nazi leader was beneath them – in social hierarchy, in education, in manners, in style, in intelligence, in almost every variable save one. He had the support of millions of voters and they did not.

The contempt many of them felt for Hitler was mirrored in the contempt many ordinary Germans felt for people of Papen's class and character. Was it not men like Papen who had presided over Germany's defeat? Wasn't Papen, a devout monarchist, a figure more reminiscent of the Kaiser's Germany? How did he represent the solution to Germany's problems? Ultimately – for millions of Germans – wasn't Papen one of 'Them' rather than one of 'Us'?

Papen could be as condescending as he liked, but it didn't solve the fundamental problem – his administration lacked legitimacy. So two of his earliest decisions were designed to appease the Nazis. The first was to reverse the ban on the Stormtroopers marching or wearing uniforms in public that Brüning's government had put in place in April 1932, and the second was to call new elections to the Reichstag. By letting the Stormtroopers back on to the streets – a force now numbering around 400,000 – Papen allowed the Nazis to display their power. As a result, that summer saw more violent confrontations between the Stormtroopers and the communists than ever before. In July alone there were eighty-six political killings.[65] Civil war had not yet broken out, but it seemed a distinct possibility.

Papen demonstrated his own anti-democratic credentials on 20 July, when he attempted to remove the Minister-President of Prussia, the Social Democrat Otto Braun, from office, claiming his administration was failing to uphold law and order. But the coup attempt soon unravelled in the face of public opposition and strikes.

Less than two weeks later a new general election was held. It was another triumph for the Nazis. On 31 July 1932, they polled just over 37 per cent of the vote and were now the biggest party in the Reichstag, although still short of an overall majority. This was not unusual. The multi-party nature of the Weimar system had meant that every previous government had been a coalition.

A powerful cognitive bias might well have played a part in the decision more than one in three Germans made to vote for the Nazis. Psychologists are aware of the tendency we all have towards 'loss aversion' – where the pain of losing what we already have would be greater than the pleasure of gaining an equivalent benefit.[66] The 37 per cent of Germans who voted for the Nazis were acutely aware of what they might lose if the political instability continued – or in many cases, given the economic catastrophe, acutely aware of what they had already lost and fearful of losing more. They craved stability in these unstable times.

Hitler had said openly during the election campaign that the only way to provide that longed-for stability was to get rid of German democracy. 'Is it typically German to have thirty parties?' he asked rhetorically in a speech in July 1932. 'We are intolerant [of this system]. I have given myself one goal – to sweep these thirty political parties out of Germany.'[67] It was this focus on the futile squabbling of democratic politicians, together with the need for Germans to pull together as one to create the mystical *Volksgemeinschaft*, that dominated Hitler's discourse during the election. His hatred of the Jews was, as it had been for several years, much less prominent in his public pronouncements. That hatred hadn't disappeared, and he never denied it. It was just that he was astute enough to realize that the violent anti-Semitic speeches that he had given earlier in his political career were not the way to gain mass support.

The communists had made modest gains in the July 1932 election, and now held eighty-nine Reichstag seats. This meant that the Nazis and communists combined had a share of just over half the electorate. This was another significant moment. It meant that a majority of Germans, in supporting either the Nazis or the communists, had voted for parties that were openly committed to destroying democracy. Germans had just used the democratic process to demonstrate that they didn't want democracy – or at least the crippled version of democracy that Hindenburg had helped create.

The 1932 election had shown that if any individual had a claim to be Chancellor – based on the traditional measure of the number of seats held in the Reichstag – it was Adolf Hitler. Schleicher certainly thought so. He tried to get Hindenburg to agree to a Hitler Chancellorship, with other right-wing figures in the cabinet to restrain him. But that wasn't a solution that President Hindenburg was prepared to contemplate. In a legendary meeting he held with Hitler on 13 August 1932, Hindenburg told the Nazi leader – according to Otto Meissner, the state secretary – that 'He [Hindenburg] could not justify before God, before his conscience or before the Fatherland, the transfer of the whole authority of government to a single party, especially to a party that was biased against people who had different views from their own.'[68]

These fine words have led some, who haven't followed the details of the history, to give Hindenburg more credit than he deserves. They forget that by pursuing a policy of governing with his Chancellor by emergency decree, and then dissolving the Reichstag when the deputies supported a motion of no confidence in his government, he had created a cycle of crisis. More recently he had shown contempt for the democratic process by appointing Papen as Chancellor, a man with no mandate to govern.

It wasn't even as if, by rejecting Hitler as Chancellor, Hindenburg had solved the problem. Predictably, when the Reichstag assembled that autumn, members put forward a motion of no confidence in Papen's government. In a moment of black comedy, Papen tried to prevent the vote being held by dissolving the parliament which had only just gathered. Hermann Göring, the new speaker of the Reichstag, ignored Papen's request and the no-confidence vote was held. The result showed the desperate state of the German political system, as a huge majority of deputies – more than 500 – voted for the motion.

Hindenburg kept faith with Papen. He dissolved the Reichstag and scheduled yet more elections for November. There seemed no end to this remorseless cycle. The Germans had voted, the crisis hadn't been averted and now they were called upon to vote again. In such circumstances one can understand why so many Germans were disillusioned with the democratic process.

Papen hoped that the Nazis' electoral success had peaked. Perhaps his authoritarian government could deliver the Nazi policies the voters liked, but without the brutality of the Stormtroopers? Maybe the voters could be convinced that the Nazis and the communists were two sides of the same coin? There were signs this might be so. The temporary cooperation of the Nazis with the communists during the Berlin transport strike in November 1932 seemed to confirm that these two radical anti-democratic parties had much in common.[69] The Nazis had intended their backing of the strike to demonstrate their support for the workers, but the price was the alienation of some middle-class voters.

The election of November 1932 was something of a setback for the Nazis – they lost 4 per cent of their vote and thirty-four of their Reichstag seats. But this didn't really change the overall situation. The results could even be interpreted as more evidence of growing crisis as the communists increased their own share of the vote by 2.6 per cent.

After more fruitless negotiations with the Nazis, Hindenburg leant towards Papen's solution to the impasse and considered authorizing what would in effect be a dictatorship under Papen's Chancellorship.

But the ever-present Schleicher raised a powerful objection. At a cabinet meeting on 2 December he presented the results of a war game organized by his adjutant, Lieutenant Colonel Eugen Ott, which demonstrated that if the Poles launched an aggressive move on Germany's eastern border at the same time as the Nazis and communists clashed in open revolt, the Reichswehr would be unable to defend the country. Even though the notion of an imminent Polish attack was far-fetched, this was received as devastating news.[70]

By this ruse Schleicher successfully plotted the downfall of Papen. Hindenburg was always anxious to hear what the Reichswehr felt, and the idea that they had war-gamed this scenario with such disturbing results was deeply troubling for him. And so on 3 December Hindenburg made Schleicher Chancellor of Germany.

Schleicher had told Hindenburg that if he was Chancellor he could do what Papen couldn't and get the Nazis to participate in government. He had been conspiring with the Nazis even before Papen's downfall and had long been in discussions with Gregor Strasser – by now the organizational head of the Nazi movement. Hitler had agreed to the talks taking place, but had then withdrawn his consent as negotiations reached a final stage at the end of November. The question of Nazi participation in the government had always been a delicate one. The benefits of demonstrating that the Nazis were more than a protest party had to be weighed against the potential marginalization of the movement if the plan was not a success. Ultimately, Hitler had seen the latter as the more potent threat.

Nonetheless, Schleicher carried on talking to Strasser, and in the first week of December offered him both the Vice-Chancellorship and the role of Minister-President of Prussia. When Hitler ordered him not to accept, Strasser was furious. In an atmosphere of crisis, on 8 December Strasser told his Nazi colleagues that Hitler didn't seem to understand the political reality – which was that Hindenburg had 'consistently' refused to offer him the Chancellorship. In the face of Hitler's intransigence, Strasser announced he was resigning from the party and 'going to the mountains to recuperate'.[71]

Hitler remained adamant that the price of Nazi participation in the government was that he was made Chancellor of a Presidential cabinet, one that did not rely on a coalition with other parties. Hindenburg had already been forced to accept, in the light of the recent election results, that if Hitler could form a majority in the Reichstag then he would have to appoint him Chancellor of a parliamentary cabinet – one that did not need Presidential cooperation via 'special decrees' – but it was obvious that the chances of Hitler putting together such a coalition in the Reichstag were slim to none.

In the face of these setbacks, Hitler tried to project a sense of optimism, telling senior Nazis a few hours after Strasser's resignation that the 'day will come' when he would be made Chancellor on the terms he wanted. 'It is probably nearer than we think,' he said.[72] But it seemed this was just wishful thinking. The party's finances – always shaky – were in disarray because of the cost of fighting so many elections. In late December, Reinhard Heydrich's phone was cut off because the bill hadn't been paid, and the following month there was no money to pay the salaries of members of his intelligence unit.[73]

However, during January 1933, Papen came to accept that the only workable way forward was for Hitler to be made Chancellor. But he was prepared for this to happen only if he was made Vice-Chancellor and several of his right-wing colleagues had places in the cabinet. Hitler would then be under their control. At least that was the theory.

Hindenburg took some convincing. As late as 26 January 1933, just four days before Hitler became Chancellor, he said, 'Gentlemen, I hope you will not hold me capable of appointing this Austrian corporal to be Reich Chancellor.'[74]

Hindenburg was brought round not just by the persuasive words of Papen and others in his inner circle, but by the appointment of a fifty-four-year-old general, Werner von Blomberg, as Minister of Defence. Blomberg was exactly the kind of officer Hindenburg liked. According to his adjutant, Blomberg was 'very elegant, good looking, tall, and was very trained in the diplomatic way of looking at various things'.[75] He was also one of many Reichswehr officers who welcomed the creation of an authoritarian state. On a visit to the Soviet Union he had been impressed by the way a one-party state functioned, and now based in East Prussia he had formed a positive impression of the Stormtroopers.

Hindenburg was finally persuaded, and he made Hitler Chancellor on 30 January 1933. And while it's true that he had concerns about the man he was appointing, the bigger picture was that he had at last achieved his aim – a government that would hopefully bring stability. Even if the cost was the destruction of democracy.

There was undoubtedly a tendency to groupthink in Hindenburg and the elite that surrounded him.[76] This psychological phenomenon occurs when members of a group convince themselves that they have reached the correct solution to a problem, even though they haven't properly considered all the negative connotations and potential alternatives. It is particularly likely to occur when decisions are made under stress and when there is a lack of diversity among members of the decision-making group. That was certainly the case here. Hindenburg and his cronies, all of whom came from the same elite background, failed to think through the consequences of appointing Hitler as Chancellor. Instead, they conned themselves into thinking that they could control him once he was in office.

Their arrogance was exemplified by Alfred Hugenberg, a nationalist politician and wealthy press baron, who believed that, after Hitler became Chancellor, he would inevitably be restrained by sophisticated politicians like himself. 'We're boxing him in,' he boasted. Franz von Papen was just as smug and felt able to crow after Hitler's appointment, 'we've hired him.'[77]

It was a tragedy. All the more so because there were signs that the worst of the depression might soon be over. At the Lausanne conference in the summer of 1932 the German delegation had successfully argued for an end to the reparation payments imposed by the treaty of Versailles. The fact was that Germany didn't need a Nazi Chancellor in order to begin the road to economic recovery.[78]

Ultimately, Hitler had been eased into power with the connivance of the German elite. Getting rid of him would prove much harder.

6. Attacking Human Rights

Once they gain power, dictators seek to destroy the human rights of their population. A free press, the rule of law, fair elections – all of them need to be annihilated if a dictator is to feel secure. Hitler was no exception, but where he was more adept than many was in his attempt to convince millions of people that their loss of freedom was for their own benefit. It was a difficult psychological task, but he had a shrewd instinct about how to make it happen.

Not that it was obvious in January 1933 that Hitler's appointment as Chancellor of Germany would mark the start of twelve years of oppression – years that would culminate in the biggest and bloodiest war the world has ever seen and the infamous crime of the Holocaust. We look upon 30 January 1933 as a terrible landmark, a blot upon history, but that was not how it was seen by many people at the time.

Josef Felder, a Social Democrat member of the Reichstag, remembered that there were colleagues in his party who 'had the disastrous belief' that socialist rule 'would still come' and that Hitler could be controlled through parliament. Their attitude was: 'if Hitler's government, constitutionally formed by the President, is operating legally, then we are the legal opposition.'[1]

Eugene Leviné, a sixteen-year-old Berlin Jew, recalled that his mother 'closed her eyes' to Hitler's rise to power. 'And I said, "Look, we are not safe here." And she laughed . . .'

Leviné and his mother were doubly at risk because they were not only Jews but devout communists as well: 'Some of us had believed Berlin could never fall to the Nazis. Berlin will always be Red, and this came as a great shock, these results.' But even now, with Hitler as Chancellor, 'Many people thought, well, he can't cope with unemployment, he can't do anything, he'll be finished. He'll make a lot of promises, he'll be finished.'[2]

The British ambassador to Germany, Sir Horace Rumbold, thought the bulk of Germans 'took the news [of Hitler's appointment] phlegmatically'.[3] It was possible to see Hitler as just one in a long line of recent political leaders. Whether he was special or not, only time would tell.

The reaction of Nazi supporters like Günter Lohse was, predictably, very different: 'Now a man was trying to clean up the stables . . . One person is saying what's what, and not fifteen. That was decisive, because they had mismanaged [everything]. And there was one more thing – the appeal to the national conscience . . . Adolf Hitler addressed the German people in a totally different way – as the "German people". The concept of the "German people" had been totally lost. Nobody used it any more . . . And people said: "He is going to push reforms through, and quickly. And things have to happen fast. There is no alternative." Above all, there was the wish to place power in the hands of a man who says: "We will do it. That's how it's done. And this is how we are going to do it, and we will succeed like this, if we all roll up our sleeves." People wanted him. The German people were – how shall I put it? – not quite humiliated but dejected. Everything was grey on grey. Nowhere was there a happy splash of colour. And now someone had come who promised: "The six million unemployed, we will get rid of them in no time." '

On the evening of 30 January 1933, Lohse watched as thousands of Stormtroopers and other Nazi supporters paraded by torchlight down the Wilhelmstrasse in the heart of the government section of Berlin. 'It was really impressive,' he said. 'This jubilation was spontaneous . . . the whole street was full of people, young, old, women, children, everybody was there. It wasn't [just] the SA [Stormtroopers]. Please understand what I mean. The SA may have arrived with torches. But there were people as far as the eye could see. And they cheered Adolf Hitler [who acknowledged the crowd from the Reich Chancellery].'[4]

But it wasn't the case, as fervent Nazi supporters wanted to believe, that Hitler was secure in power. Most people date Nazi rule to 30 January 1933, but that is somewhat misleading. Hitler was not head of state – Hindenburg was. And constitutionally Hitler could still be dismissed as Chancellor whenever the President wanted.

Then there was the question of the army, the Reichswehr. Hitler knew that one of his most urgent tasks was to get the generals onside – not just because Hindenburg was always anxious to know their mood, but because he needed the support of the army to realize his future plans. But there was one immediate problem. The army distrusted the Stormtroopers.

On 3 February, just four days after he had been appointed Chancellor, Hitler went for dinner at the home of the Commander-in-Chief of the Reichswehr, General Kurt von Hammerstein-Equord. The omens were not auspicious for the meeting. Hammerstein-Equord had been against Hitler's appointment – he was a close friend of General Schleicher's, who had briefly been Chancellor before Hitler. But, fortunately for Hitler, others at the dinner were better disposed towards him, including the Minister of Defence Werner von Blomberg and his chief of staff Colonel Walther von Reichenau.

It is a meeting that is of great importance in this history, and while there were no official minutes, there are a number of other sources for what was discussed. One is from a Russian spy – most likely one of Hammerstein-Equord's daughters, Helga[5] – who asserted that Hitler told the generals that 'Just as in the individual's life the stronger and better always prevails, it is the same in the nation's life.' But now a 'drastic change' in this natural order had occurred, caused not just by Germany's defeat in the First World War but by 'the poisoning of the world by Bolshevism'. The question they all faced was 'How can Germany be saved?'

Handily, after posing this profound existential question, Hitler told the generals he knew the answer. His preferred solution was 'through a large-scale settlement policy which presupposes an expansion of the living space [*Lebensraum*] of the German nation [*Volk*]'. He therefore set himself 'a time-limit of 6–8 years to entirely annihilate Marxism'. After that had been achieved, the army would be tasked with gaining 'the expansion of the living space of the German nation . . . the target would probably be the east. But a Germanization of the population of the conquered land is not possible. You can only Germanize soil. We will have to ruthlessly deport some millions of people like Poland and France did after the war.' Hitler ended, as he often did, with an appeal: 'I address you, my Generals, and request that you fight with me for this grand goal, to understand me and to support me . . .'[6]

These were astonishing admissions. Though Hitler had explicitly said in *Mein Kampf* in 1924 that gaining territory in the east was his intention, during his various election campaigns in the early 1930s he had been careful to avoid any mention of such a plan.

There was no necessity for Hitler to tell the generals his long-term aims at this stage. The purpose of the meeting was to reassure them that he was committed to restoring the armed forces to greatness and that they would lead any German fight against a foreign adversary in the future. The spectre of the Stormtroopers lay behind the meeting, and Hitler sought to assuage any worries the generals might have about interference in their work from Röhm's beer-hall bruisers. But none of that explains why he felt it necessary to be so revealing about his grandiose ambitions. Perhaps he was trying to excite them and gain support for his overarching vision. Still, he could have decided to deceive them about his plans, just as he was deceiving the German public.

Nonetheless, since Hitler was expressing a long-term goal, it was possible for the generals to focus primarily on his immediate message: his promise to protect and expand the armed forces and his assurance that the political instability of the previous years was now behind them. Moreover, ahead lay a chance to eradicate the humiliation of Versailles. This was a seductive vision for the generals gathered in their Commander-in-Chief's home that night. And if their new Chancellor had also indulged in some aspirational thinking about the future, well, maybe that was to be expected from a politician who often spoke in visions rather than policies.

It is also likely that among those present were some who welcomed the chance to conquer the east. After all, everyone remembered the way the German Army had humiliated the Bolsheviks fifteen years before at the treaty of Brest-Litovsk. A German empire in the east was not such a fanciful idea.

But the crucial fact remains: just four days after he was appointed Chancellor, Hitler revealed to his generals that his preferred foreign policy option was to fight a war of conquest in the east. Everything that happened in the eight years between this meeting and the German invasion of the Soviet Union in June 1941 must be understood against that background. For Hitler, the task ahead was to prepare the collective German psyche for war, but without telling ordinary Germans that this was his plan.

Though the generals supported many of Hitler's goals, the extent to which they were believers in the Nazi Party varied. While General Kurt von Hammerstein-Equord wasn't a Hitler supporter, Blomberg and Reichenau most definitely were. Reichenau had even been shunted off to East Prussia by Schleicher before Hitler became Chancellor because of his support for the Nazis, but now Blomberg had brought him back to Berlin and the centre of power. It was Reichenau, above all of those present at the meeting, who believed that the Nazis were revolutionaries and that this revolution was necessary.

These were sentiments that Manfred von Schroeder, a nineteen-year-old Nazi supporter, agreed with wholeheartedly. He thought this was the beginning of a 'new Germany' and if the communists were now targeted then people thought, 'so what?' The 'communists would have done the same thing and this is a revolution'.

Schroeder came from a privileged background and saw himself as an 'idealist'. He believed that Hitler's appointment as Chancellor broke the stalemate in government and meant the endless cycle of elections was gone forever. Though he had read *Mein Kampf*, he didn't take the contents 'really seriously' and considered the book a flight of fancy written years before. What mattered now was to 'overcome the consequences of the First World War, and especially the treaty of Versailles'. It didn't hurt, of course, that with the communists eliminated as a political force, his family's wealth was secure.[7]

On 3 February, the same day that he told his senior military commanders that he wanted the army to prepare for an 'expansion' of German 'living space', Hitler held a press conference and stated the exact opposite to foreign journalists. He now hypocritically presented himself as desperate to preserve peace. 'Anyone like myself who knows what war is', said Hitler, 'is aware of what a squandering of effort or rather consumption of strength is involved.'[8]

Two days before, on 1 February, Hitler had spoken to the German public for the first time as Chancellor. This radio broadcast was the most significant of his career so far and played a part in influencing the thinking of millions of Germans about the new regime.

What is remarkable is what Hitler didn't say in the broadcast. He didn't mention his hatred of the Jews, nor did he warn of any future conflict, nor did he propose any detailed policies. Instead, he emphasized how appalling the previous regime had been and that he was inheriting a 'dreadful' mess. 'The problem that we have to solve', he said in a flourish of hyperbole, 'is the most difficult that has been set for any German statesman since time immemorial.' But luckily, said Hitler – linking himself to Hindenburg – 'the venerable leader of the world war called upon us men in the national parties and associations to fight one more time under his leadership as we once did at the front, in unity and loyalty, to save the Reich.'[9]

In a speech full of nebulous ideas, Hitler committed his regime wholeheartedly to the most nebulous of all – the *Volksgemeinschaft*. The 'first and supreme duty' of his 'National Government' was 'to restore the unity of spirit and will of our *Volk*'. It was the ultimate feel-good politician's promise. It sounded wonderful and yet melted away when you tried to define exactly what it meant. And in a sign that Hitler recognized that the vast majority of the electorate – and many politicians – were Christians, he even said that his government would 'strongly protect Christianity as the basis of our entire morality'. He said this even though he wasn't a practising Christian. Not surprisingly, this was a promise he would not keep.

He claimed that 'Fourteen years of Marxism [that is, socialist government] have wrecked Germany' and that 'one year of Bolshevism would annihilate Germany.' The latter was a shrewd choice of foe. Many committed Nazis would have recognized the word 'Bolshevism' as a trigger to their anti-Semitism. Hadn't Hitler previously emphasized that the Jews were behind this hated ideology? But, equally, Germans less committed to the cause could take the words at face value. Most Germans were opposed to a communist revolution, even if they weren't supporters of anti-Semitic action.

It was a speech that demonstrated Hitler's understanding of one decisive fact: Nazi Party members alone were not sufficient to keep him in power. He needed the support of various other power groups – in particular the armed forces and the right-wing political elite. Above all he had to keep President Hindenburg onside. Hence the obsequious mention of the German President at various points in his address. Hindenburg's support opened the door not just to the generals' acceptance of his Chancellorship, but to the continued acquiescence of his political allies.

As for Hindenburg, from the moment the torchlit parade of Stormtroopers had marched past his window on the Wilhelmstrasse on 30 January, he had shown every sign of support for the new regime.[10] He had agreed that fresh elections could be called for March – a key Hitler demand – and that the new government could rule by Presidential decree. This, remember, was a concession Hitler had always wanted but Hindenburg had previously denied. Moreover, Hindenburg had voiced no objection to Hitler's assertion that the March elections would be the 'last' ones held in Germany. The President, like his friend Papen, welcomed the destruction of democracy and the authoritarian rule that would follow.

There was another power group that Hitler was keen to engage with that February – big business. Contrary to popular myth, Hitler and the Nazis were not propelled into power with the backing of mighty industrial concerns. While many owners of small businesses had supported the Nazis, most of the larger organizations had preferred to ally themselves to the conservative centre parties.

On 20 February a group of the richest businessmen in Germany were invited to a meeting at Göring's residence in Berlin. Hitler told them that he was committed both to capitalism and to the destruction of democracy. 'Private enterprise cannot be maintained in the age of democracy,' he said. 'It is conceivable only if people have a sound idea of authority and personality. Everything positive, good and valuable which has been achieved in the world in the field of economics and culture is solely attributable to personality . . . Now we stand before the last election. Regardless of the outcome there will be no retreat . . .'[11] The big danger to business, he told them, was communism – the creed he was determined to destroy.[12]

It was only after Hitler had finished speaking that the real purpose of the meeting was made clear. The Nazis wanted money. They needed the cash in order to finance their campaign for the March election. Göring told the businessmen that 'the sacrifices asked for ought to be made 'easier to bear' by the knowledge that 'the election of March 5 will surely be the last one for the next ten years, probably even for the next hundred'.[13] After Hitler and Göring had left, Hjalmar Schacht – a distinguished banker who supported the Nazis – asked the businessmen to open their wallets. A deluge of bank transfers to the Nazi Party followed. The major industrial concern IG Farben alone contributed 400,000 Reichsmarks[14] – several million pounds today.

The evening resembled a Mafia-style shakedown. Implicit was the threat that the Nazis planned on being in power for a long time and these tycoons had to decide whether they wanted to be on the Nazi train or not. Those left on the platform knew that life would become, at the very least, uncomfortable for them. But there was more to the evening than straightforward threat; there was also self-interest. Hitler was promising stability and the chance to make money. And what business-man present wouldn't find that attractive? The fact that this was a regime committed to destroying its enemies and persecuting the Jews – although Hitler had been careful to make no reference to Jews at the meeting – was of little concern.

On 27 February, just seven days after Hitler met with these business-men, an event occurred that would be of enormous help to the Nazis in shaping the mentalities of the German population: the Reichstag in Berlin was set alight. Hitler, Göring and other leading Nazis immedi-ately rushed to the scene. 'The Reichstag is burning,' wrote Goebbels in his diary. 'Crazy fantasy. But it is true. Barrelled down the road with Hitler immediately. The whole building is aflame . . . Hitler is enraged.'[15]

A twenty-four-year-old Dutch communist called Marinus van der Lubbe was quickly identified as the sole culprit, caught within the build-ing as the fire started around him. But Hitler, Göring, Goebbels and other leading Nazis leapt to the conclusion that there must be a vast communist plot behind him. Hadn't there been a communist uprising in Berlin after the end of the First World War, and fears just a year ago of a civil war between the Nazis and the communists? What more dra-matic signal could there be to start this conflict than the burning of the Reichstag – the symbol of the democracy the communists wished to overthrow?

'There will be no mercy now,' said Hitler at the scene of the crime, according to Rudolf Diels, head of the Prussian Political Police. 'Those who stand in our way will be slaughtered. The German people will not accept leniency. Every communist official will be shot where he is caught. The communist deputies must be hanged this very night. Every-body who is in league with the communists must be taken into custody. There will no longer be any mercy for Social Democrats either.'[16]

In talking to Hitler at the scene of the crime, Göring made much of the fact that some Communist Party members were in the Reichstag less than half an hour before the building went up in flames. But this wasn't surprising as the communists had been forced to close their offices in Berlin and so were using the Reichstag for meetings.

Yet still Hitler, Göring and others persisted in claiming that the crime was the product of a conspiracy. It was an allegation that benefited them enormously. The day after the fire, 28 February, Hindenburg signed at Hitler's request a decree 'For the Protection of People and State'. This was the moment that the basic human rights enjoyed in the Weimar years by the German people were eliminated. Free speech, the free press, the right to assembly, the right to privacy of letters and telephone conversations were all taken away. Renewed throughout Hitler's rule, this was the legal basis for much of the terror the Nazis inflicted on their internal enemies.

The journal entries of a former teacher in Hamburg, Luise Solmitz, demonstrated just how much the burning of the Reichstag smoothed over concerns about this destruction of civil liberties. While in the days before the fire she had been broadly supportive of the Nazis – she called the torchlight procession in Hamburg after Hitler came to power 'a wonderful uplifting experience for us all' – she still had criticisms of the regime. In an entry for 25 February, she wrote that she believed, contrary to Nazi ideology, that 'every race within its own sphere has to be granted its rights and respect.' And she confessed that she and her husband were undecided whether in the forthcoming election in March to vote directly for the Nazis or for their nationalist allies.

But van der Lubbe's actions had an immediate impact on her. 'The Reichstag fire was to be just the beginning,' she wrote on 1 March 1933. The communists wanted 'to take hostages of women and children . . . send murderous bands to the villages to start fires, use every weapon in the cities from the most refined to the primitive – boiling water to poison'.[17]

It is another example of the psychological power of 'Them and Us' categorization. Solmitz's fear of a communist uprising drove her towards greater support for the Nazis as she experienced a sudden rush of intense panic about what these 'murderous bands' would do. In the wake of the Reichstag fire, Luise Solmitz and millions of other Germans believed that they lived in a period of terrifying vulnerability. If it was necessary to restrict human rights in order to deal with the perils the country faced, then so be it.

The more Hitler amplified the potential communist threat, the more he and the Nazis benefited. To that end they used the kind of hyperbolic rhetoric favoured by other conspiracy theorists. As Professor Richard Hofstadter wrote in an article in the early 1960s, 'The paranoid spokesman sees the fate of conspiracy in apocalyptic terms – he traffics in the birth and death of whole worlds, whole political orders, whole systems of human values. He is always manning the barricades of civilization. He constantly lives at a turning point . . . Since the enemy is thought of as being totally evil and totally unappeasable, he must be totally eliminated . . .'[18]

Hitler and his colleagues certainly fitted into that framework. For it wasn't just that their various conspiracy theories were politically convenient. Such thinking permitted them to imagine themselves centre stage at a 'turning point' in history. Scarcely anyone before, they believed, had ever been more important. They weren't living ordinary lives, they had a transcendent purpose. But if they ever questioned the validity of their conspiracy theories, then their whole worldview would be destroyed. How can you be an epic hero if you do not have an epic enemy to vanquish?

What is even more remarkable about the Reichstag fire incident is that it became the subject of a double conspiracy. On the one hand the Nazis claimed that a nefarious group of communists had conspired to create the arson attack; on the other, many of their opponents declared that the Nazis had organized the whole event themselves[19] – this despite the fact that the bulk of the evidence supports the idea that Hitler and his comrades were surprised by the attack. Although there has been a veritable industry of books about the fire, it's still likely that van der Lubbe acted alone.[20]

It is significant that so many people over the years have been attracted to one or other of the conspiracy theories about the Reichstag fire. Part of the reason, of course, is that the event remains open to different interpretations. But some of this drive towards conspiracy also illustrates a commonly held belief – that a momentous event must have a momentous cause. It's a phenomenon that social psychologists call proportionality bias.[21] There is a tendency to argue backwards from the result – in this case the passing of a law that destroyed civil liberties in Germany – to create a conspiracy.

The trouble is that many events of enormous significance in our lives can have a trivial cause. If someone slips on the leaves on the pavement and falls into the path of an oncoming bus and is killed, the cause is trivial. Yet the consequence is catastrophic. But our psyches tend to revolt against this arbitrariness. It is not hard to imagine that those of our ancestors, many thousands of years ago, who believed significant events had to have significant causes – perhaps the gods were angry and needed appeasing – were better able to endure the vicissitudes of life than those who understood that bad things can just happen. So we are descended from people who found meaning when often there was none.

In February 1933, the effect of the civil-liberties smashing Reichstag fire decree 'For the Protection of People and State' was immediate. The American ambassador in Berlin, Frederic Sackett, sent a dispatch to the Secretary of State in Washington warning that the Nazis were arresting 'prominent pacifists, journalists, authors, educators and lawyers who defended Communists in political trials, and a number of Social Democrats'. He thought the forthcoming March election would be a 'farce' because the Social Democrats were 'so completely muzzled that outwardly at least they have ceased to exist'.[22]

The Reichstag fire decree served to accelerate the Nazis' journey along a path they were already treading. A few days before the Reichstag fire, Göring, as acting Prussian Minister of the Interior, had sworn in Stormtroopers as 'auxiliary police' and they had immediately targeted their erstwhile enemies. Wolfgang Teubert, a Stormtrooper who had previously been fighting communists in beer halls, was one of these new 'policemen' and he and his comrades 'arrested two people, one of whom was a union secretary, he was a big troublemaker, and the other one was a notorious swindler, and he got his five-year prison sentence in a proper court of law. While the union secretary was released after weeks or months.'

Makeshift prisons were created to hold people like the union secretary who were 'arrested' by Teubert and his fellow 'auxiliary policemen'. Over time these places were replaced by the concentration camps for which the Nazis would become infamous. During the 1930s these camps weren't places of mass extermination – although some of the inmates were murdered – but they did symbolize, from the beginning, the injustice of the new regime. Since the Nazis claimed that the inmates were held in 'protective custody', they never needed to bring criminal charges against anyone who was imprisoned.

When after the war Wolfgang Teubert was questioned about the concentration camps, he had trouble properly articulating his views. While he initially admitted the camps were 'not justified', he immediately qualified his judgement by saying that while 'it's quite clear to me that innocent people also ended up there, on the other hand we had no more crime. There was no crime and that was the upside, the sunny side, and wherever you have sunshine, you've got to have shadows. If you're locking up the criminals – or locking up the putative criminals – when that happens there is [bound to be] the occasional personal act of revenge, that's only human.'[23]

The revenge-filled atmosphere of these early weeks was pungently expressed by the Nazi politician Wilhelm Murr. 'We don't say: an eye for an eye, a tooth for a tooth,' he declared at a rally. 'No, if someone knocks out one of our eyes, we will chop off his head, and if someone knocks out one of our teeth, we will smash in his jaw.'[24]

For opponents of the regime, these were obviously perilous times. The young communist Alois Pfaller realized that it wasn't safe to remain in Germany and left the country. His brother, also a communist, chose to stay. 'That was his mistake,' said Pfaller. 'It cost him his life.' He was sent to a concentration camp, 'let out after eight years, mortally ill, and died a few years later'.

Alois Pfaller fled to the Soviet Union, but felt after a year that he ought to go back to Germany and help rebuild the Communist Party, even though he knew he would risk his life in doing so. On his return he was betrayed by a former Communist Party member. Taken to a police station, he was punched in the face and kicked unconscious. When he recovered, he was beaten again until his eardrum split and his blood spilled all over the room. Afterwards, 'I was given a bucket with a cloth, and I had to clean the whole desk, and the floor, had to clean off all the blood and so on, and then I was handed over to another officer, to get me back to my cell.'[25] From the police station he was taken to a concentration camp where he languished for many years.

Up to 5,000 people were arrested in the seven days between the Reichstag fire and the March general election, and many more afterwards. Altogether almost 200,000 political prisoners were detained at some point by the Nazis during 1933.[26] It was a devastating demonstration of both the regime's capacity for vengeance and their contempt for human rights.

The results of the 'final' German general election on 5 March could be spun either way. On the positive side for the Nazis, they achieved their largest ever share of the vote – 43.9 per cent – and together with their conservative political partners they had a majority in the Reichstag of just over 51 per cent. On the negative side, this was hardly a spectacular achievement given the atmosphere of bullying and coercion that surrounded the election campaign. And it remains notable that the Nazis, despite all their advantages, had still not convinced a majority of Germans to vote for their party. But regardless of how you chose to interpret the figures, the Nazis had now fulfilled their promise and held the last election. A general election offering any kind of genuine choice would not be held in Germany until after Hitler had put a bullet in his head.

'The defeat in 1918 did not depress me as greatly as the present state of affairs,' wrote Victor Klemperer in his diary on 17 March 1933. Klemperer, an academic in Dresden, had converted to Protestantism years before, but the fact that he had a Jewish background still put him at risk: 'It is shocking how day after day naked acts of violence, breaches of the law, barbaric opinions appear quite undisguised as official decree.' Surveying the effect the Nazis had already had on Germany, he declared that 'I can no longer get rid of the feeling of disgust and shame, and no one stirs; everyone trembles, keeps out of sight.'[27]

But Hitler, and his propaganda expert Joseph Goebbels, did not want to rule over a Germany in which 'everyone trembles'. They wanted to convince as many 'racially pure' Germans as they could to switch their previous allegiances and support them. So, as a first step towards creating greater unity, Goebbels tried to strengthen the public perception of a link between Hitler and the aged President Hindenburg. One tactic during the run-up to the March election had been to print posters showing Hitler and Hindenburg together, the President's head above and to the left, Hitler's lower and to the right. The visual implication was clear. Hindenburg, almost godlike, was blessing his young and vigorous successor. It was an obvious attempt to clothe Hitler in Hindenburg's respectability. This may be a Nazi revolution, the poster implied, but it was one sanctioned from above and born from German honour and tradition.[28]

The apogee of Nazi attempts to piggyback off Hindenburg's reputation was reached during the opening of the new session of parliament, little more than two weeks after the election had been held. As a result of the burning of the Reichstag, the ceremony was held on 21 March in Potsdam, just outside Berlin. The location could hardly have been more symbolic – the garrison church, the burial site of Frederick the Great, whom Hitler hero-worshipped.[29]

'Here the marriage was successful, if not forever, then at least temporarily, between the masses led by Hitler and the "Spirit of Potsdam", the Prussian tradition, represented by Hindenburg,' wrote the young German novelist Erich Ebermayer in his diary. 'What a brilliant production by the master producer Goebbels! Hindenburg, the members of the government and parliament drive from Berlin to Potsdam past a single, cohesive line of cheering millions. All of Berlin seems to be in the streets.'[30] As Goebbels had wanted, Ebermayer was struck by the significance of Hindenburg's presence as the one individual who could unite Germany's past with its future.

While Hindenburg took centre stage, resplendent in his field marshal's dress uniform, Hitler demonstrated his subservience by wearing civilian clothes. And once inside the church, he was obsequious in his praise. 'Your wondrous life', he said, addressing Hindenburg, 'is a symbol of the indestructible vigour of the German nation for all of us.' Hindenburg's 'understanding' had permitted a consummation of 'the marriage between the symbols of old greatness and young strength'.[31] Hindenburg then descended alone into the crypt of the church to pay homage to the Prussian kings in their burial chamber. As a propaganda spectacle, demonstrating Hindenburg's endorsement of the link between the new regime and the days of German glory, it could not have been bettered.

Hitler moved on to the first session of the new Reichstag, held in the Kroll Opera House in Berlin. He wanted the deputies to pass an Enabling Act that would allow him to bypass both the President and the Reichstag. But he faced a hurdle. He needed two-thirds of the deputies present to support him.

The communists were no longer an obstacle – they weren't even allowed into the building – but members of the Centre Party had to be persuaded to vote for the Nazis. Consequently, just as he had been obsequious to Hindenburg, Hitler was now obsequious to deputies of the Centre Party. The Nazi leader hypocritically professed support for their Christian beliefs, saying, 'The National Government sees in both Christian denominations the most important elements for the preservation of our nationhood.'[32]

Hitler started the debate in as dignified a manner as he could, but after Otto Wels of the Social Democrats had voiced the view that 'criticism is wholesome and necessary' and protested at the 'serious consequences' of passing the Enabling Act, Hitler's mask of statesman-ship fell away and he revealed his true nature – that of a beer-hall rabble-rouser.[33] In a speech filled with threat he claimed that the Nazis were 'restraining' themselves 'from turning against those who have tortured and tormented us for fourteen years'. He called the Social Democrats 'sissies' for 'speaking of persecution' and told them that their 'last hour has come' and they deserved their fate. 'Everything in a nation that becomes rotten, old and frail', he declared, 'will vanish and never return.'[34]

All the parties in the Reichstag, with the exception of the Social Democrats, subsequently voted for the Enabling Act, which passed by 444 votes to 94. A majority of Reichstag deputies thus voted themselves into irrelevancy.

By the time the Enabling Act was passed, the Nazis had already made determined efforts to secure control of the security apparatus of the state. Heinrich Himmler, for instance, had become acting police chief of Munich on 9 March after the Minister-President of Bavaria, Heinrich Held, had been forced out of office.

At a press conference a few days after taking office, Himmler announced that 'I have made quite extensive use of protective custody . . . I felt compelled to do this because in many parts of the city there has been so much agitation that it has been impossible for me to guarantee the safety of those particular individuals who have provoked it.'[35] The cynicism of Himmler's concept of 'protective custody' was breathtaking. He wanted his audience to believe that he had imprisoned opponents of the regime to 'protect' them from the righteous anger of other Germans. He thus maintained that he was doing them a favour by locking them up.

Given the decentralized structure of the state, the Nazi takeover of the security forces had to be conducted piecemeal, and it wasn't until 1936 that Himmler formally became chief of all the German police. But from these early days, policemen understood that they faced a stark choice – support the new regime or be forced out. The Law for the Restoration of the Professional Civil Service, passed in April, gave legal backing to the removal of any members of the police who opposed the Nazis. This, coupled with the appointment of police leaders who were members of the party, swiftly created a police force loyal to the new regime.

142 *The Nazi Mind*

Not that there needed to be much of a purge. Most German police officers stayed on and served the Nazis. They decided to do this even though their new bosses were often the very people they had been targeting as dangerous revolutionaries just a few months before. Reinhard Heydrich, for instance, who had been conducting a variety of illegal operations prior to Hitler's Chancellorship, now became head of the political section of the police in Munich.

One of the policemen that Heydrich inherited was Heinrich Müller, a thirty-two-year-old career officer. Although Müller loathed communism, he had never been a supporter of the Nazis. Yet even though the Nazis were aware that Müller's loyalties had been directed elsewhere, his career flourished and he eventually became head of the Gestapo. In 1937 a revealing appraisal of him by the local party stated that while Müller had acted against left-wing groups before 1933, 'It is no less clear, however, that Müller, had it been his task, would have proceeded just the same against the right.' The report concluded: 'With his vast ambition and relentless drive, he would have done everything to win the appreciation of whoever might happen to be his boss in a given system.'[36] As a description of human pragmatism, it could hardly have been bettered.

Heinrich Müller was not alone in demonstrating this fundamental psychological trait. Enormous numbers of other Germans swiftly changed their previous allegiance and conformed to the new order. Over a million joined the Nazi Party in early 1933.[37] It would be naive to think that all these people suddenly recognized the validity of Hitler's arguments in a kind of collective Road to Damascus moment. Many of them were surely opportunists.

The novelist Erich Ebermayer encountered one such character in April 1933. He was shocked to discover that a friend, who 'until now had been anything but a Nazi', was 'wearing a party badge under his jacket, on his waistcoat! I am aghast. He explains to me, in a cold and sober manner, that he is not keen on being pushed against the wall by the Nazis. You must take part in this, and whether your heart is in it or not doesn't matter.' Ebermayer was astonished, especially given that his friend was the 'most talented young actor in Leipzig – why should politics concern him?'[38]

Three years later, a member of the now illegal political party the SPD reached the doleful conclusion that 'The average worker is first and foremost interested in work and not in democracy. People who once enthusiastically defended democracy don't show any interest in politics. One must be clear about the fact that in the first place men are part of a family and have professions, and that politics is of secondary importance and then only when they hope to get something out of it.'[39]

Psychological research has demonstrated that most of us feel a profound 'need to belong'. We are social animals and 'lack of attachments is linked to a variety of ill effects on health, adjustment, and well-being.'[40] This 'need' can be fulfilled by participating in social groups independent of the state, but this became increasingly difficult in Nazi Germany as the regime sought to push its influence into every organization. This invasion of the individual's personal space was one of the many sinister sides to the utopian dream of the *Volksgemeinschaft*.

While Erich Ebermayer's actor friend in Leipzig was able to accommodate himself to the new Germany, it was impossible for anyone the Nazis considered a Jew to do likewise. Less than 1 per cent of Germans were Jews, so they were a minority that was easy to oppress. During these early months of the regime the Jews were particularly at risk of arbitrary attacks from Stormtroopers in actions that were often designed to humiliate. Rudi Bamber, from a Jewish family in Nuremberg, remembered how his father was taken to a sports stadium and made, along with other Jews, to cut the grass with his teeth.[41]

Hitler openly expressed his own anti-Semitism just a few days after the passing of the Enabling Act. In a proclamation to all party organizations, he blamed German Jews for supposedly helping to orchestrate protests about Nazi atrocities from foreign nations, and repeated the conspiracy theory that Jews plotted with each other across national boundaries.[42] Jews, he believed, owed their loyalty to other Jews – not to the countries in which they lived.

However, this proclamation was not all it seemed. Though it was inconceivable that it could have been issued without Hitler's input, it was nonetheless only signed 'Party Leadership'. And while the proclamation called for a boycott of Jewish shops and businesses, it also emphasized that the Jews were not to be physically abused. Disingenuously, the *Völkischer Beobachter* reported on 30 March that Hitler had said one reason for the boycott was the risk that 'the *Volk*' might rise up against the Jews in actions that would 'perhaps assume undesirable forms'.

Just as Himmler had said people should be imprisoned in concentration camps to 'protect' them from the wrath of the populace, so Hitler now asserted that Jews should be persecuted by the state in order to safeguard them from spontaneous attacks by ordinary Germans. It was a nonsensical argument, not least because it presupposed that the Nazis couldn't police their own population.

The reason for this twisted logic was that Hitler knew he had to balance competing interests. Local party activists had already been targeting Jews, and while he needed to keep their support he also had to ensure that traditional conservative elements – including the army, his cabinet colleagues and President Hindenburg – didn't think that Germany was now at the mercy of a lawless rabble.

Hitler was right in his proclamation in one respect. There had been protests abroad about the Nazis' actions against Jews, most notably a rally on 27 March in New York attended by more than 50,000 people. But Hitler omitted the reason why people were protesting – the Nazis were already persecuting German Jews. Though he had tried to present the Nazis as the wronged individuals in the dispute with the Jews, he and his comrades had caused the problem in the first place. Hitler frequently used this kind of duplicitous argument. He would light a fire and then blame other people for trying to put it out.

The night before the boycott of Jewish shops and businesses was due to start, Goebbels announced that it would last for just one day. This was likely because Hitler realized that there wasn't widespread support for the action within Germany and that a longer boycott risked aggravating foreign trading partners still further.

The boycott when it took place on 1 April was traumatic for German Jews. Stormtroopers positioned themselves outside Jewish shops and intimidated people into staying away. For the Jews it brought the realization that not only would the state not protect them, the state actually wished them harm. 'I felt as if I was falling into a deep hole,' said one German Jew, a teenager in Stuttgart. 'That's when I intuitively realized for the first time that the existing law did not apply to Jews.'[43]

Wolfgang Teubert, along with his Stormtrooper comrades, stood 'outside the Jewish shops for a whole day and said "nobody is allowed to buy anything here"'. He willingly accepted Hitler's lie about the reason for the Jewish boycott. 'We should always be aware of a natural law in such cases,' he said, 'effect and cause. No effect without cause. And that boycott that we held against the Jews, for one day, was caused by the declaration of [economic] war [by foreign Jews].'[44]

For Nazi supporter Günter Lohse, this action against the Jews was a fulfilment of the 'pronouncements of Hitler and Goebbels' that the Jews 'occupied all the significant positions – in the banks, in industry, with the authorities, in university chairs, there are Jews everywhere. And for months that was presented. And so I thought that some correction was not inhumane, but rather I should say that I didn't give it much thought. But for me the significance lay in the background. They [the Jews] rule everything here, that shouldn't be the case. Something like that.'[45]

Günter Lohse was an intelligent man. A student when the Nazis came to power, he later went on to work in the German Foreign Office. Yet he could parrot the lie that the Jews 'rule everything here' when it was obvious that the people who 'ruled' Germany and had been instrumental in appointing Hitler – Hindenburg, Papen and others in the German elite – were demonstrably not Jewish. And though there were Jews in 'significant positions' within German society it was ludicrous to claim they were 'everywhere'.

Representatives of Germany's former adversaries were taking note of what was happening. None more so than Sir Horace Rumbold, British ambassador to Berlin, who wrote a perceptive long telegram to the Foreign Office in London on 26 April 1933. Rumbold spotted that though the 'Reichswehr and the President are probably still in a position to check and possibly even to control Hitlerism', the problem was that 'sooner or later, especially if the President dies, the Reichswehr may be expected to throw in their lot with the present regime.' Moreover, since Hitler believed that 'only brute force can ensure the survival of the race' he was set on a course of rapid rearmament. While that goal was being achieved, Rumbold thought that Hitler would try 'to lull the outer world into a sense of security'. Simultaneously, the 'new regime' would attempt to convince Germans of the rightness of their aims, and 'To this end it has embarked on a programme of political propaganda on a scale for which there is no analogy in history.'[46]

Rumbold was one of the first to spot the talents of Joseph Goebbels, whom he described as 'a man of infinite resource and invention'. Goebbels, newly installed as the Minister for Popular Enlightenment and Propaganda, made his desire for control over the press explicit at the first press conference he gave. 'It goes without saying', he told journalists, 'that you will still be given information here [at the Propaganda Ministry], but you will also receive instructions. You will know not only what is happening, but also what attitude the government takes to it and how you can most appropriately convey that to the nation.'[47]

Cultural institutions were threatened with abolition if they didn't fall into line and purge themselves of elements the regime opposed. Some, like the Organization for German Students – the Deutsche Studentenschaft – even volunteered lists of 'corrupting' literature. During this process of pseudo-renewal, unique cultural collections were destroyed, including Magnus Hirschfeld's pioneering sexology institute.[48]

The books from Hirschfeld's institute, snatched on 6 May 1933, were among those destroyed at the infamous book burning in Berlin held four days later. Students threw works by Bertolt Brecht, Erich Maria Remarque, Sigmund Freud and a host of other famous writers on the bonfire. In Leipzig, when he heard news of the book burnings, Erich Ebermayer was worried that his own works might be destroyed as well. A few days later, on 14 May, he received terrible news – his books were indeed to be banned.[49]

Even joining the Nazi Party was no guarantee of safety, as the immensely wealthy industrialist Günther Quandt discovered that spring. He became a member of the party in early May but shortly afterwards was arrested and accused of currency and business irregularities. He was imprisoned, forced to pay a large amount to gain his freedom on bail and then placed under house arrest. Only after he had 'donated' still more money to the Nazi cause was he allowed to resume his normal life. It was just one example of the many protection rackets that the Nazis operated.[50]

Hitler was initially ambivalent about such excesses. But by 6 July 1933 he was sufficiently worried by the lawless atmosphere to warn in a speech to Nazi leaders that 'revolution is not a permanent condition, and it must not develop into a permanent one. The energy released by the revolution must be channelled into the safe bed of evolution.' Businessmen shouldn't be 'removed' merely because they weren't Nazis, since 'in business, the only crucial thing is ability.' Moreover, 'the ideas of the programme don't oblige us to act like fools and overturn everything.'[51]

It was all very well for Hitler to say these things, quite another to make his followers – especially the Stormtroopers – abide by them. And the abuses continued long after he had given his speech. This was a growing problem for both Hitler and Goebbels in their quest to convince the millions of Germans who had opposed the Nazis to support the new regime. It was obvious that the *Volksgemeinschaft* couldn't be created in an atmosphere in which almost everyone was at risk of attack or extortion.

But that was not the only difficulty that Hitler faced. A more immediate problem was that Ernst Röhm was not falling into line. He had written an article in June 1933 in which he said that while 'A victory on the road to the German revolution has been won,' it was 'not absolute victory!' And 'as long as the real National Socialist Germany still awaits fulfilment, the fierce and passionate struggle of the SA and SS will not stop.'[52] Furthermore, despite Röhm saying that the Stormtroopers were not a threat to the established army, there were signs, as they searched for a role in the new Germany, that they could be. The Stormtroopers had evolved into a powerful force – several million by the end of 1933 – and this huge expansion in membership only exacerbated the problem of enforcing discipline.[53]

A confrontation between Hitler and his old comrade Röhm seemed inevitable. On 1 February 1934, Röhm sent Blomberg, the Minister of Defence, a memo in which – according to Blomberg – he said that he wanted his Stormtroopers to oversee the army.[54] This was in direct opposition to Hitler's policy – he wanted to rearm the established armed forces, not increase the influence of the Stormtroopers. During a speech to military leaders later that month, Hitler explicitly said that while the Stormtroopers might be used for 'tasks of border protection and premilitary training' this was only to happen during a 'transitional period' to allow the established armed forces to grow. He reiterated that the army were to become the sole 'weapon carriers' of the nation.[55]

That same month, Blomberg wanted to demonstrate the army's support for Hitler. So he insisted that the 'Aryan paragraph' was enforced and Jews removed from the ranks.[56] He also oversaw a change in the uniforms of the armed forces. From now on an eagle clutching a swastika would be seen on all military jackets. It is another example of how individuals and organizations came forward to volunteer change to please the new regime, and of how their perception that Hitler had to 'balance' various power groups was often the motivation behind that change.

Röhm was not well that spring. The French ambassador, André François-Poncet, met him for dinner in May and remarked that he 'looked absentminded and ill'.[57] It is possible that Röhm was despondent partly because he believed that others were moving against him. The Stormtroopers were unpopular not only with the armed forces but with President Hindenburg and Franz von Papen as well.

Events soon reached crisis point. On 8 June, four days after meeting Hitler, Röhm told the Stormtroopers that he was going on sick leave and that they should take time off as well, reconvening on 1 August. He reassured them that 'The SA is and remains Germany's destiny.'[58] That, however, was not how others saw the future of the Stormtroopers. On 17 June, Papen gave a speech at Marburg University in which he insisted that 'the government must represent the people as a whole' and that 'the government is well aware of the selfishness, the lack of principle, the insincerity, the unchivalrous behaviour, the arrogance which is on the increase under the guise of the German revolution.'[59]

The situation worsened for Hitler on 21 June, when both Hindenburg and General Blomberg told him that he should bring 'the revolutionary troublemakers . . . to reason'.[60] Hitler had a powerful motivation to do as he was asked. He was aware that crushing Röhm would help his chances of becoming head of state after Hindenburg's death. What better demonstration would Germans need of his commitment to the nation than turning on his own supporters?

Hitler ordered Röhm to convene a meeting of Stormtrooper leaders at the spa town of Bad Wiessee on 30 June. Early that morning, while they were still asleep, Hitler arrived with an entourage that included two dozen SS men. He stormed up to Röhm's room and arrested him while he was still in his pyjamas. Thirteen Stormtrooper leaders, including Röhm, were then taken thirty miles north to prison in Munich. The next day, Röhm, having declined the opportunity to commit suicide, was shot by two SS men, Theodor Eicke and his junior colleague Michael Lippert.

The choice of Eicke to lead the murder squad was significant. Like Reinhard Heydrich he owed his career entirely to Heinrich Himmler. A dangerous revolutionary, Eicke had been sentenced to prison in 1932 for plotting to use bombs against the Nazis' political enemies. He had escaped by fleeing to Italy while on bail, only to return after Hitler came to power. Thinking that he had previously been betrayed by Josef Bürckel, a Nazi Gauleiter, he sought revenge but was captured and sent to a mental asylum. Bürckel considered Eicke 'syphilitic and completely mad', although a doctor at the asylum pronounced him sane.[61] Shortly afterwards, Himmler stepped in and saved Eicke's career by appointing him commandant of the concentration camp at Dachau.

Once again Himmler's ability to find recruits in unlikely places paid dividends, as Eicke proved uniquely suited to the task. 'He hates his enemies behind the barbed wire,' said one of Eicke's SS colleagues at Dachau, Max von Dall'Armi. 'He speaks of their destruction and annihilation. He instils this hatred into the SS through speeches and conversations. Eicke is a fanatical SS officer and ardent National Socialist for whom there is no compromise.' Dall'Armi also recalled Eicke's saying that 'SS men must hate . . . The heart in their breasts must be turned to stone.'[62]

Eicke repaid Himmler for rescuing him from the mental asylum with his unquestioned loyalty. Not only did he throw himself into the reorganization of Dachau, making it the 'model' camp within the Nazi system, infamous for its ordered brutality, but he was willing to fulfil whatever special tasks the Reichsführer SS gave him. That is why, in the early evening of 1 July 1934, Eicke found himself inside cell 474 at Munich's Stadelheim prison pointing a loaded gun at Ernst Röhm. 'I am proud', he allegedly said, 'that I shot this faggot swine with my own hands.'[63] Back at Dachau, Eicke and his men gloried in the chance to kill the other Stormtroopers who were delivered to them, turning the whole event into a bacchanal and drinking barrel-loads of beer.[64]

At his own headquarters in Munich, Hitler had told a group of his followers that Röhm had been planning a coup. He omitted to mention that there was no real evidence that this was the case. Röhm had shown no inclination to go against Hitler. Rather than thwarting a coup in turning against Röhm, Hitler had acted out of his own narrow self-interest, realizing that his career was at risk if he displeased Blomberg and Hindenburg. Röhm's death also offered him other benefits – it destroyed the power base of the Stormtroopers and reassured the army that Hitler was committed to their pre-eminence as a military force.

The sheer lawlessness of what became known as the Night of the

Long Knives was remarkable. For this wasn't just an action against the Stormtroopers; Hitler also relished the opportunity to eliminate those who had previously angered him, including General Schleicher, Gregor Strasser and many others. Altogether around 150 people lost their lives.

The accused were never allowed a chance to plead their innocence before a court of law, just summarily dispatched. The SS even killed people in error. On the evening of 30 June they snatched the music critic of one of Munich's leading newspapers from his flat as he was playing the cello. His wife told the SS there must be some mistake and started searching for documents to prove her husband's identity. She stopped when the SS pointed their guns at her. Two days later she learnt that he had been shot at Dachau 'by accident'.[65] The SS had mistaken him for another journalist of the same name.

The killers were similarly reckless when they went to kill General Kurt von Schleicher, the man who had been Chancellor of Germany just the year before. They killed not only Schleicher but his wife as well. She had started screaming when she saw her husband targeted. Afterwards the Gestapo reported to Himmler that Schleicher had died while 'resisting arrest' and his wife had been killed in the ensuing firefight. The phrases 'resisting arrest' and 'attempting to escape' were to be used as all-purpose justifications for murder throughout the twelve years of Nazi rule. Another euphemism the Nazi security forces employed was 'suicide' – this was how Gregor Strasser's death was described after he had been shot on the night of 30 June in his cell in Gestapo Headquarters in Berlin.[66]

Hitler's justification for these killings would have fallen apart at the merest investigation. Not only was there no substantive evidence that a coup was imminent, but the list of non-Stormtroopers who had been killed demonstrated that this was an obvious settling of old scores. The marginalized Schleicher and Strasser, for instance, were hardly leaders of a credible plot to overthrow the regime.

On 3 July, Hitler did his best to explain to his cabinet why the killings had been necessary. He told them that Röhm had betrayed him and that Strasser and Schleicher had been seeking to overthrow the government. After Blomberg thanked Hitler, the whole cabinet agreed that the actions were 'justified as defence of the state'. There was to be no retrospective investigation into the truth of Hitler's claims.[67]

Hindenburg, no doubt much to Hitler's relief, also expressed his gratitude that these 'treasonable intrigues' had been quashed and that Hitler had 'saved the German nation from serious danger'.[68] Hitler thus managed to fend off the risk to his Chancellorship from the combination of Hindenburg, Blomberg and Papen.

In a final stunning display of hypocrisy, Hitler also claimed to be shocked by the evidence of homosexuality within the Stormtrooper movement, even though he had known about Röhm's sexual proclivities for years. Immediately after Röhm's arrest, he said that he wanted 'every mother to be able to give her son to the SA, to the party or the Hitler Youth without fear that he might become ethically or morally corrupt'.[69]

The reaction of army officers to the Night of the Long Knives was predictable. The aristocratic Johann Adolf Graf von Kielmansegg, then twenty-seven years old, spoke for many of his comrades when he later said that Röhm 'wanted to make it his army. Of course he didn't say it like that, but it was becoming increasingly clear. That came on top of our simple rejection of the SA because of their ways, because of their behaviour, because, well you can call it mob rule if you want . . . But the revolution eats its own children, that's always been the case, hasn't it?' Above all, what mattered to officers like Kielmansegg was the imprimatur of President Hindenburg: 'He had given his blessing to Hitler's behaviour. This was the important thing for us. You know, for the army, Hindenburg was not Hitler.'[70]

Kielmansegg's words were another vindication of Hitler's tactic of leaching off the reputation of Hindenburg during the first year and a half of his Chancellorship. It was psychologically much easier for Kielmansegg and his colleagues to support the new regime because 'Hindenburg was not Hitler'. This endorsement by the aged Field Marshal was crucial.

Hitler waited nearly two weeks before he spoke to the Reichstag deputies about the killings. It was a potentially sensitive moment given that he had presided over the murder of several of their Reichstag colleagues. But his speech on 13 July was defiant. He not only gave detailed – if spurious – reasons for his actions, he even said that 'If someone holds it against me why we didn't call on the courts of law for the sentencing, I can only say: in this hour I was responsible for the destiny of the German nation and therefore I was Supreme Judge of the German people!'[71]

Göring echoed Hitler's words, telling Reichstag deputies that 'if today, foreign countries think that chaos is happening in Germany, the German *Volk* will reply with a single cry: "All of us always approve what our Führer does." '[72] Even one of Germany's leading legal theorists, Professor Carl Schmitt, supported Hitler's action in an article called 'Der Führer schützt das Recht' (The Führer protects justice).[73] Hitler was indeed, said Schmitt, the supreme judge of right and wrong.

All semblance of the previous rule of law was gone. But what is still more notable is that Hitler's popularity in Germany increased after the Night of the Long Knives. The Nazi control over the press meant that the killings could be spun as Hitler's heroic attempt to restore order in the country. He had used the minimum necessary force, people read in the newspapers, to prevent violent disorder. Moreover, he had been prepared to punish his own erstwhile supporters for the greater good of the nation. Was not this dramatic evidence of how he saw himself as governing for all Germans – or at least those deemed racially acceptable – not just those who had voted Nazi?

Reports reaching members of the Social Democratic Party, who had been forced into exile to escape persecution, made gloomy reading. 'Large, evidently very large, sections of the population are even extolling Hitler for his ruthless determination, and only a very small portion has been set thinking or been shocked,' read one summary of the information they received from Germany. 'Large sections of the working class have also become enslaved to the uncritical deification of Hitler.'[74]

It was an astonishing demonstration of what can happen when people have access to only one voice across all media. With German radio stations and newspapers all parroting the same government line, millions of people not only forgave Hitler for his crime but lauded him for it.

Destroy the rule of law. Eliminate the free press. Suborn the police and the army. Hitler demonstrated that would-be dictators should do all three as soon as they can. Then they have a chance to reap benefits similar to the ones he enjoyed, from a population that has no one else to turn to for justice or information or protection but the newly corrupted institutions of the state.

Less than three weeks after Hitler declared to Reichstag deputies that he was 'Supreme Judge of the German people', President Hindenburg died, and Hitler was about to become the undisputed leader of the country.

Goebbels had called the previous year for a 'mobilization of mind and spirit in Germany'.[75] Now, in August 1934, that task could begin in earnest.

7. Exploiting Faith

Adolf Hitler believed he knew a great secret about the human mind. 'Be assured,' he said in 1927, 'we too put faith in the first place and not cognition. One has to believe in a cause. Only faith creates a state. What motivates people to go and do battle for religious ideas? Not cognition, but blind faith.'[1]

It is one of the most important statements Hitler ever made. He was not a religious believer in any conventional sense, yet he did all he could to create a faith-based state in Germany – one in which the population had 'blind faith' not in a supernatural being but in him and the Nazi regime.

Hitler also thought he knew the best way to engender faith. The key was to reach people not through logic but through emotion. 'The art of propaganda', he wrote in *Mein Kampf*, 'lies in understanding the emotional ideas of the great masses and finding, through a psychologically correct form, the way to the attention and thence to the heart of the broad masses.'[2]

President Hindenburg's death on 2 August 1934 allowed him to put these ideas into practice. The day before, the cabinet had passed the Law Concerning the Head of State of the German Reich, which on Hindenburg's demise would make Hitler not just Chancellor but Führer of the German Reich as well – a plan which was rubber-stamped by a referendum held amid much intimidation on 19 August.

Now that Hitler was proclaimed the new head of state, every member of the armed forces was ordered to swear an oath of allegiance to him personally. For a soldier like Johann Adolf Graf von Kielmansegg this marked a symbolic return to past glory. 'Prussian-German history is full of personal oaths of loyalty,' he said. 'Indeed we almost preferred that to swearing loyalty to a piece of paper. Before we had been sworn in on the Weimar constitution, which nobody knew.'[3] Nonetheless swearing this oath to Hitler represented a permanent obligation. 'A German officer', he said, 'does not break an oath sworn before God.'[4]

For many, this demonstration of their emotional commitment to the

'Führer' was life changing. Air force officer Karl Boehm-Tettelbach said that the oath 'accompanied me my whole life to the end. I mean oath is oath . . . I can't break the oath, otherwise I might [have to] commit suicide.' The oath represented a permanent obligation.[5]

Some oath ceremonies – particularly those of the SS – were held at night, under torchlight. Every opportunity was taken to create a spiritual atmosphere, reminiscent of a sacred ritual. It was a deliberate attempt to generate faith in Hitler as the all-powerful leader.

In focusing on faith not cognition, Hitler benefited from a reality psychologists have known for years. It is almost impossible to convince people who have formed a strong emotional belief that they are wrong by using reasoned argument. Since faith is not dependent on reason, how can reason be used to convince anyone they are mistaken?[6]

Hitler linked all these ideas to one further notion. He thought human beings in large groups were basically dim. 'The receptivity of the great masses is very limited,' he wrote, 'their intelligence is small, but their power of forgetting is enormous.' As a result, 'all effective propaganda' had to be both simple and repeated over and over.[7]

This was a view shared by his Propaganda Minister, Joseph Goebbels. Wilfred von Oven, Goebbels' personal attaché, remembered his boss telling him that 'Propaganda is like a convoy in the war which has to make its way to the target under heavy military protection. It has to adjust its marching speed to suit the slowest of the unit. That's how it is here. We have to do the same with our propaganda. All sophisticated propaganda is quite out of place. The masses don't understand irony. One has to concentrate quite simply on the basic message which one wants to achieve with the propaganda and one has to get it to the masses in the most popular and graphic way possible.'[8]

This didn't mean, said Goebbels, that the propaganda message had to be solemn or earnest. On the contrary, as he told an audience of German radio executives in March 1933, 'First principle: at all costs avoid being boring. I put that before everything.'[9] Unlike many totalitarian propagandists, Goebbels came to understand that it was counter-productive to try and ram an ideological message down the throats of the audience.[10] 'He kept telling his film people,' remembered Wilfred von Oven, ' "Don't come to me with political material. All political films have turned out dreadfully" . . . He kept repeating, "Hands off political films." '[11]

Goebbels rephrased this view for public consumption in an article in the *Völkischer Beobachter* in February 1934: 'If I believe that there is an honest artistic attitude behind a film, then I will protect it . . . I do not demand that a film begins and ends with National Socialist parades. The Nazi parades should be left to us, we understand them better.'[12]

Subsequently the vast majority of films produced during Goebbels' time as Propaganda Minister contained no explicit propaganda at all – they were primarily pieces of entertainment. According to Arthur Maria Rabenalt, a film director who worked for him, Goebbels felt well qualified to judge their worth. 'He was movie crazy,' said Rabenalt, 'and he liked to look at pretty women. So he basically liked exactly what the audience wanted.'[13]

Goebbels understood, however, that these entertainment films performed a valuable service within the Nazi state. They had a 'political purpose' which was to allow the audience to escape from their 'household cares and family worries'.[14] What was more, by the choice of subject matter – love stories, for instance, that supported the idea of the *Volksgemeinschaft* – Goebbels sought to influence Germans without them realizing it.

'Even entertainment can be politically of special value,' wrote Goebbels, 'because the moment a person is conscious of propaganda, propaganda becomes ineffective.'[15] It was this insight – more than any other – that marked Goebbels out as the leading propagandist of his time. And, incidentally, explains why a modern-day propagandist aiming to use Goebbels' methods would seek to influence people at least as much through the storylines in soap operas or entertaining content on social messaging sites as via traditional media.

Goebbels had set himself an immense task. 'If this government is determined never and under no circumstances to give way,' he said on his appointment as Propaganda Minister in 1933, 'then it has no need of the lifeless power of the bayonet, and in the long run will not be content with 52 per cent behind it and with terrorizing the remaining 48 per cent, but will see its most immediate task as being to win over that remaining 48 per cent.'[16]

This focus on entertainment films was a key part of Goebbels' plan to 'win over' the 48 per cent. But he faced formidable obstacles. The first was that, despite his exhortation that propagandists should avoid being boring, that was precisely what much of the news produced under his aegis was. Newspaper circulation dropped by 10 per cent between 1933 and 1939, largely because journalists could no longer write what they wanted; instead they had to stick to the line produced by Goebbels' ministry. As a result, there was little variety or spice in their articles.

The second problem Goebbels faced was even more intractable. There was a fundamental disconnect between the Nazis' economic 'vision' and the reality. The Nazi Party had proclaimed itself the party of small businesses and farmers. Yet Hitler's commitment to rearmament meant that the focus had to be on large industrial concerns and modern methods of production. Mega-companies like Krupp, the giant steelmaker and armaments conglomerate, were much more valuable to the regime than any number of artisans working in small workshops. Goebbels might rail against the 'asphalt' culture of the big cities[17] and praise the beauty of the German forests, but it was in the grimy industrial heartland of the country – with not a tree to be seen – that the weapons Hitler so desperately wanted were being constructed.

The solution Goebbels and his colleagues found to these difficulties was to continue to promote the fuzzy vision of the *Volksgemeinschaft* for the 'in-group' of racially acceptable Germans, while emphasizing the continuing danger from the 'out-group' – primarily the Jews.[18] In this context Goebbels understood a great truth of his own: it is often easier for members of a political party to define themselves by what they hate rather than by what they like. But in propaganda terms this presented a problem. Different people felt different levels of hatred. At one extreme were the thugs of the SA, at the other the former socialists Goebbels hoped to convert to the Nazi cause.

That disparity in levels of hatred was one reason why Goebbels was wary of producing anti-Semitic films during the 1930s – indeed, it wasn't until the war began that German cinemas started to show overtly anti-Semitic work like *Der ewige Jude* (The Eternal Jew) and *Jud Süss* (Jew Süss). Goebbels must have realized that he risked provoking uncontrolled aggression from the extreme Jew-haters within the party if they were incited via what he thought was the immense power of film.[19]

Nonetheless, the Nazis remained ideologically committed to 'educating' the German public about the Jewish 'danger'. This was attempted in two main ways – by the written word, in books and newspapers, and by the changes to the educational system which were discussed in a previous chapter.[20] Among newspapers, Julius Streicher's hate-filled publication *Der Stürmer* continued to voice the most extreme anti-Semitic propaganda. The 'Jewish Murder Plot' edition in May 1934 was one of the most notorious. It featured caricatures of Jewish men collecting the blood of German children to make unleavened bread, and claimed that the history of the Jews was 'an unbroken chain of mass murders and bloodbaths'. After protests both from outside Germany and from Christians within the country the edition was eventually banned. But none of this prevented *Der Stürmer* from publishing still more grotesque lies about the Jews in subsequent editions.[21]

It is hard to read *Der Stürmer* today without thinking that the man behind it, Julius Streicher, possessed a sick mind. Even his own defence lawyers at the Nuremberg war trials after the war suspected this was the case. But after an examination by a panel of psychiatric experts he was proclaimed sane enough to participate – although they determined that he suffered from a 'neurotic obsession' and possessed the 'lowest IQ' of any of the prisoners at Nuremberg. Even in his prison cell he continued to spout anti-Semitic hatred, telling the American psychologist Dr Gustave Gilbert that he was 'the only one in the world who clearly saw the Jewish menace as an historical problem'.[22]

Underpinning all this hatred lay the terrible reality of the concentration camps, but even here – at least during the 1930s – attempts were made to 're-educate' many of the inmates. And in order to understand how, for the Nazis, terror went hand in hand with a desire to reshape minds, we need to remember that the camps of this period weren't yet the factories of death that were to come during the Holocaust and nor did they contain predominantly Jews.[23] Most of the inmates in the early years of Nazi power were their political opponents.

While the regime in the camps was brutal and a minority of prisoners were murdered, most were eventually released back into German society, normally after about eighteen months of incarceration. It was thus in the SS guards' own interests to try and 're-educate' the prisoners in their charge, many of whom were socialists or communists. Cruel methods were often used to break their spirit – inmates could be starved or whipped or beaten with fists. But a number of the other techniques the SS employed were more psychologically sophisticated. One was the indeterminate nature of the sentence. No one sent to a concentration camp knew how long they would be held. They might be released the next day, or never at all. Because they had been sent to the camp for their 'own protection' it was entirely up to their captors how long they stayed. 'The uncertainty of the duration of their confinement was something with which they could never come to terms,' said one SS officer who worked at Dachau. 'It was this that wore them down and broke the strongest wills.'[24]

Alongside 'breaking wills' the SS tried other methods of remoulding those they thought reclaimable as citizens of the new Germany. A prisoner at Börgermoor concentration camp, in the north-west of the country, revealed one technique the SS used in an attempt to convert the inmates. On Christmas Eve, at the start of Hitler's Chancellorship, the commandant of the camp spoke 'with feeling' to the prisoners, after they had been told to sing a Christmas carol that has a special place in German culture – 'Stille Nacht, heilige Nacht' (Silent Night, Holy Night).

'You are not bad people,' said the commandant, 'you are not sub-human.' And even if this Christmas was bad, 'the hour of freedom will come for you too! Then help build our great, new German fatherland. Give willing allegiance to our wonderful People's Chancellor and Führer Adolf Hitler, who also fights for your happiness, for your future and who is now safely standing under the tree of lights and thinking of his people . . . To be German means to be a National Socialist. With this in mind, we are celebrating the first National Socialist Christmas.'[25]

It was an obvious attempt to use the emotion of Christmas to make the prisoners think of the Nazis as 'Us' rather than 'Them', and to use their collective sense of 'Germanness' to create 'faith' in Adolf Hitler.

Some Germans, of course, were harder to convert into National Socialists than others. That was especially the case with Jehovah's Witnesses. Their passionate faith in God Almighty, combined with their overt pacifism, meant that the Nazis considered them a direct threat.

The Witnesses were unique among the groups targeted by the Nazis. If they renounced their faith they had a chance of immediate release. Yet many chose to endure horrific abuse sooner than take that step. Always at risk of arrest from the moment Hitler came to power, they found their jeopardy increased still further by an order issued in May 1937. From this point onward they could be imprisoned in a concentration camp if they were merely suspected of opposing the regime.

The same prisoner who experienced Christmas at Börgermoor camp described how the SS tried to break the will of one Jehovah's Witness. He was a man of about forty who 'gave everyone a friendly look' and 'tirelessly swept the cell and the corridor, fetched water and made himself useful to everyone'. But he refused to raise his arm and say 'Heil Hitler' in greeting because he believed that God had told him not to.

For this offence against regulations, he was taken to the punishment block and beaten. After his return the other prisoners tried to get him to say 'Heil Hitler' by reassuring him that when they greeted the guards that way they were 'just pretending'. But he still refused. So he was taken outside by SS guards and battered unconscious until his 'blood froze' on the hard ground. But even after he came round, he still would not raise his arm and say 'Heil Hitler'. He was then thrown into a cell along with 'career criminals' and made to carry the 'toilet bucket at a run'. His life now alternated 'between arrest, beatings and toilet cleaning'. The SS guards enjoyed tormenting him and made bets with each other on whether he would eventually crack. When after 'many weeks' of this torture he was sent back to his original barracks, his fellow inmates saw him raise his arm 'awkwardly' when he passed an SS man. His 'blood-caked hand' stretched out and he finally whispered 'Heil Hitler!'[26]

Mistreatment of Jehovah's Witnesses occurred at other camps. At a post-war trial of members of the SS who worked at Sachsenhausen concentration camp outside Berlin, the court was told that a Witness had been buried up to his neck and then two SS men had urinated on his head. He was left buried for an hour before he was released.[27]

But the relationship between the SS and Jehovah's Witnesses was not just one of contemptuous oppression. The SS also envied the fanaticism of the Witnesses. Rudolf Höss, later commandant at Auschwitz, was 'deeply moved' by the way two Witnesses behaved when sentenced to death at Sachsenhausen. When they were told of their fate 'they went almost mad for joy and ecstasy and could hardly wait for the day of execution.' Taken out to be shot, 'they wished on no account to be bound, for they desired to be able to raise their hands to Jehovah. Transformed by ecstasy, they stood in front of the wooden wall of the rifle range, seemingly no longer of this world.'[28]

It wasn't only Rudolf Höss who was impressed by the absolute commitment of the Witnesses. Both Heinrich Himmler and Theodor Eicke, commandant of Dachau, were as well. They proclaimed that 'SS men must have the same fanatical and unshakeable faith in the National Socialist ideal and in Adolf Hitler that the Witnesses had in Jehovah. Only when all SS men believed as fanatically in their own philosophy would Adolf Hitler's state be permanently secure.'[29]

While it was a remark that illustrated how much the leadership of the SS understood that they were running a faith-based organization, it also brought to the surface a fundamental problem Himmler faced in constructing the mentality he required of an SS man. On the one hand he wanted everyone in the SS to believe as 'fanatically' as Jehovah's Witnesses did, but on the other he had to construct an alternative belief system for them to feel 'fanatically' about. That was no easy task, especially given that Hitler was not willing to declare outright war on Christianity. Even though Himmler believed that 'Christian doctrine has been responsible for the destruction of every nation,' Hitler had forced him to say publicly that 'he valued highly peaceful relations between state and church.'[30]

Himmler's stance was made even more complicated by the fact that he despised atheists. He preferred that each member of the SS declare that they were 'believers in God' (*Gottgläubigen*) – rather than believers in the doctrine of Christianity. His challenge was thus to formulate a belief system which included 'God', but which ignored more than a thousand years of Germanic Christian culture. He attempted to do this by reaching back to the beliefs of the Teutons, a German tribe who had fought the Romans in pre-Christian times. In the process he adapted a hotchpotch of ideas, including a form of ancestor worship based on racial superiority.

Himmler was acutely conscious of the need to develop rituals that replaced the often deeply felt ceremonies of the Christian faith. Psychologists have long recognized, for example, that funerals are fundamental to the human psyche because of the need to process grief.[31] And even though he would have been unaware of the psychological research that underpinned his actions, Himmler spent time devising ceremonies by which members of the SS could exit this world. In the preface to a booklet entitled *Suggestions on How to Conduct a Funeral* he outlined his philosophy: 'The meaning of all dying is in life: mothers suffer death in order to give life to children; countless fighters and soldiers have died so that our nation [*Volk*] could live. In previous times, our ancestors passed away in peace when they knew that the fruits of their labour and difficulties were in good hands with their children and grandchildren. For us, there is no fright at death. It is a great and sacred event that is filled with meaning by life and its laws. The individual dies, but in his children, his nation rises above him in his own time. But since we love the future of our nation's life more than ourselves, we freely and bravely consent to death wherever necessary.'[32]

The funeral itself, Himmler thought, should be of an 'uplifting' and 'heroic nature', a ceremony that would be 'memorable' and 'powerful' for the relatives. The booklet specified that 'the decoration of the room' should be 'light and bright' to create a 'festive mood'. Furthermore 'plant arrangements must not be of foreign origin – especially no palms! Plastic flowers and other artificial means of decoration are not part of our ceremonies.' Himmler's pernickety ideas even extended to the type of coffin to be used. In 1936 he complained in a speech to SS leaders about the use of 'terribly tasteless and unstylish, factory-made coffins with hideous cast-iron fittings which are an insult to every eye and also to the dead'. Consequently, he instructed an SS major to 'make designs [of SS coffins] that are truly simple and plain and still beautiful without this over-ornate, foolish and silly pomp of the 1870s to 1890s, this peak of bad taste'.[33]

Himmler's suggestions for the content of the valediction were also revealing: 'No one knows how long a single oak tree will stand . . . But that's not what is crucial, for we know that oak as a species, as a genus will continue to exist . . . the age of a person can also not be determined in advance, but we know and believe that our species will continue to exist in the eternal life of our nation [*Volk*] . . . The individual may die, but the life that bore him, the life of his tribe, of his nation, stays. And in realizing this, we not only understand how this is a kind of immortality, but we also receive meaning and purpose.'[34]

It was the ultimate racial vision of the 'in-group'. You belonged to your 'tribe' even after death through the 'purity' of your offspring. It was a straightforward idea that was easily internalized by members of the SS. In an essay he wrote which is contained in his personal file, SS man Joseph Altrogge talked of the 'holy obligation' he and his comrades should feel to 'keep our blood pure and pass it on to our children and grandchildren'. As long as they did this, they had the chance to become 'truly immortal'. In a corruption of the Christian idea of the 'Trinity', Altrogge wrote that by propagating racially pure offspring, 'one day the objective – the Trinity of the Reich, the *Volk* [the People] and the Faith – will be accomplished.'[35]

No wonder, then, that Johannes Hassebroek, commandant of Gross-Rosen concentration camp, told an interviewer after the war that 'I was full of gratitude to the SS for the intellectual guidance it gave me. We were all thankful. Many of us had been so bewildered before joining the organization. We did not understand what was happening around us, everything was so mixed up. The SS offered us a series of simple ideas that we could understand, and we believed in them.'[36]

This didn't mean that Himmler was only interested in 'simple' people joining the SS. Far from it. Some of the cleverest young men in Germany became members, many serving in the SD, the section of the organization run by Reinhard Heydrich. Two of the most notorious were Franz Six and Otto Ohlendorf, who both went on to command Einsatzgruppen murder squads during the war.

The backgrounds of these killers might seem incongruous. Six gained a doctorate from the University of Heidelberg and by the mid-1930s was a professor of journalism at the University of Königsberg. Ohlendorf received his doctorate in jurisprudence from the University of Pavia in Italy and later became a specialist in economics. But they had more than their academic achievements in common: both had been too young to fight in the First World War, though old enough to have vivid memories of the conflict; both were committed to the Nazi cause as young men and had joined the party before Hitler came to power; and both devoted their intellectual gifts to Heydrich's SD during the 1930s.

Even though they would end up as murderers in the killing fields of the east, we need to remember that Ohlendorf and Six were originally selected for the SD in large part because of their intellectual gifts. They were certainly not ignorant thugs with an obvious capacity to kill. Ohlendorf was specifically told by Professor Reinhard Höhn, who acted as an academic talent spotter for the SD, that Heydrich's unit 'needed critical intellects like his'.[37]

Ohlendorf was excited by the challenge of creating a new Germany based on Nazi principles. And he believed there was much to put right. At his post-war trial he claimed that he had become a Nazi because of the 'spiritual, religious and social disintegration' that his generation experienced in the years before Hitler became Chancellor. It was a time when 'Thirty or more parties were fighting for state power' and the 'social future was hopeless'.[38]

But it is also important to recognize that Otto Ohlendorf and Franz Six were not conventional intellectuals. Unlike normal scholars who feel able to debate a variety of theories with their colleagues, Ohlendorf, Six and the other Nazi intellectuals saw everything through one prism – race. If you weren't a racist then you were not part of their club. In that respect they were faith-based intellectuals, as unwilling to question the validity of their racial beliefs as a fanatical Christian is the existence of God.

In proclaiming the centrality of race to the human experience they were, of course, aping their leader, Adolf Hitler. Writing in *Mein Kampf* back in 1924, Hitler had expressed his racist beliefs in extreme terms: 'In the blood alone resides the strength as well as the weakness of man . . . Without the clearest knowledge of the racial problem and hence of the Jewish problem there will never be a resurrection of the German nation. The racial question gives the key not only to world history, but to all human culture.'[39]

Nazi intellectuals found scholarly confirmation for their racist beliefs in the work of academics. Professor Hans Günther, for instance, preached of the glories of the 'Nordic race', claiming that 'if an illustrator, painter or sculptor wants to represent the image of a bold, goal-determined, resolute person, or of a noble, superior and heroic human being, man or woman, he will in most cases create an image which more or less approximates the image of the Nordic race.' That explained, said Günther, why 'the relatively great number of Nordic people among the famous and outstanding men and women of all Western countries is striking'.[40]

Warped theories like this were, to the intellectuals of the SS, inspiring insights, especially since they considered themselves members of this 'noble, superior and heroic Nordic race'. But they also knew they couldn't just sit back and bask in their superiority, because they felt they were under demographic threat – chiefly from the Slavic states to the east. As Werner Conze, later appointed a professor at the Reich University in Posen and an esteemed historian in post-war Germany, put it just before the Second World War: 'In large areas of eastern Central Europe, rural overpopulation is one of the most serious social and political problems of the present day.'[41]

This would prove to be a crucial building block in the thinking of many of the perpetrators of the Holocaust. Their starting point was that Germans were a nation of victims. The loss of the First World War and the suffering in the years immediately afterwards had been the consequence of betrayal by internal enemies – many of whom were not truly German – and the perfidious behaviour of other nations. As if that wasn't bad enough, in the years since the end of the war Germany had been threatened with racial annihilation by the increase in the Slavic population to the east. It was a situation the Jews, who controlled Bolshevism, had helped orchestrate.

It followed that those charged with the epic task of righting this wrong felt in no way responsible for the original cause. Rather they were the solution to a problem not of their making. All of this was lies, of course, but if you accepted the lies which underpinned this argument as truth, and took the rest as articles of faith, it had a kind of coherence.

Nazi intellectuals like Ohlendorf and Six believed they were taking part in a quest to create a utopia – a wonderful new world in which all racially pure Germans would live a life in the sunlight. The fact that creating this paradise would involve inflicting suffering on millions of others was understood, but their racism meant that they accepted this as a necessary consequence of the 'natural' order of things.

The Nazis were also helped by their belief that they were radical thinkers – the only people who were prepared to face up to the realities of this world, however brutal those realities were. It followed that the majority of these Nazi intellectuals were never content to just sit behind a desk. They were activists, in a hurry to get things done.[42]

It is not surprising that what they respected in the British, beyond the fact that they were mostly of an acceptable race, was the aggressive way they had pursued their goals. Hermann Göring told the British ambassador to Berlin, Sir Nevile Henderson, that the British 'he really admired were those whom he described as the pirates, such as Francis Drake, and he reproached us for having become too "debrutalised"'.[43] This idea that the British had lost something precious since the time of Drake was developed further by the poet and literary author Hermann Burte, who argued in a speech in 1940 that Shakespeare belonged to the Germans just as much as to the English. He claimed that the Nazi regime was closer to the 'spirit' of Elizabethan England than the British were, because the

Nazis had fully embraced Shakespeare's rejection of Shylock, the Jewish moneylender of *The Merchant of Venice*.[44]

The buccaneering spirit so prized by the regime generated enormous excitement in many of these Nazi intellectuals about the limitless possibilities ahead. If you believed that the strongest could take whatever they wanted, then you could embark on a new age of piracy. The only precondition for success was to ensure that you were stronger than your enemies.

The Nazis' quasi-Darwinian struggle for supremacy was not just directed at those living outside Germany's borders or confined to internal enemies such as communists or Jews. It was fought out within the regime itself. Dr Günter Lohse, who started work at the German Foreign Office in the mid-1930s, remembered that much of his time was spent battling rival departments within government. His regular opponent was Goebbels' Propaganda Ministry. There was a fight, for instance, over the wording on the stamp that he used when censoring foreign newspapers. Once he had checked a foreign article, he stamped it 'Passed by the Foreign Office Press Department', but after a fierce battle and objections from Goebbels' staff the wording was changed to 'No reservations, Foreign Office Press Department'. Lohse felt 'the subtle difference was earth-shattering' and he remembered that 'there were grotesque situations like that almost every day, in the smallest daily tasks.'

Lohse believed that the fundamental reason for all this infighting was 'the struggle for good standing with the Führer' – a conflict that was exacerbated by the fact that Hitler 'liked to give two people the same or closely related tasks' and then was loath to arbitrate between them when disputes occurred. As a result, normal bureaucratic structures fractured and split under the strain.

What mattered was not your official title but how close you were to Hitler. According to Lohse, party officials 'would refer to the Führer's decisions, to something the Führer had said', and this would then be reported as 'the will of the Führer', although 'it was really questionable' whether Hitler had actually said what was claimed or had intended a casual remark to be acted upon.[45]

An added complication was Hitler's belief in his own genius. He was the opposite to most leaders, who seek to consult with their comrades before deciding on the way forward. So much so that he didn't just avoid discussing policy, on occasion he actively tried not to know what other leading Nazis were thinking. On 5 June 1935, for example, his adjutant Fritz Wiedemann returned a document to Martin Bormann, Hitler's secretary, with a note that said 'The Führer had this document in his hands but then returned it to me immediately unread. At the next party rally he wants to give a big speech on this question and so doesn't want to be influenced in his views by others.'[46]

All this meant that the administrative system was clogged up in unexpected ways. 'If the Führer introduced a new instruction,' said Lohse, 'because of a new idea or something, then, you could almost say, Parkinson's law came into effect. Everyone made an institution out of the instruction. And these institutions grew and grew and grew.' While Lohse and his colleagues were clear on Hitler's overall vision – 'the Germanic race has to be the dominant one, at least in Europe', and that it was necessary 'to free the world of Bolshevism' – it was difficult to imagine how all this structural confusion could help bring about the desired end.[47]

What this method of government did do was to create immense dynamism. That's because everyone knew that Hitler prized radical thinking, and so the way to get his attention was to come up with a radical solution to any problem. Hitler didn't necessarily adopt the suggestion, but he was likely to admire the person who made it. This partly explains the rise to prominence of Joachim von Ribbentrop, who became Nazi Foreign Minister in 1938. He specialized in parroting back to Hitler views he knew his Führer already held, and then adding his own radical twist. Ribbentrop was despised by many other leading Nazis who considered him pompous and stupid, but despite his many personal shortcomings he possessed one priceless talent. He knew how to manage his boss.[48]

The Nazis' conviction that life was a constant battle penetrated every public sphere – medicine in particular. Doctors were called upon – in an utter corruption of their Hippocratic ideals – to serve the state more than their patients. As a result the medical profession was primed to play an important part in the psychological conditioning that led to the Holocaust.

The starting point, predictably, was race and the belief that the worth of a human being should be determined by the extent of their contribution to the 'national community'. While the first precondition of usefulness – predictably – was racial composition, even those who passed this racial test could still be targeted if it was thought they didn't measure up in other ways. Most insidious of all was the Nazi belief that selected categories of the disabled posed a potential threat.

Not all the disabled were assessed equally. The largest category of disabled in Germany were veterans of the First World War, and the Nazis professed to treat them as heroes who had sacrificed themselves for their country. In July 1934 a law was passed which gave these disabled war veterans a special pension. Hanns Oberlindober, head of the NSKOV, the organization charged with overseeing veterans' interests, praised the new legislation as an important victory in the 'fight for the honour of the German soldier'.[49]

The rest of the disabled were more vulnerable to mistreatment – and had been so even before the Nazis came to power. Around 30 per cent of the population of German asylums – just over 140,000 people – died during the First World War. This appalling mortality rate was primarily the consequence of a wartime environment in which care of the mentally ill ceased to be a priority.

Against that background, in 1920 a book was published in Germany which suggested a radical answer to the 'problem' of the disabled. The suggested solution was evident from the title: *Die Freigabe der Vernichtung lebensunwerten Lebens* (Allowing the Destruction of Worthless Life). The work was a collaboration between two academics, Professor Karl Binding, a prominent legal thinker, and Professor Alfred Hoche, a psychiatrist. Split into two sections, with Binding focused on the 'judicial' justification for killing the severely disabled and Hoche providing 'medical comment', the book expressed the authors' views in candid terms. 'We will never cease to treat as best we can the physically and mentally ill,' wrote Hoche, 'as long as there is any prospect that we can change their condition for the better; but we may one day mature into the view that the elimination of those who are mentally completely dead is not a crime, nor an immoral act, nor emotional cruelty, but a permissible and beneficial act.'[50]

Hoche recognized that doctors had to wrestle with 'enormously complicated' ethical questions but argued that there was no 'absolute' requirement to 'preserve the life of others under all circumstances'. A doctor only had a 'relative' duty to save life, and this could change once circumstances were 're-examined'. Keeping alive people who were incurably ill could be a 'torture' for them and was just as wrong as repeatedly keeping awake 'a healthy person who was tired'. But lest anyone think that Hoche was arguing for medically sanctioned killing purely out of compassion, he also pointed out the cost savings to asylums if doctors eliminated their severely mentally disabled patients.[51]

Binding and Hoche's book stimulated a debate which rumbled on through the 1920s with passionate advocates on either side. Meanwhile the crisis in the care of the disabled worsened during the early Weimar years and deteriorated still further once the depression hit. But while killing selected disabled patients remained a step too far, another less dramatic solution began to find favour – sterilization.

This was not a policy in which Germany was a pioneer. Several states in America had already adopted a policy of compulsorily sterilizing selected mentally and physically disabled people. So it was in that context that German doctors debated whether sterilization was an ethical option.

It was obvious that sterilizing the disabled in asylums would not accomplish much, since those confined in secure hospitals were not likely to reproduce. But, equally, sterilizing selected Germans within the general population would be a radical move. Where would the line be drawn? Exactly who would be forcibly sterilized?

At a conference in Bavaria in 1931, Professor Oswald Bumke made a prophetic contribution to the debate. While he recognized that sterilizing some of those with mental illness might prevent the suffering of future generations, he warned against taking this action just in order to save money as the 'logical conclusion' would be that 'one should do away with all those people who at the time seem dispensable for financial reasons.' Bumke also cautioned against sterilizing people using purely racial criteria.[52]

But there were plenty of medical professionals in Germany who took a different view. Professor Hans Luxenburger, a leading psychiatrist, said that doctors should become 'the executors of the eugenic will of the nation' and in 1932 he proposed that the law should allow people to be sterilized for eugenic reasons.[53] Hitler agreed, and the following year, six months after he became Chancellor, the Law for the Prevention of Hereditarily Diseased Offspring was passed.

The law was based on a draft that the Prussian government had composed the year before, but all elements of consent were now dropped. Moreover the new legislation didn't just apply to Germans who were suffering from mental illnesses such as schizophrenia, but also encompassed those who were suffering from hereditary blindness or deafness or any severe hereditary deformity. It even included those who were alcoholics.

Not only did this give medical professionals enormous power; it changed the nature of their jobs. Doctors now had to balance the care of the individual alongside the perceived welfare of the state. They no longer had to abide by moral strictures which forbade them to cause harm to their patients – they could now cause them immense harm if they thought the state would benefit. Their task, according to Gerhard Wagner, the pre-eminent Nazi doctor, was the 'promotion and perfection of the health of the German people . . . to ensure that the people realise the full potential of the racial and genetic endowment'.[54]

It was a seismic change in outlook. Yet there was little protest from within the medical profession. Why was this so? How could doctors who were trained to protect patients be so easily corrupted? A clue to the answer is found in one key statistic. Around half of all the doctors in Germany voluntarily became members of the Nazi Party before Hitler came to power. This was a far greater proportion than in any other profession.

A 2012 study conducted by researchers across the disciplines of psychiatry, psychology, law and political science investigated the reasons why such a large number of doctors found Nazism so attractive.[55] Some of their conclusions are already familiar to us: the idea that Nazi ideology was itself a pseudo-science and thus potentially attractive to medical professionals; the effect of the savagery of the First World War on doctors – almost 25,000 of whom had fought for their country and nearly one in ten died in combat. This led one researcher to conclude that many German doctors 'became brutalized by the slaughter'. As a result, they had a tendency after the war to be 'practical and technical physicians, lacking in human compassion'.

A further possible reason why so many became Nazis builds on another phenomenon we encountered earlier – the psychological pressure to conform. But the researchers concluded that with doctors this tendency was exacerbated by the rigid nature of their training, which emphasized 'obedience to authority'.

In addition, doctors were likely influenced by a motivation that has existed throughout history – economic self-interest. It was obvious that if the Nazis came to power Jewish doctors risked losing their jobs, and that meant more career opportunities for 'Aryan' doctors. Moreover, during the Weimar years medical salaries had been relatively meagre and there was considerable unemployment in the profession. A Nazi regime promised not just to eliminate those problems but to raise the status of doctors. Their profession was now pre-eminent, and many were no doubt inspired by the words of Rudolf Hess, the Deputy Führer, who declared in 1934 that 'National Socialism is nothing but applied biology.'[56]

Just as Nazi intellectuals were excited by the seemingly limitless opportunities ahead, so were many medical researchers. The destruction of the injunction 'first cause no harm' opened up the possibility of medical research unhindered by traditional ethical considerations. In the future there might even be the chance to reshape the racial composition of Germany. Was that not a more thrilling prospect than merely treating individual patients?

All these factors contributed to the decision made by large numbers of doctors to join the Nazi Party – and not just the Nazi Party. More doctors also joined the SS than members of any other single profession, and many of these medical professionals would go on to play an important part in the murders of the Holocaust.

Few people could have imagined, when the sterilization law was passed in 1933, that German doctors had begun their journey to mass killing, especially since no other country which had adopted similar measures followed the same path. But nowhere else did the leader of the country have a secret agenda in mind from the very beginning – the murder of selected disabled citizens. Hitler explicitly said as much in private in 1935, although he accepted that it would be best to pursue such a policy only during wartime.[57]

There was a major propaganda effort during the 1930s to prepare the way for more radical measures to be taken against the disabled. One device was to allow thousands of Germans to visit mental asylums and witness the patients for themselves. The Nazi activist Bruno Hähnel saw conditions at the mental hospital at Aplerbeck near Dortmund and was appalled: 'The most shocking thing, that never left me, and which I saw in front of my eyes again and again, was the ward with the schizophrenics. It was a room in which there were, let's say, forty cots, not really beds, but simply wooden planks. And on these forty beds lay naked emaciated people . . . and the professor said that this was the final stage of schizophrenia and that the disease could attack any of us tomorrow, through some kind of mutation in the brain. This really worried me terribly, that this could really happen, and more than anything else I came away from this room with the understanding that the right thing to do was to kill people who are in such a state, not keep them alive, not like the way that the Christian Church teaches that each person is valuable . . . in my view the lives of such people were no longer worth living. That's what I took away from this ward.'[58] Many other Germans went on similar visits – one institution in Bavaria received over 20,000 visitors between 1933 and 1939.[59] It was one of the most dramatic examples of the regime's attempt to reinforce a sense of 'Them and Us'.

Part of the reason so many Germans were shocked at the sight of the mentally ill was the conditions in which the patients were kept. Bruno Hähnel was horrified to see 'naked emaciated people' in Aplerbeck mental hospital and concluded that this was a result of their illness. But it was at least as much a symptom of the lack of care they received. Ensuring budgets were adequate for such institutions was not a priority for the regime, and underfunding had the added advantage of creating the very environment in mental hospitals that confirmed the Nazis' pre-existing prejudices about the mentally ill. They were perceived as 'life unworthy of life' in part because the regime had forced them to live the way they did. The Nazis would later practise a similar type of deception as they escalated their persecution of the Jews.

The regime didn't just organize visits to asylums; propaganda films proclaimed that this was a problem that urgently needed a solution. In 1937 the documentary film *Opfer der Vergangenheit* (Victims of the Past) asked why the mentally ill were 'living in palaces' while 'normal people' had to make do with 'hovels'. The answer, said the film's commentary, was because the 'laws of natural selection' had been disregarded by successive governments. As a result 'our race' was marching to 'its destruction'. Significantly, given that this was unsubtle propaganda of the sort Goebbels disliked, the film was commissioned not by his ministry but by Dr Gerhard Wagner, the Reich Health Leader. The conclusion of the film – which was shown in every cinema in Germany – could not have been more explicit: 'By humanely terminating their wretched and helpless lives, we shall be observing our Creator's law of natural selection and order.'[60]

It is important to note the reference to the 'Creator' in the last line of the commentary. It's an example of the continuing care with which the regime approached the church. The word 'Creator' was deliberately ambiguous. Those Nazis who were committed Christians could see it as synonymous with the Christian God, and those SS who were 'God Believers' could think it referred to the ancient Germanic beliefs that Himmler proselytized. Hitler spoke in the same ambiguous terms in his public pronouncements. In one speech in March 1936 he referred to the guiding force of 'providence' in his life, saying 'I follow the path assigned to me by providence with the instinctive sureness of a sleepwalker.'[61] But he never explained who or what providence actually was.

Hitler, to many Germans, began to assume a quasi-religious aura himself. Sir Nevile Henderson, British ambassador to Berlin during the late 1930s, concluded that 'though God might still be worshipped' in Germany, 'He must be a purely German one, to whom Hitler was so closely allied as to be barely distinguishable from the Deity himself.'[62]

Letters were sent by devoted followers to Hitler in huge numbers – so many that extra clerks had to be hired to deal with the massive amount of correspondence. The letter writers ranged from a barber who begged to be allowed to cut Hitler's hair[63] to an entrepreneur who wanted approval to market a 'Hitler cigarette',[64] from proud parents who sent a photo of their ten-month-old daughter who was already able to 'greet' a photo of her 'Führer with a Heil Hitler!'[65] to a teacher who wanted to take her class to Berlin because 'none of my girls have ever seen you yet, my Führer, and you cannot even imagine how great the desire of every girl is to see you at least once.'[66]

There was even correspondence from religious devotees. A sister in the Order of St Francis wrote to Hitler saying that '*Mein Kampf* has bewitched me!' She asked him to send her a personal copy of the book as 'our income is barely enough to live on.' As a thank-you, she promised to educate 'the teenage girls entrusted to me as a teacher' in a 'national way' and would 'pray on a daily basis for many blessings and the success of your beautiful task'.[67]

This nun was clearly entranced by Hitler. But the church as a whole was less enthralled. The Nazi regime had signed the Reichskonkordat with the Catholic church in July 1933, a treaty which purported to

guarantee the rights of the church in Germany in exchange for a promise that priests would keep out of politics. But the clerics were right to
be wary of the deal, as the regime mounted a series of attacks on the
church after the treaty had been signed.

While there was no denunciation of the institution as a whole – that
risked alienating Nazis who were Catholics – Heydrich and Himmler
focused on exposing alleged 'perverted' priests. In 1934 Heydrich even
recruited Albert Hartl, a Catholic priest, into the SD to help with the
task. Hartl had joined the Nazi Party the year before and later left the
priesthood after he had informed on one of his religious colleagues.

Alongside this attempt to destabilize the church by accusing selected
priests of sexual misconduct, Goebbels orchestrated a propaganda
campaign, warning parents of the danger of sending their children
to religious schools. Who knew how the priests might treat their
progeny?

These attacks coincided with a more proactive approach to others
who were considered a threat. By 1935 the vast majority of those who
had been imprisoned in 'protective custody' in the concentration camps
had been released. But Heydrich didn't see this as the end of oppression –
quite the reverse. In 1935 he wrote a series of revealing articles detailing
the way forward, published as a book the following year called *Transformations of Our Struggle*.[68]

Heydrich warned against believing that all 'enemy organizations'
had been crushed, since 'the driving forces of the enemy stay the same
eternally: world Jewry, world Freemasonry and a large number of political priests who abuse their denominations . . . their objective remains
the destruction of our *Volk* . . .' He claimed that 'the struggle has become
deeper' as the enemy was 'sitting in all branches of our *Volk*'s life and
within the state structure'. It would take 'years of bitter struggle finally
to push back the enemy in all areas, to destroy them, and to secure Germany both physically and spiritually against new incursions'.

He was careful – as was Hitler – to assert that religious and cultural
values 'were not in danger at all', but that 'piles of documents show how
mendacious representatives of the church could be as they fought for
"domination"'. Alongside these 'mendacious' priests, the Jews remained
a constant threat since they had 'always been the mortal enemy of all
Nordic-led and racially healthy peoples'.

Heydrich divided Jews in Germany into two groups, the Zionists and the assimilated. Of the two he claimed it was the assimilated Jews who were the most dangerous, because while they uttered 'all kinds of declarations of loyalty' to the state, they still worked behind the scenes to usurp the regime. To defeat these menacing foes it was necessary for the SS – 'the ideological shock troops' of the nation – to be 'hard' even at the risk of becoming 'notorious for being uncontrolled brutes'.

Heydrich's approach was psychologically astute. His central message – that while overt enemies of the regime might have been conquered, hidden foes still remained – was impossible to disprove. If you could find no trace of these internal enemies, well, that simply showed how effect-ively they had hidden themselves. It was a false argument reminiscent of some of the most devious anti-Semitic propaganda, such as the children's book *Der Giftpilz* (The Poisonous Mushroom) published in 1938. The book warned children that 'just as it is often very difficult to tell the poi-sonous mushrooms from the edible mushrooms, it is often very difficult to recognize Jews as thieves and criminals.'[69] Therefore Jews were not just dangerous when they were an obvious threat, but potentially even more dangerous when they hid their true nature behind a duplicitous façade.

Such sentiments played into the human tendency towards negative bias. This phenomenon, demonstrated in many academic studies, is caused by the brain's predisposition to focus on negative stimuli more than positive ones.[70] For instance, we dwell more on harsh words that are spoken to us than on complimentary ones, and are hard-wired to be sensitive – in many instances over-sensitive – to potential threats. Here Heydrich activated all that anxiety but added an extra level of stress by claiming that the new threat was hidden.

This was a different psychological tactic from that employed during the same period by the leader of the Soviet Union, Joseph Stalin, and his head of secret police Lavrenti Beria. In the Soviet Union the terror was indiscriminate in a way it never was in Nazi Germany. Stalin's purges were often conducted by quota. Various party organizations were told to give up a prearranged number of 'enemies of the people'. Meetings were held so that party members could decide who among them should be 'denounced'. The pressure on those who attended these gatherings was immense: should they speak out and denounce someone else, or stay silent and risk being denounced themselves? And what exactly did you have to do to be an 'enemy of the people'? Beria's definition was not much help in deciding. He claimed that anyone who 'doubts the rightness of the party line' was an 'enemy of the people' – a description so vague that it could encompass virtually anyone.[71]

Oppression in Nazi Germany in the 1930s was not so random. Unlike Stalin's purges, army officers were not culled en masse, nor were Nazi leaders told to offer up specific numbers of allegedly unreliable members of the party. Moreover, the SD and the Gestapo were much smaller in numbers than Beria's own NKVD. For the whole of Lower Franconia in Bavaria, for example, a district of a million people, there were just twenty-eight Gestapo officers.[72] However, they did have the benefit of underlying assistance. Surveillance was often conducted by 'block wardens', Nazi supporters who kept an eye on apartment blocks or streets of houses.[73]

Pioneering work on the Gestapo in the early 1990s challenged the popular idea that the regime relied primarily on terror. Instead, it supported the notion that there was considerable support for Hitler and his policies among the German population.[74] Other historians came to agree with that judgement, with one overview, published this century, concluding that 'National Socialism did indeed gain widespread popularity during the Third Reich.'[75] This view has been challenged by others, who point out that since the Nazis outlawed free speech – it was even a crime to tell jokes about Hitler – it is difficult to talk of 'consent' at all.[76]

It is possible, however, to reconcile these different viewpoints. The key is to understand the fundamental difference between the Soviet system of oppression and the Nazi one. While the Nazi regime did keep a watch on ordinary Germans, the threat was not as arbitrary as it could be in the Soviet Union. In Nazi Germany you knew if you were in a particular group that was at risk from denunciation – for instance, if you were Jewish, a communist, a priest or a Social Democrat still openly critical of the regime.

When an 'ordinary' German like Hubert Lutz was asked if there had been a 'climate of fear' during the Third Reich, he replied 'absolutely not . . . After all, I didn't do anything they could denounce me for.'[77] It was a revealing answer. Unlike in the Soviet Union, millions of Germans felt they could rest easy in their beds as long as they professed support for the Nazi state.

★

In pursuit of their goal of the 'mobilization of the mind' one of the most vital tasks for the regime was to target the working class. Now that the Nazis had outlawed trade unions, there was a recognition that more had to be done to convince the ordinary worker to support the new Germany. The regime's answer was Kraft durch Freude (Strength through Joy), an organization that sought to improve working conditions in factories and provide after-work leisure activities.

Kraft durch Freude was part of the German Labour Front, run by one of the most corrupt Nazis of them all – Robert Ley. Yet another veteran of the First World War and an early supporter of the Nazi Party, Ley siphoned off money from the Labour Front to fund his notorious drinking and womanizing. His corruption allowed him to build a palatial estate near Waldbröl in North Rhine-Westphalia. The manor house featured a marble hall and an enormous mural featuring a naked Nazi goddess driving a chariot.[78] He was considered an incompetent drunk by many other Nazis, but Hitler always stood by him, because Ley was loyal, and that – as we've seen – was the quality Hitler prized.

Despite Ley's many weaknesses, Strength through Joy did contribute to support for the regime. Conditions in some factories improved and holidays at discounted prices were offered to workers. Wolfgang Teubert, a Nazi Stormtrooper, remembered Strength through Joy as one of the 'successes' of the 1930s: 'The factories were working again, the workshops were working again, and everything progressed. And now the workers could go on proper holidays with Strength through Joy, where they only had to contribute a fraction of the cost. They did their trips to Upper Bavaria – for example from Silesia to Upper Bavaria – where they were warmly welcomed, and suddenly they saw what a *Volksgemeinschaft* really looks like. And the next lot went to Madeira by ship, on KdF [Strength through Joy] ships. First it was with hired ones, and then with purpose-built ships to Madeira and other places, where they would never [otherwise] have got to in those days.'[79]

The opposition group New Beginning understood the part that Strength through Joy events played in convincing opponents of the regime to change their minds about the Nazis. One report, from June 1935, noted that 'A good number of former Social Democrats, communists and trade unionists with whom we talked came back from such events – especially from holiday trips which had been organized as part of the KdF – filled with enthusiasm. The trend towards the creation of a *Volksgemeinschaft* is obviously consolidated by this. In this respect, the regime is most successful in its attempt to win the "soul of the German worker".'[80]

But Strength through Joy was far from being an unalloyed success. The most prestigious scheme – the promise to provide a 'people's car' – was an abject failure. In spring 1934 Hitler had met with Dr Ferdinand Porsche, the automotive engineer, and told him that he wanted a Volkswagen built – literally a 'people's car' – that would cost less than a thousand Reichsmarks. The design also had to be capable of being altered in the future so that military vehicles could be produced rather than cars. Porsche embraced the task, and just three years later Goebbels was test-driving the new Volkswagen, commenting that 'The car has fabulous pulling power, climbs well and has excellent suspension.'[81]

Meanwhile, several hundred thousand excited Germans paid money up front to be the first owners of the new Volkswagen. But the cars were never delivered. The few hundred that were built in the late 1930s were given not to the workers but to Nazi leaders, and during the war the Volkswagen was converted into the Kübelwagen military reconnaissance vehicle.[82]

The 'people's car' was just one example of a key promise of the *Volksgemeinschaft* that was not fulfilled. There were many others. In January 1936 a Nazi report into the mood of the population in Berlin mentioned that 'moaning' was on the increase, because 'the income of wide circles of the population is still grossly disproportionate to living expenses, especially compared to the prices of important groceries which have increased considerably . . .'[83] A few weeks later in March, a report from the Prussian Secret State Police talked of how the 'small shortages' of consumer goods could be 'easily accepted if there was only general trust in the government and in the movement'. But 'it is widespread opinion that most of the higher- and middle-ranking leaders of the state and the party live in great luxury . . . The term "corruption" can be heard time and time again.'[84]

Yet that very month – March 1936 – Hitler would be fêted by millions of Germans when he ordered troops to re-enter the area of the Rhineland that had been demilitarized in the wake of Versailles. A plebiscite held at the end of March declared that 99 per cent of Germans approved of Hitler's decision. Even allowing for the social pressures on the population to conform and evidence of electoral fraud, there is little doubt that Hitler's action was widely popular.

Nothing illustrates the vagaries of the concept of the *Volksgemeinschaft* better than the contrast in March 1936 between support for Hitler over the issue of the Rhineland and the continued 'moaning' of the population about rising prices.[85] While one aspect of the *Volksgemeinschaft* was going badly, another was going well. It is a dichotomy that reveals something fundamental about the notion of 'consent' in Nazi Germany that is often forgotten. People could embrace some of the regime's policies while simultaneously being opposed to others.

It was the presence of Adolf Hitler that helped unify Germany and resolve these contradictions. The Prussian Secret State Police report of 1936 also mentioned that there was a widespread public perception that 'the Führer is surrounded by an invisible wall through which truthful reports cannot reach him any more.' The idea that Hitler was unaware of the problems the public faced – often expressed in the phrase 'If only the Führer knew' – became one of the central myths of the regime. It allowed millions of Germans to keep their faith in Hitler while 'moaning' about the corruption of other Nazi leaders.

Still, there was a huge amount of rhetoric – and not just from Goebbels' Propaganda Ministry – about how Germany was changing for the better. A manual on how to write letters, published in 1936, proclaimed that 'our new state is a state of the *Volksgemeinschaft*!' Germany was now a country where 'The performance determines the value. The little gas worker who does his work conscientiously and thoroughly is worth more than a director general who is not fitted for his post.' If you visited a government office you would find 'a human being, a national comrade [*Volksgenosse*] like you and me, with the same worries, pleasures and needs, a man with whom one can talk decently'.[86]

Books like this reveal that the *Volksgemeinschaft* existed largely in the mind. It was an emotional feeling, a psychological gift rather than an economic reward. It was about everyone feeling equally important, not the price of vegetables at the greengrocer.

Crucially, the *Volksgemeinschaft* was a statement of intention. It promised a bright new Germany awaiting all true believers, a utopian ideal to strive for rather than a practical aim that could be accomplished next month. It was, above all, a question of having faith in the future, faith in Hitler to deliver on his pledge.

In turn, this gave the concept enormous psychological power. Scientific research has demonstrated that dopamine – crudely defined as the feel-good hormone in your brain – is released as we move towards the goal we desire. As Professor Robert Sapolsky wrote, 'dopamine is more about anticipation of reward than about reward itself.' Moreover, as long as people believe their goal is achievable, they can 'delay gratification for insanely long times'.[87]

Paradoxically, it may even have helped the regime that the goal of the *Volksgemeinschaft* was never fully realized. That is because research also shows that it can be disappointing to fulfil one's ambitions.[88] Human beings, it turns out, are often happiest when they are travelling towards a goal rather than when they attain the goal itself.

Millions of Germans, fuelled by their faith in Hitler, thus continued to strive towards the goal of the *Volksgemeinschaft* – only to find it always just out of reach.

8. Valuing Enemies

The Berlin Olympic Games marked the high point of Nazi Germany on the international stage. 'One felt the effort to show the world the grandeur, the permanency, the respectability of the new regime,' wrote Sir Henry 'Chips' Channon, a strongly pro-German, British Conservative politician, in his diary on 6 August 1936. 'Certainly the Olympic Games, as they were intended, have made Berlin the rallying point, if only for a fortnight, of the grand and the chic of the earth.'[1] As the Games ended Channon gave his final verdict: 'Mankind has never staged anything so terrific, or so impressive.'[2]

All of which prompts the question – why couldn't the Nazis have stayed on this course and carried on earning plaudits for their 'grandeur' and 'respectability'? The answer reveals a great deal about the mentalities of the Nazis and the radical mind of their leader, Adolf Hitler. In particular, it tells us how they saw potential enemies everywhere.

It wasn't, of course, that everyone in 1936 perceived events in the rosy way that Channon did. Beforehand there had even been talk of a boycott, but it transpired that that was all it was – talk. Avery Brundage, the president of the American Olympic Committee, had visited Germany in 1934 to judge for himself how the regime was treating German Jews. Accompanied everywhere by representatives of the regime, he unsurprisingly heard few complaints.

Yet Brundage must have known that Jews were suffering in Nazi Germany – especially given the boycott of Jewish businesses that had taken place the previous year – but he remained unperturbed. His experience of Nazi Germany seems to have reminded him of home, as he commented that Jews were barred from joining his gentlemen's club in Chicago.[3]

Brundage's stance was all the more surprising given that the Nazi regime had been open in banning Jews from sporting organizations. 'There is no room in our German land for Jewish sports leaders, for pacifists, political Catholics, pan-Europeans and the rest,' wrote Bruno

Malitz, a senior Nazi sports official. 'They are worse than cholera and syphilis.'[4]

Insightful American diplomats were aware of the potential dangers of a German Olympics. George Messersmith, serving in Austria, wrote in a dispatch to Washington in December 1935 that 'the Games should be non-political, but the Germans have made a political matter of them and I can conceive of few things, outside of a lack of complete Anglo-French co-operation in Europe, which would be a greater misfortune for Europe than the holding of the Games in Berlin in 1936.'[5]

While serving in Berlin two years before, Messersmith had concluded that 'A psychology is being developed that the whole world is against Germany and that it lies defenceless before the world.'[6] Messersmith was perceptive – this focus on the myriad threats that the country faced was an essential part of the way the regime sought to influence the mentalities of ordinary Germans.

Now, in December 1935, Messersmith wrote that he had lost 'confidence in a good many friends' as he saw how they had fooled themselves about the way the Nazis would use the Games. He quoted the president of the Austrian Olympic Committee, who was half-Jewish and yet supported the idea of a German Olympics. When asked how he could take this position given 'none of the principles of sport and fair play' existed in Germany, he replied that 'we are not going to Berlin, but we are going to the Olympics.'[7]

The Nazis were aware that not everyone in the Olympic movement would be so amenable. So they announced that they would allow German Jews to compete – as long as they met the required standard of the German team. In 1934 they held 'Olympic training courses' for twenty-one Jews to assess if they were good enough. Predictably, it was judged that none of them were. Only one German of Jewish ancestry took part in the summer games – a fencer called Helene Mayer.[8] But even this was not what it seemed. Mayer was half-Jewish and had been living in America for several years. Blonde and statuesque, she looked 'Aryan' and even 'awkwardly' gave a Nazi salute on the podium after winning a silver medal.[9]

The 1936 Olympics are famous for the actions of one man – Jesse Owens. A black American, he won four gold medals, and in the process supposedly demolished the notion of 'Aryan' racial superiority and angered the Nazi regime. But, once again, the truth is not that simple.

Goebbels' Propaganda Ministry had issued an edict on 3 August 1936 that 'the racial point of view should not in any form be a part of the discussion of the athletic results. Special care should be exercised not to offend Negro athletes.'[10]

Far from being offended by Owens' success, the predominantly German crowd in the Olympic stadium cheered him on. Nor was it the case that Hitler snubbed Owens by refusing to shake his hand. After the first day of competition, the Nazi leader had been told by Olympic officials that he should either congratulate every winner on their success or none. It is possible – perhaps probable – that he chose not to meet with all of them in order to avoid greeting non-Aryans, but it is not the case that he singled Owens out for discourteous treatment.[11] As far as Jesse Owens was concerned, 'there was absolutely no discrimination at all.'[12]

There was another reason why the success of Jesse Owens did not offer the stark contrast between the rest of the world and Nazi Germany that is sometimes supposed. The Nazis were not the only ones committed to racial discrimination. In many southern states of America black people were persecuted. They could not visit certain theatres, sit where they liked on trains or buses or join various clubs or universities. In the 1930s, both the segregated southern states of America and Nazi Germany were, according to one scholar, 'two unapologetically racist regimes, unmatched in their pitilessness. In the early 1930s the Jews of Germany were hounded, beaten, and sometimes murdered, by mobs and by the state alike. In the same years the blacks of the American South were hounded, beaten, and sometimes murdered as well.'[13] The Nazis even looked to American racial laws in the mid-1930s for inspiration in the creation of their own anti-Semitic legislation. Roland Freisler, who would later become infamous as president of the People's Court during the war, remarked in 1934 that American racial 'jurisprudence would suit us perfectly, with one single exception', which was that in America 'the Jews, who are also of interest to us, are not reckoned among the coloureds.'[14]

No one who knows the history would claim an exact equivalence between the two systems in the 1930s, not least because there were no concentration camps in America, but the substantive point remains. If you were a black American athlete, you were familiar with racial prejudice both at home and abroad.

Nor was anti-Semitism confined to Nazi Germany. The president of the International Olympic Committee, a Belgian aristocrat, Count Henri de Baillet-Latour, wrote to Avery Brundage before the Berlin Games, saying, 'I am not personally fond of Jews and of the Jewish influence.' But he was insistent that 'I will not have them molested in any way whatsoever.'[15] Acting on that sentiment, he insisted that anti-Semitic signs be taken down at the Winter Olympics, held at Garmisch-Partenkirchen in Bavaria in February 1936.[16] Like so many at the time, his disagreement with the Nazis over their anti-Semitism was one not of principle but of practice.

Victor Klemperer, who had lost his university post in Dresden because of his Jewish heritage, found the Berlin Olympics 'odious'. He thought the world was being conned into thinking that 'one is witnessing . . . a spirit of the Third Reich, which lovingly embraces the whole world'. He saw through this lie and recognized that the vicious anti-Semitism of the regime, which had only been on pause for the duration of the Games, would return in earnest as soon as they were over.[17]

Avery Brundage always maintained that the Olympics were not about politics. But in Berlin in 1936 it was impossible to make that distinction. The influence of the regime was everywhere, from the swastika flags flying throughout Berlin to the lavish hospitality offered to visiting dignitaries. Ribbentrop, Goebbels and Göring each held parties of fabulous extravagance. 'Chips' Channon wrote that after a 'whole corps de ballet danced in the moonlight' at Göring's extravaganza, 'suddenly with no warning' the end of the vast garden 'became floodlit and a procession of white horses, donkeys, peasants, music[ians] appeared from nowhere'. No wonder 'the staggered guests wandered about dazed by such lavish hospitality.'[18]

Channon wasn't naive, he understood that the Nazis could be 'v[ery] hard and ruthless . . . when occasion demands', but he thought this was an insignificant concern when set against the dangers of communism.[19] He believed that it was 'due to Hitler' that Germany was not communist, and that England should 'wake up. You in your sloth and conceit are ignorant of the Soviet dangers and will not realise that . . . Germany is fighting our battles.'[20]

The founder of the modern Olympics, Baron Pierre de Coubertin, concluded that the Berlin Games had 'magnificently served the Olympic ideal', and Avery Brundage was pleased that he had defeated those who had wanted to boycott the Games, insisting that 'once again this great quadrennial celebration has demonstrated that it is the most effective influence toward international peace and harmony yet devised.'[21]

Hitler basked in the success of the Olympics. Germany had not just 'magnificently served the Olympic ideal' but had won more medals than any other country. The Führer's authority was unquestioned, his position on the world stage never more admired. Plenty of other dictators would have been satisfied with all this and wallowed in the glory. But not Hitler.

A hint as to why was captured on film during the hammer-throwing competition in Berlin's Olympic stadium. Leni Riefenstahl's *Olympia* contains a shot of Hitler smiling broadly. It is one of the few moments when, in public at least, he spontaneously expressed joy.[22] He was happy because Germans took gold and silver in the event, and he was likely thinking that Germans who could throw a hammer further than anyone else in the world were also Germans who could fight. That's because a future war was very much on Hitler's mind that August.

Though the vast spend on armaments had risked destabilizing the German economy, Hitler could still have decided in 1936 to alter his priorities and focus on building up the domestic economy instead. But in August 1936 – the very month in which Nazi Germany hosted the Berlin Olympics – Hitler reaffirmed his choice. His overwhelming priority remained rearmament – at whatever cost necessary.

That August, Hitler wrote a memo in which he outlined the reasons why he believed war was inevitable. While most leaders frequently commit their political views to paper, it was extremely unusual for Hitler to do so. That he did it in this case revealed a great deal about his mentality.

'Since the outbreak of the French Revolution, the world has been moving with ever increasing speed towards a new conflict,' he stated didactically at the beginning of the memorandum, 'the most extreme solution of which is called Bolshevism, whose essence and aim is solely the elimination of those strata of mankind which have hitherto provided the leadership and their replacement by worldwide Jewry.'

As an accurate political analysis it was lamentable, but it did have the benefit of clarity. Once again Hitler's conviction was on show – a crucial aspect of his appeal. To his close followers he was an intriguing combination of patriarch and intellectual superior. There was no equivocation, you knew what he believed. And if you didn't believe it yourself then you had no future in the movement.

Hitler talked in the memo of Germany's 'destiny' – which was to be 'the focal point of the Western world in face of the Bolshevik attacks'. If 'Bolshevism' triumphed it would likely lead to 'the most gruesome catastrophe . . . which has been visited on mankind since the downfall of the states of antiquity'.[23]

This was another example of Hitler's hyperbolic rhetoric. As we have seen, he often posed dramatic either/ors. Either we win or we are destroyed. It was a form of thinking that had been present from the earliest days of his political career. Remember that the declaration of the original party programme in 1920 had even ended with a promise that the leaders of the movement were prepared to 'sacrifice their very lives' to fulfil their goals.

It is easy for refined political thinkers to ridicule this approach. But it was enormously effective. Everyone wants to think that their lives matter. And how could your life matter more than if you were tasked with preventing 'the most gruesome catastrophe' since ancient times?

These were truths that George Orwell spotted instantly. In 1940, in an essay about *Mein Kampf*, he commented on the 'rigidity' of Hitler's mind and the fact that 'his world-view *doesn't* develop'. He recognized that 'Hitler could not have succeeded against his many rivals if it had not been for the attraction of his own personality . . . He is the martyr, the victim, Prometheus chained to the rock, the self-sacrificing hero who fights single-handed against impossible odds. If he were killing a mouse he would know how to make it seem like a dragon . . . Whereas Socialism, and even capitalism in a more grudging way, have said to people "I offer you a good time," Hitler has said to them "I offer you struggle, danger and death," and as a result a whole nation flings itself at his feet.'[24]

It was no accident that Hitler had seen Wagner's opera *Lohengrin* again and again. This story of a knight on a quest to protect a wrongly accused noblewoman played perfectly into his vision of the world as a stage for heroic struggle. For Hitler, life was a monumental fight – a fight against enemies that either wanted what you had or had what you wanted.

It was this that heightened Hitler's 'Them and Us' rhetoric to a level seldom seen in other dictators. Enemies were essential to his worldview;

he believed that only death could end the individual's struggle against them. Indeed, without enemies his worldview would have collapsed. He understood their profound value.

With this mentality it was inconceivable that he would have scaled back rearmament in 1936 in order to stabilize the German economy. As Professor Adam Tooze puts it: 'the idea that the Nazis could have somehow just extended the prosperity of the 1930s into some sort of peaceful VW future of modernity and satisfaction is just not on the cards for Hitler's regime. It's a fundamental misunderstanding that many people succumb to, but it's really not what's on Hitler's mind at all.'[25]

It was also clear, even as early as this memo in 1936, that Hitler cared only about winning the forthcoming struggle – not about how the Germans won: 'Nor will posterity ever ask us by what methods or by what concepts, views, etc., which are valid today, we achieved the salvation of the nations, but only *whether* we achieved it.' It didn't matter how cruel or heartless you had to be, victory was all that counted.

Moreover, by confronting 'Bolshevism' by whatever means necessary Hitler claimed that Germany would be solving not only an ideological problem but a practical one as well. Since Germany was 'overpopulated', the answer 'lies in extending the living space of our people and/or the sources of its raw materials and foodstuffs. It is the task of the political leadership one day to solve this problem.' In addition, economic issues – such as Germany's lack of raw materials – would become 'solely a *question of will*. And the National Socialist State leadership would possess the will, and also the resolution and the toughness, to solve these problems in the event of war.'

It was obvious that the Jews faced still worse persecution. Hitler wrote that he wanted the Reichstag to pass a law not only 'providing the death penalty for economic sabotage' but also 'making the whole of Jewry liable for all damage inflicted by individual specimens of this community of criminals upon the German economy, and thus upon the German people'.[26]

These words, remember, were written while much of the world was admiring Germany for the way it had staged the Berlin Olympics – the ultimate gathering for peaceful competition. What is even more significant is that the twin goals that Hitler had outlined in *Mein Kampf* – the need for Germany to expand to the east and the importance of confronting the 'Jewish problem' – were yet again on display.

This despite Hitler's public rhetoric remaining one of a desire for peace.

Among members of Hitler's immediate political circle there was broad acceptance of his aggressive intentions. Earlier in 1936, Walther Darré – the Minister for Food and Agriculture – had told officials at the Reichsnährstand, the State Food Society, that Germans would seize land in the western part of the Soviet Union, justified by the right that a 'superior people' had to 'conquer and to own the land of an inferior people'. 'Europe has been released from the paralysis of the Peace of Versailles,' he said. 'Ten years will not pass before the political landscape of Europe will again look quite different from today.'[27]

When Hitler's memo was discussed by the cabinet on 4 September 1936 there was little surprise at the contents – which were succinctly paraphrased by Göring as starting 'from the basic premise that show-down with Russia is inevitable'.[28] Goebbels was even more bullish. In February 1937 he wrote in his diary: 'In 5–6 years, he [Hitler] expects a great world conflict . . . He imagines brilliant prospects for the future. In a future battle, Germany will triumph or not go on living.'[29]

While each of these three leading Nazis – Darré, Göring and Goebbels – accepted Hitler's ambitious plans, their psychological reasons for doing so were subtly different. Göring was a hard man who had no problem in trampling over his opponents. Above all, as he wrote in 1934, he had formed the view that Hitler was 'sent to us by God to save Germany . . . There is no quality that he does not possess to the highest degree . . . For us the Führer is simply infallible in all matters political and all other issues concerning the national and social interest of the people.'[30] Twelve years later, talking to an American psychiatrist in his cell at Nuremberg, he was still parroting the line that Hitler was a 'genius'.[31]

Walther Darré was an altogether different case. Unlike Göring, he was an intellectual who was obsessed with racial theory. He whole-heartedly supported the idea of gaining more 'space' in the east via a war of aggression. To him it made not just political but intellectual sense.

Goebbels combined aspects of both. Like Göring he was a believer in Hitler's genius, and like Darré he considered himself an intellectual, but he added something else to the mix – his intense emotional feelings for Hitler, feelings which in 1926 he had described as 'love'.[32] Goebbels, unlike Göring and to a certain extent Darré, had no real constituency within the Nazi movement. He was utterly a creature of Hitler's.

There is also a curious psychological phenomenon that unites not just all three of these leading Nazis but everyone else who followed Hitler. They all waited passively for their Führer to make the strategic decisions. 'At the Führer's at noon,' wrote Goebbels in his diary in February 1939. 'He will go to the mountain now and think about his next foreign policy measures.' What these new 'measures' would be, Goebbels simply didn't know.[33]

While this certainly wasn't how democratic leaders are supposed to work – Hitler seldom, as we have seen, canvassed opinion before deciding on major issues – it wasn't the way that conventional dictators work either. That is because, far from being didactic, Hitler allowed his acolytes to take initiatives, have ideas, pursue original solutions, all in the service of his Big Idea. It was a symbiosis that created in his followers the sense that he was leading on behalf of 'all of us'.[34]

But at a level above this 'Us-ness' Hitler continued to offer something that was enormously powerful psychologically – certainty. He was capable of acting as a father-figure and triggering the feelings of a child towards its parent in the hearts of many of his supporters, most notably in his relationship with Goebbels.

Göring, in his trial testimony at Nuremberg, referred to the 'Leadership Principle', which he defined as a 'reversal' of previous governance. 'In German parliamentary procedure in the past,' he said, 'responsibility rested with the highest officials, who were responsible for carrying out the anonymous wishes of the majorities, and it was they who exercised the authority. In the Leadership Principle we sought to reverse the direction, that is, the authority existed at the top and passed downwards, while the responsibility began at the bottom and passed upwards.' Göring wholeheartedly supported this new form of government, 'because the system which previously existed, and which we called parliamentary or democratic, had brought Germany to the verge of ruin'.[35]

Hitler was well aware of the importance of projecting himself as an all-powerful father not just to his committed followers but to the broader population, once remarking that the 'broad mass' of Germans were in need of an 'idol'.[36] And though he was obviously capable of enormous cruelty – even, as he had in 1934, targeting his own supporters if necessary – he could not understand the actions of Joseph Stalin in the late 1930s, when the Soviet leader presided over mass purges of party activists and military officers. 'Stalin is probably sick in the brain,' he told Goebbels in July 1937, 'otherwise you can't explain his bloody regime.'[37]

This approach had downsides, of course. Since he had conducted no Stalinesque purge, Hitler had to rely not just on the authority of his position but on his powers of persuasion to get his way. While the Minister of War, Werner von Blomberg, was a Hitler believer[38] – his attaché claimed that 'there was hardly a trip back [from a meeting with Hitler] when he didn't praise him and said that he had a good idea'[39] – other leading military figures were less effusive. Ludwig Beck, Chief of the General Staff of the army, was immune to Hitler's supposed charisma, as was the head of the army, General Werner von Fritsch.

In the late afternoon of 5 November 1937, Hitler decided it was time to update his military commanders on his plans. At a meeting at the Reich Chancellery, attended by the heads of the army, navy and air force and by Konstantin von Neurath, the Foreign Minister, he began by announcing that the subject he was about to discuss was of immense importance and that 'in the event of his death' the contents of the meeting should be taken as 'his last will and testament'.

For the military leaders, this all came as a shock. They had expected the meeting to be about resolving a squabble over the allocation of raw materials. But now Hitler was suggesting something momentous. He stated that his overall 'aim' was 'to make secure and to preserve the racial community [*Volksmasse*] and to enlarge it. It was therefore a question of space.'[40] While this was an ambition that he had mentioned to German generals within days of becoming Chancellor in 1933,[41] it had now moved from a goal that might be accomplished in the distant future to one that would be achieved within a few years. In a chilling message that would have murderous repercussions, Hitler said that 'It is not a matter of acquiring population but of gaining space for agricultural use. Moreover, areas producing raw materials can be more usefully sought in Europe in immediate proximity to the Reich than overseas . . . Germany's problem could only be solved by means of force and this was never without attendant risk.' Hitler declared that he would 'solve Germany's problem of space' at the 'latest by 1943–45'. The first stage towards this goal was to move against the Czechs and the Austrians. He did not, on this occasion, make any mention of the Soviet Union.

The minutes of the meeting reveal that both Field Marshal Blomberg and General Fritsch were worried that these aggressive actions might result in Britain and France declaring war on Germany. Fritsch was so spooked that he told Hitler he thought he ought to cancel the holiday he had planned that was due to start in a few days' time. Hitler reassured him that wasn't necessary as the forthcoming 'conflict' was not so imminent.

Blomberg's and Fritsch's concern was understandable. Both had fought in the First World War and had no desire to fight the British and French in western Europe once again – at least not until they thought Germany had a good chance of winning. Hitler tried to reassure them that Britain and France were unlikely to cause a problem. But his arguments were not convincing. His plan was obviously one that involved immense jeopardy.

Ludwig Beck, Chief of the Army General Staff, was informed of the meeting a few days later and captured on paper his views on Hitler's plans. It was a wholly negative appraisal, and in understated terms he dismissed as 'little thought through' the idea of solving Germany's economic problems by an expansion of living space. Instead of refusing to participate in the world economy, Germany ought to trade with others – otherwise 'the German people would slowly waste away.'[42] Moreover, like Fritsch and Blomberg, he warned that it was dangerous to underestimate French and British opposition to Hitler's plans.

Matters now took a dramatic turn. In a matter of weeks both Blomberg and Fritsch were removed from office. But this was not, in the manner of Joseph Stalin's 'bloody regime', a series of night-time arrests followed by torture and execution. Blomberg and Fritsch exited the scene in a much less violent way, and their removal was partly occasioned by happenstance.

Blomberg, a widower of fifty-nine, married a secretary in her mid-twenties on 12 January 1938, with both Hitler and Göring attending the wedding. Shortly afterwards Göring learnt that Blomberg's young wife had posed for pornographic pictures. She was also, as testimony at the Nuremberg trials after the war revealed, 'registered as a prostitute in the files of seven large German cities'.[43] In the status-conscious world that German aristocratic officers inhabited, the idea that one of their own had married such a woman was an outrage.

Blomberg brought this scandal on himself – no one forced him to marry a young woman with a 'past'. But that wasn't the case with what happened to General Werner von Fritsch. Shocked by the news about Blomberg, Hitler remembered that there had previously been a suggestion of a scandal involving Fritsch. Two years before, Heydrich had gathered incriminating material that alleged Fritsch had been intimate with a rent boy. The intelligence was largely based on the testimony of an infamous criminal called Otto Schmidt, and Hitler had dismissed the report back in 1936. Whether that was because he recognized that it was unreliable or because he just didn't care about Fritsch's sexuality – as for years he hadn't cared about Röhm's – is unclear. But now this old report was revisited.

At the Reich Chancellery on 26 January, with Hitler and Göring looking on, Fritsch met his accuser, Otto Schmidt. On his word of honour as a German officer, Fritsch denied all the allegations. Nonetheless, Hitler sacked him.[44] He also seized the chance to remove another dozen generals who he thought he couldn't completely trust. Almost four dozen more were shifted to jobs where they couldn't cause trouble.[45]

The next day Blomberg resigned. But, despite his plotting, Göring was deprived of the chance to take Blomberg's place. During his final meeting with Hitler, Blomberg had suggested to the German leader that he should take the job himself. Hitler agreed, even though such an appointment was bound to disrupt the chain of command given that he was now, as Minister of War, responsible to himself as Chancellor. Shortly afterwards Hitler changed the title of the job and made himself Commander-in-Chief of the armed forces instead, but the administrative muddle remained.

The days following 27 January were potentially fraught for Hitler and the Nazi leadership. As always in a dictatorship, the greatest potential threat to those in power comes from the armed forces, and now the state was without Blomberg as Minister of War and Fritsch as head of the army. Moreover, the Chief of the General Staff of the army, General Ludwig Beck, was not enamoured of the Nazi leader. So why didn't he come forward and make a concerted protest? At least one senior officer called on Beck to offer leadership in this crisis, but he declined to.

The question of Beck's mentality at this crucial moment is even more intriguing because of what was to come – six years later he would be a part of the 20 July 1944 plot to kill Hitler. But at the start of 1938 he felt he had to stay loyal. In part this was because of the circumstances surrounding the removal of Blomberg and Fritsch. Much as Beck distrusted Himmler and the SS, they could hardly have been behind Blomberg's ill-fated marriage. Nor was he in a position to judge the accuracy of the claim against Fritsch. While Fritsch had given his word of honour that there was nothing behind the sexual allegations, could Beck condemn Hitler for acting as he did? Yes, he might have behaved precipitously, before a court martial had been convened, but these were serious charges.

There was also the broader context. While he was worried that sudden action by Hitler might cause a war with the British and French, Beck nonetheless approved of the overall policy of rearmament and righting the supposed 'wrongs' of Versailles. He had also been devastated by the removal of one German head of state, the Kaiser, and was not keen to act against another.

In addition, like many who would go on to become leading figures in the resistance, Beck initially fell for the lie that Hitler was overly influenced by allegedly more sinister figures such as Himmler and Göring. But in doing so Beck was neglecting his own advice. Three years before, in a speech at the war academy, he had warned of the 'danger' that an officer faced if 'he did not reckon with things as they are, rather than with how he wished them to be'.[46]

There was another difficulty Beck had to confront: many younger officers were ideologically committed to the regime. By now, the regime's focus on indoctrinating future soldiers in the Hitler Youth was bearing fruit. When these young men joined the army they brought with them both a belief in the brilliance of Hitler and an intimate connection to the ideals of the regime.

As for middle-ranking officers, a number of them now saw a glorious future as the armed forces expanded, and they viewed Beck as a relic of the past. Major Rudolf Schmundt, for example, confided to his colleagues in 1938 that Beck just couldn't grasp 'the dynamism of the new regime'.[47] Committed to this 'dynamism', Schmundt subsequently died of injuries sustained in the bomb attack against Hitler in July 1944 – a victim of the resistance plot supported by Beck.

In the immediate aftermath of Fritsch's sacking, Beck complained to a colleague that Hitler had not consulted him over the military re-organization as he had promised he would. His colleague called him a 'fool' for trusting Hitler's word in the first place.[48] But still Beck, deeply unhappy though he was, hesitated to take action.

Ultimately, Beck's character told against him. 'Environment is not just something that "happens to us",' wrote Professor Essi Viding, a developmental psychopathologist at University College London. 'Individuals create, select, and modify their own environment. We are co-creators of our social ecologies.'[49] While the extent to which human beings can create their own environment obviously varies – the Nazis' prisoners in concentration camps could do little to alter their 'social ecologies' – Beck had certainly chosen his own world: one steeped in the traditions of the Prussian military. He had sworn an oath to be loyal to Adolf Hitler and he would stand by it. He summed up his position in 1938 in this famous statement: 'Mutiny and revolution are words not to be found in a German officer's dictionary.'[50]

Hitler managed to exploit the Blomberg–Fritsch crisis by appointing two malleable generals in their place. Fritsch's replacement as head of the army was General Walther von Brauchitsch. Not only was he more weak-willed than Fritsch, but his wife, Charlotte Schmidt, was a committed Nazi. The second appointment was General Wilhelm Keitel, as Chief of the Armed Forces High Command. He was one of the most compliant figures of all. Interviewed by an American psychiatrist in his cell at Nuremberg after the war, Keitel appeared bemused by what had befallen him. 'I can see today that perhaps I was much too uncritical in my entire character,' he said.

Despite all the evidence of Nazi atrocities, Keitel still believed after the war that Hitler was a 'genius' with 'such extensive ability to look into the future, with a tremendous ability to feel things, with such extensive knowledge of historic and military matters'.[51] The psychiatrist, after talking to Keitel, was not impressed by the human material in front of him. 'Keitel is the wooden soldier,' he said, 'the wooden ingratiating smile, yet suffering from the human woes of love of attention, desire for approval.'[52]

Keitel and Brauchitsch had been in their new jobs for only a few weeks when they were thrown into a crisis – one caused by Hitler's designs on Austria. Hitler had long wanted Austria, the land of his birth, to be under his control, and had escalated existing tensions by making a series of threats to the Austrian Chancellor, Kurt Schuschnigg, at a conference in Berchtesgaden on 12 February 1938. He had warned Schuschnigg that 'perhaps you will wake up one morning in Vienna to find us [the Germans] there – just like a spring storm. And then you'll see something.'[53]

Hitler was emboldened in his bullying of the Austrian Chancellor by the knowledge that the British were wavering in their commitment to the Versailles treaty. Lord Halifax had visited Hitler at Berchtesgaden in November 1937 and told him that vexed issues such as Austria, Danzig and Czechoslovakia 'fell into the category of possible alterations in the European order which might be destined to come about with the passage of time'.[54] Halifax was not yet Foreign Secretary when he spoke those words – he would only get that job in February 1938 – but it was clear to Hitler that he spoke for the Prime Minister, Neville Chamberlain. Halifax was not suggesting, of course, that the British would support armed aggression to break the provisions of Versailles, but the idea that they might accept 'possible alterations' was still significant.

Nevile Henderson, the British ambassador to Berlin, had said in a memo on 4 May 1937 that he felt that it was dangerous to regard the treaty of Versailles as 'sacrosanct' and that 'many seeds for future wars remain unless it is modified by peaceful negotiation . . .' Henderson – echoing Hitler's racist view – also said that 'The German is certainly more civilised than the Slav,' and so 'it is not fair to endeavour to prevent Germany from completing her unity or from being prepared for war against the Slav.'[55]

The mentalities of Henderson, Halifax and Chamberlain are not hard to penetrate. Their chief aim, after the horrors of the First World War, was to do all they could to prevent another conflict – especially one fought over the provisions of a treaty that many now thought unfair. They also believed that Germany was not just a powerful player in Europe but also a potential bulwark against the lack of 'civilization' in the Slavic east – a threat symbolized by Stalin's Soviet Union.

The thawing of the British attitude towards the Nazi regime also demonstrated the growing success of Hitler's diplomatic strategy. He sought to conceal his ambition to create a vast new empire behind his professed desire to regain territory lost at Versailles and to unite all German-speakers. In that apparent quest, Austria was Hitler's easiest target. Not only had the Austrians been prevented from joining Germany by the Versailles treaty, but they were German-speakers as well.

As tension mounted between the two countries, Schuschnigg made a fateful decision – he decided to call a referendum, to be held on 13 March 1938, asking whether Austrians wished to retain their independence. And in a blatant attempt to fix the result, he refused to let people under the age of twenty-four vote in the poll. The Austrian Chancellor clearly understood the extent to which Nazism appealed to the young.

Hitler's response was powerful and dramatic. On the morning of 12 March German troops marched unopposed into Austria. This was the first of three significant actions that helped shape Nazi mentalities during 1938.

Emil Klein, now a regional commander of the Hitler Youth, followed units of the Wehrmacht as they entered Austria that March, and wasn't surprised by the 'indescribable' enthusiasm with which they were greeted: 'When I went to Austria [before the invasion] people were always asking, when will the annexation be, when will we be annexed? At that time Hitler wasn't even talking about annexation! They spoke about Germany as if it was His Holiness. That was the Austrians. They longed for us! The majority longed for it, the unification with the Reich was so holy to them. One has to have lived through it!' Another Nazi supporter, Bernd Linn, also witnessed the 'excitement' as he marched into Austria. He claimed he was offered 'wine by the bowl or rather by the bucket . . . everyone cheered . . . And later – to cap it all – there was this celebration in Vienna at the imperial palace. [It was] the best atmosphere. There was no resistance or anything else.'[56]

But it wasn't all flowers and buckets of wine. The Nazis knew that a sizeable number of Austrians opposed them, and so Himmler and Heydrich had flown into Vienna in the early morning of 12 March – reaching the capital even before the rest of German forces arrived in the city. They and their Security Police had prepared extensive lists of over 20,000 people they wanted to arrest. Some were taken across the border to Dachau concentration camp outside Munich, others would be imprisoned in a new camp at Mauthausen near Hitler's home city of Linz. Mauthausen was to become one of the deadliest concentration camps of all.

The Jews, predictably, became a special target, and the intensity and immediacy of their suffering rivalled anything yet seen under Nazi rule. That was partly because there were proportionately more Jews in Austria than in Germany. Fewer than 1 per cent of Germans were Jews, whereas in Austria about 2.8 per cent of the population were Jewish, with a high concentration of Jews living in Vienna.

Such was the extent of the violence and looting in Austria that even Heydrich became worried. Austria, after all, was a fellow German-speaking nation. In public he tried to blame the Nazis' enemies for the excesses. 'Communist Party followers, misusing official party uniforms, try to threaten public security and order by illegally carrying out confiscations, house searches and arrests,' he wrote in an article in the *Wiener Neueste Nachrichten* on 17 March 1938. 'The state police will step in against such criminal activities by the harshest means and act with merciless severity.'[57]

However, the problem wasn't 'Communists' in 'official party uniforms' but the Nazis themselves, as Heydrich admitted in a note he wrote to the leading Austrian Nazi, Josef Bürckel, on the same day his article appeared in the Vienna newspaper. 'Unfortunately,' he said, '[Nazi] party members' appeared 'to have committed infringements in a totally undisciplined manner'. And while he had publicly blamed 'Communist Party followers' for the crimes, he privately warned 'our own party comrades' against launching unsanctioned operations, adding that 'it would be unfortunate if the state police had to take action against party comrades on a larger scale.'[58]

As in Germany in 1933, it was proving hard to control Nazi supporters after fuelling their hatreds. Arguably it was even harder to do so in Austria than in Germany, given the number and prominence of Jews in Vienna, the city that had been the home to world-famous Jewish figures such as Sigmund Freud.

Infamously, the Nazis made Austrian Jews scrub the streets clean. One young Viennese Jew remembered, as he was scouring the street, seeing a 'well-dressed woman' holding up 'a blonde, lovely girl with these curls, so that the girl could see better how a twenty- or twenty-two-year-old man (a Nazi Stormtrooper) kicked an old Jew who fell down because he wasn't allowed to kneel . . . And they all laughed, and she laughed as well – it was a wonderful entertainment – and that shook me.'[59]

The pioneering work of Professor Susan Fiske, a psychologist at Princeton University, helps us understand the mental processes of those who were tormenting the Jews on the streets of Vienna. Her research into stereotyping and prejudice identified two key questions that we ask when, for example, a new neighbour moves next to us. First, we ask if they are likely to be friendly or unfriendly – benevolent or malevolent – and second, are they competent or incompetent at fulfilling that role.[60]

The Jews in Vienna were mostly seen by the Nazis as competent and malevolent. But the act of humiliating them pushed them into a much less threatening category. 'What the Nazis pioneered,' says Professor Robert Sapolsky, 'by having Jews on their knees scrubbing the side-walks with their toothbrushes amid mocking crowds, was to turn them from competent and malevolent to powerless and malevolent.' It was transforming 'the people who you view as highly competent and highly malevolent – you believe they're controlling the banks and all of that – into a dramatically different category of Them'.[61] As we shall see, the humiliation of Jews – turning them in the eyes of the Nazis from 'competent and malevolent' to 'incompetent and malevolent' – would be practised on a still greater scale once the war began.

More systematic persecution went hand in hand with the street atrocities. The Gestapo stole valuable art collections from the Viennese Jewish elite, and the new regime banned Jews from a whole variety of professions, such as the arts and academia. An 'Aryanization' process forced Jews to sell their businesses and property at a fraction of the real value. Simultaneously, Adolf Eichmann, Heydrich's 'Expert on the Jews' in the SD, put in place a bureaucratic system that allowed the Nazis to rob the Jews and then deport them. By the end of the year 80,000 Jews had been forced out of Austria.[62]

No other nation offered to come to Austria's aid militarily as the Germans swallowed the country up, and Hitler easily dismissed diplomatic objections to his actions. '50,000 German Troops Seize Austria' read the headline in the *San Francisco Examiner* on 12 March; 'France and Britain Merely Protest'.[63]

Hitler had originally intended just a union with Austria, but the rapturous reception he received on entering his home city of Linz helped convince him to incorporate the country fully into the Reich. The adulation was repeated on a gigantic scale when he gave a speech in the Austrian capital three days later – as many as 200,000 people gathered in the Heldenplatz in front of the Hofburg Palace in Vienna to hear him proclaim Austria's new status.

This moment in Hitler's life – his triumphant return to the homeland in which he had failed so badly as a young man – was transformative for him. Scientific research has demonstrated, as we have seen, that 'brains and cultures coevolve'.[64] The mind has a plasticity that means circumstances can help change the way our brains process and perceive what is around us. This, almost certainly, was just such a moment of change for Hitler. If he had fulfilled this one dream, why could he not fulfil all his dreams?

Franz von Papen would have agreed with this analysis. He wrote that the German leader was in 'a state of ecstasy' in Vienna. Hitler's success – 'in spite of all warnings and prophecies' – had, according to Papen, a profound effect: 'The result was that Hitler became impervious to the advice of all those who wished him to exercise moderation in his foreign policy.'[65]

Hitler's triumph in Austria didn't, of course, just have an effect on him. It also made others reassess their view. It didn't matter now that General Fritsch was exonerated at his court martial and the machinations of Heydrich and Himmler were laid bare. As General Keitel said to the American psychiatrist who interviewed him at Nuremberg, 'nothing convinces a soldier more than success.'[66]

The subjugation of Austria had another consequential effect – one that is the second of the three significant events of 1938 that had an impact on Nazi mentalities. Just a few days after German troops entered Austria, President Franklin Roosevelt announced that he wanted to convene an international conference to discuss the plight of those who sought to leave the Reich because of Nazi persecution. The current problem had been succinctly expressed in 1936, by the president of the World Zionist Organization, Chaim Weizmann: 'the world is divided into places where they [the Jews] cannot live and places where they cannot enter.'[67]

On the face of it, Roosevelt's response to the Austrian crisis seemed humane and compassionate. It was also an initiative welcomed by Hitler – albeit in oblique and sarcastic terms. In a speech he gave on 25 March 1938, he said that he hoped the rest of the world, 'which feels so deeply sorry for these criminals [the Jews], is at least generous enough to turn this compassion into practical help'. He even said he was prepared to 'offer these criminals luxury ships to get to these countries'.[68]

But Roosevelt's initiative was not what it seemed. He knew from the beginning that it was unlikely that anything positive for the Jews would emerge from the proposed conference. A State Department

'Memorandum on Refugees', not made public at the time, revealed that the aim of the conference was to 'get out in front and attempt to guide the pressure, primarily with a view toward forestalling attempts to have immigration laws liberalized'.[69] In other words the whole thing was a sham, a smokescreen to make it look as if America was doing something in theory, while it did nothing in practice to help Jews who desperately sought a safe haven.

A cursory reading of the invitation sent out by the Americans should have immediately made refugee activists suspicious. It explicitly stated that no country that attended the conference would be asked to take more refugees than current legislation allowed. Nor was it honest enough to talk openly of the whole reason for the conference – the Nazi persecution of Jews. It only referred to 'political refugees'.

Another sign that little except talk would be accomplished at the meeting was the fact that the Nazis were robbing Jews before letting them leave. This made taking them even less appealing. On the day the conference opened in Évian in France, the British ambassador to Berlin, Sir Nevile Henderson, asked Ribbentrop, recently appointed German Foreign Minister, if Germany would allow Jews to leave the country with their assets, as 'no country was prepared to receive the emigrating German Jews, particularly if they were without means.' Ribbentrop rejected any idea of 'collaboration' over this issue as it was 'an internal German problem that was not subject to discussion'.[70]

A further clue as to the real purpose of the Évian conference was the list of countries that were not invited, including Hungary, Poland and the Soviet Union – almost all of them places where large numbers of Jews lived. Though never admitted openly, it was obvious that these countries weren't asked to Évian because they might want to discuss removing some of their own Jews. Indeed, inside the British Foreign Office it was acknowledged that this was the case.[71]

There was one final piece of cynicism in the run-up to the conference. Understandably, Jewish groups wanted to discuss the possibility of sending large numbers of refugees to Palestine, then under British control. But this option was to be explicitly excluded. The British had sought to keep a delicate balance between Jewish and Arab claims in the Middle East, but by 1938 it appeared the balance was coming down on the side of the Arabs.[72] Lord Winterton, the British representative at the Évian conference, was on record as a supporter of the Arab cause in Palestine.

Given that background, it's not surprising that the Évian conference in the summer of 1938 achieved nothing of significance. It was a forum for each invited country to express sympathy for the 'refugee' problem but offer little in terms of practical help. This, no doubt, fitted perfectly with Roosevelt's aims for the gathering. He could demonstrate that America was concerned with the human cost of the Nazi persecution of the Jews at no real price to himself or his country – this despite the fact that large numbers of Jews were in desperate need. In a further bitter irony, the conference gave the lie to Hitler's assertion that the Jews were enormously powerful, secretly controlling governments across the world. What Évian demonstrated was what little power and influence they actually possessed.

The reason Évian matters so much in the context of the mentalities of the Nazis is because of the hypocrisy that pervaded the conference. 'Now that the protests have become overwhelming,' said Hitler at the Nuremberg rally on 12 September 1938, and Germany was 'no longer willing to be sucked dry by these parasites [the Jews], it is now that there is great complaint abroad. However, these democratic countries don't exchange this hypocritical protest for helpful acts. On the contrary, they coldly say there is no space free there!' Hitler summed up the attitude of those in the international community who complained about the Nazi treatment of Jews as 'no help. But morals!'[73]

Hypocrisy has a powerful psychological effect, with one study showing that, 'remarkably, hypocrites were rated as less trustworthy, less likable and less morally upright than those who openly lied.'[74] It was understandable, therefore, that the hypocritical attitude that suffused the Évian conference had a profound impact on the Nazis, allowing Hitler to portray Roosevelt and the other leaders who had supported Évian as politicians who only pretended to care. It all fitted into the worldview that Hitler sought to project of a Germany victimized by nations that did not practise what they preached. 'Neither Mr Roosevelt nor an English archbishop nor any other prominent Democrat would put his daughter into the bed of a sleazy east European Jew,' said an article in the SS journal *Das Schwarze Korps* on 24 November 1938, 'but when it comes to Germany, they know at once no Jewish question, but only the "persecution of the innocent for the sake of their faith", as if we had ever been interested in what a Jew believes or does not believe.'[75]

The failure to take Jewish refugees also played into Hitler's obsession with 'space'. In the same speech in which he accused the 'democratic' countries of offering 'no help. But morals!' he also pointed out their apparent hypocrisy over the question of 'colonies'. 'Without ever caring about the natives' opinion, they have subjugated continents with bloody force,' he said. 'But now that Germany reclaims its colonies, they declare, dismayed at the poor natives' lot, that under no circumstances can they be left to such a fate.'[76]

Hitler thus perceived a grand, overarching hypocrisy: other nations had plenty of space in which to place Jewish refugees but still refused to take them, while the very same countries simultaneously denied Germans the right to gain space for themselves.

During the same period that he was pushing for a solution to his imagined 'Jewish problem', Hitler was manoeuvring towards war. Although it is common knowledge that 1938 was the year Hitler contemplated the destruction of Czechoslovakia, what is not so well known is how, during May 1938, he made the decision to escalate matters.

Hitler hated Czechoslovakia for many reasons. He saw the country as a creation of Versailles, a false construct containing a variety of different ethnic groups – including just over three million German-speakers, primarily in the Sudetenland in the border region of the country. Czechoslovakia was also a democracy with links to western powers – both issues guaranteed to irritate him.

In late March 1938, after the successful occupation of Austria, Hitler called the leaders of the Sudeten Germans to Berlin. He told them that they should tell the Czech government that they wanted a whole series of changes to the administration of the Sudetenland – demands that they knew would be unacceptable to the Czechs. But while this was intended to increase the tension, it didn't mean that Hitler was suddenly ready to use the Sudeten question as a pretext to crush Czechoslovakia. On 20 May he informed military leaders that he wouldn't move on the Czechs unless an unexpected opportunity arose. Yet at the end of May he told his generals that he wanted the Czech issue dealt with now. 'The Führer's intention not to touch on the Czech problem as yet is altered,' wrote Colonel Jodl in his diary.[77]

Hitler hadn't radically revised his timetable because of some dramatic geopolitical event. He had changed his mind chiefly because he felt slighted. He had been forced, after 20 May, to deny rumours that Germany might move on the Czechs, largely because of protests from the British and French. Over the next few days, turning all this over in his mind, he became overwhelmed by a sense of humiliation. 'Because of Germany's self-restraint,' wrote Jodl, 'its consequences lead to a loss of prestige for the Führer, which he is no longer willing to take.' Ernst von Weizsäcker, the state secretary at the Foreign Ministry, later confirmed in his own diary that Hitler's 'resentment from 22 May, when the English had accused him of shrinking back, led him on to the path of war'.[78]

It was an extraordinary situation. One man's sense of 'loss of prestige' risked changing the fate of millions. That this didn't lead to war in 1938 was primarily due to the appeasement of the British Prime Minister Neville Chamberlain. After he met Hitler at Berchtesgaden on 15 September, the Czechs were forced to hand over the Sudetenland to the Germans. Hitler was shocked when he heard that the Czechs had submitted to his demands. The final agreement, signed at the Munich conference in the early hours of 30 September, gave Hitler what he had ostensibly wanted, the Sudetenland, but not what he had really desired, a refusal by the Czechs to hand over the territory and a pretext for war – a conflict in which he hoped the British and French, having seen the recalcitrance of the Czechs, would not be involved.

Just as disappointing for Hitler was the increasing evidence that most Germans didn't share his desire for war. An SD report from August 1938 described the mood as 'often gloomy' because 'there exists in the broadest sections of the population the most serious concern that sooner or later a war will kill off economic prosperity and have a terrible end for Germany.'[79] Goebbels even dared to voice this opinion in front of Hitler, saying at lunch – according to Weizsäcker – that on the subject of war the population was less than enthusiastic.[80]

It was a reminder of the tension that existed between the ambitions of Hitler and the practical questions that stood in his way. He was never all powerful as a leader. For all his ability to change his policy as a result of a slight to his 'prestige', he always had to persuade others to follow him. And in that task he was helped by the fact that many of those who disagreed with his methods agreed with his goals. Even Ludwig Beck, Chief of the Army General Staff, recognized that the existence of Czechoslovakia was a problem if Germany wanted to expand. His argument with Hitler was only a practical one over whether action against the Czechs would provoke war with the British and French.

Hitler was astute enough to realize that he was partly responsible for the unwillingness of millions of Germans to embrace the possibility of war, given that he had consistently said in public that he didn't want another conflict. He admitted as much in a speech he delivered in early November 1938 to an audience of senior media figures.

During his talk he was frank about the deception he had practised thus far. 'Circumstances have forced me to talk almost exclusively about peace,' he said. 'Only by continuing to emphasize the German desire and intention for peace' had it been possible to build up German armaments. But the trouble was that this peaceful rhetoric ran the risk of creating a 'defeatist' attitude among the German population. He said he had recently attempted to change this stance, and so German propaganda now needed to emphasize that 'there are things which, if they cannot be enforced peacefully, must be enforced by means of violence.'

Hitler accepted that such a change in the mentality of the population could not be achieved suddenly. Nor could the government just tell people what to think. The way to effect change was to 'illuminate certain events in such a way that the conviction is gradually and automatically aroused in the brains of the broad masses of the people that if you can't put an end to it in a good way, then you have to put an end to it by force, but it cannot go on like this'.[81]

Goebbels also favoured this approach. He would write in his diary in July 1941 – ironically in the context of a dispute with Hitler about the way the newsreels were made – that 'I prefer to let the pictures speak for themselves and to explain only those things in the commentary that the audience doesn't otherwise understand. I consider this more effective because the viewer doesn't realize the intention behind it.'[82]

Hitler told the assembled journalists in November 1938 that he credited the single-mindedness of the German press with helping to gain the Sudetenland. Only by carrying on with this unity could the great aim of increasing the 'self-confidence' of the German people be achieved. While he recognized that there would always be people in authority who were ineffectual in one way or another, what was important was for the press never to report their failings. The message should be that the leadership was always right. This maxim, repeated again and again, would create a 'psychological' situation that would allow the leadership to survive in times of crisis.[83]

Hitler gave this confidential briefing to German journalists on 10 November, the day after the final event of 1938 that had a profound impact on the mentalities of the Nazis – Kristallnacht. Significantly, Hitler didn't mention this sudden outpouring of violence against the Jews in his lengthy talk to the journalists. Since many Germans opposed the atrocity, there was no benefit to him in talking about it.

In response to an attack on a German diplomat in Paris by a young Jewish man, Nazi thugs smashed up Jewish shops, desecrated synagogues and attacked individual Jews. Up to a hundred Jews were murdered and as many as 30,000 were sent to concentration camps. It was an action that appalled not just the world but many ordinary Germans. The district leader of Swabia in Bavaria reported that while many people had 'expected that the national government would take some action' after the murder of the diplomat, 'the greater portion of the populace had far less understanding and sympathy for the manner in which the spontaneous action against the Jews was implemented . . . these events prompted an unneeded sense of sympathy for the Jews in towns and rural areas.'[84] A Jewish resident of Munich wrote that he and his family had received help from his non-Jewish neighbours, and revealed that a leading Munich banker had confessed to him through tears, 'I am ashamed to be a German.'[85]

But this sense of indignation was by no means universal. There were also Germans who celebrated the violent action taken against the Jews. One Jewish teenager in Nuremberg remembered that the morning after Kristallnacht passers-by threw stones at the damaged front of his family home.[86]

The common perception was that Kristallnacht was the consequence of a spontaneous public reaction to the death of the diplomat Ernst vom Rath, who had been shot by a seventeen-year-old Jewish man called Herschel Grynszpan. But this wasn't the case – there was little spontaneity behind it. Leading Nazis were in Munich on 9 November for the annual commemoration of the Beer-Hall Putsch, and so it was easy for them to coordinate the attacks. 'I present the matter to the Führer,' wrote Goebbels in his diary. 'He decides: let the demonstrations [against the Jews] continue. Withdraw the police. The Jews are to experience the rage of the people. That's right. I immediately issue appropriate instructions to police and party. Then I briefly speak to the party leadership to that effect. Rapturous applause. Everyone dashes to the telephones. Now the people will act.'[87]

Goebbels was being misleading. It wasn't so much the people who would act, but Nazi thugs. And he also omitted to mention that the Nazis themselves had helped create the very circumstances that led to Kristallnacht.

In response to concerns that Polish Jews living in Germany would be denied citizenship by the Polish government, the Nazis decided on 28 October to force Polish Jews out of Germany over the border into Poland. This caused enormous suffering. Many of these Jews had lived in Germany for years, and now they were snatched from their homes and transported to a country that didn't want them. Some died when they were trapped overnight in no man's land between the two borders.[88]

Herschel Grynszpan's parents were among those deported to Poland. Devastated by what they had endured, he shot Rath in a revenge attack. But while Grynszpan pulled the trigger, the first link in this chain of causation remained clear – the Nazis' persecution of the Jews. Everything stemmed from that.

This psychological sequencing – of creating the seeds of a problem, waiting for a reaction, and then acting and blaming others – was central to how Hitler led Germany, not only against the Jews, but throughout the Second World War. Hitler came close to admitting as much in a secret speech he gave to leading military figures on 10 February 1939. 'At the beginning,' he said, 'naturally one could not foresee the right moment' to take the 'daring step' of 'proclaiming to the world' that Germany had embraced a policy of rearmament. Similarly, while he had long wanted to 'solve' the Austrian and Czech 'problems', he had been waiting for the moment when it was favourable to act.[89]

It was a curious way of leading a country, because it meant that while long-term goals existed, they could often only be achieved by a sudden action in response to the behaviour of others.

An even more extreme example of this kind of thinking was Hitler's view of Poland. When the Polish Foreign Minister, Józef Beck, visited Berlin for talks in January 1939, Hitler was still uncertain whether or not he would have to march on Warsaw. He was keen to learn from Beck if the Poles would do a deal over the city of Danzig, which as a result of the Versailles agreement had become a 'free' city under the auspices of the League of Nations. Danzig had been German before the First World War, and now sat in a 'corridor' of Polish land which split East Prussia off from the rest of Germany.

If Poland had accepted Hitler's demands – and had also agreed to become a German satellite, as Slovakia did two months later – there would have been no need for the Nazis to invade the country in order to make their way east. But Beck and the Polish government prevaricated.

The situation changed radically in March 1939, when the German Army marched on to Czech territory and occupied Prague. It was this action that resulted in Britain and France offering a guarantee to Poland. If Poland was invaded by the Germans, then the Allies would go to war. Polish equivocation could now be replaced with certainty. There would be no deal with Nazi Germany.

Events now accelerated, driven in large part by Hitler's own personality. A new factor had come to the fore – his fear of his own mortality. In explaining to his military leaders why it was necessary to go to war, just ten days before German tanks crossed into Poland, Hitler revealed his bloated egotism. 'Essentially all depends on me,' he said, 'on my existence, because of my political talents.' Yet he worried that he could be 'eliminated at any time by a criminal or a lunatic'. Moreover, 'no one knows how much longer I shall live. Therefore, better a conflict now.'[90]

As war neared, Hitler concluded the most astonishing of all his foreign policy upsets. While his long-term aim of seizing a new empire in the west of the Soviet Union remained, in order to deal with the short-term problem of the recalcitrance of the British and French, the Nazi regime did a deal with Joseph Stalin and the Soviet Union.

The Nazi–Soviet pact of August 1939 was a monument to the abject failure of Hitler's method of leadership – of having a long-term goal, provoking a response from others and then responding swiftly. That was why he ended up in a non-aggression pact with his ideological enemy, and at war with Britain, one of the rare countries in the world that he had originally wanted as his friend.

SS man Bernd Linn was 'very surprised' by this new arrangement, as were many other committed members of the Nazi Party. But he personally rationalized what was happening as merely a pragmatic response to a 'power struggle' with the Allies.[91]

For Linn, like countless other Nazis, potential enemies were everywhere. So much so that it was understandable if on occasion you had to pretend that your greatest enemy was your friend.

9. Eliminating Resistance

They were unlike any invaders that had come before. In September 1939 the Nazis didn't just seek to conquer Poland – they wanted to reshape the country, ideologically and racially. Their plans were ambitious and murderous, and as a result millions of innocent people would die. Not only did the actions of the Nazi killers in Poland lay the ground for the Holocaust, but they revealed the extent to which human beings can commit horrific murders and yet feel their actions are justified.

Part of the reason all this was possible was because in principle the idea of invading Poland was popular among senior German commanders. Under the terms of the hated Versailles settlement, territory containing ethnic Germans had been incorporated into Poland, and this meant that Johannes Blaskowitz, commander of the German Eighth Army, felt able to tell interrogators after the war that he felt the attack on Poland was 'regarded as a sacred duty, though a sad necessity'.[1] What Blaskowitz likely didn't realize in September 1939 was that the Nazis didn't just want to eliminate Polish resistance, they were prepared to turn on any army officers who disagreed with their murderous way of crushing the Poles.

On 29 August 1939, just three days before the German invasion, the Quartermaster General of the Wehrmacht met with Reinhard Heydrich and his SS colleague Werner Best. Eduard Wagner wrote in his diary that he thought both of them were 'inscrutable types' and that Heydrich was 'particularly unsympathetic'.[2] But this didn't stop all parties reaching an agreement that special 'security' units called Einsatzgruppen would follow the army into Poland. These troops, formed under Heydrich's aegis, subsequently committed a whole series of atrocities.

The commanders of the Einsatzgruppen – many transferred from Heydrich's SD – were no mere thugs. Most were highly educated and several held doctorates. Crucially, they were all ideological believers in Nazism. The majority had been members of the nationalist Freikorps and had already shown they were prepared to fight for their beliefs.[3] They were also firm believers in 'Us and Them'; and in the context of the war in Poland the ethnic Germans were 'Us' and the rest of the Polish population most definitely 'Them'.

So imagine how members of the Einsatzgruppen processed the news that Poles in Bydgoszcz, north-west of Warsaw, had killed several hundred ethnic Germans on 3 September – especially when Nazi propaganda dubbed the incident 'Bloody Sunday of Bromberg' (Bromberg was the German name for the city). Why Polish units shot the ethnic Germans is still unclear. Testimony from eyewitnesses, gathered immediately after the war, said that the ethnic Germans fired at retreating Poles – details omitted from some other contemporary documents. There were even claims that the SD had organized the original attack on the Poles, an idea disputed by a leading Polish academic who believed that the Poles just 'lost it' as they were retreating and started shooting wildly.[4]

Whatever the cause of the killing of ethnic Germans by the Poles – either provocation from the ethnic Germans or the retreating Poles panicking – the impact of 'Bloody Sunday' was immense. Hermann Göring even ludicrously claimed at his Nuremberg trial that the action was one reason for the German invasion of Poland – an impossibility, given that the killings happened two days after the conflict started.[5] Writing after the war, Melita Maschmann, a former Nazi supporter and member of the BDM, the Nazi youth movement for girls, remembered making the same mistake: 'my clear recollection was that we only made the attack on Poland after the news of the "Bloody Sunday" had reached Berlin. In point of fact the events happened in the reverse order. But my version, which I held to until a few months ago, was much better for easing our bad political conscience.'[6]

The number of ethnic Germans killed by the Poles during the invasion was wildly exaggerated by the Nazis; instead of the reality of several hundred in Bromberg and a few thousand elsewhere across Poland, Nazi propaganda declared that 58,000 had died. The incident played perfectly into Nazi claims that ethnic Germans were at risk on Polish territory. 'The shadows of death have hung over Bromberg these past few days,' read an article in the *Völkischer Beobachter*. 'In every road and garden lie the most bestially mutilated bodies of murdered *Volks-deutsche*.'[7] Reports like these incensed the German invaders. At Bromberg, together with local German 'protection' units, the Einsatzgruppen murdered around 1,200 Poles in reprisal.[8]

A key reason the incident at Bromberg had such an impact on the psyche of many Germans was the way the ethnic Germans had died. Claims that ethnic Germans had been shot by Polish snipers from church towers generated a particular kind of loathing. In the First World War snipers had been hated more than any other type of soldier, and that detestation continued into this conflict. An Allied soldier who fought in Normandy in 1944 remembered that, 'if captured', snipers on both sides 'were shot on the spot without ceremony', as troops 'hated the thought of a sniper taking deliberate aim to kill by singling them out'.[9]

The Germans were also worried, not just in Bromberg but across Poland, that they might be shot at by partisans – combatants dressed in civilian clothes. This was a heightened concern after the regular Polish Army had been defeated and resistance elements took over the fight. Just like snipers, these partisans were loathed. It was considered a dishonourable, cowardly way of fighting.

Himmler issued an order on 3 September – the same day as the Bromberg incident – that 'Polish insurgents caught in the act or with a weapon' should be 'shot on the spot', with his definition of 'insurgent' encompassing anyone who 'threatened vital facilities or goods'. A few days later the Wehrmacht altered its own previous position on Polish civilians suspected of firing at German soldiers. Instead of an investigation being conducted into each incident, those accused were to be shot at once, together with others who were merely 'located at the house and farmsteads from which our troops had been fired on'.[10]

The 'partisan threat' had a powerful psychological element to it. How could you trust anyone you met in Poland, if civilians might be prepared to fire at you? Much better, many of the German invaders felt, to shoot first and worry about whether the person you feared was a genuine partisan afterwards.

In the eyes of Einsatzgruppen officers, such as SS-Sturmbannführer Helmuth Bischoff, a combination of these fears justified the killing of hostages. In Bromberg in the days after the deaths of the ethnic Germans, Bischoff ordered over a dozen Polish civilians – a mix of Jews and non-Jews – to be rounded up and placed in front of the entrance to the hotel in which the Einsatzgruppen were lodged. He then announced that every time a shot from an alleged partisan was heard, a hostage would be killed. Every one of the hostages was murdered that night.[11]

Even this early in the war, a belief was forming among German security units that resistance from civilians, real or imagined, justified indiscriminate reprisals. There appears to have been no thought given, for instance, to the notion that while the Poles shooting from hiding places in Bromberg were guilty of threatening the Germans, the hostages who were killed in response were likely innocent of any crime. To the Einsatzgruppen they were all part of the same mass of threatening Poles.

Added to this was the sense, as one German soldier put it, that the behaviour of the Poles in fighting back was 'characteristic of primitive people'. The Germans were thus 'civilised men' involved in a life and death struggle against 'savages'.[12] This belief, of course, meant that many felt justified in abandoning all normal restraint.

Crucially, there was also the − erroneous − belief that Polish Jews were largely responsible for the partisan threat, with Heydrich telling the leaders of the Einsatzgruppen, on 21 September, that the Jews had been 'crucial participants' in the attacks and in 'plundering operations'.[13] Fear and the desire for revenge are two of the most powerful human emotions, and the Einsatzgruppen were boiling over with them. And filled with such toxic fuel, security forces murdered 300 men and women − more than half of them Jews − at Częstochowa in early September, and locked Jews in synagogues in Mielec, Będzin and other locations and set them on fire. Several hundred lost their lives.[14]

After the Bromberg action, Helmuth Bischoff and his Einsatzkommando pressed on into Poland. Like many of his colleagues Bischoff was an educated man, with a doctorate in law. But, having first joined the Hitler Youth in the late 1920s and then the Nazi Party in 1930, he believed that whether or not he and his unit could behave ruthlessly in Poland was a fundamental test of their character. One of his men later recalled that Bischoff had told them that 'in this action, anyone can prove he's a real man.'[15]

Overlying their visceral feelings of aggression and the desire to prove they were 'real men' lay an intellectual approach − as deadly in its way. Nazi economic thinkers, many of whom were relatively young, claimed that the fundamental problem with Poland was easy to identify − there were just too many Poles living there. Helmut Meinhold, an economist in his twenties, calculated in 1941 that nearly six million Poles were 'surplus population'.[16]

This was a 'problem' that the Nazis believed was exacerbated by the presence of around three million Jews in Poland. This was a gigantic number compared to the few hundred thousand Jews who remained in Germany. 'For many Germans this is probably the first time in their lives that they have seen so many Jews en masse,' wrote Eduard Könekamp of the German Foreign Institute on a visit to Poland in December 1939. He thought the Jews 'just vegetate' in ghettos which were 'just about the filthiest places you can imagine . . . Exterminating these subhumans would be in the best interests of the whole world. But exterminating them poses incredibly difficult problems. There are too many of them to shoot. And one can't simply shoot women and children.'[17]

Notwithstanding Könekamp's utopian dream of 'exterminating' the Jews, the policy towards the Polish Jews during this first phase of the Nazi occupation was primarily one of ghettoization – confining the Jews in ghettos while they awaited deportation to an as yet unnamed destination. The pace of ghettoization varied – the Łódź ghetto was 'sealed' in April 1940 and the Warsaw ghetto in November 1940 – but the Jews were targeted for persecution from the very beginning. Just as in Austria, deliberate attempts were made to humiliate them: to change them in the eyes of their persecutors, as psychological research suggests, from 'malevolent and competent' to 'malevolent and incompetent'.[18] In Warsaw, for instance, a Jewish Pole called Emanuel Ringelblum recorded in his diary in February 1940 that Jewish workers were 'ordered to beat one another with their galoshes' and 'a rabbi was ordered to shit in his pants',[19] while 'women in fur coats' were 'ordered to wash the pavement with their panties, then put them on again wet'.[20] Such actions also, of course, suggest a number of the perpetrators were motivated by sadism, sexual or otherwise.

Alongside the persecution of the Jews, the Nazis wanted to reorder Poland by destroying the 'leadership class'. Landowners, teachers, even pharmacists, were at risk from imprisonment in concentration camps or execution. Heydrich's team had compiled a list of just over 60,000 prominent Poles who were to be targeted in an action known as Operation Tannenberg. The name was significant. It referred not just to Hindenburg's famous victory over the Russians in August 1914 but to the First Battle of Tannenberg in the early fifteenth century between the Teutonic Order and Polish and Lithuanian forces.[21] Though the Teutonic Order had lost the battle it nonetheless symbolized the idea that this land had for centuries been a site of German expansion.

Einsatzgruppen commanders had enormous latitude in how they behaved, so much so that some were even accused of excessive brutality by the Nazis themselves. Heydrich's Reich Security Head Office investigated the actions of a leader of an Einsatzkommando called Alfred Hasselberg, a qualified lawyer in his early thirties. Fritz Liebl, one of his men, told investigators in December 1939 that he had concluded as a result of working under Hasselberg's command that in Poland 'human life has absolutely no value.' He was 'especially disgusted' by having to kill prisoners by shooting them in the back of the neck on the edge of a pit. He didn't object to murdering these Poles in principle, it was just that in practice he thought 'the members of the execution squad were just not trained for these tasks.'[22]

The investigation revealed that Hasselberg had ordered his men to enter Polish apartments shouting 'Your money or your life' and that they 'had ripped rings off Jewish women's fingers, even breaking fingers in doing so; and had then stripped them naked and examined them closely'.[23] No wonder that one of his men thought that Hasselberg 'rejoices in torturing people' and 'had sadistic tendencies'. Another member of the Einsatzkommando complained that the 'constant fear' of working for Hasselberg 'settles on the men's souls as an anxiety psychosis'.[24]

Some suggestions as to why a man like Hasselberg might reveal his cruelty in these circumstances, while a number of the killers working for him had difficulties in carrying out their tasks, are discussed in the following chapters.[25] As for the Hasselberg investigation, Heydrich ended this in January 1940 when Hasselberg asked to be transferred to the Wehrmacht.[26]

Heydrich revealed in a letter he wrote to his wife, to be read in the event of his death, how he expected those close to him to behave, including his own children. He called on his wife to 'educate our children to believe in the Führer and Germany; to be loyal to the ideas of the Nazi movement; to obey the fundamental laws of the SS; to be tough with themselves; to be generous to the people of our own *Volk*; to be hard on all enemies at home and in foreign countries'. Finally, 'when time has

. Posters in Berlin prior to the first round of the Presidential election in March 1932.
otice how, on the left, the slogan under Hindenburg reads 'choose a man, not a Party!'
his was an obvious attempt to position him as the elder statesman, above the fray of
)mmon party politics.

20. The aristocratic German elite take tea during the tumultuous election year of 1932. From the left, Chancellor Franz von Papen, Interior Minister Wilhelm Freiherr von Gayl, President Paul von Hindenburg and Minister of Defence Kurt von Schleicher. The leading civil servant, Otto Meissner, has his back to the camera.

21. That same year, 1932, Adolf Hitler gives an election speech in Munich. The problem the governing elite faced was that Hitler and the Nazis had the support of the masses, and they did not. Their solution? Appoint Hitler as Chancellor in January 1933 but control him. It was a plan that did not work.

22. Adolf Hitler shakes hands with President Hindenburg, shortly after being appointed Chancellor of Germany. Notice Hitler's deliberately obsequious manner and attire – dressed in civilian clothes with not a swastika armband to be seen.

23. A poster from 1933 with Hindenburg's face on the left and Hitler's on the right – designed to give the impression that the old war hero blessed the new Chancellor with his personal imprimatur.

24. One of the seminal events of the Nazis' early years in power – the burning of the Reichstag on 27 February 1933 by a young Dutch communist. In the immediate aftermath of the destruction of the German parliament, the Nazis passed legislation that destroyed human rights in Germany.

25. Inmates forced to work at Dachau concentration camp near Munich in 1933. Dachau, one of the first concentration camps established by the regime, was primarily used during this early period to imprison the Nazis' political enemies.

26. A mass protest meeting against Nazi atrocities, held in Madison Square Garden in New York on 27 March 1933. Around 20,000 people were inside the stadium and many more demonstrated outside.

7. The Nazi boycott of Jewish businesses held on 1 April 1933. The Nazi leadership claimed that this was simply a reaction to the recent foreign protests against their actions, but in reality their commitment to the persecution of the Jews had long been a core part of their ideology.

28. This cover of a Nazi calendar for 1938, issued by the Party Office of Racial Policy, depicts an idealized family. It represents the Nazi dream – a country peopled only by healthy 'Aryan' members of the Volksgemeinschaft, the people's community.

60 000 *RM*

koſtet dieſer Erbkranke
die Volksgemeinſchaft
auf Lebenszeit

*Volksgenoſſe
das iſt auch
Dein Geld*

Leſen Sie

**neues
Volk**

Die Monatshefte des Raſſenpolitiſchen Amtes der NSDAP

9. Another image from the Party Office of Racial Policy, issued that same year, 1938, reveals a
ore sinister side of Nazi policy. It complains about the cost of keeping a disabled person alive,
lling the healthy members of the Volksgemeinschaft, 'Folks, it's your money too!'

30. Adolf Hitler drives past cheering crowds in Vienna on 16 March 1938. Imagine how he must have felt during this triumphant return to his homeland, especially after proving wrong those who had warned that it was too risky for the Nazis to attempt the 'Anschluss' of Austria.

31. Austrian Jews were immediately targeted after the Nazis arrived. Here, in front of a watching crowd, Jews are forced to scrub the streets clean.

healed' she should 'give the children another father, but it must be a real man, like the one I wanted to be'.[27]

The difficulty that the Hasselberg case had surfaced was this: what exactly was a 'real man'? If you enjoyed killing innocent civilians, close up and in cold blood, did that mean that you were no longer adhering to the 'fundamental laws of the SS'? As we shall see, Himmler often emphasized that it was important for his men to behave 'decently'.[28] But once you became involved in this kind of killing how was that possible? One Polish eyewitness testified that he had heard SS men come into a pub after shooting a group of Poles 'boasting' of their actions and saying 'the damned brains just squirted everywhere.'[29] That was certainly 'hard' on the Nazis' 'enemies', but how could it be 'decent'? It was an issue that would become still more problematic for the Nazis as the murders escalated.[30]

For the most part the German Army cooperated with the Einsatz-gruppen. In Bromberg the High Command told units on the ground not to interfere in any of the reprisal killings. But the collaboration went further than that. Major General Braemer gave up 500 prisoners held in an army barracks to be shot, and approved the killing of twenty Poles in the Market Square in retaliation for the death of one Wehr-macht soldier.[31]

Not every interaction between the army and Heydrich's security units went so smoothly. There were senior army officers who objected to what they saw. And how they went about protesting tells us a great deal not just about their mentality but about the psychology of re-sistance generally. For example, in November 1939, General Walter Petzel, military commander of the Warthegau in occupied Poland, complained in a note to the overall head of the Reserve Army that SS units were forming a 'state within a state'. Not only were they organ-izing public executions but the 'selection [of victims] was often incomprehensible'. In addition, 'all Polish landowners have been arrested and detained with their families.' Petzel was also concerned that 'in a number of cities, actions against Jews have been carried out which degenerated into serious assaults.' In one Polish town 'a number of Jews were driven into the synagogue and had to crawl through the pews singing, during which they were constantly beaten with whips by the SS people. Then, they were forced to lower their trousers in order to be beaten on their naked buttocks. One Jew who had soiled his trousers through fear was forced to rub the faeces on the other Jews' faces.'[32]

Other military leaders echoed Petzel's concerns, most notably the new overall commander of the army in Poland, General Johannes Blaskowitz. He composed a memo of complaint which was handed to Hitler by his adjutant on 18 November 1939. 'At first he [that is, Hitler] calmly acknowledged' the contents of the document, wrote Hitler's adjutant. But then he started to make 'serious accusations against "childlike attitudes" in the leadership of the army', saying, 'you don't wage war with Salvation Army methods.' As far as Hitler was concerned, the memo only served to confirm his 'long-cherished aversion' to Blaskowitz.[33]

Having received no formal response from Hitler to his memo, Blaskowitz circulated details of the atrocities in Poland to other senior officers. General Wilhelm Ritter von Leeb was so incensed when he learnt the news that he wrote to General Franz Halder, the Chief of Staff of the Army High Command, that 'there are rumours on many sides, and it seems to me very credible ones, that the behaviour of the police in Poland is unworthy of a civilized nation.'[34]

Blaskowitz carried on collecting examples of atrocities and compiled another report which he presented to the Commander-in-Chief of the army, Walther von Brauchitsch, on 15 February 1940. 'It is perverse to slaughter some 10,000 Jews and Poles as is happening now,' wrote Blaskowitz, 'for in view of the size of the population, this would neither kill off the Polish idea of the state nor eliminate the Jews. On the contrary, the manner of the slaughter is most damaging, complicating problems and making the Poles far more dangerous than they would have been . . .' Blaskowitz further claimed that 'enemy propaganda' would benefit from the killings and that 'the acts of violence against Jews that happen in public not only engender the religious Poles' deepest disgust, but also generate compassion for the Jewish population which the Pole was more or less hostile to until now.' But the greatest damage would be to the Germans themselves, as 'extreme brutalization and moral degeneration will spread in no time like a plague among precious German human material.'[35]

Blaskowitz included a long list, which he had gathered from his subordinates, of 'typical cases' of atrocities – all of them committed by either the police, the SS or others in the Nazi administration. From the story of a botched execution where one Pole, only wounded, fell into a pit full of bodies and screamed out that he wanted to be shot again so as to be put out of his misery, to a description of how 250 Jews were stripped naked and searched for valuables in the 'bitter cold' with the women's 'genitals examined by policemen' for hidden treasures.

Perhaps most horrific of all was the mistreatment by German security forces of two Poles, a man and a woman in their twenties, witnessed by three Wehrmacht soldiers who later made an official complaint about the incident. The Polish man was accused of shooting someone and the woman of 'hiding bullets'. Both were ordered to dig their own graves in front of a crowd of locals. As they were digging, a policeman started to beat them with a spade and 'hit the woman's back in the coccyx area with all his strength. The woman cried out in a tearful and accusing tone in Polish: "Please, Sir, I do work, don't I?" Thereupon, the police officer jumped into the pit in front of the woman and with the back of his hand dressed in a leather glove hit her in the face so violently that there was a bang like a gunshot . . . She fell backwards on the bottom [of the pit] and opened her legs. At the same time, a heavy stream of blood rushed from her nose and mouth . . . Still unable to get up, she spread her legs and lifted her skirt so that one could see that her underwear was completely soaked in blood . . . That's when the police officer, who was still standing in the pit in front of her, said: "Now on top of everything she's got her period, so fucking her is out of the question."'

It was the stuff of nightmares. But notice how the policeman, fuelled no doubt by his anger at these two 'partisans', clearly felt they deserved to be treated in this appalling way – since in his eyes they were also Slavs and so unworthy of proper consideration.

As for Blaskowitz, he must have known that by cataloguing these horrors he was telling his superiors things they did not wish to know. While other officers had voiced their outrage on hearing from him about the atrocities in Poland, none of them had wanted to confront Hitler about it. Heinrich Nolte tried in vain to raise the issue with his boss, General Franz Halder, Chief of Staff of the Army High Command. 'I expressed my dismay and my anger to Halder in a private conversation,' wrote Nolte after the war. '"This should not be tolerated etc." Halder tried to calm me down. Eventually, he broke off the conversation by saying something like: "Little Nolte, what do you want? There are many other things that are much worse. There's nothing that can be done about it now."'[36]

Not surprisingly, committed Nazis had come to despise Blaskowitz and other Wehrmacht officers who had dared to complain about the actions of the security forces. Hans Frank, head of the General Government – the largest district in Nazi-occupied Poland – voiced his annoyance to Joseph Goebbels. 'At Frank's in the evening,' wrote Goebbels in his diary on 2 November 1939. 'He describes his difficulties. Especially with the Wehrmacht who are pursuing a wishy-washy bourgeois policy instead of a racial one. But Frank will prevail in the end . . . These [Poles] are no longer humans any more, they are animals. For this reason our task is not humanitarian but surgical. Steps must be taken here, and they must be radical ones, make no mistake . . . Otherwise Europe will perish from the Jewish disease.'[37]

Blaskowitz must have known he was damaging his career by voicing these protests. So why did he do it? It wasn't because he disagreed with the invasion of Poland. His argument was with the way the Poles – Jews and non-Jews alike – were being treated, not with the German decision to conquer this land in the first place.

The reasons for Blaskowitz's behaviour are to be found, once again, in the complex relationship between his genetic predisposition and his cultural circumstances. It might seem strange to claim that there is a genetic component to resistance, but Professor Essi Viding, a specialist in developmental psychopathology, is adamant that 'Like any human characteristic I would be incredibly surprised if there wasn't a genetic predisposition – that some people are more likely to resist and others less so. I don't know of any human characteristic that does not show some genetic influence.' She professes 'not to know why people don't want to accept' that we can be predisposed to have the character we do, as we're perfectly happy to accept that 'physical traits' have a genetic basis.[38]

In addition to this 'genetic predisposition', it's easy to see how Blaskowitz must have been shaped by his environment. His father was a minister in a church in an East Prussian village and was known as 'Thundering Blaskowitz' for the power and force of his sermons. Both father and son were deeply committed Christians – General Blaskowitz carried a Bible with him and read it each night.

Born in 1883, Blaskowitz was sent to a Prussian cadet school and later to the Central Cadet Corps School at Gross-Lichterfelde near Berlin. During these impressionable years he was taught to be loyal and honourable and to practise self-denial. But in a reminder that such an education does not inevitably create an officer with unshakeable principles, one of his comrades at Gross-Lichterfelde was Walther von Brauchitsch, who in early 1940, as Commander-in-Chief of the army, heard Blaskowitz's complaints about the atrocities in Poland and then clearly wished he had not.[39]

A combination of all these factors – his genetic predisposition, his hard-line Christian upbringing in a village in East Prussia, his education at strict military schools and the situation he was confronted with in Poland – led Blaskowitz to act as he did. These preconditions also limited the form his resistance took. He chose to protest, but within the structure that had been his life for many years – the German Army. He didn't, perhaps couldn't, move outside of it.

Other protesters, not brought up in such a rigid framework, took a very different approach. In November 1939, as Blaskowitz was gathering evidence of atrocities in Poland, another German took more direct action against the regime. A thirty-six-year-old carpenter called Georg Elser made an audacious attempt to blow up Adolf Hitler. Elser knew that on 8 November Hitler would give a speech at the Bürgerbräukeller in Munich on the anniversary of the Beer-Hall Putsch, and so he resolved to make a bomb and conceal it in the woodwork close to the speaker's rostrum. Over several days he concealed himself in the beer hall, waited until closing time and then worked through the night to create a hiding place for the explosive device.

The bomb exploded as planned just before 9.30 p.m. on 8 November and killed eight people, wounding many more. But Hitler escaped. Because of bad weather he had decided to take the train back to Berlin rather than flying, and so had brought forward the time of his speech. He was stupendously lucky to have survived.

Elser was not so fortunate. Hardly a master criminal, he was arrested as he tried to cross into Switzerland on the night of 8 November. When the border guards ordered him to turn out his pockets they found a wealth of incriminating material, including a postcard of the Bürgerbräukeller. Despite repeated torture by the Gestapo, Elser stuck to his story. He had acted alone. This was contrary to the conspiracy theory the regime wanted to project – that Elser was part of a wide-ranging scheme orchestrated by British intelligence.

All the evidence uncovered since supports Elser's claim that no one else was involved in the attempt to kill Hitler. He was the classic lone assassin – an oddball who found it hard to fit in wherever he went, often changing jobs, unable to sustain a long-term relationship, given to brooding over his personal situation and the state of Germany as a whole. He had voted communist in the past and was concerned about the role of workers within the country, but he was too introspective to form a resistance group with others. He had worked out on his own what needed to be done to save Germany – and what was needed was a Germany without Adolf Hitler.

This type of lone killer is hard to stop. No amount of surveillance of resistance groups by the Gestapo would have detected him. Elser, for all his lack of formal education, knew one vital truth – the definition of a secret is something only one person knows.

Elser also illustrates a psychological reality about resistance. The spread of variables among a large population – of genetic predisposition, of parenting, of education, of the myriad other factors in the environment – mean that, as Professor Viding says, 'you will always have a few people who will absolutely resist.'

The fault in this case, as far as the Nazis were concerned, was not so much the inability of the Gestapo to find Elser before he started building his bomb as the lax security at the Bürgerbräukeller that made his attempt possible. Not that any of that mattered to Georg Elser – his attempt failed, he was sent to a concentration camp and executed just before the war ended.

General Blaskowitz's protest took a different course. Unlike Elser he was steeped in a culture that had twin pillars – his religion and his military code. His age – he was forty-nine when the Nazis came to power, fifty-six when the war began – meant that he had formed his worldview before Hitler had any influence on his career.

It is important to note that an officer like Blaskowitz could never have troubled Stalin – during the 1930s the Soviet leader had eliminated any Red Army officer whose loyalty was remotely suspect. But Hitler, as previously discussed, had decided against a mass purge of the German Army, chiefly because he intended to launch a war of conquest and didn't want to risk destabilizing the command structure. One of the risks of that approach, from his perspective, was the emergence of a general who felt he could protest against the actions of the Nazis' ideological fighters.

But Blaskowitz's background was also a bar to his resistance. He had spent his whole adolescence and adult life following a collective code of honour, and so believed that the only way he could protest was through the chain of command. Like many senior army officers, he initially found it hard to believe that Hitler, the head of state to whom he had sworn an oath of allegiance, was aware of the crimes being committed in his name. Blaskowitz and his colleagues tended to see the problem as a battle for Hitler's attention: if only Hitler knew in detail what the SS was doing, then things might change.

Blaskowitz's resistance focused entirely on events in Poland. What he didn't know was that his colleagues back in Berlin faced what they considered was a more existential threat – Hitler's decision to move against western Europe as quickly as possible. As early as 27 September 1939 Hitler had demanded that 'immediate plans' be made for a strike west. This was devastating news for the army commanders close to him. We find it hard to imagine their shock, because we know that the campaign when it began in May 1940 would be an overwhelming success. But in order to understand the way the mentalities of those in positions of power in the regime developed during the war, we need to grasp just how threatening they felt Hitler's plans were at the time.

Unlike the Polish armed forces, the British and French presented a formidable obstacle. Not only did they possess more tanks than the Germans, but many of them were superior to any of the tanks the Wehrmacht could put into battle. The considered judgement of a large number of German military experts was that the earliest a war in the west could be fought with any real chance of success was 1941, while others thought that French fortifications were so daunting that 1942 was a more realistic option.[40] In the opinion of General Stülpnagel, as quoted in the war diary of the Wehrmacht High Command, 'the [German] heavy tanks have been so battered in the east [in the war against Poland] that they must first be thoroughly overhauled, and the supply of new equipment is insufficient for the time being; and light combat vehicles cannot be considered to be adequate for full-on warfare.'[41]

The British and French agreed. They were confident that they would win an immediate conflict in the west. The military intelligence experts at the French Deuxième Bureau thought that any attack on France by

Hitler would result in the Germans suffering 'enormous human sacrifice' that 'could bring about the fall of the Nazi regime'.[42] Just before the outbreak of war Winston Churchill had visited French soldiers on the Maginot Line fortifications and been impressed by their 'calm and resolute morale', whereas the German troops he could see across the border appeared 'dead beat, or half starved, perhaps both'.[43]

The two most senior German generals – Brauchitsch, Commander-in-Chief of the army, and Halder, Chief of Staff of the Army High Command – were torn. They had sworn an oath of loyalty to Hitler, and both their training and centuries of military tradition taught them to be unquestioningly loyal. Moreover, Brauchitsch tended to wilt under pressure from Hitler, and since his new wife was a staunch Nazi believer he could count on little support at home for any opposition to Hitler's plans. Halder appeared to present a more resolute stance, but he also found it hard to disobey an outright order from the Nazi leader. Set against this was their belief that an attack on western Europe was doomed to fail. At best it would lead to stalemate and a repeat of the horrors of the First World War – a conflict both remembered all too well. At worst it meant the destruction of Germany.

That is the background to one of the most astonishing entries in Halder's war diary, written on 14 October 1939 after a meeting with Brauchitsch: 'Three possibilities: attack, wait, change.'[44] These five words contain within them the possibility of something shocking – rebellion. We can't know for certain what Halder intended by the third possibility, 'change', but it is possible it meant that Hitler would be pushed aside, much as the Kaiser had been sidelined by Hindenburg and Ludendorff during the last war, or even that Halder thought there was a possibility of arresting Hitler if he ordered the attack against France and the Low Countries.[45]

Halder also discussed various options to hinder Hitler's plans with other generals and potential resisters in the Abwehr (military intelligence) and the German Foreign Office. But Brauchitsch remained anxious about the consequences of radical action, and was made even more frightened by a calamitous meeting with Hitler on 5 November. After he told Hitler that the army was not prepared for an attack in the west and questioned the morale of the soldiers, the German leader became furious. He was infuriated by the suggestion that the army was not ready and demanded specific examples of the problems Brauchitsch had mentioned. He was so incensed that Brauchitsch emerged from the meeting shattered. He would now play no part in any attempt to unseat Hitler, indeed he was worried that Hitler already knew – or at least strongly suspected – that senior officers were plotting against him.

Meanwhile Halder had discovered that although some generals shared his view that the proposed attack in the west was 'mad'[46] there was a seemingly insurmountable problem. Even if senior officers might be prepared to break their oath and overthrow Hitler, they could not count on their men supporting them. As one general of the armoured corps wrote after the war, it would have been 'futile' to attempt a mutiny as the 'majority of the young soldiers' had too much belief in Hitler.[47]

Once again we see the split in mentalities, between the old guard who had largely formed their views before the Nazis came to power and those who followed afterwards who had been 'educated' by the regime. Officers like Halder and Brauchitsch had an intense loyalty to the army as an institution. When they thought of 'Them and Us' there was still a temptation in moments of stress to class the army as 'Us' and Hitler and the Nazis as 'Them'. But there was no such conflict in the minds of many of the younger soldiers. They had been raised in a system that preached that Hitler was profoundly one of 'Us'.

Another problem the resisters faced was the reaction of the public to Elser's failed assassination attempt on 8 November 1939. Reports by the SD and the local police emphasized the outrage felt at the attempt to kill Hitler. 'Nearly the entire population was disgusted by this heinous deed,' said one typical report from the police in Waischenfeld. 'One could hear repeatedly that "God is obviously on the Führer's side and it is such a relief that he didn't come to any harm."'[48]

No less significant was the motivation behind this potential mutiny. Halder and Brauchitsch weren't acting out of principle. They hadn't decided – as Blaskowitz had – that a stand had to be taken over the atrocities that were being committed in Poland against innocent civilians. No, they were concerned with a purely practical issue – if the army fought a campaign in the west they would lose. In theory, they relished the idea of seeking redress for Versailles by defeating the French – they just disagreed about the timing. They weren't martyrs, they were pragmatists, something which placed them firmly in the mainstream of human experience.

Though Brauchitsch was prepared to raise Blaskowitz's complaints with Heinrich Himmler during 1940, he was easily reassured after a few platitudes from the SS leader. Revealingly, Brauchitsch and many of his colleagues were more passionate about another instruction issued by Himmler. At the end of October 1939, in what became known as the 'procreation order', Himmler had said that soldiers should do all they could to leave a child behind them. They should 'procreate' regardless of whether they were married or not. But, as Himmler recognized in an instruction issued to 'all of the SS and police' dated 30 January 1940, this had been 'misunderstood by some' to mean that SS men 'would be asked to approach the wives of soldiers fighting on the battlefield'. Claiming to be outraged by the suggestion that German women were not themselves acting as 'guardians of their honour' Himmler nonetheless stated unequivocally – and much to the reassurance of Brauchitsch and others in the army – that 'you don't approach a comrade's wife.'[49]

There was a coda to the row two years later, when the head of the SS court wrote to Himmler to ask for clarification. 'Lately,' said the letter, 'the number of cases in which members of the SS and the police have engaged in sexual intercourse with the wives of conscripted soldiers has increased.' But the fault was not always on the side of the SS since 'the women make it very easy for the young men.' One case was also quoted where the SS man 'had the intention to marry the woman after her divorce'. So the question was what should be done if 'a proper romantic relationship with serious marriage plans has developed'.[50]

Six weeks later, in March, Himmler made his view clear. 'Not every violation is to be legally punished,' he said. 'It rather depends on the individual case . . .'[51] That wasn't, of course, what Brauchitsch had been promised two years before. But a lot had changed since then: Brauchitsch had retired after suffering a heart attack in December 1941; the German Army was involved in a life-and-death struggle on the Russian steppes; and the SS were committing atrocities on a scale that dwarfed anything they had perpetrated in Poland in 1939.

Himmler, despite the platitudes he had expressed in early 1940 to reassure the army leadership about the SS, did not alter his hard-line ideological stance towards the Poles. Quite the reverse in fact. Because he wasn't just trying to terrorize the Polish population; he was attempting one of the biggest ethnic-cleansing actions in history. Under the deal with Stalin arranged by Ribbentrop, the Baltic States and other territory in eastern Europe that contained large numbers of ethnic Germans now fell under Soviet control. Himmler and Hitler, in their pursuit of 'racially pure' blood, wanted to 'rescue' these people from the clutches of the Bolsheviks. Appointed in October 1939 as Reich Commissioner for the Strengthening of German Nationality, Himmler organized transport for tens of thousands of these ethnic Germans – around 60,000 from Estonia and Latvia alone – and relocated them to Poland.

To find room for the ethnic Germans, the Nazis deported more than 200,000 Poles in less than two years into the General Government in the east of the country. The suffering of these Poles was immense. Franz Jagemann, whom we met in a previous chapter when he revealed how much he objected to life in the Hitler Youth, was drafted as an assistant interpreter to help the SS as they deported the population of entire Polish villages. He was initially misled by the equivocal language the Nazis used: 'It was all very carefully put. They would say something like, this or that person has to be "evacuated" and must give way to a German, but it was said in such a way that you could not imagine the reality that I then later experienced.'[52]

The Nazi regime had, from the beginning, used euphemisms to conceal the brutal truth of their actions. Prisoners in concentration camps were said to be in 'protective custody' in order to be 're-educated'. But with the outbreak of war and the increasing number of atrocities, the number of euphemisms grew, until during the Holocaust almost every action had its own camouflage term. Jews were 'resettled' not 'deported' and those to be murdered were subject to 'special treatment'. After 97,000 Jews had been killed, one report blandly said they had been 'processed'.[53] The best-known example of a euphemism, of course, was the name the Nazis gave to the Holocaust itself – the 'Final Solution to the Jewish Question'.

There was an obvious advantage in the use of euphemisms. As Maria Otero Rossi has pointed out, it 'simplifies' the 'later negation' of crimes.[54] Anyone examining documents after the war would find no mention of the murder of the Jews, just their 'special treatment'. It was a ruse that even today helps facilitate Holocaust deniers.

This anodyne language offered the Nazis another benefit, one that is more psychologically profound. In the words of Professor Albert

Bandura, euphemisms help perpetrators to 'detach and depersonalize' themselves from their actions. There is even psychological evidence that 'people behave much more cruelly when assaultive actions are given a sanitized label than when they are called aggression.'[55]

It was a technique of moral disengagement, however, that didn't work for everyone. It didn't stop Franz Jagemann feeling devastated as he witnessed the deportation of Polish civilians from their homes. 'People were kicked, punched, pistols were waved in their faces,' he recalled. 'It was like a proper hold-up.' After the villagers had been loaded on to trucks and taken away, 'The SS people took the Catholic paintings of saints, ripped them off the walls together with little mementoes, little statues and the like, and threw them in a heap in the courtyards, so that they all splintered up. Then straw was thrown on to them and then the whole thing was set on fire and burnt. It was a sort of symbolic appropriation – de-Catholicizing, or de-Polonization. Here Polish rule is at an end.' Once the deportations and associated destruction were complete, the SS left for a nearby inn and 'got really drunk'. Jagemann remembered that 'the SS were always very satisfied with themselves, because from their perspective through their brutality and recklessness they had shown who was the boss.'

Jagemann was filled with 'horror' at the actions of the SS and claimed to have mounted a small act of resistance. He found out where and when the next forced deportations were taking place and tried to 'get a warning' to the villages targeted. The reason he took this risk was straightforward – his own part-Polish heritage meant that he felt conflicted. Was he a Pole or was he German? Who were 'Us' and who were 'Them'? The answer, as he participated in these brutal ethnic-cleansing actions, was that Jagemann started to lean more towards his Polish side.

Once, during a deportation, Jagemann said he tried to 'talk soothingly' to a young woman and told her, 'I am one of you.' And 'when I saw that this seemed to help these people in such a bleak situation, I did it again later. And so one day I was staggered when I heard one of them saying of me: "He's one of us." Without any nasty comment. It was even in a respectful tone.'

Not that Jagemann considered himself brave – he reproached himself after the war for a lack of courage. 'You sometimes felt bad about yourself,' he said. 'You didn't like yourself any more.'[56]

These deportations were just part of the Nazis' vision for Poland.

They saw the country as a gigantic racial sorting ground, a vast experiment in separating 'Them' from 'Us'. The content of your character, your intelligence, your education, your guilt or innocence of any crime, none of that mattered. All that concerned the Nazi administrators was their judgement of your racial composition.

'We need to be clear about one thing,' Himmler told Nazi Gauleiters on 29 February 1940. 'I believe that our blood, the Nordic blood, is the best blood on this earth . . . We are superior to everything and everyone else. Once we are liberated from inhibitions and restraints, there is no one who can surpass us in quality and strength.' Because 'Nordic blood' was so superior, added Himmler, the Nazis needed to search for people not currently living in the Reich who possessed this 'best blood on earth' and take them to Germany: 'now that the time has come when we are strong, we have to see to bringing back all of our blood, to do everything in our power to make sure that no blood of ours will ever be lost to the outside again.'[57] In pursuit of this policy of 'bringing back all of our blood' Himmler ordered that young Polish children who were deemed 'racially' acceptable should be kidnapped and raised as Germans.

Himmler's racial fanaticism was so great that, even if you committed a crime that the Nazis considered merited your execution, you could be saved if your 'race' was reclassified. That is what happened to a number of Polish workers who had consensual sexual relationships with German women. Initially any Pole who committed this 'offence' was sentenced to death, but in 1941 the order was changed so that any perpetrator who 'showed elements of Nordic race' and was of 'favourable' character could escape execution. If a Pole passed this racial test – after a physical examination which included an examination of cheekbones and hair and eye colour – he would be sent to a concentration camp for a 'short time' and afterwards be 'Germanized'.[58] If his cheekbones and hair didn't measure up then he would be murdered. Your 'race' was everything.

In parallel with the racial reorganization of Poland, the Nazis pursued another policy that created appalling suffering – 'euthanasia' actions against the disabled. This deadly scheme has not penetrated the public consciousness today as much as it should. That is partly because these killings were subsequently dwarfed by the enormity of the Holocaust,

but it is also a consequence of the effectiveness of yet another euphemism. The Nazis called the operation the 'euthanasia' of the disabled,
and that implied that there was an element of consent in the killing. In
reality there was none. This was a scheme to murder selected disabled
civilians who were wholly innocent. Their only misfortune was to be
considered a 'burden' on the Nazi state.

The 'euthanasia' actions are also of importance in understanding the
mentalities of those who would later plan and implement the Holocaust,
because many of the psychological mechanisms used to facilitate the
murder of the disabled would later be employed by the killers in the
death camps.

In an earlier chapter we saw how even though Hitler pushed through
legislation to sterilize selected disabled Germans, he had always wanted
a more radical policy.[59] As war neared in the summer of 1939, he seized
his chance. Philipp Bouhler, head of the Führer's Chancellery, brought
a letter to Hitler's attention written by the father of a baby who was
severely disabled. The father wanted the child to be killed as an act of
'mercy'. Hitler agreed, and from this one case developed the 'child
euthanasia scheme'.

Three doctors would separately examine reports on each child and
then mark the form with a plus or a minus. Two or more minus marks
meant the child was sentenced to death. Responsibility was thus shared
among the doctors for the decision. Rather like a firing squad where no
single shooter can feel entirely to blame for the death of the condemned
prisoner, so no single doctor had to bear the guilt for killing a child. There
are obvious psychological benefits in this diffusion of responsibility.

Not all doctors supported the plan to kill children. Dr Friedrich
Hölzel was one of those who wasn't happy about participating. He
worked for one of the most notorious enthusiasts for the scheme, a
committed Nazi called Dr Hermann Pfannmüller, director of the
Eglfing-Haar mental hospital in Bavaria. In a letter to Pfannmüller, Dr
Hölzel said that even though he thought the 'new measures' were 'convincing' it was 'one thing to approve of the measures of the State with
full conviction and another to carry them out oneself in their final consequence'. He felt 'somehow emotionally bound' to the children, and
admitted at the end of his letter that he was 'too weak for this task'.[60]

Notice once again how Hölzel took refuge in euphemistic language –
the killings were 'new measures' or simply 'the task' ahead. What's also

significant is that he does not criticize the correctness of the plan, only his own ability to carry it out. Once the Holocaust began, similar excuses were used by members of the killing squads who were unable to shoot Jews.[61]

Shortly after he had authorized the murder of selected disabled children, Hitler ordered the scheme to be expanded to the adult disabled. This presented a number of 'challenges' for the killers. Children had been murdered either by medication – such as an overdose of luminol – or by starvation. But these measures wouldn't be sufficient for the much larger number of disabled adults that were expected to be selected for these 'new measures'. In search of another way of killing, officials working on the euthanasia plans contacted a scientist – Dr Albert Widmann, the twenty-seven-year-old head of the Criminal Technical Institute.

Widmann was told that 'animals in human form' were to be killed and that he should come up with ideas for how this should be done. Initially he suggested that carbon monoxide could be pumped into hospital wards to gas the patients as they slept.[62] But there were practical difficulties in hermetically sealing a ward, so the plan was modified. The disabled patients selected to die would now be told they had to take a shower, and then carbon monoxide, rather than water, would be pumped into the shower room.

This is a crucial moment, not just in the evolution of the Nazi process of mass murder, but in the way the killers were able to cope mentally with their work. That's because gassing by the fake-shower method offered the killers something vital – distance. Psychological studies have demonstrated that it is much easier to kill from a distance than from close up. As we saw earlier in the context of the First World War, to stab someone with a bayonet as you look into your victim's eyes is much harder than launching an artillery shell at them from miles away.[63]

The added advantage of killing via artillery is that you don't commit the act as an individual. You act as part of a team and so gain 'group absolution'. This process is so freeing psychologically that one expert wrote that 'In years of research and reading on the subject of killing in combat I have not found one single instance of individuals who have refused to kill the enemy under these circumstances, nor have I found a single instance of psychiatric trauma associated with this type of killing.'[64] Similarly, by shifting from injecting children with a deadly chemical to ushering adults into what purported to be a shower room and turning on the gas valve, those involved had made their crime psychologically easier to commit.

The invention of the shower/gas chamber provided other psychological benefits for the killers. There were cases of children protesting and pleading as they were taken away for lethal injection, which could be distressing for the nurses and doctors involved. But now, with the adult scheme, the medical staff would be 'spared' upset, as long as their victims believed until the moment they started breathing the poison gas that they were taking a shower. But as their work progressed not all the disabled targeted by the Nazis were ignorant of their fate – eventually it proved impossible to keep the murders a secret. This led to heart-rending scenes, with patients selected for transports to the killing centres begging and shouting, 'I just want to live, I just want to live.'[65]

There were many ways in which the mindset of the euthanasia killers resembled that of the perpetrators of the Holocaust to come. Most notably in the strong sense of justification that the medical staff felt. They took their lead from Hitler, who at a meeting about the adult euthanasia scheme had said he felt it right to destroy 'life unworthy of life'. He painted a gruesome picture of mentally ill people eating 'their own excrement' and sleeping on the bare ground because they 'would soil themselves constantly'.[66] This kind of rhetoric made it easier for those involved to believe they were carrying out the killings almost out of kindness.

Even long after the end of the war some of those involved in the murders still protested their innocence. Dr Georg Renno, who worked at Hartheim killing centre in Austria, said in 1997: 'I don't feel guilty – like somebody who has shot someone or anything. After I saw how the people died, I told myself that this was no ordeal for them, I would rather say, in quotation marks: "It was a relief."' Renno was ninety years old when he said these words and was sufficiently relaxed about his past crimes to remark, 'I pass into eternity confidently.'[67]

Werner Dubois, an SS man assigned to the euthanasia scheme, remembered that he and a colleague 'were shown photographs of seriously mentally ill people' and told that they were to be involved in 'mercy killings'.[68] He was also informed that there was an economic benefit to their actions, since 'billions of Reichsmarks were being spent on these incurably ill people and that doctors and nursing staff were tied down caring for them, although they and the money were needed for other purposes.'[69]

Many of those appointed to run the killing centres were not only committed Nazis but young for the level of responsibility the job entailed. Dr Horst Schumann was just thirty-three when he became director of the Grafeneck euthanasia centre, Dr Rudolf Lonauer was the same age when given the job of running the killing centre at Hartheim in Austria, and Dr Irmfried Eberl was younger still – only twenty-nine – when appointed to lead the team at the euthanasia unit at Brandenburg.

Eberl, in particular, was a fanatical believer. While a student he had mimicked Hitler's appearance, cultivating both a short moustache and Hitler's penetrating stare. He also hated Christians and Jews and had written a parody of the Lord's Prayer which included the lines: 'Unimportant be Thy name. Thy kingdom we want to destroy,' and 'Lead the comrades not into temptation, but deliver them from the Jews and priests.'[70]

Another doctor involved in the euthanasia scheme described Eberl as 'very vain and arrogant' and 'cocksure of himself and his ability'.[71] Circumstances had conspired to offer Eberl an opportunity to make a mark as a Nazi, and he relished the chance to show his worth. Like many involved in the killing of the disabled, Eberl would go on to play an important part in the Holocaust.

The disabled in Poland were an early target for the Nazis, with Einsatzkommandos killing Polish patients in West Prussia at the end of September 1939. Though these disabled Poles lost their lives because of Nazi ideology, there was a link with the population transfers that were causing chaos in the country. Some of the buildings that were emptied by the killings were later used to house ethnic Germans who had arrived looking for a new life.

Gassing experiments were also conducted in Poland during which an entirely new method of delivering gas to the disabled was used. Since it was onerous to transport the Polish patients to the killing centres in Germany to be murdered, a way was found of bringing the killing apparatus to them. Herbert Lange, a thirty-year-old SS officer, pioneered the use of a mobile gas chamber – a gas van. Lange's men drove between mental hospitals in the Warthegau in Poland in a van emblazoned with the words 'Kaiser's Kaffee Geschäft' (Kaiser's Coffee

Company) picking up selected patients, cramming them in the back of the van and then turning on the gas.[72]

Lange and his men began their work on 7 December 1939, when they arrived with their gas van at the Dziekanka psychiatric hospital thirty miles north-east of Poznań. They then proceeded over the next few weeks to kill over a thousand patients across the area, before moving on and killing thousands more. Alcohol clearly helped them in their task – after clearing the psychiatric institution at Warta in April 1940, men in Lange's unit drank so much that they passed out.[73]

Like Dr Eberl, we shall meet Herbert Lange and his gas van again.

While Lange, Eberl and their SS colleagues murdered thousands of disabled people in gas chambers and vans, German generals remained focused on their own concerns – chiefly, how to stop Hitler destroying Germany by invading France. Since rebellion was not a practicable option, and it was impossible to change Hitler's mind, their only recourse was to try and delay the attack. Bad weather became one of their most effective excuses, and a whole series of dates for the invasion were announced and then cancelled.

Hitler did not know it at the time, but this was his first lucky break in what would turn out to be a series of lucky breaks. The plans for the November 1939 invasion of western Europe amounted to little more than a repeat of the failed campaign of 1914, and his generals were right to think the attack would fail. But then something surprising happened – because the generals knew that an attack west was inevitable, they started to consider a more imaginative approach to the campaign.

This new idea, famously championed by General Erich von Manstein,[74] favoured a powerful thrust south through the Ardennes forest towards the French city of Sedan on the River Meuse. Once over the river, German forces could sweep across the plains of northern France to the sea. Here they would meet up with the second army group involved in the attack, which was tasked with moving west via the 'traditional' invasion route from Germany through the Netherlands and Belgium. 'This is an operation of unprecedented logistical risk,' said one scholar who has studied the plans in detail. 'The gamble bears the possibility of total victory . . . but also a risk of catastrophic defeat, which they're fully conscious of.'[75]

The 'gamble' was that Allied forces would not detect German troops as they made their way through the Ardennes forest. If discovered in the forest, where they would be vulnerable to air attack, the Germans would almost certainly lose the war. Nonetheless, Hitler – who was fond of risk-taking – was enthusiastic about the new plan.

The gamble worked. The British and French, largely due to their incompetence and complacency, didn't react to the movement of the Germans through the Ardennes until it was too late. The psychological shock of the appearance of German armoured units at Sedan, combined with a devastating attack by Stuka dive bombers, led to the infamous 'panic of Bulson' on 13 May 1940 when units of the French Army turned and fled. At 7.30 in the morning of 15 May, Paul Reynaud, Prime Minister of France, rang Winston Churchill and said dramatically, 'We have been defeated.'[76] It was an incredible victory for the Germans – just five days after they had launched their offensive. The French did not sign the armistice with the Germans until 22 June, but the war was over long before that.

Just imagine how the German generals now felt. During their attempt to conquer France in the First World War, they had been stuck in a ghastly war of attrition in the trenches for four years. Now they had defeated the French in a matter of days. It was almost unbelievable. Halder's war diary in the first months of 1940 contains numerous references to the anxieties and concerns of the generals – he prefaces one entry on 25 February with the single word 'Worries'. But even during the difficult planning phase of the campaign that spring, Hitler had always been 'manifestly confident of success'.[77]

You don't have to have studied the psychology of leadership to understand the immense consequences of what Hitler had just achieved. He had been proved right and his naysaying generals had been proved wrong. German generals would remember this moment the next time they were tempted to doubt Hitler. Wasn't it now sensible just to ape what Göring, Himmler, Goebbels and the other Nazis had been doing for years and have faith in the Führer?

The effect of the triumph over France on the psyche of millions of Germans cannot be overestimated. As a result of the victory, resistance to Hitler became more difficult than ever. Who could oppose him now, when the victory parade in Berlin on 6 July was unlike any seen before, with screaming crowds delirious with happiness?[78]

10. Escalating Racism

In the early morning of Sunday 22 June 1941, the Germans and their allies launched the biggest and bloodiest war in the history of the world. Almost four million soldiers pushed on to Soviet territory in three giant thrusts, aiming for the Baltic States, Moscow and Ukraine.

Just as with the war against Poland nearly two years before, Einsatzgruppen killing squads entered enemy territory behind the fighting units. But in this new conflict they would commit atrocities on a different scale and perpetrate an unparalleled orgy of bloodlust and hatred. Nazi killing squads murdered well over a million people, perhaps as many as one and a half million. These were close-up killings, conducted in circumstances which meant the killers could not be distanced from their actions. Intimate murders, with blood, brains and fragments of bone reaching the shooters.

This war was to be the great reckoning for the Nazis. In Hitler's eyes the Soviet Union was the home of a double threat – Bolsheviks and Jews. Moreover, he believed that 'the rulers of present-day Russia are common bloodstained criminals' who represented the 'scum of humanity'. Scaling the heights of hyperbole, he claimed they were responsible for the 'most cruel and tyrannical regime of all time'.[1]

Hitler was so desperate to confront this 'scum' that he decided to commit Germany to a two-front war. His original plan had been to win the war in the west before turning east. But because Britain would not give up, the war in the west was still under way. He tried to convince his generals that victory over Stalin would help defeat Britain, claiming that the British hoped that eventually the Soviets would become their ally. But it was a false argument – Britain's great hope was the United States, not the Soviet Union. The British believed their saviour would be Roosevelt, not Stalin.

This had been a racist conflict from the moment German tanks crossed into Poland on 1 September 1939, but that racism was now to be escalated to a new level. Hitler announced to his military commanders that the war against the Soviet Union was to be a 'war of extermination' and ordered that the political leaders of the Red Army, the 'commissars', together with the 'Communist intelligentsia', should be killed rather than taken prisoner. It was vital, he said, to remember that a 'Communist is no comrade before or after the battle' and that German commanders 'must make the sacrifice of overcoming their personal scruples'.[2]

Despite the radical nature of Hitler's words, there was little protest from his generals. They knew of the atrocities that had taken place – and were still taking place – in Poland. So that was the basis on which the new brutalities could be judged. Chivalrous principles of war had long since been discarded, and if you hadn't mutinied over the actions of the security forces in Poland, why would you mutiny now – especially since Hitler's prestige as a military leader had never been higher after the triumph in the west the previous year?

But there was another reason why Hitler's generals didn't object to this 'war of extermination': many of them shared his racial prejudice against the inhabitants of the Soviet Union. 'The history of all Russian wars shows that the Russian, as a combatant, is illiterate and semi-Asian, and thinks and feels differently [from us],' wrote General Blumentritt of the Fourth Army.[3]

Colonel General Küchler was even more outspoken, writing two months before the invasion, 'There is a profound abyss that separates us from Russia ideologically and racially.' It was important, he said, to remember that 'we are fighting against racially alien soldiers.'[4] Another message to the troops, signed by Colonel General Falkenhorst, warned that the 'Russian' was a 'master of every means of chicanery, fraud and propaganda' and that enemy soldiers were 'capable of every sadistic bestiality'.[5]

Many times during this investigation we have seen the impact of 'Them and Us' thinking on mentality and action. But we have now reached what, for the Nazis, was the ultimate war of 'Them and Us', one in which their dehumanizing of the enemy would reach almost transcendent levels.

Every German soldier who took part in the invasion was primed to expect the worst from their new adversaries. They were told their opponents were not just racially inferior – subhuman, in fact – but would not fight by the rules of war. Consequently, the triggering of fear and aggression in the minds of many of these invaders would have been immense.[6] This war was more akin to a struggle against animals than one against human beings. Just as you couldn't trust a snake, so you couldn't trust a Russian. Our brain tends to see our friends as individuals and our enemies as a collective – and the 'Russians' were perceived as one single horde of wild beasts.

We have already seen how the belief among the German forces in Poland that their enemy was prepared to undertake 'partisan' warfare was a factor in the Nazis' often pre-emptive brutality. That emotion would now be magnified many times over in the invasion of the Soviet Union. And, given that they were told in advance to expect 'every kind' of 'chicanery' from Red Army units, German soldiers were already predisposed to treat their enemy with great brutality.

Senior figures in the SS were well aware that this was to be a war of murderous colonization. Heinrich Himmler held a conference for senior SS leaders at Wewelsburg castle shortly before the invasion and announced that 'thirty million' people were expected to die in the occupied Soviet Union.[7] The Nazis, it transpired, wanted the land but they didn't want millions of the people who currently lived on it.

German soldiers were told to steal food from the locals, and enormous numbers of civilians were expected to die of hunger. Nazi officials ordered the soldiers not to feel sorry for those they starved to death. 'Poverty, hunger and thrift have been the lot of the Russians for centuries,' said Herbert Backe of the Department of Food and Agriculture. 'Their stomachs are elastic – so let us have no misplaced pity.'[8]

Four Einsatzgruppen, a total of around 3,000 men, were given the more immediate task of murdering 'Jews in the service of the party or the state' and 'Communist officials'. But this was the bare minimum they were expected to kill, as their instructions also said they should incite pogroms by convincing locals to rise up against the Jews.

Given the heinous crimes they were about to commit, there is a tendency to think that the members of the Einsatzgruppen were all bloodthirsty sadists. It's a comfortable way of thinking about the history, but it's wrong. Whatever else motivated these killers, it wasn't mass psychopathy.

Two of the four commanders of the Einsatzgruppen, Arthur Nebe, head of the Criminal Police, and Walter Stahlecker, who had led security forces in Norway, volunteered for the job.[9] The others were appointed, including the intellectual Otto Ohlendorf of the SD. He wasn't the only cerebral commander within the ranks of the killing squads. In Einsatzgruppe A, eleven of the seventeen most senior leaders were lawyers; nine held academic doctorates.[10]

Many members of the Einsatzgruppen were both young and ambitious. One entire class of the Security Police leadership school in Berlin was sent east to join the killing squads. The vast majority had been born after 1910, so virtually their whole life as policemen had been spent under Nazi rule. Bruno Streckenbach, the SS officer in charge of personnel at Heydrich's Reich Security Head Office, later commented that 'without exception they all proved themselves splendidly.'[11]

Others were drafted into the Einsatzgruppen from the Waffen SS and the police. One SS sergeant was even called back from his job as a plumber.[12] But while they were all committed Nazis with a background in the security forces, few had track records as killers, although they were all predisposed to accept violence as a solution to the problems they perceived Germany faced, and they believed that though their job was hard and difficult they were acting together to create the utopia they desired. They felt both privileged and burdened – they had been given tasks that no one before or after them would have the courage to undertake.

The philosopher and sociologist Zygmunt Bauman believed that the two great 'archetypes' of Nazism were medicine and gardening.[13] In the last chapter we saw how doctors were told that by killing the disabled they were treating the body of the state, and now Hitler told senior Nazis on 16 July 1941 that he wanted to build a 'Garden of Eden' in the east. The tools this gardener wanted to use to create this paradise were 'shooting' and 'resettlement'.[14]

The SS director of one of the euthanasia centres, Dr Irmfried Eberl, thought he combined both roles – doctor and gardener. He justified the killing of the disabled by using a gardening metaphor, telling a colleague that just as a gardener needed to destroy 'all weeds' to allow healthy plants to flourish, so 'people not worthy to live ought to disappear.'[15] As we shall see, Dr Eberl would later become commandant of Treblinka, one of the most notorious of the Nazi death camps, where he would practise his 'gardening' on a horrendous scale.[16]

The Nazis were keen to stir up racial tension among the locals as they crossed into the Soviet Union, and some of the earliest atrocities were not perpetrated by Germans but by the indigenous population. When Einsatzgruppe A arrived in Kaunas in Lithuania, for example, just a day after the invasion had started, they found locals who were keen to start killing Jews. They watched as one Lithuanian clubbed to death a group of Jews with an iron bar. When he had murdered all of them, he climbed on top of their bodies, picked up his accordion and played the Lithuanian national anthem to an appreciative crowd.[17]

That same month, in Lviv in Ukraine, locals murdered Jews in much greater numbers. With German support they killed around 4,000 Jews in an action that haunts the city to this day. Both the Lviv and Kaunas killings were committed by perpetrators fuelled by a mix of anti-Semitism and vengefulness. They had suffered badly under Stalin's rule – in Lviv the Soviet secret police had killed Ukrainian prisoners just before the Red Army retreated, and in Lithuania thousands of people had been deported to the wilds of the Soviet Union. Now the locals unjustly blamed the Jews for these Soviet crimes.

Soldiers of the Romanian Army, which invaded the Soviet Union as an ally of Germany, also committed the most appalling atrocities. As they recaptured former Romanian territory taken by the Soviets, they murdered more than 100,000 Jews. Once again, the combination of 'traditional' anti-Semitism coupled with the erroneous belief that the Jews were behind communism proved a deadly mix. So dreadful were the frenzied actions of the Romanians that one German general even complained about their conduct.[18]

Nazi killing squads tended to operate on a more definite schedule and in a more systematic way. But there was no set method of committing these murders dictated from above. Each unit commander was free to devise his own technique of shooting innocent civilians. At Nuremberg, Otto Ohlendorf claimed that he ensured that his 'executions were carried out in a military manner, by firing squads under command'.[19] But some commanders paired each shooter with a victim and the killings were conducted face to face. Others shot kneeling victims in the back of the neck. Still more made the Jews strip naked and lie in a pit on top of those who had already been shot, thus maximizing the number who could be killed in each pit.

We can gain some insight into the mentalities of these killers from the results of the most famous experiment in social psychology. In the summer of 1961, a Yale psychologist called Stanley Milgram oversaw a series of experiments to test the nature of obedience. He wanted to discover whether an ordinary person – the 'subject' – would be prepared to deliver electric shocks to someone else, on the orders of an authority figure. Unbeknown to the subject, the person supposed to suffer the shocks – the 'victim' – was an actor, and no electric shocks were given. Neither the subject nor the victim could see the other during the experiment, but the subject was told there was a microphone connection between them.

An authority figure in a white coat told the subject to administer electric shocks to the victim after the wrong response had been given to a memory question, starting at 15 volts and incrementally increasing to 450. Both the authority figure and the subject sat in the same room throughout the experiment. As the shocks increased, the subject heard protests from the victim, which were pre-recorded on tape. The two highest levels of shock were marked on the machine 'Danger: Severe Shock' and 'XXX'.

The results of the experiments were unexpected. Most of the initial group of forty subjects – around 65 per cent – were prepared to administer the highest level of shock. They did this despite hearing the victim protest by making a banging noise, and for the final shocks hearing nothing at all.

The subjects carried on administering the shocks even though they believed the victim was likely in distress, and despite the fact they were free to walk away from the experiment whenever they wanted. Even when, in a variation of the experiment, the subject heard the victim scream out and beg for the experiment to stop, twenty-five of the forty subjects still carried on and delivered the maximum shock.[20]

There are, of course, obvious differences between the Milgram experiment and the actions of the Nazi killers. The subjects Milgram selected, for example, were told by the experimenter that the shocks they were administering would not cause permanent damage. Nor did they think, as the Nazis did, that they were hurting 'inferior' people. However, albeit with qualifications, Milgram's work does still offer valuable insights into the mentality of those who kill.[21] For Milgram himself, the most 'fundamental lesson' was that 'ordinary people, simply doing their jobs, and without any particular hostility on their part, can become agents in a terrible destructive process.'[22]

The role of the authority figure and the imprimatur of Yale University were two crucial reasons why it was possible for so many of the subjects to carry on administering the shocks on the scale they did. Both at the individual level – the authority figure radiated confidence – and at the institutional level – Yale is one of America's most distinguished universities – Milgram succeeded in creating an environment in which most of the subjects were prepared to inflict pain on another human being.

The neuroscientist Professor Robert Sapolsky noticed a similar legitimizing effect from both individuals and institution in his laboratory at Stanford – like Yale one of America's top universities. He observed a split among his students once they were faced with experimenting on animals. Some 'weren't bothered in the slightest' by the task and so he tried to find 'some means to get them out of the lab because something's wrong with you if this isn't bothering you'. Others just couldn't cope with the work and dropped out. Finally, there was the middle group of students who, while they found the work emotionally difficult, were still 'trying to understand if it's worth it'. Sapolsky revealed that when he sent these students to a hospital to observe patients who 'were the ones who were having their lives destroyed, because we hadn't figured out the answers to this [disease] yet', then 'the students would suddenly realize, "Wow, that's why I'm doing this!" '[23]

In Milgram's case, the authority figure also emphasized how important the work was, and made a pre-scripted series of legitimizing statements when the subjects objected to administering the electric shocks. From 'please go on' to 'the experiment requires that you continue' and 'it is absolutely essential that you continue.' Fascinatingly, the least effective statement was the last one given – 'You have no other choice, you must go on.' This was the only request that could be characterized as an 'order'.

It might be thought that this 'order' failed because it was the last comment, spoken at a point when the subjects were at their most stressed. But even when in later versions the order was switched so that it came earlier in the experiment it was still the least effective prompt.[24] The inescapable conclusion was that reassurance was the most powerful tool the authority figure possessed.

Another insight contained within both Milgram's study and Sapolsky's anecdotal experience is the prevalence of the search to justify one's actions – what psychologists call the 'just world' hypothesis.[25] And the consequent revelation that a significant number of people can be led to believe that inflicting suffering is necessary, so long as they are reassured by an authority figure that this is so.

Certainly, in the context of the Nazi killers, the role of the authority figure was crucial in legitimizing the actions of the group. Both Heydrich and Himmler were aware of this, and took a close personal interest in the actions of their killing squads. In the early weeks of the war against the Soviet Union, when they were concerned about what they saw as the slow pace of the killings, they went on a tour of the killing zone and talked to members of the Einsatzgruppen, emphasizing the importance of their task and congratulating those who had achieved the most kills.

Heydrich and Himmler reassured their men that the state supported their actions and that they should not feel 'guilt' for the killings, all of which were necessary for the security of their fellow Germans. It was a leadership technique the psychoanalyst Erich Fromm would have recognized. He was one of the earliest thinkers to suggest that passing on responsibility to others could be attractive, calling it 'escape from freedom'.[26]

Broadly speaking, each group of killers could be divided into three. There were those who found they enjoyed killing. There were those who, from the moment they started, found it all but impossible to kill. And there were those who found it difficult to shoot, but discovered they could do it nonetheless. This three-way split, with the majority of people in the middle group, is something we will see repeated again and again in the context of the killing mentality.

Within a few weeks of the start of the war against the Soviet Union, a moral Rubicon was crossed. Word from above was passed between the murder squads over the summer and early autumn of 1941 that the killing was to be expanded to include Jewish women and children. This coincided with the reinforcement of the Einsatzgruppen with thousands of extra SS and security forces.

There was never a formal explanation given for this widening of the killing, although Himmler did come close when he said two years later, in an infamous speech he gave to leading Nazis at Posen on 6 October 1943, that he didn't want to let these children 'grow up to take revenge on our sons and grandsons'.[27]

In the summer of 1941, Himmler was careful how he described this change in policy. On 1 August, he sent an order to the SS Cavalry Brigade, operating in the Pripet Marshes – one of the areas in the occupied Soviet Union where the killing squads were wreaking havoc. 'All Jews must be shot,' said Himmler. 'Drive the female Jews into the swamps.' In response he received a reply from Franz Magill of the 2nd SS Cavalry Regiment, which read, 'Driving women and children into the swamps did not have the success it was supposed to have as the swamps were not deep enough for sinking under to occur.'[28] It is clear from this exchange that despite Himmler's euphemistic language, Magill understood perfectly that the order meant that his unit should murder the women and children.

It is tempting to think that these killers were psychopaths or had psychopathic tendencies. But there aren't huge numbers of such people in the population – only around 1 per cent of people in the population today can be diagnosed as psychopaths. However, since individuals with these tendencies tend to gravitate towards jobs that allow them to behave cruelly, there would likely have been a greater proportion of them among the Einsatzgruppen. One recent study of people who committed atrocities under the Pinochet regime in Chile, for instance, found that these perpetrators had higher levels of core psychopathic traits than not only the general population but also other prisoners.[29]

It is much harder to estimate how many people have sadistic tendencies – those people who enjoy inflicting harm. For psychologists it's an area fraught with definitional and experimental difficulties, so much so that, depending on the criteria used, estimates 'vary wildly' for the prevalence of sexual sadistic tendencies among the population from a few per cent to considerably more.[30] There are certainly more sadists among us than psychopaths.

For the sadists in the Nazi murder squads, the extension of the killing to women and children offered more opportunities for gratification. Alfred Metzner, a driver for one of the Nazi commanders, remembered that 'pregnant women were shot in the belly for fun and then thrown into the pits . . .'[31] And Walter Mattner, an officer charged with organizing a ghetto clearance, recounted his actions to his wife in October 1941: 'I aimed calmly and shot with confidence at the women, children and numerous babies . . . The babies flew in great arcs and we shot them to pieces in the air before they fell into the ditch and the water . . . Oh, Devil take it! I'd never seen so much blood, filth, flesh. Now I understand the expression "blood-drunk".'[32]

Surprisingly perhaps, within the Einsatzgruppen it was impossible to predict who would enjoy killing and who would not. Take the case of Martin Weiss, a heating engineer from Karlsruhe in south-west Germany. Before his service in an Einsatzkommando those who knew him said he was a model citizen with 'a sense for everything noble and good'. Yet in his actions against the Jews and in the partisan war he behaved with great cruelty.

At his post-war trial it was revealed that he shot half a dozen Jews merely because he thought they didn't 'behave properly'. He remarked during the war that if he didn't 'see blood every day, I would be thirsty'. Yet when he returned home between killing assignments, he changed back into the respectable character his friends in Karlsruhe remembered.[33] Weiss presumably had brutal tendencies that did not manifest themselves when he was working as a plumber, but that were triggered by the opportunities offered to him by the war in the east.

Himmler's attitude to men like Weiss rested on a strange conception of 'decency'. In a speech to SS leadership figures at Posen on 4 October 1943, he said it was important to be 'honest, decent, loyal and comradely' only 'to those of our own blood'. He added, however, that since Germans 'alone on this earth' have a 'decent attitude to animals' the SS applied 'a decent attitude to these human animals, but it is a crime against our own blood to worry about them and to apply ideals to them . . .'.[34] This muddled reasoning could be difficult for individual members of the SS to process. They were supposed to have a 'decent attitude' to 'animals in human form' but were simultaneously ordered not to 'worry about them'. It was all symptomatic of the illogicality and inhumanity of the whole murderous scheme.

Not surprisingly, many of the killers found it hard to kill women and children at close quarters. Consequently, some commanders tried to make their killers' task less difficult by absolving them of individual responsibility. Felix Landau described how his Einsatzkommando was ordered to kill Jewish women by firing as a group at each individual. 'Six of us had to shoot them,' he wrote. 'The job was assigned thus: three at the heart, three at the head. I took the heart. The shots were fired, and the brains whizzed through the air.'[35]

Psychological research confirms that the key to making the killer's task easier is to dehumanize the victim as much as possible. One study reveals, for instance, that if a kidnap victim is forced to wear a hood, it becomes easier for the killer to pull the trigger.[36]

Equally, and as psychologists could have predicted, the more the killer during the Nazi actions had eye contact with his victim, and the more he had a sense that he was murdering an individual, the harder it was to pull the trigger. That partly explains why so much effort was put into portraying these victims as 'Them'.

Away from the killing fields this dehumanization process could sometimes break down. One member of a Reserve Police Battalion that was assigned to the killing of Jews wrote in letters to his wife in strikingly different ways about the Jews he encountered. En masse he referred to the Jews sarcastically as the 'chosen people' and noted without emotion that they were 'being totally exterminated'. But when referring to two Jews who worked as his servants, he changed his tone. 'We give our bread [to them],' he wrote. 'I cannot be so tough.'[37]

The second practical device to aid the killing – one that had been used by murder squads from the start of the war against the Soviet Union – was alcohol. Many reports from murder scenes mention that the killers were drinking. A member of Reserve Police Battalion 101 testified that their officer, Lieutenant Gnade, was so drunk while shooting that he was 'in constant danger of falling' into the murder pit. Some non-German killers, who shot alongside the Reserve Police Battalion, were so inebriated during one action that they became incapable of killing.[38]

Another non-German killer, a Lithuanian called Petras Zelionka, confirmed that alcohol made the killing easier. 'After you have a drink,' he said, 'everyone is braver then.' Alcohol was also important for Zelionka and his comrades immediately after the murders. He remembered that back in their barracks the killers were allowed to drink as much vodka as they liked to 'throw out' of their minds any 'unpleasant' images. 'When you are drunk,' he said, 'it is different.'

Zelionka mentioned another primitive expedient that helped the killers do their work – greed. 'They [the Germans] used to search them [the Jews] and take all golden things from them, watches etc., everything made of gold . . . Our former warrant officer also had a suitcase where he used to put those things.'[39]

Despite Himmler's claim that his killers had behaved 'decently', the reality was that theft from the Jews was widespread. 'Don't let's kid ourselves, there was always something up for grabs during the Jewish actions,' said a police official from the Kraków region. 'Everywhere you went there was always something for the taking.' He revealed that most of his colleagues were 'quite happy to take part in shootings of Jews . . . There was great hatred against the Jews; it was revenge, and they wanted money and gold.'[40]

There was one last factor that helped facilitate the killing – the power of the group. Psychological research over the years has revealed the immense pressure that a group dynamic can place on the individual. In a pioneering experiment in the 1970s, for example, Henri Tajfel and his team demonstrated that even if people were divided into groups by purely arbitrary criteria, they subsequently treated members of their own group preferentially.[41]

Evolutionary psychology provides a straightforward explanation for this phenomenon. To be expelled from a group of hunter-gatherers meant death. No one could survive as an individual, and the 'stone age' minds with which we operate are hard-wired to be concerned about such a fate.[42] Even though today many people live outside of a group, for most of us this evolutionary tendency remains.

Amid the multiple stresses of a killing squad, the group offered support and anonymity. Not just that, but the leader of the group could give quasi-paternal comfort to those who found the killing difficult. In such circumstances the pressure to conform was enormous.

Four thousand miles away from the war against the Soviet Union, soldiers of the Japanese Imperial Army also demonstrated the power of the group dynamic to shape human behaviour. In China, they perpetrated a series of atrocities both before and during the Second World War. And even though their crimes were not directly comparable with the ultimate horror of the Holocaust, there were striking similarities between their group behaviour and that of the Germans.

Like the Germans, the Japanese soldiers were told that they were fighting their racial inferiors. 'The Chinese didn't belong to the human race,' said Yoshio Tshuchiya, who served in the Kempeitai, the Japanese secret military police. 'That was the way we looked at it.'[43]

Shortly after he arrived in China, Tshuchiya was ordered to bayonet civilians during training: 'I didn't have courage at the beginning, but I couldn't escape from it. I would be labelled as "chicken". So I had to do it . . . The first time you still have a conscience and feel bad. But if you are labelled as courageous, and honoured and given merit, and if you're praised as having this courage, that will be the driving power for the second time. If I'd thought of them as human beings I couldn't have done it. But because I thought of them as animals or below human beings, we did it.'[44]

Another member of the Imperial Army, a young recruit called Hajime Kondo, participated in a barbaric 'pacification' action during which the rape of Chinese women was commonplace. When he was in his third year in the army one of the older soldiers 'summoned me and said, "Kondo, you go and rape."'[45] Kondo said that he felt he 'couldn't turn it down' and so became a rapist himself.

It is important to remember that notwithstanding group pressure there was always a choice. Though the pressure on them to conform was huge, Hajime Kondo and Yoshio Tshuchiya could have decided to act differently. Indeed, both of them chose to go against the group just over fifty years later by agreeing to be interviewed about their experiences. It was a decision that wasn't easy in the context of the times. 'Veterans don't really talk about the war openly,' said Kondo. ' "Don't talk about bad things", they say, "as it would shame Japan. Keep quiet." '[46]

Of course, a group dynamic is not necessarily bad. Groups can be directed towards positive goals as well as negative ones – think, for example, of the achievements of groups formed to protest against slavery or civil rights abuses. What psychological research has shown, however, is that groups tend to make more extreme decisions than individuals. They push people further than they otherwise might have gone – for good or ill.[47]

Even given all these psychological pressures, not every member of the Nazi killing squads found they could pull the trigger. In his famous study of a German Order Police unit, Christopher Browning revealed that several policemen told their superiors they were not up to the task. One said he was not prepared to shoot 'defenceless women and children',[48] another that he found the work 'repugnant'. Both were re-assigned to other duties, such as guarding the perimeter. Even when one officer told two policemen that they risked being shot if they didn't comply, they were still merely reassigned.[49]

After the war many of the killers tried to hide behind the 'acting under orders' defence. And while superficially this was true – they had been ordered to kill – at a deeper level it was false. It was false because no one was shot for refusing to kill. In fact, most were treated with an element of compassion, or at least condescension, since they were perceived as 'weak'. And second, it was false because 'acting under orders' implied that the killers would have committed any crime if they had been 'ordered' to. This was demonstrably not the case. When Willi Seibert, deputy commander of Einsatzgruppe D, was asked at his trial after the war if he had been ordered by a superior officer to 'shoot his own parents' would he have done so, he replied that he 'would not do so' because 'it is inhuman to ask a son to shoot his parents.'[50] At a stroke his defence of 'acting under orders' collapsed.

It was evidence such as this that led a panel of German judges in Koblenz in June 1961 to express the reality succinctly: 'Historical research did not reveal a single case when resistance against orders of this kind was punished particularly harshly.'[51]

One reason these refuseniks escaped draconian punishment at the time was because they were relatively harmless as long as they didn't attempt to convince their comrades not to shoot. More troublesome for the commanders of the killing squads was a much larger group – those who pulled the trigger but suffered psychological damage as a result.

Professor Essi Viding is not surprised by this phenomenon. 'Yes, most people can probably be trained to behave in ways that are callous and cold, or to switch off their emotions in particular situations, at least some of the time,' she said. 'However, people are not blank slates. You can't train everyone to be the same. You're still limited by a natural propensity. The cost will be different to different individuals. Only those who have naturally high levels of psychopathic traits can do those things without any cost to their own psyche.'[52]

The psychological problems developed by many of the Nazi killers are well documented. Rudolf Höss, the commandant of Auschwitz, wrote in his memoirs after the war that 'Many members of the Einsatzkommandos, unable to endure wading through blood any longer, had committed suicide. Some had even gone mad.'[53] One member of Einsatzgruppe C said that after shooting only 'five times' he had to be relieved as he 'began to feel unwell' and felt he 'was in a dream'.[54] Paul Blobel, commander of a killing squad and a notorious drunkard, suffered 'a nervous breakdown' and 'completely lost his mind'.[55] After the war, before he was executed for his crimes, Blobel even went as far as to claim – outrageously – that 'our men who took part in these executions suffered more from nervous exhaustion than those who had to be shot.'

He went on to say that 'our men had to be cared for' as they 'experienced a lot, psychologically'.[56]

When the killers travelled back on leave to Germany they took their mental problems with them. Bernd Linn, an SS man, met 'a mate' on a train who told him in desperation, 'I'm not going back to the unit.' It was only later that Linn learnt that his friend had been involved in the killing of Jews. 'He was in the police, and they sent police patrols to carry out these liquidations . . . So he'd experienced it and couldn't cope.'[57]

These were exactly the kinds of problems that Erwin Schulz, commander of Einsatzkommando 5 in the Ukraine, had predicted would happen once the killing was extended to women and children. At the end of August 1941, he returned to Berlin and protested about the murders to Bruno Streckenbach, an SS officer who played an important part in overseeing the organization of the killers. Schulz, according to testimony he gave in 1956, told Streckenbach that the risk of psychological damage to the killers was acute.[58] While Schulz's protest did not stop the killings, he was able to escape further involvement in the murders himself. And the fact he was considered not 'hard enough' for the task of killing innocent civilians did not hurt his career, because two months later he was promoted.[59]

As the war in the east dragged on, and the partisan war intensified, ordinary soldiers from the Wehrmacht became more involved in committing atrocities against civilians. Wolfgang Horn, for instance, a soldier in a Panzer artillery unit in his early twenties, took part in punitive actions against villages in the occupied Soviet Union. He burnt down houses in which partisans were suspected of hiding and left the villagers without shelter. Speaking many years after the war was over, he sought to justify his actions by saying that these were 'primitive Russian houses' that were 'much below our standards' and so he and his comrades 'didn't take it so seriously to fire a Russian house or damage them'. As for the villagers who were thrown out into the cold and snow after their homes had been destroyed, he dismissed any concerns for their welfare by arguing that 'Russians are quite resourceful' when 'coping with cold'.[60]

Horn was an intelligent man – after the war he became an academic – but he saw nothing wrong in what he did. He must have known that many of the women and children he cast out into the snow would likely freeze to death, but he sought to defend the inhumanity of his actions by imagining that Russian civilians living in these 'primitive' houses were somehow immune to suffering. Moreover, if partisans had been suspected of hiding in their village they somehow all collectively 'deserved' their fate. And if they 'deserved' what happened to them, how could the perpetrators be guilty of anything?

Paul Blobel, commander of a killing squad, uttered similar sentiments at his trial after the war. He revealed that he and his men had managed to convince themselves that their victims were so profoundly 'other' that they didn't possess normal emotional feelings: 'Human life was not as valuable [to them] as it was with us. They did not care so much. They did not know their own human value . . . they were resigned to their fate, and that is the strange thing about these people in the East.'[61]

In part, Horn's and Blobel's inability to accept responsibility for their actions would have been the result of a mental defence mechanism. 'You cannot engage with it [that is, suffering] to the same degree you would if it had happened to your own family members,' said Professor Essi Viding. 'I think evolutionarily our mind has been designed not to engage with every horrible thing, because I don't think we could cope with it . . . so you will probably stop thinking about these people as individuals. You do part of it as a self-protective thing.'[62]

However, there was a conceptual difference between Wolfgang Horn burning down supposed partisan villages and Paul Blobel's men killing Jewish civilians by shooting them. In Horn's case he could tell himself that he was fighting a war and was at risk of being attacked himself, whereas Blobel's killers had a more difficult time convincing themselves they were doing anything other than shooting women and children. Mentally the former task was less psychologically troubling than the latter.

Like Wolfgang Horn, Adolf Buchner – a member of an SS Pionier-Bataillon – took part in the campaign against the 'partisan threat'. Buchner's personal motivation for killing suspected partisans was based on the simplistic emotions of hate and fear: 'It was said that: "This is a partisan and he must be removed, because partisans kill your family, so you have to kill him first before he kills your family!" So he has to go. It's either him or me, one of the two. In that case it isn't your brain that takes charge – [asking] "should I or shouldn't I?" – but simply a reaction. You don't think about what kind of nonsense you are about to embark on, you just start shooting. He hadn't done me any harm, I hadn't done him any harm, but I had to kill him. After all, you don't know what he might do. So I have to do it. Let's say that the two of us were enemies, you would think that you had better hit me first before I hit you – that's roughly how it is.'[63]

Buchner remembered how over time his unit progressed to murdering children. When he asked why the children had to be killed, he was told, 'a child might also be holding a weapon.' But that wasn't the only reason. Once their parents had been killed, the children were an unwanted encumbrance: 'The child has to be fed, so they'd sooner simply get rid of it, put it in a ditch and the matter was over and done with. That was the terrible thing, the children.'

In these violent circumstances, where anyone was at risk of being killed as a 'partisan', sadists emerged once again. 'There were some bastards,' said Buchner. 'They undressed them [the villagers] until they were naked and they killed them once they were naked . . . among our own people there were those who were really hot for it, to be able to let them have it . . . Was there any need, for example, to shoot the children in front of the women and then shoot the women after that? That happened too. That is sadism. There were officers like that, they liked sadistic things, they liked it when the mothers were screaming or children were screaming – they were really hot for that. In my view those people are not human.' And yet, he said, 'if they survived the war and returned home, they were as tame as lambs, well-behaved little men, and they had been such pigs out there.'[64]

Himmler, the man who prided himself on 'decency', had no difficulty in tolerating sadistic behaviour when he felt it helped his cause. The most infamous example of this double standard was the special group he formed under the command of Oskar Dirlewanger. Himmler ordered that poachers, currently in prison for their crimes, be released to form a unit that would be used primarily to hunt partisans. Over time Dirlewanger's motley group was reinforced with members of the SS who had bad disciplinary records, and with prisoners from concentration camps who had previously supported the Nazis' political opponents but now wished to demonstrate their loyalty to the new regime.

Dirlewanger – like so many in the movement – had fought in the First World War, served in a Freikorps and subsequently joined the Nazi Party. But he also had a distinctly chequered personal life. He was deeply unstable, often drunk, and had been arrested in 1934 for having sex with a fourteen-year-old girl. Like Reinhard Heydrich, Theodor Eicke and others, Dirlewanger now joined the long list of SS men who owed their rehabilitation to the Reichsführer SS.[65]

In the partisan actions in Belarus, Dirlewanger's men raped, pillaged and killed. They used villagers as human mine detectors to clear the road of hidden explosives and committed countless other atrocities. Wilhelm Kube, the Generalkommissar of the region, complained in 1943, together with his staff, about 'the erroneous psychological treatment of the population' by occupying forces, and singled out Dirlewanger and his men as the worst offenders: 'When women and children are shot en masse or burned alive, there is no longer a semblance of humane conduct of war. The number of villages burned during sweep operations exceeds that of those burned by the Bolsheviks.'[66]

The following year, Dirlewanger's soldiers helped suppress an uprising by Polish freedom fighters in Warsaw. Mathias Schenk, a Belgian, was drafted into the German Army as an assault engineer and attached to Dirlewanger's unit during the action. He could not believe the sadistic cruelty he witnessed. A child was shot as she had her hands up trying to surrender, other children had their heads smashed open with rifle butts and women were stripped and raped. For a 'joke' a teenage Polish boy had a hand grenade slipped into his pocket and was then told to run away. It exploded and killed him.[67]

Schenk, who was a devout Catholic, 'trembled' and 'threw up' when he saw how Dirlewanger's unit behaved. Once, he saw them tear the robes from a priest and beat him. The soldiers then drank the communion wine and 'urinated' on a crucifix that lay on the floor. Schenk gathered four or five of his comrades and they 'immediately ran back and pulled the priest out' of the church. There was no protest from Dirlewanger's men as they 'were very drunk and didn't even notice'.

Schenk was distraught about what he saw in Warsaw. Even long after the war, he could swiftly be reminded of the days in the Polish capital when Dirlewanger's soldiers set fire to buildings. 'Just the smell of smoke raised my hackles,' he said. 'The pictures came back and the feeling of being there was absolutely present.'[68]

Himmler was well aware of the problematic nature of Dirlewanger's unit. While they performed a useful purpose for him, they scarcely had a 'decent attitude' even towards 'animals in human form'. Significantly, even though Dirlewanger was an SS officer, his men were not technically in the SS until the last year of the war. Before that Himmler described them as serving in the SS but not belonging to it.[69] That distinction was clearly important to him. Even though Dirlewanger's men were useful to him, he wanted some distance from these ill-disciplined thugs.

Himmler had agreed to the formation of this group of reprobates and placed an unstable drunk in charge, so he shouldn't have been surprised they acted as they did. Imagine the mentality of the poachers who originally formed the unit. They had been caught stealing, had suffered imprisonment and had now been given the chance to go back hunting – this time for human beings.

Like many of the locals the Germans recruited to assist the Einsatzgruppen in killing Jews, these poachers were country folk used to slaughtering animals. The sight of blood and guts was not unusual for them. But even among these groups it was often necessary for the killers to dull their senses with alcohol.

This human response to committing murder at close range presented Himmler with a dilemma. He knew that ways had already been developed of killing the disabled by gas vans or gas chambers – methods of murder that distanced the killers from the crime. But technical problems meant that the type of gas chambers used in Germany could not be replicated on the eastern front,[70] and though in the coming months gas vans were made available to the Einsatzgruppen, they only ever killed a minority of those the Nazis targeted in the occupied Soviet Union – not least because the roads were so bad that the vans often broke down.[71]

Set against that was the knowledge that it was possible to murder vast numbers of Jews by shooting them. In September 1941, at Babi Yar in Ukraine, Nazi killers murdered more than 33,000 men, women and children in just two days. None of the later death camps – not even the biggest, Treblinka and Auschwitz – ever approached that number of murders per day.[72]

The killings at Babi Yar proved that the extermination of the Jews could have been accomplished by shooting alone. But on 15 August 1941 Himmler learnt first hand why that was not necessarily the best way forward for his killers.[73]

In Minsk he watched as men from Einsatzgruppe B shot a mix of around a hundred 'partisans and Jews'. Afterwards, one of the most senior officers present, Erich von dem Bach-Zelewski, claimed he said to him, 'Reichsführer, those were only a hundred [that had been shot] . . . Look at the eyes of the men in this Kommando, how deeply shaken they are. These men are finished for the rest of their lives. What kind of followers are we training here?'[74]

Bach-Zelewski was – to all appearances – one of the hardest of the hard men. He had been wounded twice in the First World War and awarded the Iron Cross First Class. He joined the Nazi Party in 1930, the SS the following year and in 1940 took part in the forced removal of tens of thousands of Poles from their homes and villages. More recently, in the early weeks of the Soviet invasion, he had supervised the killing of Jews in Riga and Minsk. And yet it wasn't just the 'men in this Kommando' who were 'deeply shaken' by what they had done – he was himself. In spring 1942 an SS doctor reported to Himmler that Bach-Zelewski was experiencing mental health problems, 'especially from visions in connection with the shootings of Jews that he himself had led, and from other difficult experiences in the east'.[75]

In August 1941, after hearing of Bach-Zelewski's concerns for his men at the murder site in Minsk, Himmler must have grasped the central truth about his killing squads – a sizeable number of them struggled with the emotional consequences of their bloody work.

Himmler gave a short speech to the killers in Minsk to try and build up their morale. He emphasized that the laws of nature proved that 'Those who didn't want to fight simply perished . . . we humans were in the right when we defended ourselves against vermin . . .' The task his men were entrusted with performing was unquestionably 'hard', but they must be 'hard' themselves 'and stand firm'.[76]

That, however, was easier said than done. Walter Frentz, an air force cameraman who was part of Himmler's entourage for the visit, was approached by one of the killers after the murders. He pleaded with Frentz, saying, 'I can't take it any more. Can't you get me out of here?', before adding in desperation, 'I can't take it any more – it's terrible.'[77]

Himmler emerged from this experience determined to find a 'better' method of murder – 'better' for his men, not for their victims. And the way the Nazis tackled this ghastly task would reveal much about their mentalities as killers.

11. Killing at a Distance

While Hitler, Himmler and other Nazi leaders were responsible for the overarching vision of the Holocaust, those tasked with making it happen often came up with new ways of committing murder themselves. They were not so much 'SS robots'[1] as zealous problem solvers — when the problem they had to solve was how to kill as many people as possible while sparing their own emotional feelings.

As the Milgram experiment revealed, 'ordering' people to inflict pain on others is not generally as effective as persuading them to cause suffering.[2] Similarly, explaining to SS officers why certain people had to die, and then leaving them the choice of how to accomplish the gruesome task, was more psychologically astute than just 'ordering' them to kill.

The murder of Soviet commissars in concentration camps during 1941 demonstrated this phenomenon in horrific fashion. These commissars were supposed to be shot on the front line straight after their capture, but several thousand escaped this fate and were only later identified in prisoner-of-war camps. From there, along with other prisoners considered especially 'undesirable', they were sent to concentration camps to be murdered.

In Auschwitz in the summer of 1941, the SS decided to work the Soviet commissars to death in gravel pits. 'It was just a few days,' said Kazimierz Smoleń, a Polish political prisoner who witnessed their suffering, 'and then they ceased to exist. It was the torture and murder of hundreds of people. It was a cruel death they died. It's like in a horror movie, but such a movie will never be shown.'[3]

The SS in other concentration camps chose their own method of murdering the Soviet commissars. In Dachau they were shot. In Flossenbürg and Gross-Rosen they were killed by lethal injection. But at Sachsenhausen, after discussing various killing possibilities, the SS devised a much more elaborate system.[4] The prisoners were taken one by one into a room to be measured, and as they stood with their back to the wall they were shot in the neck through a hatch from next door. The killing room was then cleaned, the body removed and the next prisoner ushered in.

The SS at Sachsenhausen were proud of their innovation and demonstrated it to other concentration camp commanders. As a consequence, similar execution chambers were established at Buchenwald and Mauthausen. But such a killing method had serious flaws from the Nazi perspective. There remained an intimate connection between the killer and his victim, and each murder had to be conducted individually. It might have been a 'better' method of killing than the bloody horror of the Einsatzgruppen murders in the occupied Soviet Union or working prisoners to death in the gravel pits of Auschwitz, but potential psychological issues for the killers still remained.

The SS who conducted these murders were ideologically committed to the regime, and had previously participated in the cruel treatment of inmates. They also considered the Soviet prisoners subhuman – a low-grade type of 'Them'. But this was relentless murder, and just as on the eastern front their ability to carry out the task varied. A proportion of the SS gloried in their work, boasting of how many Soviet prisoners they had dispatched. A few refused to participate, and though none were executed at least one was disciplined and sent to a penal unit. Most – just as we saw with the Einsatzgruppen – were in the middle group and took part in the killing with various degrees of difficulty. Once again, alcohol offered a temporary respite. Holidays were organized for them to relax, and a group of murderers from Sachsenhausen took a trip to Italy where several got drunk and smashed up their rooms.[5]

Shortly after the killing of the commissars in the concentration camps had begun, Dr Albert Widmann travelled to Minsk with a truck carrying several hundred kilograms of explosives and two lengths of gas hose. Widmann, who had helped devise the gassing technique used to kill selected disabled people in Germany, had been given a new task by Arthur Nebe, commander of Einsatzgruppe B and former head of the Reich's Criminal Police. Widmann testified after the war that Nebe had asked him to travel east 'because the Russians had left behind in Minsk incurably mentally ill people' and 'his men could not be expected to have to shoot these mentally ill people one by one.'[6]

It wasn't possible for Widmann simply to replicate the same method of killing that had been devised to murder the disabled in the gas chambers in Germany and Austria. That relied on the use of bottled carbon monoxide. Not only was it impractical to transport large quantities of the gas all the way to the east, but the gas was expensive as well. So, in the search for another way of killing that would spare the Einsatzgruppe killers the psychological upset of murdering the mentally ill 'one by one', Widmann and Nebe conducted two gruesome new killing experiments.

The first, incredibly, was an attempt to blow their victims up. A group of mentally ill were confined in a bunker along with explosives. But immediately after the explosives had been detonated it was obvious that the experiment – from the Nazi perspective – had failed. 'The sight was atrocious,' remembered Wilhelm Jaschke, an officer with Nebe's Einsatzgruppe; 'some wounded came out of the bunker crawling and crying.'

The bunker was quickly patched up, the surviving mentally ill pushed back inside and more explosives detonated. Jaschke recalled the macabre legacy of the experiment: 'body parts were scattered on the ground and hanging in the trees.' The next day he and his men tried to collect up the human remains but 'left the body parts which were in the unreachable parts of the trees where they were'.[7]

Driving away from the murder site, Widmann and his colleagues were 'depressed' because 'the people had not [all] died instantaneously' as anticipated.[8] They concluded that murdering people by blowing them up was not sustainable as a method of mass murder. They needed another way forward.

In the search for a solution Nebe remembered how he had once fallen asleep in his car in his garage with the engine running and had suffered 'slight carbon monoxide poisoning'.[9] Maybe that experience offered a clue to another way of producing deadly gas? Perhaps engine exhaust could replace bottled gas as a killing agent? Nebe and Widmann realized this method of killing not only might be easier than transporting bottled gas to the murder site, but would be cheaper than 'buying the gas from a chemical company'.

They now conducted a gassing experiment in a mental hospital in Mogilev, two hours' drive east of Minsk. Mentally ill patients were locked in a room and one end of a hose was shoved in through a gap at the side of the brickwork. The other end of the hose was connected to the exhaust of a car and the engine started up. They soon discovered that the exhaust gases from a car weren't sufficient to kill people as quickly as desired, so a lorry engine was connected as well.

The breakthrough had been achieved. Nebe told Widmann that he was planning to write to Himmler to let him know that while blowing people up wasn't an option – since 'the ensuing cleaning-up process is most unpleasant' – killing with exhaust fumes was 'feasible'.[10]

Widmann later said that he saw the killing of the mentally ill in Minsk and Mogilev as 'lawful' and merely an extension of the existing euthanasia policy. 'I have to say', he testified, 'that I was of the opinion at the time that the state could order and execute something of this kind.' He claimed that 'I am merely a small cog in the machine. I am not the sort of person who likes to be obstructive, so I carried on being a small cog.'

He was asked at his trial what the psychological limits were of his life as a small unobstructive cog. Would he, for example, have 'taken his own life' if Nebe had 'ordered' him to? Widmann replied that he would have refused. He was only prepared to follow those orders he considered 'legitimate'.[11]

Despite his commitment to the regime, and the enthusiastic way he devised new methods of murder, the conclusion Widmann came to after his experience working for the Nazi regime was that 'I no longer want to have anything to do with state authorities. We wanted to do our best and we were shamefully abused.'[12] It was a revealing statement – Widmann considered himself to be a victim. In devoting his time to researching effective killing methods he had only wanted to do his 'best work'. He now hoped people would feel sorry for him and understand that he had acted lawfully within the context of the situation in which he had found himself. But he omitted to mention that it was only the fall of the regime that had caused him to feel 'shamefully abused'. If the Nazis had won the war, he would likely have carried on in much the same vein and felt proud of his work.

Not all death camps would use Widmann's and Nebe's preferred method of gassing. At Auschwitz, which would become the biggest death camp of all, the SS devised their own technique of choice. It was Karl Fritzsch, the deputy commandant, who took the initiative while his boss, Rudolf Höss, was away from the camp.

Fritzsch was a fanatical Nazi who gave every sign of loving his job.

He joined the SS in 1930 while in his twenties, and subsequently served at Dachau concentration camp. By the time he reached Auschwitz he was infamous for his cruelty. At Auschwitz he relished selecting prisoners to die in the starvation cells. There were even reports that he tortured prisoners to death.

Yet prior to his service at Dachau he had shown no sign that he was a sadist. After an unsettled childhood, he had decided on a career working on the boats that sailed up and down the River Danube. But in 1933 his desire to settle down and start a family made him swap careers and take the job at Dachau.

Once he started working at the concentration camp, Fritzsch came to value the comradeship of the SS. 'That friendship eventually became everything to him,' recalled his widow. Interviewed after the war, she denied that her husband had committed the crimes he so obviously had. None of this happened, she said, it was all lies. On the contrary, he was 'the best man in the world'.[13]

In late August 1941, Fritzsch made a momentous connection between the Soviet prisoners – the 'animals in human form' – who had recently arrived in Auschwitz and a deadly insecticide called Zyklon B used in the camp to disinfect clothing and kill lice. Why not, he thought, put the two together? What could be a greater demonstration of the 'otherness' – the 'Them-ness' – of his enemies than by killing them with a chemical used to exterminate vermin?

The Nazis were fond of such animal imagery. The previous year in *Der ewige Jude* – one of the most infamous propaganda films ever made – shots of rats had been intercut with images of Jews in the Warsaw ghetto. 'Goebbels demanded rat scenes,' said Fritz Hippler, the film's director, 'because rats were portrayed as a symbol for Jews.' Hippler remembered that Hitler had taken a keen interest in the editing of the film, demanding that it be made more horrific: 'Hitler wanted to bring the "evidence" so to speak with this film that the Jews are a parasitic race within men, who had to be separated from the rest of men.'[14]

The Jews were not yet targeted en masse for gassing. But it's easy to see why psychologically, once Auschwitz became the largest death camp of the Holocaust, murdering by insecticide offered the Nazis not just a 'simpler' way of killing, but one which must have reinforced Hitler's idea that the Jews were a 'parasitic race'. As we saw earlier, not only is killing people much easier when you don't believe you're killing people at all, but thinking people are rats – or other creatures that spark revulsion – triggers an instant and powerful negative response in the brain.[15]

At the start, Fritzsch had no idea if his innovation would work effectively. Zyklon B is based on cyanide and comes in crystal form. Exposed to the air the crystals create a poisonous gas. But how much was needed to kill people, and under what circumstances? So he started to experiment. He ordered basement cells in Block 11 at Auschwitz main camp to be made airtight, and Soviet prisoners shut inside. 'But it turned out that the gas didn't work that well,' said August Kowalczyk, a Polish prisoner in Auschwitz who observed the activity around Block 11. 'Many of the inmates were still alive the next day.' As a result, 'they strengthened the dose. More crystals were poured in.'[16]

It is almost impossible to imagine the suffering of the prisoners forced to participate in Fritzsch's 'experiment'. Choking, gasping for breath for hour upon hour, they died the most painful death. But through trial and error the SS found what they considered the 'optimum' dose of Zyklon B. They also discovered that the gas worked best when the cell was crammed with prisoners and was warm. These were findings that would help them as they moved towards creating purpose-built gas chambers.

When the commandant, Rudolf Höss, returned to the camp he watched a demonstration of the new killing method and was pleased with what he saw. He wrote that he had 'always shuddered at the prospect of carrying out exterminations by shooting' because of the 'vast numbers' involved. Now he was 'relieved' that 'we were to be spared all those bloodbaths.' He also thought this would spare the 'suffering' of those he was killing.[17] But this was a lie that he told himself to feel better about the crime. Those he murdered by gas would suffer a terrible death.[18]

Though these were the first Auschwitz inmates to die by gassing in the camp, they were not the first prisoners from Auschwitz to be gassed. A few weeks before Fritzsch began his experiment, several hundred prisoners had been deported from the camp under a scheme known by the code 14f13. Selected because they were sick, the prisoners were transported to Sonnenstein euthanasia centre in Germany where they were killed in a gas chamber built to murder disabled patients.

By now, rumours about the existence of these killing centres for the disabled were circulating among ordinary Germans. And in August

1941 Clemens von Galen, the Bishop of Münster, attacked the whole idea. In a sermon in Münster cathedral he talked about the 'widespread suspicion, bordering on certainty', that the Nazis were killing 'innocent human beings' because 'their life is of no value for the people and the state'. Making a direct link with the congregation in front of him, he warned that this practice might be extended to the 'brave soldiers' who returned to the homeland 'seriously disabled'.[19]

Galen's words were an obvious problem for the regime. Inflicting harm on German soldiers who returned to the Fatherland debilitated by injury was most definitely targeting 'Us'. And that was something that the Nazis could not do with impunity.

Adding to the difficulties Hitler and his comrades faced after Galen's sermon was the timing of the Bishop's protest. A few months earlier, Adolf Wagner, the Gauleiter of Bavaria, had ordered the removal of crucifixes from schools in predominantly Catholic Bavaria. There was an outpouring of protest. One woman at a demonstration later shouted out, 'I am a hundred per cent Hitler supporter and have been a National Socialist since 1923. But this is going too far. The Führer doesn't want this, and certainly knows nothing of the removal of the crosses.'[20]

Her comments amounted to saying 'if only the Führer knew' – a common way of letting off steam and criticizing the regime's policies. But the protests didn't stop there. In a sign that the crucifix scandal was in danger of damaging Hitler's own reputation, one anonymous letter sent to a Nazi official read: 'If our Führer lets such scoundrels rule, it will soon all be over with Heil Hitler.'[21]

The men and women who publicly protested over the crucifix issue were not rounded up and sent to concentration camps. The regime listened and changed policy – not just over the issue of the crucifix but in relation to 'euthanasia' killing as well.[22] After Galen had spoken it was thought too risky to carry on busing disabled people to their deaths across Germany and the practice ceased.

It wasn't that the whole policy was abandoned – hospitals still carried on killing selected disabled by starvation or lethal injection – but the specialized murder centres like Sonnenstein stopped gassing patients. As for Bishop Galen, he wasn't arrested, wasn't sent to a concentration camp and wasn't beaten up by the Gestapo. Though Hitler was furious, and several leading Nazis wanted Galen executed for treason, he escaped violent retribution.

It seems remarkable that Galen was spared under a regime that was so oppressive. But Galen, like the crucifix protesters, was offering criticism as a member of the 'in-group', and he wasn't challenging the fundamentals of the regime. Galen wasn't a Nazi, but he hated Bolshevism, despised the treaty of Versailles, believed the German Army had been 'stabbed in the back' in the First World War and approved of the invasion of the Soviet Union. When he was inaugurated as Bishop of Münster in 1934, Stormtroopers had paraded by torchlight past the Bishop's palace, and Nazi officials had welcomed Galen with their arms outstretched in the traditional Nazi greeting.

After the war, Galen told Allied occupying forces that imposing democracy on Germany would 'bring communism' and he requested that black soldiers not be allowed on to the streets at night. He also referred to the tribunal at Nuremberg, where leading Nazis were held to account for war crimes, as 'show trials'.[23] Consequently, Galen cannot be portrayed simplistically as an out-and-out 'resister'.

Goebbels recognized that targeting Galen for his euthanasia protest risked alienating the Catholic German soldiers fighting on the front line. 'I take the view that it would be best to defer the church affair now in principle,' he wrote in his diary on 18 August 1941. 'The church problem needs to be solved after the war . . . Once the victory is ours, it will be easy to get rid of all the problems in one go.' He thought Martin Bormann, who had been instrumental in the crucifix controversy, 'now begins to realize that in some respects the action he takes is too harsh and that radicalism in this field can cause more harm than good, at least in the present times'.[24]

It is also important to note what Galen's sermon did not contain – which was condemnation of the persecution of the Jews. Nor were there vociferous public protests about their fate, as there had been over the removal of the crucifixes.[25] Yet there was plenty of evidence that the Jews in Germany and elsewhere in the Nazi empire were suffering abominably. But the Jews, unlike the disabled, were most definitely not perceived by Galen and many other Germans as members of the 'in-group'. Goebbels took careful note of this distinction. 'It is different with the Jewish question though [as opposed to the church protests],' he wrote in his entry of 18 August. 'Currently, all Germans are against the Jews. The Jews need to be put in their place.'

When the Jews of Münster – Galen's own city – were deported, there was no protest from him. And while it would be wrong to label Galen as an outright anti-Semite, he was certainly no friend to the Jews. In a sermon on 14 September 1941, he even referred to the 'Judaeo-Bolshevik rulers in Moscow'.[26]

In contrast to Galen, in his own city of Münster there were German clerics who were unambiguous in their resistance to the regime. August Wessing, for instance, acted compassionately towards foreign workers the Nazis considered subhuman, and refused 'to be hostile to anyone, whether Polish, Russian or Jew'.[27] The price Wessing paid for his humanity was high – he was sent to Dachau and died there two months before the war ended.

None of this means that Galen was not brave – he undoubtedly was. He expected the Gestapo to arrest him for his euthanasia protest, and he was ready to be a martyr. But he was selective in what he chose to protest about, and like many senior Catholic figures he focused a great deal on the damage the Nazis were doing to the institution of the church.

In large part his resistance was rooted in his faith in Catholicism. As we've seen before with the case of General Blaskowitz,[28] that resistance is often predicated on support from an alternative belief system – the most powerful of which in Nazi Germany was the church.

The months following Galen's sermon – from August to December 1941 – would see radical changes in the development of the Holocaust and the killing methods used to murder the Jews. Understanding the mentalities that underpinned these changes is not an easy task. But one useful way of approaching the question is to see the wild fluctuation in mood among the Nazi leadership during this crucial period as almost replicating – in a more concentrated psychological form – the journey we saw in the First World War, as Germans went from euphoria to despondency.

The first weeks of autumn that year were a gloriously optimistic time for the Nazis. In September the Wehrmacht won a great victory at Kiev, when in one of the largest encirclement actions of modern times over 650,000 Soviet troops were captured or killed. Shortly afterwards German tanks pushed on towards Moscow in Operation Typhoon. The progress they made was extraordinary. They advanced thirty miles a day and entered the city of Orel as the trams were still running. Hitler was ecstatic, and in a speech in Berlin on 3 October he boasted that 'this enemy is already broken down and will never rise again.'[29] Less than a week later his press secretary, Otto Dietrich, told journalists that 'For all military purposes, Soviet Russia is done with.' The German newspapers the next day splashed headlines that proclaimed 'Victory in the east'.[30]

None of this publicity was authorized by Goebbels. The fractured nature of decision making within the Nazi regime meant that Dietrich felt able to take responsibility for this PR blitz himself. But, from the point of view of the Nazi leadership, it was a mistake not to have concentrated all press power in Goebbels' hands. 'I hope to God', wrote Goebbels in his diary on 10 October, 'that the military actions will keep developing in a way that we don't suffer a psychological setback.'[31]

Goebbels was right to be concerned. The German Army became bogged down outside Moscow, and Goebbels was forced in December 1941 to make a public appeal for warm clothing. Nothing symbolized the Germans' humiliating collapse more than the contrast between the front-page headlines 'Victory in the east' in October and the soldiers of the mighty Wehrmacht reduced by December to wearing fur coats and hats donated by the public.

Little wonder that Goebbels wrote in January 1942 that Dietrich's premature victory pronouncement 'probably constitutes the greatest psychological mistake of the entire war'.[32] Significantly, Goebbels didn't blame Hitler for saying that the Red Army would 'never rise again', which had been the catalyst for Dietrich's boastful declaration. Events had not yet reached the stage where Goebbels felt comfortable criticizing Hitler directly for such a major blunder.

Two weeks after his diary entry criticizing Dietrich, Goebbels wrote: 'the people are much more primitive than we imagine. Therefore, the essence of propaganda is constant simplicity and repetition. Only those who are able to reduce problems to the simplest formula and who have the courage to repeat them eternally in this simplified form, even against the objections of intellectuals, will achieve fundamental success in influencing public opinion.'[33]

It was precisely because Goebbels thought that the German public was 'primitive' that he was so incensed by Dietrich's propaganda mistake. Dietrich had delivered a 'simple' message – the war was effectively won – and it had turned out not to be true. And Goebbels knew that it was imperative not to promise the public something specific that you later failed to deliver.

Goebbels was vehemently opposed to telling the public lies that could subsequently be found out. 'Lying doesn't get us anywhere,' he told his attaché, Wilfred von Oven. 'One has to represent the truth in such a way that it becomes clear to the simplest of men, with perhaps a correction here and a correction there. But on the contrary, straightforward lies, one day they come back and turn counter-productive.'[34]

The difficulty of reconciling Dietrich's false October message of victory with what was happening on the ground grew still worse as two more problems of epic proportions arrived for the Nazis in December 1941. The first came from an unexpected source. On 5 December, twenty-seven Soviet divisions smashed into the German front line as the Red Army mounted a major counter-attack – something the Wehrmacht had not been expecting. One German tank commander remembered these days as a 'terrible experience . . . the war had changed completely'.[35]

Two days later came another shock. On Sunday 7 December the Japanese bombed the American Pacific Fleet at Pearl Harbor in Hawaii. This immediately brought the United States and its economic might into the war as an enemy of Japan. But even though Germany was Japan's ally Hitler was not obliged to join in and fight the Americans. Yet on 11 December he announced that Germany was declaring war on the United States.

Many people who don't know the detail of this history think this an incomprehensible decision. But from Hitler's perspective it made sense. Roosevelt was already helping the British, and in September had ordered American ships to 'shoot on sight' any U-boats in the north Atlantic. So, by declaring war on the United States, Hitler believed that he was merely anticipating the inevitable. From the Nazi perspective the hope was that the Japanese would keep the Americans occupied in the Pacific long enough to enable both the Wehrmacht to defeat the Red Army and German U-boats to break the supply line between America and Britain in the north Atlantic.

There were, of course, large elements of wishful thinking in this scenario. Everyone knew that the entry of America into the First World War in 1917 had caused dire problems for the Germans. And the geography hadn't changed since then. New York was still 4,000 miles from

Berlin. So how exactly did Hitler think he could defeat the United States?

But, regardless of the practicalities, Hitler was certain he knew the underlying reason why the Americans were now his enemy. His monomania about the Jews made him convinced that the Jews were behind President Roosevelt just as they were behind Joseph Stalin. His anti-Semitism was so outlandish that he thought the Jews controlled both capitalism and Bolshevism. As far back as July 1922 he had said that the Jews 'pursue one common policy and a single aim. Moses Kohn on the one side encourages his association to refuse the workers' demands, while his brother Isaac in the factory incites the masses and shouts, "Look at them! They only want to oppress you! Shake off your fetters . . ." His brother takes care that the fetters are well and truly forged.'[36] Nineteen years after he uttered these remarks, Hitler told Reichstag deputies on 11 December 1941 that a 'circle of Jews' around Roosevelt, who were 'driven by Old Testament greediness' and 'satanic perfidy', were to blame for Germany's current situation.[37]

It might seem puzzling that Hitler could have held what appear at first sight to be contradictory views – that the Jews were behind capitalism and Bolshevism. But psychological research demonstrates that such apparent inconsistencies are not uncommon among believers in conspiracies. Professor Karen Douglas and her colleagues have found that some conspiracy theorists can agree both with the idea that bin Laden is still alive today and with the idea that he was dead long before the Americans claimed to have killed him. Such contradictions, she said, 'make some sense if people also believe that they can't trust anything they're told'. They reason: 'If that could be true, another conspiracy is also possible and so on.'[38]

Hitler had 'prophesied' in a speech in January 1939 that the Jews of Europe would be 'annihilated' if he believed they ever 'caused' another world war.[39] Now, nearly three years later, he explicitly referred to this 'prophecy' when talking to leading Nazis on 12 December 1941, the day after Germany declared war on the United States. 'As regards the Jewish Question, the Führer is resolved to clear the air,' wrote Goebbels. 'He prophesied to the Jews that if they were to bring about another world war, they would experience their own extermination. This was not a hollow phrase. The world war is here, the destruction of the Jews must be the inevitable consequence.'[40]

It would be easy to think this was the moment that the 'Final Solution' was definitively agreed – the absolute moment of decision. It would fit the view that many people have about how crimes are conceived. Just as in the narrative arc of a crime drama there is the gathering of conspirators, the meeting at which the final decision is taken and ultimately the implementation of the crime. It is all straightforward and easy to comprehend. But it is a pattern that doesn't fit the development of the Holocaust.

On the one hand, Jews were being murdered in large numbers in the occupied Soviet Union and deported to the east from Germany before Hitler said that he wanted to 'clear the air' on 12 December 1941, and on the other his remarks didn't result in a sudden dramatic expansion in the killings elsewhere. The movement towards the Holocaust was a gradual one, and while 12 December was an important moment in the evolution of the crime, it wasn't the single point of decision – because there wasn't one.

In fact, the piecemeal way the Holocaust developed may even have made the crime easier for the perpetrators to commit. Research shows that many people are more comfortable making a series of small decisions rather than one big one. This process is known, colloquially, as the 'foot-in-the-door' technique after one of the earliest psychological experiments.[41] One consequence of this incremental decision-making process is that it can lead to a more radical outcome than if one single decision had been taken in the first place.

Evidence for this kind of incremental decision making exists throughout the Nazis' progression to the Holocaust. Nazi functionaries, for instance, had been considering various radical solutions to their 'Jewish problem' for months before America entered the war. An SS officer called Rolf-Heinz Höppner wrote in an infamous memo to Adolf Eichmann in July 1941: 'This winter there is a risk that there will not be enough food to feed all the Jews. Serious consideration should be given to the possibility that the most humane solution might be to despatch the Jews who are unfit for work by some fast-acting agent. This would certainly be more pleasant than allowing them to starve to death.'[42]

Höppner, who worked in the Warthegau, an area of occupied Poland that contained some of the most overcrowded ghettos, was responding to a crisis that the Nazis had created themselves. They had imprisoned Jews and denied them adequate food and care. Now he was suggesting killing some of them to resolve the Nazis' self-generated problem. It's an example of a phenomenon identified by the psychologist Professor Ervin Staub: 'As they begin to harm the victim group, the perpetrators learn by and change as a result of their own actions, in ways that make the increasing mistreatment of the victims possible and probable.'[43]

It wasn't just Höppner who wanted a 'fast-acting agent' to be found to murder Jews. By late 1941 two separate killing sites were already under construction in Poland, and it was Hitler who had helped start the chain of causation that led to both these factories of murder. In September 1941, he had authorized the deportation of Jews from Germany and Austria, making this decision after a number of his subordinates – including Joseph Goebbels, who was angry that Jews remained in Berlin – had lobbied him vociferously. But Hitler had given no written directive about what exactly should happen to these Jews after they were deported east. What was certain, however, was that he wanted to 'get rid' of them one way or another.

Shortly after Hitler had decided on the deportations, Himmler notified Arthur Greiser, the ruler of the Warthegau, that he wanted to send 60,000 Jews east to the Łódź ghetto. Greiser protested – the ghetto was already overcrowded. So Himmler agreed to reduce the number to 20,000 Jews. But this was still a huge problem for Greiser, as he didn't even want many of the Jews he already had.

In the Łódź ghetto the Jews were forced to work long hours to produce goods which were then sold, and so Greiser had no use for Jews who couldn't work. He had already been in discussions with Himmler about this issue, and it may well be that Höppner's reference to a 'humane solution' for the 'Jews unfit for work' in his memo back in July referred to discussions about the use of gas vans to kill these supposedly 'unproductive' Jews.

The imminent arrival of thousands of Jews from the west only accelerated Greiser's desire to build a base for gas vans to kill the Jews who couldn't work. Hence the idea of setting up a killing facility at Chełmno – a remote village within easy reach of the Łódź ghetto.

The use of a gas van to kill Jews rather than the disabled appears to have first occurred to the Nazis in mid- to late September 1941. Jews from the ghettos of Grodziec and Rzgów were transported in groups to a nearby forest to be killed in the van. The proposed new base at

Chełmno was intended to make the murder process more streamlined from the killers' point of view.

District leaders like Greiser were given enormous flexibility in decision making within their own realm, as long as they understood that the Jews were the enemy they should target above all others. We can get a hint of just how much latitude Greiser possessed from a note he wrote to Himmler in 1942, in which he said that Hitler had told him 'that I should act according to my best judgement' as far as the Jews were concerned.[44]

Greiser faced an enormous challenge. He had been made ruler of an area which contained around five million people – of whom about 4.2 million were Poles, approximately 400,000 were Jews and 325,000 were ethnic Germans.[45] Yet even though the Germans were the smallest minority this was a district that had to be 'Germanized'. To compound Greiser's difficulties, he also had to accommodate ethnic Germans within the Warthegau who were arriving from other countries, including the Baltic States.

It is the kind of situation that we see occurring again and again in this history. Encouraged by Hitler to have vast ambition in pursuit of their shared vision, leading Nazis sought to reach often unachievable targets. In their attempt to do so they created further crises that had to be solved, which resulted in yet more difficulties that needed to be addressed. The Nazis had a long-term vision and a series of short-term goals but often lacked a strategy to connect the two together. What these Nazi functionaries did know for sure was that if they acted 'radically' they would almost certainly never be criticized. Mix all that together and it was a recipe for an immensely dynamic decision-making process.

By the time Hitler told leading Nazis in Berlin, on 12 December 1941, that the Jews would 'experience their own extermination', the murder facility at Chełmno was up and running. But the two things aren't directly connected. Chełmno was a local solution to a local problem. It was, however, one more step along a path that demonstrated to the Nazis that an even more radical way of solving their 'Jewish problem' might be possible.

The suffering of those killed in the gas van at Chełmno was every bit as appalling as that of those killed by shooting. One villager was still haunted long after the war by the screams of the Jews as they died in the back of the van.[46] But for the SS this was not just a labour-saving method of killing; it was also potentially less psychologically damaging than shooting the Jews face to face, especially since they forced prisoners to do the horrific work of clearing the bodies out of the van and burying them.

For Kurt Moebius, one of the SS guards at Chełmno, the 'justification' for his work seemed obvious. He said that at the time he 'believed the Jews were not innocent but guilty' because Nazi propaganda declared they were 'criminals and subhumans' who were responsible for Germany's problems after the First World War.[47]

As Moebius and his SS colleagues operated the gas-van installation at Chełmno, a second killing facility was under construction in the east of occupied Poland. Once again this had been planned before Hitler's December talk, and once more it was a local solution to a local problem. It was also more significant in this history than Chełmno, because this new camp in the remote village of Bełżec would be the first static murder factory designed to kill Jews.

Bełżec was in the General Government, the area of Poland under the control of Hans Frank. As we saw previously, the General Government – much to Frank's annoyance – had been used as a 'dumping ground' for thousands of Poles not wanted in the areas of Poland that were to be Germanized. But Frank had received 'good' news as a result of the invasion of the Soviet Union. He was told there had been a change of plan and that his area was eventually to become 'German' as well, with all the unwanted 'elements' removed further east. Frank even imagined sending the Jews in the General Government into the wasteland of the Pripet Marshes in the occupied Soviet Union.

However, since the war in the east was not yet won, Frank embraced a more immediate solution to his 'Jewish problem', one which Himmler and Odilo Globocnik, the SS and Police Leader in Lublin, discussed in the autumn of 1941. They planned to create an extermination camp at Bełżec in eastern Poland, seventy miles from Lublin. Large numbers of Jews from the General Government would no longer be deported elsewhere, but would be murdered on their home soil.

Globocnik, who would become one of the worst perpetrators of the Holocaust, was yet another whose troubled past meant that he owed his career entirely to the patronage of Heinrich Himmler. Born in 1904 in Trieste, in what was then the Austro-Hungarian Empire, he moved as a teenager to southern Austria and later joined the Nazi Party. In May

1938, after the German takeover of Austria, he was appointed Gauleiter of Vienna. It was at this point that his career started to unravel, as he proved himself too unreliable for the job. After an investigation – including allegations of financial irregularities – he was sacked as Gauleiter in January 1939. Disgraced, he served in the SS as an NCO in the Polish campaign before Himmler decided to rescue him and appoint him to the top SS job in Lublin.

Himmler judged Globocnik – or 'Globus' as he was nicknamed – to be a man of ambition with a 'can-do' attitude. Himmler, like Hitler, hated those who worked for him to exude anything but positivity. When, for instance, doubts had been raised about the creation of a giant new camp at Auschwitz Birkenau because the proposed site had drainage issues, Himmler had simply stated, 'Gentlemen, it will be built. My reasons for constructing it are far more important than your objections.'[48] But positivity doesn't solve problems on its own – the drainage difficulties were never resolved, and plagued the camp throughout its existence. One SS man who worked at Birkenau remembered that 'feet sank into a sticky bog at every step.'[49]

Globocnik would never have let such practical matters interfere with his breezy enthusiasm. But those who worked closely with him soon noticed that he consistently promised more than he delivered. Rudolf Höss, commandant of Auschwitz, found him a 'pompous busybody' who spun 'fantastic plans' that could never be realized. Höss was 'rather shocked' by Globocnik and was puzzled that Himmler held him in such 'high regard'.[50]

In pursuit of his ambitious killing aims, Globocnik was fortunate in one respect – he was able to employ proven experts in mechanized killing. After the gas chambers in German euthanasia centres had ceased operation in the summer of 1941, many of the specialist staff who had worked there were unemployed. So around a hundred of them were now transferred to the General Government and told to use their skills to murder Jews.[51]

One of these euthanasia veterans was Christian Wirth, who was appointed the first commandant of Bełżec. A ruthless former policeman, he was older than many involved in the murders – fifty-five when appointed to run Bełżec – but he remained a man of formidable energy. He also possessed a vast capacity to hate. Franz Stangl, another former euthanasia operative who subsequently became commandant of a death camp, remembered that Wirth expressed himself with 'awful verbal cruelty'. Wirth once said that 'sentimental slobber' about 'doing away with useless mouths . . . made him puke'.[52]

While Wirth and his savagery remain infamous, the individual that Wirth relied on to perform the most essential task in the death camp – operate the gas chambers – is less well known. Lorenz Hackenholt was another veteran of the euthanasia killings, and he not only had a hand in the building and operation of the murder apparatus at Bełżec, but subsequently helped manage the gas chambers at Treblinka and Sobibór, two new death camps opened in 1942.

Hackenholt's SS file reveals that he was born in 1914 in Gelsenkirchen, became a bricklayer after he left school and joined the SS when he was nineteen years old in 1933.[53]

Six years later, in the summer of 1939, he and an SS colleague were selected to join the euthanasia scheme. They were 'shown photographs of mentally ill persons at the most serious stages' and told that it was important to destroy these people to save medical resources.[54] They both accepted the assignment without protest, although Hackenholt's colleague later claimed that when he 'first saw the bodies' at a euthanasia facility he 'vomited and was ill for over a week'.[55]

Hackenholt was also a mechanic, and before his transfer to Bełżec in the autumn of 1941 had worked primarily as a driver for the euthanasia scheme. By all accounts, he was a tough character – over six feet tall and heavily built – and was prepared to use his fists. In January 1941 he hit an innkeeper in a tussle over prostitutes. The police investigated the incident but charges were eventually dropped.[56]

Once Hackenholt was at Bełżec, Wirth used his technical skills to great effect. Under Wirth's direction Hackenholt was instrumental in the construction, maintenance and operation of the killing method that Nebe and Widmann had pioneered in the occupied Soviet Union – the use of exhaust gas from a vehicle engine to murder people.

Jews from the surrounding area were first transported to Bełżec in March 1942, and Karl Schluch, an SS man who worked at the camp, later described the practicalities of the killing process and Hackenholt's role in it. 'After the Jews entered the gas chambers, the doors were closed by Hackenholt himself or by the Ukrainians subordinate to him. Then Hackenholt switched on the engine which supplied the gas. After five or seven minutes – and this is only an estimate – someone looked through the small window into the gas chamber to verify whether all inside were dead . . . The Jews inside the gas chambers were densely packed. This is the reason that the corpses were not lying on the floor but were mixed up in disorder in all directions, some of them kneeling, according to the amount of space they had. The corpses were besmirched with mud and urine or with spit.'[57]

As well as orchestrating the gassing, Hackenholt killed Jews by a more traditional method. 'He shot Jews who couldn't walk,' said Schluch, 'Jews who weren't able to cover the distance to the gas chamber. I also saw with my own eyes that he shot a Jew of the work detail who didn't behave the way Hackenholt wanted him to.' Hackenholt remained, according to Schluch, a 'reckless, tough, brutal man without any sense of honour, and I want to say unscrupulous and indifferent. He drank a lot of alcohol and was often locked up for that.'[58]

Willy Grossmann, another SS colleague of Hackenholt's, described him as 'stupid and insolent. He was also feared a great deal. Hackenholt was often drunk, especially at the end. He was unruly, even towards superiors.'[59] But perhaps the most insightful remark about Hackenholt was made by Robert Jührs, another SS man who worked at Bełżec: 'He wanted to go pissing with the big dogs but couldn't lift his leg.'[60]

Hackenholt was an uneducated working man who had been presented with an unexpected opportunity to play God. People entered his world of the gas chamber and never returned. For the most part he appears to have relished his work, and he went on to play a key part in the creation of the improved gas chambers at Bełżec that began operation in July 1942. In his honour a sign was placed over the new building that read 'Stiftung Hackenholt' – 'Hackenholt Foundation'.[61] These were the last words the Jews would read before they died.

By the time the 'Hackenholt Foundation' was in operation at Bełżec, the Holocaust was under way. In January 1942, at an infamous conference held at Wannsee in south-western Berlin, Heydrich had announced that the Nazis sought to include all European Jews in what they called their 'Final Solution' to the 'Jewish problem'. Initially Heydrich had said that the Jews were to be worked to death building roads in the east, but soon that policy changed to one of outright murder. It is likely that this further escalation was discussed during a series of meetings that Hitler held with Himmler between 23 April and 3 May.[62]

Heydrich, however, didn't live to see the expansion of the murder programme – he was shot in a suburb of Prague and died in hospital on 4 June 1942. After his death, the three camps that focused solely on murder – Bełżec, and the new death camps at Sobibór and Treblinka – were known collectively as the Operation Reinhard camps in Heydrich's 'honour'. All three were built in remote areas next to railway lines but still relatively close to cities that contained large numbers of Polish Jews. The largest of them, Treblinka, was around fifty miles north-east of Warsaw, and many of the 700,000 to 900,000 Jews who died in the camp were from the Warsaw ghetto. Altogether, about one and a half million people would be murdered in the Reinhard camps – the vast majority Jews, but also thousands of Sinti and Roma (known to the Nazis as Zigeuner or Gypsies) together with thousands of Poles.

Auschwitz, which would become the largest single killing centre, didn't start killing in huge numbers until 1943 when new brick-built crematoria/gas chambers opened at Auschwitz Birkenau.[63] Smaller gas chambers in converted peasant huts had been operating at Birkenau since the previous year, but it was the creation of these new buildings at Auschwitz that marked not just the final evolutionary stage of the Holocaust, but one of the key reasons why this genocide is different from others. The gas chambers at the Reinhard death camps were temporary constructs, but the solid factory-like killing centres at Auschwitz were designed to have permanence. They, more than any other structures, were the physical embodiment of the Nazis' attempt to eliminate an entire people – swiftly and via a quasi-industrial process. The pernicious ideology of the Nazis thus came to be represented in the brick crematoria/gas chambers at Auschwitz Birkenau.

They were also a perverse statement of modernity. As the Soviet correspondent Boris Polevoy pointed out in an article written for *Pravda* days after the liberation of the camp, the crematoria/gas chamber facilities at Auschwitz resembled an 'enormous industrial plant'.[64] Modern technology and innovation had been harnessed together to create a new kind of genocide. But what was less commented on were the immense psychological advantages that this 'modern' method of killing offered the perpetrators. The Nazis had done everything they could to make committing mass murder easy for themselves – and had succeeded.

Unlike the Einsatzgruppen in the east who had to witness the emotional trauma of their victims – all of whom knew they were about to die – the SS in the death camps could pretend to new arrivals that they had no intention of committing murder. The practice of telling Jews as they entered the gas chambers that they were about to take a 'shower' seems to have emerged at Auschwitz in the late autumn of 1941. It wasn't an entirely new idea, since the gas chambers of the euthanasia centres were also disguised as showers. But this was the first time this method of calming was used in the context of the extermination of the Jews.

Pery Broad, an SS man at Auschwitz, observed how the procedure worked in Auschwitz main camp early in 1942 when the killings were conducted in a converted room in the crematorium. On arrival Jews were told by an SS officer that they needed to 'bathe and be disinfected. We don't want any epidemics in the camp. Then you will be brought to your barracks where you'll get some hot soup. You will be employed in accordance with your professional qualifications. Now undress and put your clothes in front of you on the ground.' After they heard these words, Broad noticed that the Jews 'All felt relieved after their days full of anxiety.' Moments later they were ushered into the gas chamber, the door locked and Zyklon B crystals poured in from a hatch above. The screams of the dying were so loud, and the crematorium in the main camp so close to other buildings, that a truck engine was turned on to try and drown out the cries.[65]

The 'fake shower' deception could be enormously effective. Toivi Blatt, a Jewish prisoner at Sobibór death camp, vividly recalled the arrival of about 3,000 Jews from the Netherlands.[66] The new arrivals were told to leave their luggage close to the gate and then walk 'straight to a big yard, and there a German we called "the angel of death" talked to them so nicely. He apologized for the three-day journey from Holland but now he said they're in a beautiful place, because Sobibór was always beautiful. And he said, "For sanitary reasons you need to have a shower, and later you will get orders to leave here." Then people clapped, "Bravo!", and they undressed themselves nicely . . . This trap was so perfect that I'm sure that when they were in the gas chambers and gas came out instead of water, probably they were thinking that this was some kind of malfunction . . . When the job was finished, when they were already taken out of the gas chambers to be burnt, I remember thinking to myself that it was a beautiful night [with] the stars – really quiet . . . Three thousand people died. Nothing happened. The stars are in the same place.'[67]

The SS were careful, as Blatt said, to ensure that 'Sobibór was always beautiful.' Under commandant Franz Stangl every effort was made to disguise the function of the place. The hut by the arrival ramp was made to look like a normal station with fake timetables on the wall, and flowers were planted in pots by the side of the platform.

In psychological terms, Stangl was trying to support confirmation bias in the new arrivals. A term first used by the psychologist Peter Wason in the 1960s, confirmation bias is the tendency most of us have to look for evidence that confirms what we already think.[68] In this case the Nazis sought to reinforce the view held by many of the Jews that they had arrived at a transit camp where they would merely be showered and disinfected.

Even some Polish Jews en route to Treblinka, who had heard rumours that they were being sent to their deaths, still clung to the hope that they were on a train to a work camp. Samuel Willenberg, dispatched to Treblinka in 1942, remembered that 'it was hard to believe' that a place like Treblinka could exist. 'I was here,' he said, 'and still I could not believe it at first.'[69]

At Auschwitz Birkenau the SS were careful to tell the new arrivals not to be concerned when they were selected for one of two groups – those judged fit for work and those unfit. The SS claimed that the old, children and mothers with babies were to be sent to a different camp to be looked after. It was a lie, of course. There was no other camp. They were destined for the gas chamber, and most of those found unfit to work were dead in a matter of hours after their arrival.[70]

While it was the usual practice to select the fit from the unfit at Auschwitz, at the Operation Reinhard camps almost everyone was sent immediately to the gas chambers. Only occasionally was a selection held to pick strong and healthy people to work within the camp. Many of these Jews worked in the Sonderkommando and performed the nightmarish tasks of emptying the gas chambers and burning the bodies.

The behaviour of the SS who worked in the killing factories varied wildly. Some SS even formed tolerable working relationships with members of the Sonderkommando. Morris Venezia, a Greek Jew forced to work as a Sonderkommando at Auschwitz, remembered that one SS man 'treated us sometimes to a cigarette' and was 'a very, very good man' – although this 'good man' was still 'always willing to go and kill people'.[71] In contrast, another SS man at Auschwitz, Otto Moll, was greatly feared. He was a sadist who once threw children alive into the flames of an open cremation pit.[72]

Everything was done to ensure that people were 'processed' not just calmly but quickly. The SS at the Operation Reinhard camps were particularly focused on speed, as they wanted to prevent new arrivals spotting the lack of accommodation barracks in which to house them. Moving new arrivals through the camp swiftly also helped the SS to perceive the Jews as an amorphous mass. There was no possibility of forming any kind of relationship with someone who passed by in a matter of moments. It was thus easier to see them as the 'other' when they were naked, forced quickly down the pathway to the gas chambers.

The key to running a death camp, from the Nazis' perspective, was thus to keep the true function of the place a secret until the last possible moment. Consequently, the number of transports had to be carefully balanced with the camp's killing capacity – if too many people arrived then the infrastructure could collapse. And that was exactly what happened at Treblinka in August 1942.

The commandant Dr Irmfried Eberl – another veteran of the euthanasia programme – was acting in pursuit of a grandiose goal. 'Dr Eberl's ambition', remembered August Hingst, an SS man at Treblinka, 'was to reach the highest possible numbers and exceed all the other camps.'[73] He certainly achieved that during the summer of 1942, when the numbers arriving to be murdered from the Warsaw ghetto could reach almost 10,000 a day. But the consequence was that the camp started to fall apart. The vital link between the arrival of a new transport, killing them in gas chambers and disposing of the bodies – all before the next transport arrived – had been broken. Overwhelmed with people to kill, the SS and their Ukrainian helpers started shooting new arrivals, which caused more panic. Rotting bodies lay all over the camp and the smell was appalling.

When Odilo Globocnik found out about the chaos at Treblinka he was outraged. It didn't matter that this grotesque situation had resulted from Eberl overpromising – and thus acting as Globocnik regularly did himself. Eberl was sacked, Franz Stangl was brought in from Sobibór death camp as the new commandant, and the trusted death-camp fixer, Christian Wirth, was tasked with helping sort out the mess.

Globocnik's ability to bring in hardened murderers like Wirth and Stangl demonstrated a further advantage the gas chambers offered the perpetrators. Since so few people were now needed to orchestrate the killings, there had been an element of self-selection among the specialists that remained. Wirth and Stangl, with their background in the euthanasia scheme, now had years of experience in mass murder and could be relied on to turn around a difficult situation.

All new transports to Treblinka were cancelled while the camp was cleaned up. Franz Suchomel, another veteran of the euthanasia programme, remembered that in one area of the camp 'The corpses had bloated beyond recognition under the influence of the heat and were in the process of decomposition. Beneath them, there was a cesspool formed of blood, faeces and other excrements that was almost 15cm high.'[74]

Wirth ordered an SS man called Erwin Kaina to organize a group to clean this up, but according to Suchomel, 'Nobody wanted to do this work. The work Jews [*Arbeitsjuden*] to whom this task was assigned would rather be shot, because beating was of no use any more.' Wirth, infamous not just for his cruelty towards the disabled and Jews, but also for his fury when his wishes were not carried out, now threatened Kaina. If he couldn't get a work detail to clear up the bodies, said Wirth, Kaina would have to do it himself. If he still didn't finish the task then he would be sent to a concentration camp. Kaina knew this wasn't an idle threat. When he was working at the euthanasia centre at Hadamar he had been sent to Buchenwald concentration camp for several months because he had gossiped about his work to ordinary Germans.[75] At Treblinka, Kaina told Suchomel that 'he didn't want to go to a concentration camp any more' and shot himself.[76]

It is important to note that Kaina hadn't refused to be part of the killing process at either the euthanasia centre or Treblinka death camp. He was in trouble only because he spoke out of turn at Hadamar and because he objected to cleaning up the bodies at Treblinka. Ultimately, the horror of the Treblinka clean-up had proved psychologically too much for him.

Treblinka was back in operation by the autumn of 1942, but like all the Reinhard camps it was destroyed the following year. Treblinka, Sobibór and Bełżec had been designed to perform just one function – murder – over a relatively short period of a year or two. So, by the end of 1943, and after the vast majority of the Polish Jews in the surrounding area had been killed, the Nazis ploughed all these camps back into the earth. Auschwitz was now the centre of the murder operation and able to cope on its own with the Nazis' killing demands.[77]

While the Einsatzgruppen operations in the occupied Soviet Union were labour-intensive, now little more than two dozen SS were needed to supervise the operation of one crematorium/gas chamber complex at Auschwitz Birkenau. Altogether there were four such killing factories, each of which could murder up to 2,000 people at a time.[78] The psycho-logical and practical benefits to Himmler and the SS from this system of killing were obvious.

Most of the SS who worked at Auschwitz were employed not in dir-ectly murdering people, but as guards or in the various administrative departments of the camp. It was this separation of tasks that meant that one of the SS, who worked at the camp in the economic section count-ing the money stolen from the Jews, could say long after the war that he had made 'friendships' in the camp that 'I'm still saying today I like to think back on with joy'.[79]

There was one final 'benefit' the SS gained by the killing operation at Auschwitz – the use of doctors to oversee the selection of new arrivals. Since trained medical professionals decided who could live, at least temporarily, and who should die at once, the Nazis could try and con-vince themselves that this process didn't resemble the blood- and brain-spattered killings of the Einsatzgruppen, but was a cold, well-thought-through medical procedure. It was a massive demonstration of the power of the cognitive bias known as the 'just world' hypothesis. These people 'deserved' to die, the SS at Auschwitz could pretend, as qualified doctors had made the decision. And who could argue with their professional judgement?

Up to now, we have discussed only the work of men as perpetrators. But women were also involved. This may come as a surprise, as the Nazi regime preached that a woman's first duty was to be a wife and mother – especially the latter. 'The highest service a woman can render to the community', said the Deputy Führer Rudolf Hess in December 1939, 'is the gift of racially healthy children for the survival of the nation.'[80]

But that wasn't all that women did. Starting in the late 1930s and accelerating still more during the war years, women were of growing importance in the workplace. They didn't take part in the fighting;

that was still anathema to the all-male leadership of the Nazi Party. In the Soviet Union there were women serving as fighter pilots, as tank commanders, as snipers, even as interrogators in SMERSH, the counter-intelligence service. While that would have been inconceivable in Nazi Germany, women did still work in industry, in armaments factories and as typists and secretaries and in other administrative posts for Nazi functionaries.

There were also women who were killers – primarily nurses working within the euthanasia scheme. At a mental hospital in Kaufbeuren in Bavaria, Pauline Kneissler volunteered to give lethal injections to selected patients.[81] Tried for her crimes after the war, she never considered herself a murderer. 'I never understood mercy killing as murder,' she said. 'My life was one of dedication and self-sacrifice . . . Never was I cruel to persons . . . and for this today I must suffer and suffer [the legal consequences].'[82]

Other crimes were committed by women in the occupied territories in the east. One study revealed that the wife of an SS man shot six Jewish children.[83] Women also contributed to the torment of those sent to the camps. Before the war, they had been employed as *Aufseherinnen* (overseers) of female inmates at concentration camps, primarily at Ravensbrück, which was the largest camp for women as well as the central training centre for *Aufseherinnen*. They weren't formally inducted into the SS – Himmler was loath to accept women as full members – but they worked alongside male SS guards.

Surprisingly, one might think, a scholarly study of the *Aufseherinnen* who served at Majdanek concentration camp, on the outskirts of Lublin, concluded that their motivation for joining up was seldom ideological.[84] Of the twenty-eight female guards at Majdanek, there is detailed evidence available for the motivation of thirteen. Only one of them had expressed previous commitment to the regime by joining the BDM, the female equivalent of the Hitler Youth. Most had decided to become *Aufseherinnen* because the job offered more money and better working conditions than their current employment.

Margarete Buber-Neumann, a prisoner who worked in the administration office at Ravensbrück, remembered that 'recruiting drives' were organized to entice more women into becoming *Aufseherinnen*. The recruiter made no mention of the exact nature of the job, except to say that the 'pay was good and the food ample'. Buber-Neumann estimated that 'almost half' of those who took the job would start 'weeping' during their first week and 'ask to be allowed to go home'. But when they were told that they had to speak to the commandant about their request, few had the 'courage to do so'. They stayed, and over time most became habituated to the work.

'Again and again one could observe the same transformation,' wrote Buber-Neumann. 'These young working women were soon every bit as bad as the old hands, ordering the prisoners around, bullying them and shouting as though they had been born in a barracks. There were, of course, exceptions, but not many.' For some of the *Aufseherinnen* the change from ordinary factory worker to tough concentration camp guard happened as soon as they put on their new uniform. Buber-Neumann noticed that their high leather boots and forage cap immediately 'gave them a feeling of confidence and superiority'.[85]

The 'transformation' of these women, which Buber-Neumann observed, should not come as a surprise to those who know the details of the Stanford prison experiment.[86] In the early 1970s, a Stanford University psychology professor called Philip Zimbardo arbitrarily split volunteers into two groups: guards and prisoners. Soon, each group started to conform to their new roles. Some of those chosen as 'guards' embraced the job so enthusiastically that the experiment had to be cut short.

It is an experiment that remains controversial and has spawned an immense amount of scholarly literature.[87] Nonetheless, along with Stanley Milgram's work, the Zimbardo experiment remains one of the most significant psychological attempts to understand behaviour that is relevant to our investigation. Crucially, if the level of change that Zimbardo observed could happen to young people living in a democracy, it's easy to imagine how so many of these young German women could quickly turn into 'old hands' as Nazi prison guards. Even though the majority of them were not hard-line Nazis, they had been raised in a culture that preached racial supremacy and which warned of the dangers posed by the very people they were now guarding. By working in the camps these women were told they were performing a vital service for the state, employed in jobs that were much more valuable than labouring in a factory or as a typist.

Their feeling of increased self-worth was amplified by the accommodation they were given in the camp. The *Aufseherinnen* had their own rooms with wash-hand basins, and there were communal areas where they could meet and chat. 'Well, I want to be quite honest,' said Herta Ehlert after the war, 'I had never such a good life as in the beginning at Ravensbrück when I arrived.'[88]

This changed when twenty-eight of them were posted to Majdanek concentration camp in the heart of Globocnik's killing empire in the east. Similar to Auschwitz in function if not in scale, Majdanek was both a concentration camp and a death camp. It also shared something else with Auschwitz – the killings in the gas chamber were conducted with Zyklon B.

For the *Aufseherinnen*, this new environment was a shock. Not only was Majdanek a place of systematic murder as well as incarceration, but as women they were a minority amid hundreds of SS men who worked in the camp. The level of day-to-day brutality was also much higher than at Ravensbrück. At Majdanek the *Aufseherinnen* could carry riding crops and beat prisoners whenever they liked. This was in addition to the more formal 'floggings' when a female prisoner would be tied down and whipped. One inmate remembered how '*Aufseherin* Rosa . . . administered 25 blows on our buttocks, along with a 26th blow, to our head, using the metal grip of the whip.'[89]

Some *Aufseherinnen* discovered they enjoyed beating the prisoners, but others held back. *Aufseherin* Hermine Braunsteiner behaved with 'brutality and an evident sadistic satisfaction', while Hermine Brückner was praised after the war by survivors as 'humane'. One recalled that 'When she [Brückner] was in charge of roll call, we knew that no blood would flow that day.'[90]

The disparity in the levels of violence that different *Aufseherinnen* chose to employ mirrors the disparity we have already observed among groups of male perpetrators. In a quite astonishing parallel, one of the most sadistic SS men working at Treblinka, Kurt Franz, set his dog on prisoners in the same way that one of the most sadistic *Aufseherinnen* did at Majdanek. Franz, known as 'Doll' because of his looks, would order his St Bernard to attack prisoners with the command 'Man, grab the dog!'[91] And Hildegard Lächert ordered her dog to attack a prisoner at Majdanek with the words 'Human, go get that dog.'[92] Both were clearly referring to their dogs as humans and the prisoners as dogs.

Little wonder that one German scholar who has studied the subject has concluded that 'in terms of arrogance and self-righteousness, inventiveness in kinds of torment and unbounded sadism, there was no gender-specific difference in women's favour.'[93]

Women who had previously led 'normal' lives in Nazi Germany went on to commit terrible crimes once they had the opportunity. It is remarkable, yet it is a pattern we have often seen in this history – not just with women but with men as well. As the Polish philosopher and sociologist Professor Zygmunt Bauman remarked: 'The most poignant point, it seems, is the easiness with which most people slip into the role requiring cruelty or at least moral blindness – if only the role has been duly fortified and legitimized by superior authority.'[94]

But now, with the Nazi regime under ever increasing pressure, the Germans were about to discover what happens when the 'superior authority' of the state begins to fracture, and previous certainties split apart.

12. Stoking Fear

In the whole of German history there had never been a defeat like it. At the Battle of Stalingrad 400,000 German soldiers were killed, wounded or taken prisoner. And the great goals of the regime – of victory over Bolshevism, of access to vast resources, of glory to rival anything in the pages of German history – were under dire threat.

After the disaster of the surrender at Stalingrad on 2 February 1943, the challenge for the Nazi leadership was clear. In such a psychologically fraught atmosphere, how could they keep people loyal and still prepared to fight to the last?

One way was just to hope people would have faith that all would turn out well in the end. Emil Klein, an 'old fighter' who had taken part in the Beer-Hall Putsch, was one of those who did his best to keep that faith alive. He remembered thinking: 'Speaking with my head, we are losing the war, but according to my heart we have to win it!'[1] Jutta Rüdiger, the leader of the BDM, the Hitler Youth for girls, took solace from the knowledge that setbacks had 'happened in history quite frequently, let's just take Frederick the Great as an example. He had almost lost everything, too, and then he managed to turn the tables after all.'[2]

Friedrich Kellner, a civil servant who opposed the Nazi regime, wrote in his diary in the summer of 1943 that, while it was 'not possible to determine the percentage of optimists versus pessimists' in the German population, 'the number of the hopeful is still considerable. Hope seems indestructible.'[3]

Hermann Göring, in a speech delivered on 30 January 1943, announced that the Germans who had died at Stalingrad had made a heroic sacrifice, and fantasized that the Red Army was now drained of all reserves. But he also made a remark that was psychologically interesting. He asked how the rise of Hitler to power, and all the successes since, could possibly 'be meaningless' just because of the German travails at Stalingrad.[4]

What Göring had done – almost certainly unconsciously – was highlight the disconnect that had occurred in the Nazi psyche, between knowledge of the past successes of the Nazi regime and the reality that hundreds of thousands of German soldiers had just been defeated by a better-armed, better-motivated, better-led opponent.

This is an example of one of the most significant phenomena in psychology – cognitive dissonance. 'A man with a conviction is a hard man to change,' wrote Professor Leon Festinger, who conducted pioneering research in the field. 'Tell him you disagree, and he turns away. Show him facts or figures and he questions your sources. Appeal to logic and he fails to see your point.'[5]

What Festinger and his colleagues discovered was just how much human beings strive to avoid internal contradictions. He highlighted the extent to which we are anxious to avoid a conflict between our beliefs and reality. The result is often an attempt to reframe reality to fit the previous mental construct. 'Suppose', said Festinger, that someone 'believes something with his whole heart; suppose further that he has a commitment to this belief, that he has taken irrevocable actions because of it; finally, suppose that he is presented with evidence, unequivocal and undeniable evidence, that his belief is wrong: what will happen? The individual will frequently emerge, not only unshaken, but even more convinced of the truth of his beliefs than ever before. Indeed, he may even show a new fervour about convincing and converting other people to his view.'[6]

Festinger's classic 1950s study, of a small quasi-religious group who believed in the imminent arrival of visitors from outer space, demonstrated how beliefs can survive the most powerful 'dis-confirming evidence'.[7] When the extraterrestrials failed to turn up on the predicted date, an obvious conflict occurred between the group's beliefs and reality. Those who had the strongest belief came up with various excuses for the non-fulfilment of the prophecy. In many cases their belief was strengthened. Others chose reality as the best option and abandoned the group.[8]

It's a phenomenon of obvious relevance to this history. Similarly, once Germans learnt of the setbacks on the eastern front, there were those whose faith in Nazism remained strong or even intensified, and there were those who felt increasingly disconnected from the regime.

There were already signs that this split was happening some weeks before the loss at Stalingrad. SD intelligence operatives had reported 'a greater degree of evidence for war weariness in some parts' caused by 'the increasing difficulties in supply, three years of cutbacks in all areas of daily life, enemy airstrikes steadily increasing in intensity and scope' and 'fear for the lives of relatives at the frontline'.[9]

Joseph Goebbels – that truest of true believers – now faced his most difficult psychological task so far. He had to convince those whose faith was cracking to hold fast in the face of adversity. His first, and most infamous, attempt to do this came in his 'Total War' speech on 18 February 1943 – less than three weeks after the German defeat at Stalingrad. He didn't just call on Germans to redouble their effort and ask that they have faith that the regime would turn matters around, he also did his best to generate fear, saying that if the Red Army won this war it would mean 'the liquidation of our entire intelligentsia and leadership, and the descent of our workers into Bolshevik-Jewish slavery'.[10]

Goebbels knew that fear was the key to motivating Germans to continue the fight. From now until the end of the war he would stay committed to this message – it's in your personal interest never to give up, because the 'subhumans' from the east are approaching, intent on rape, murder and revenge. Surrender would just make these barbarians arrive more quickly.

It was a straightforward, emotional message – the sort Goebbels preferred. But in the context of the defeat at Stalingrad he made what for him was a rare propaganda mistake. He agreed with Hitler that the regime should announce that every single one of the more than 90,000 troops of the German Sixth Army who had been taken prisoner by the Red Army had been killed. 'Surrender demanded twice by the enemy has been proudly refused,' said Hitler's message from his military headquarters on 3 February 1943. 'The last battle took place under the Swastika flag, which was hoisted conspicuously on the highest ruin of Stalingrad. Generals, officers, non-commissioned officers and other ranks fought side by side to the last bullet. They died so that Germany can live.'[11]

This outright lie was a terrible idea. Officials in the German Foreign Office realized at once that the Allies would trumpet the news that these soldiers were still alive and in captivity. Anxious relatives would bombard German officials wanting news of their loved ones and it would be impossible to maintain the falsehood. They were right to be concerned – as Allied propaganda outlets like Radio Moscow soon broadcast the truth.

It was all part of a bigger problem for the regime. The trouble was that the German public was becoming aware of the disconnect between Nazi propaganda and reality, and in particular the knowledge that crimes had been committed – and were still being committed – in the east. It was increasingly difficult to portray the Nazis as fighting an 'honourable' war when just two months before Goebbels' 'Total War' speech the Allies had released a collective statement detailing the existence of the Holocaust and the 'bestial policy of cold-blooded extermination'.[12]

Goebbels knew the Allied claims were true. The Nazis were indeed murdering millions of Jews in a crime that would haunt the imagination of the world. Such a situation might have crushed a lesser propagandist, but not Goebbels. He decided to launch a gigantic campaign based on a technique popularized today as 'whataboutism'. Goebbels announced at a propaganda conference a few days before the Allies' statement on the Holocaust that because 'attack is the best form of defence' the Germans should start an 'atrocity propaganda' campaign against their enemies. The focus should be 'on English atrocities in India, in the Near East, in Iran, Egypt etc., wherever the English are located. In doing so, we can refer to completely vague sources just like the English do, by saying for instance: "Trustworthy men who have just arrived in Lisbon coming from Cairo report that a certain number of prominent Egyptians have been shot dead, etc." '[13]

Goebbels knew that it was impossible for the Nazis to take on the Allies' claims about the Holocaust directly. 'We cannot respond to these things,' he had said at a conference on 14 December 1942. 'If the Jews say that we have executed two and a half million Jews in Poland by firing squad or deporting them to the east, we cannot respond that it was only about 2.3 million. So, we are not in a position to enter into a debate – at least not in front of the world public. Furthermore, the world public doesn't know enough detail about the Jewish Question that we could risk saying: "Yes, we did this, and for the following reasons." We wouldn't get a chance to speak anyway.'[14]

True to his belief that the best way to influence the mentality of the German people was through emotion, Goebbels understood that a diet of fear-generating 'atrocity propaganda' had to be augmented by more cheerful topics. In March 1942 he had written in his diary that 'In these times of highest strain, film and radio must offer some relief to the people. The good mood must be preserved.'[15]

It followed that Goebbels thought that one of the most effective ways of destroying the enemy's morale was to prevent them from having fun. To that end he had talked to Hitler during 1942 about bombing British 'cultural centres, seaside resorts and civic centres'. He argued that 'the psychological effect would be much stronger there, and the psychological effect is what matters the most at the moment.' Consequently, and in response to the British bombing of German cities, Goebbels and Hitler wanted to 'level English sites of cultural interest to the ground'.[16]

Goebbels' belief in the 'psychological effect' of culture and in the importance of creating a 'good mood' among the German public led to a bizarre juxtaposition of messages in the spring of 1943. On the one hand, in his 'Total War' speech of 18 February, he talked of the need for self-sacrifice. But on the other, less than two weeks later, he released one of the most expensive fantasy-entertainment films ever made in Germany. *Münchhausen* was a colour feature film that told of the adventures of an imaginary German baron. It featured a sorcerer, a hot-air balloon journey to the moon, lavish banquets and topless young women bathing in a harem pool.

Arthur Maria Rabenalt, a film director who worked for Goebbels, understood the motivation behind films like *Münchhausen* – the tremendous power of escapism: 'The towns were burning [after a bombing raid] and the people were still queuing in the streets so that they could watch films about a fashionable and elegant world.'[17]

In early April 1943, one month after the release of the *Münchhausen* film, Goebbels received a propaganda gift, one that supported his core message of why Germans should be terrified of the evil, murderous Bolsheviks. Outside the city of Smolensk, in the German-occupied Soviet Union, thousands of bodies had been discovered buried in the forest of Katyn. It was easy for German investigators to trace this crime to the NKVD, the Soviet secret police. Tens of thousands of prominent people, taken from the eastern area of Poland occupied by the Soviets, had disappeared in the spring of 1940, and this was all that was left of many of them.[18]

Was this not firm evidence of the Bolshevik 'atrocities' that Goebbels had warned about? What hypocrites the Allies were, complaining about German crimes, when the Allies themselves were so obviously guilty of mass murder. 'We are exploiting it with all the tricks of the trade,' wrote Goebbels gleefully in his diary on 17 April.[19]

The bodies found in the forest of Katyn also reinforced Goebbels' key theme – the savageness of the Bolsheviks. He may not have known the physiological reasons why the emotion of fear can be triggered so immediately and so powerfully within the brain,[20] but he did know that frightened people were liable to fight to protect themselves. And that link was tremendously useful to him.

Just two days after Goebbels had written that he was 'exploiting' the discovery of the bodies at Katyn, the Nazi regime suffered a further setback. Jews in the Warsaw ghetto rose up en masse against the Germans. The majority of Jews in the ghetto – almost 300,000 – had been deported to the murder camp of Treblinka the previous summer. At the time the Jews hadn't known for certain that they were being sent to their deaths. The fiction peddled by the Nazis that the Jews were only being 'resettled' had not yet been disproved. But by April 1943 the remaining Jews in the ghetto – up to 60,000 – knew what fate awaited them if they climbed aboard a German transport.

Having smuggled weapons into the ghetto, on 19 April 1943 the resistance fighters opened fire on the Germans. 'It was the first time we saw Germans running away,' remembered Aharon Karmi, a twenty-one-year-old Jew. 'We were used to being the ones who ran away from the Germans. They had no expectation of Jews fighting like that. There was blood and I couldn't take my eyes off it. I said, "German blood." '[21]

The resistance fighters held out in the ghetto for nearly a month, forcing the Germans to clear each building from basement to attic. Eventually, with little ammunition, Aharon Karmi and a few of his comrades managed to escape the ghetto through the sewers. In practical terms little had been accomplished; the vast majority of Jews in the ghetto at the start of the uprising still lost their lives, murdered by the Germans. But in psychological terms a huge amount had been achieved. More than anything else, the Warsaw uprising gave the lie to the idea that the Jews did not fight back against their oppressors.

Yet Franz Stangl, commandant of Treblinka, continued after the war to express a scornful view of the Jews. Interviewed in 1971 he said: 'They [the Jews] were so weak; they allowed everything to happen – to be done to them. They were people with whom there was no common ground, no possibility of communication – that is how contempt is born.

I could never understand how they could just give in as they did. Quite recently I read a book about lemmings, who every five or six years just wander into the sea and die; that made me think of Treblinka.'[22] Stangl's contempt for what he saw as the passivity of the Jews was further evidence of a cognitive bias we have encountered before – the 'just world' hypothesis, the fallacy that people always deserve what happens to them.[23]

Even though the Warsaw uprising demolished that outrageous suggestion, the idea still lingered in other quarters as well. Surprisingly, it existed in Israel in the immediate years after the war. Halina Birenbaum, a survivor of both Majdanek and Auschwitz camps, was taunted after she arrived at a post-war kibbutz with the words 'You didn't defend yourselves. Why didn't you defend yourselves? What happened to you? You're to blame. You didn't do anything. That kind of thing wouldn't happen to us. Don't tell us about it. It's a disgrace. Don't tell the young people, you'll crush their fighting spirit.'[24]

Moshe Tavor, a Jew who fought in the British Army, said that he 'couldn't understand how six or eight German soldiers could lead one hundred and fifty people into vehicles and take them away . . . But I'm a different type of person than those Jews who lived in small towns in Poland. As kids we'd pretend we were old Jewish heroes and fight mock wars. I feel very connected to the people who fought here [in Israel] two thousand years ago, and I was less attached to the Jews who went like sheep to the slaughter – this I couldn't understand.'[25]

Moshe Tavor was unquestionably a courageous man. After the war he was part of the Israeli team who went to South America to capture Adolf Eichmann and take him back to Jerusalem for trial. But the sentiment he expressed about his fellow Jews going 'like sheep to the slaughter' is a calumny.

In the first place, as we've seen, large numbers of Jews who were transported to death camps were deceived by the Nazis about their fate. Up until the last moment many believed they were stepping into a shower, only to suddenly discover the terrible reality when it was too late to mount any resistance. Even if they did suspect what might be about to happen to them, their arrival at a death camp was overseen by guards in watchtowers with automatic weapons.

In the pit killings in the east the circumstances were different. But even here escape was fraught with difficulties. Most of the local population were not inclined to help, and the Jews had few friends prepared to risk everything to hide them. There was also, as with the arrivals at the death camps, the overwhelming problem faced by mothers with children. It is an outrageous slur to say that women caring for their small children and so unable to run should be compared to 'sheep to the slaughter'.

More than all that, Moshe Tavor's criticism omits the immense bravery of the Jews who did resist – not just the Jews in the Warsaw ghetto, but the Jews who fought back in the death camps of Treblinka and Sobibór. There were uprisings in both places during 1943 and several hundred prisoners managed to get past the barbed wire to the forests beyond. Significantly, the majority of those involved in the successful escapes were young men, unencumbered by a young family or older relatives. At Sobibór, for instance, the resisters were led by a core of Jews previously trained as Red Army soldiers.[26]

Leon Festinger would not have been surprised at the response of many Nazis to the news that the Jews could be fierce fighters. Logically – if one can use such a word in the context of Nazi ideology – these events should have caused a reassessment of their previously held opinion. Nazi propaganda had for years presented an image of the Jews as cowardly and sly, as shirkers who plotted in the shadows. And yet here was 'unequivocal and undeniable evidence' that this judgement was wrong. But, as Festinger could have predicted, prominent Nazis were now 'even more convinced of the truth' of their 'beliefs than ever before'. The fact that the Jews had resisted became merely another 'proof' of how dangerous they were. It was thus one further reason why they had to die.

A similar transformation was also taking place in their assessment of the Red Army in the wake of the loss of Stalingrad. Many German commanders had believed, before the invasion of the Soviet Union, that while the soldiers of the Red Army might be brutal and primitive, they were also ineffective. General Jodl had summed up this mood by saying, 'The Russian colossus will prove to be a pig's bladder, prick it and it will burst.'[27]

When the 'pig's bladder' had most definitely not 'burst', this assessment seamlessly shifted. Now the very success of the soldiers of the Red Army was yet more evidence of their brutality and 'proof' of the correctness of the original decision to invade. Because Red Army soldiers possessed the ability to fight in a ruthless fashion – and were using this to overcome their more 'civilized' opponents – it was even more necessary than before to defeat them.

This argument had to be deployed with greater force after the major setbacks the Germans suffered in the summer of 1943. At the Battle of Kursk, 280 miles south-west of Moscow, the Red Army held firm against several thousand German tanks. At Kursk, the Wehrmacht possessed more sophisticated military equipment than their enemy, but the 'primitive' technology of the Soviet T-34 tank enabled the Red Army to put more vehicles than the Germans on to the battlefield.

A few weeks before the German disappointment at Kursk, Goebbels had tried to place the best gloss possible on the difficulties the regime faced. He wrote in the weekly newspaper *Das Reich* that past military successes had ensured 'an absolutely stable position from which we can head for victory with virtual certainty'. Yes, there would be setbacks and 'moments of crisis from time to time', but though these 'cannot shake the core of our political and military position . . . they do bring with them certain stresses, particularly of a psychological nature'. However, it was important not to 'mistake a temporary although significant difficulty for a real crisis'.[28]

For a skilled propagandist like Goebbels, it was an extremely weak argument. Goebbels always strove as much as possible to avoid a disconnect between the message he projected and the evidence that the public saw around them. But that was just what he had created here. How could the public ignore the 'setbacks' and simultaneously be confident that victory would arrive, when all the evidence in front of them was that Germany was losing the war, especially given that in the weeks after he wrote his article there was even more bad news? Not just the Battle of Kursk, but the Allied firebombing of Hamburg at the end of July 1943 – the most destructive air raid the Germans had yet suffered.

There was also an overarching 'psychological' problem, not so much the elephant in the room as the elephant that was not in the room – Adolf Hitler. He had refused to appear in public for months. He gave one short speech in Berlin on 21 March 1943 on Heroes Memorial Day and said nothing more in public until he talked to an audience of officer cadets in November. The previous year, by comparison, he had given six major speeches.

Although Goebbels longed for Hitler to be more visible to the

German people, it is doubtful how much that would have helped the situation. An appearance by Adolf Hitler was supposed to generate enthusiasm, but the views he was now expressing were anything but upbeat. In his New Year proclamation to the Wehrmacht on 1 January 1943, there had been a trace of self-pity in his words. 'Even when we were compelled into this war,' he said, 'we did not know the concept of hatred – particularly towards our Western enemies.' He commented balefully that he had only ever wished to 'live in friendship' with Britain, France and America. 'We never demanded anything of them', he said, 'that could have hurt or even offended them.'[29]

It was as if he couldn't understand how Germany came to be in this position. Why were the Western Allies against him? Couldn't they see that his focus remained on his twin obsessions – the Jews and Stalin's Soviet Union? The idea that Western countries had allied themselves with his hated enemies was not just anathema to him, it was incomprehensible. 'May God have mercy on Europe', he said, 'if the Jewish–Bolshevik–capitalist conspiracy succeeds.'[30]

In a subsequent proclamation, one he issued to his soldiers on 19 February 1943, Hitler did offer some hope. 'I know how hard your struggle is,' he said, 'how great your sacrifices are,' but he told them they had to hold fast to give him time to deploy new divisions. Moreover, 'unknown, unique weapons are on their way to the front line.'[31]

By now Hitler was not only grasping at straws himself but encouraging his allies to do likewise. In January 1943, Count Ciano, the Italian Foreign Minister, heard rumours 'about the German secret weapon, which is supposed to do wonders: a multiple-barrelled electric gun; no armour could withstand its blow'. Ciano asked whether there was 'Any truth in it?' or was it 'the usual hot air?'[32]

It is not hard to see why Hitler was forced into fantasizing about 'wonder weapons'. Charismatic authority, as the proponent of the concept, Max Weber, stated, is 'unstable' and extremely vulnerable once things start to go wrong.[33] As a charismatic leader, Hitler had demanded that Germans have faith in his ability to lead Germany to greatness. But now events suggested he had failed. If ever there was a situation that could provoke immense cognitive dissonance – a split between belief and reality – this was it.

As a charismatic dictator he wasn't bound by the normal restraints of stable government. Instead, he had created a series of different power groups who competed against each other for his favour. One downside of this was that his most loyal followers awaited his visionary thoughts as if they were delivered by a deity from the skies. It was a tendency that had intensified since the victory over France in 1940, and led Ribbentrop to remark to Ciano in 1941 that 'every decision is locked in the impenetrable bosom of the Führer.'[34] It was also the reason why Goebbels felt he could write in his diary in October 1943, 'I have no idea what the Führer's going to do in the end.'[35]

Now, as increasing numbers of people recognized that the war was slipping away from the Germans, his dedicated followers waited for Hitler to tell them the new fruits of his genius and point to a way out of the situation. But there was no escape – short of either the unconditional surrender the Allies demanded or the destruction of Germany.

The fundamental problem Hitler faced was that many Germans were losing faith in him. And he knew that faith was everything. As far back as 1927, he had remarked that 'only faith creates a state.'[36] It was something that Benito Mussolini, his fellow fascist dictator, and an inspiration to the Nazis with his March on Rome in 1922, also believed. 'Faith moves mountains because it gives us the illusion that mountains do move,' wrote the young Mussolini. 'This illusion is perhaps the only real thing in life.'[37] But in both Germany and Italy 'faith' was diminishing rapidly. In Italy, by the summer of 1943, it had run out entirely.

In a development of enormous concern to Hitler and the Nazi leadership, the Italian King told Mussolini on 25 July 1943 that he was to be replaced with immediate effect as Prime Minister. 'It is downright shocking', wrote Goebbels, 'to imagine that a revolution that has been in power for twenty-one years can be extinguished in such a way.'[38] Even worse for the Nazi leadership was the timing of Mussolini's forced exit, coming on top of all the other various setbacks in the first half of 1943.

Just two days before he wrote of the 'shocking' departure of the Italian dictator, Goebbels had confided his other concerns to his diary. He was worried by the letters he had received from the public asking 'why the Führer does not pay a visit to the areas hit particularly hard by the air raids' and 'especially why the Führer does not even speak to the German people in order to give information on the current situation. I feel it necessary for the Führer to do this, despite the strain of the events in the military sector. One cannot ignore the people for too long; in the end, it is the centre of our warfare. If the German people lost its inner robustness and its faith in the German leadership at some point, it would create the most serious leadership crisis that we have ever faced.'[39]

But Hitler wasn't about to tour the bomb-damaged areas. He wasn't even prepared to speak the truth in public about the devastation caused by the bombs. Like most charismatic leaders – or indeed most politicians generally – he didn't want to be associated with bad news. That didn't mean, however, that he wasn't worried about his position. One immediate response was to make sure that key positions within the government were held by people he absolutely trusted. Hence, in August 1943, he made Heinrich Himmler Minister of the Interior.

While it was understandable that Hitler wanted the man he called 'loyal Heinrich' to take the job, the question Hitler didn't address was whether he was up to the task – not only because of Himmler's copious other commitments, but because he, almost as much as Hitler, was dealing with the collapse of his dreams. In the summer of 1942, with the Germans advancing south towards the Caspian Sea, Himmler had fantasized that the vision of a Greater Germanic Reich was still realizable. Under the provisions of the General Plan for the East a vast new empire would be created. This was to be no 'ordinary' occupation but the ethnic reshaping of an enormous area – one that would result in the deaths of tens of millions of innocent people.

But now, with that dream disintegrating, Himmler was torn. On the one hand, within the SS he found he had to compromise his principles in the face of reality. At a meeting in May 1943, SS judges called for a reassessment of the restriction on SS men having sex with 'women from an ethnically alien population' as 'at least 50 per cent' of the members of the SS and police in the occupied eastern regions were breaking the prohibition. As a result, the rule was relaxed – Himmler's rigid racial attitude, it turned out, was weaker than the sexual desire of his men.[40]

On the other hand, any hint of nonconformity in the general population was ruthlessly targeted, as Goebbels noted with approval. 'The never-ending moaning has decreased considerably', he wrote on 12 November 1943, 'since we have been giving death sentences to defeatists, which we have carried out and made public.'[41]

The previous month, in Posen in German-occupied Poland, Himmler had resorted to a startling measure to ensure that potential 'defeatists' within the Nazi leadership were neutralized. In two lengthy speeches on 4 and 6 October he told SS leaders and senior Nazi officials explicit details about the greatest secret of the Reich – the extermination of the Jews. Himmler took this extraordinary step because he wanted to implicate everyone who heard this news. As the war turned against the Germans, they could no longer pretend that they knew nothing of the crime. They were all conspirators now. Their shared guilt bound them together.

For those seeking to understand Himmler's mentality, the Posen speeches are the richest of sources. To begin with, his remarks were framed by his pride in the SS. Only his men, he boasted, could have accomplished the killing of the Jews. Only they were 'decent' and strong enough. 'I am talking now about the evacuation of the Jews,' said Himmler to his audience on 4 October 1943, 'the extermination of the Jewish people. It's one of the things that is easy to say: "The Jewish people will be exterminated," that's what every Party comrade says, "fair and square, it's in our programme, elimination of the Jews, extermination – we'll do that." And then they all come to us, the 80 million honest Germans, and every one of them has their decent Jew. Of course, the others are bastards, but this one, he is a great Jew. Not one of those who talk like that has seen it, has got through it [that is, the killings]. Most of you know what it means when 100 corpses lie about together, when 500 lie there or when 1000 lie there.' But, said Himmler, his SS men had been strong enough to 'have stood this' and 'except for cases of human weakness – to have stayed decent, that has made us tough'.[42]

According to Himmler, the justification for the extermination of the Jews was self-evident: 'we know how difficult it would be for us if today – with the bombing raids and the hardships and burdens of war – we still had in every town the Jews as secret saboteurs, agitators, and rabble-rousers. We would probably by now have reached the stage of 1916–17 if the Jews were still lodged in the ethnic body of the German nation.'[43]

Once again, the conspiracy theory that the Jews had been instrumental in the defeat of Germany during the First World War was used to validate their destruction in the Second. This was the most obvious lie that Himmler told in the speech, but there were many others. One of the most significant was his assertion that his SS men had 'stayed decent' throughout the killing process. But as the evidence presented in the previous two chapters has demonstrated, this was as much a fantasy as the idea that the Jews had lost Germany the First World War.

Equally, Himmler claimed that all 'the wealth' the Jews possessed had been turned over to the Reich, apart from a small amount that had been stolen by a handful of SS men who would be executed, following his promise that 'anyone who takes as much as a single Mark will die.' This was nonsense. Not only was theft of money and valuables from Jews widespread, but only a fraction of the SS who committed the offence were ever punished for it. 'They [the SS] did steal,' remembered Toivi Blatt, a Jewish prisoner at Sobibór death camp. So 'they could live like kings.'[44]

Stealing was also widespread at Auschwitz. Oskar Groening, an SS man at the camp, revealed after the war that theft was 'absolutely common', and Linda Breder, a prisoner who worked in the area of Auschwitz Birkenau where Jewish belongings were sorted, said that 'all' of the SS who supervised her 'used to steal'.[45] 'They were taking home lots of gold and other valuables, nobody counted it – it was a bonanza for them.'[46]

Theft at Auschwitz was so widespread that in 1943 an SS judge, Konrad Morgen, went to investigate. He later testified that 'The conduct of the SS staff was beyond any of the standards that you'd expect from soldiers.' They seemed to him like 'demoralized and brutal parasites'. And when he examined their lockers he found 'a fortune of gold, pearls, rings, and money in all kinds of currencies. One or two lockers even contained genitals of freshly slaughtered bulls, which were supposed to enhance sexual potency. I'd never seen anything like that.'[47] Even the commandant, Rudolf Höss, was implicated in the corruption.[48] But like most of the SS who broke Himmler's rules, he escaped punishment.

Professor Leon Festinger, theorist of cognitive dissonance, would have been familiar with the reasons behind Himmler's creation, during his speeches in Posen, of an alternative reality – one peopled by SS men who didn't steal and who conducted the murder of the Jews in a 'decent' manner. The gap between the picture that Himmler had in his head of the SS as an honourable but 'hard' organization and the corrupt reality was so great that he had chosen to live in the fantasy.

Himmler's Posen speeches are infamous for the sections in which he talked about the extermination of the Jews. But other less well-known parts are also important in understanding how he was now furnishing his fictional mental world. Take his bizarre way of finding positives in the Allied bombing campaign that was devastating German cities. Himmler asserted that the destruction meant that the population would be 'driven out onto the land by the good Lord' and that living in the countryside would be 'pretty good' in the short term: 'Some will say: "Well, it's not nearly as bad in the countryside, I have a goat, someone else has a pig, we have a few potatoes. This is a solid basis. Besides, there's not so many things falling on our roof."'

Himmler even claimed that the Allied bombers had performed an unintended but valuable service for German urban planners. 'We could never have found the money for tearing down the towns,' said Himmler. 'Now fate has torn them down, we will probably rebuild them in a reasonable and less congested way.'

If claiming that there were positives to be taken from the Allied bombing campaign wasn't outlandish enough, Himmler also told his audience that 'we will be a poor people after the war' and that he found this idea 'downright exhilarating'. The problem, he said, was that 'if we were really rich and prosperous, we would probably be unbearable. We would not know what to do with ourselves because of our megalomania.' If Germans were wealthy and could employ servants, this would lead to them imitating the ancient Romans and ruining themselves 'racially' by relying on foreign slaves. This last statement, of course, was hugely hypocritical since Himmler knew that 'at least 50 per cent' of his SS men were already 'racially' compromising themselves by having sex with 'alien' women in the east.

Above all, said Himmler, it was vital never to give up the fight: 'Only he who surrenders, who says, "I have no more faith or will to resist any more," will lose, because he lays down his weapons. He who is fighting and standing to the last, until one hour after peace has been agreed, has won.'[49]

This notion, of course, was just as unreal as the idea that Germans would benefit from the Allied bombing and from living in poverty. What was needed was not more stubbornness but the resources necessary to defeat the enemy. There was no point in 'standing to the last' when armed with a pistol and confronted by a tank.

Not that Himmler would have accepted any of this criticism. The idea that the SS were so 'hard' and 'decent' that they could perform immensely difficult tasks in adverse circumstances was central to his vision. In his second speech at Posen, on 6 October, he talked openly to the assembled Gauleiters and other senior Nazi officials about the 'hardest' task they had ever faced – killing Jewish children: 'I did not consider myself entitled to exterminate the men, to kill or have them killed, and to let avengers grow up in the form of their children for our sons and grandchildren. The difficult decision had to be made to let this people disappear from the earth.' The killings, he claimed, were 'carried out without – I believe I can say – our men and our leaders suffering damage to their spirit and soul'.[50]

Of all the attempted justifications for the killing of innocent children this was one of the most repellent. But it is also possible to understand how, for those already deeply imbued with Nazi ideology and with a commitment to the exterminatory nature of the regime, Himmler's argument might appear persuasive. In essence, it amounted to saying, 'You need to kill these children in order to save your own.' In other words, 'You demonstrate your love for your own child by murdering this other child.' It was a warped logic that Oskar Groening, an SS man at Auschwitz, understood. 'The children are not the enemy at the moment,' he said. 'The enemy is the blood in them. The enemy is their growing up to become a Jew who could be dangerous. And because of that the children were also affected.'[51]

As he intended, Himmler's speeches detailing the killing of the Jews compromised all of those who listened to his words. During his 6 October speech he explicitly told his audience, after he had 'concluded' talking about the 'Jewish Question', that 'now you know about it, and you'll keep it to yourself.'[52]

Consequently, it was hard for any of those present to claim after the war that they had been ignorant of the crime. Some still tried – most notably the Minister of Armaments, Albert Speer. He did everything he could at his war crimes trial to present himself as a Nazi with a conscience. He pretended that he had been thrust into the power politics of the Nazi elite and as a qualified architect he was merely an artist who had been led astray.

Central to the myth Speer tried to propagate was his alleged ignorance of the Holocaust. As he told journalists after his release from prison, even when he had visited an armaments factory staffed by concentration camp workers, he 'didn't look to the left or to the right [at] what was happening there'.[53] There was one looming problem with all this. Speer had been present at one of Himmler's speeches in Posen. Searching around for some possible way to defend himself, he claimed – ludicrously one might think – to have left before Himmler gave details about the killing of the Jews. Already a tenuous excuse, it collapsed completely when a letter Speer wrote in 1971 was discovered after his death. In it he said, 'There is no doubt – I was present as Himmler announced on October 6, 1943, that all Jews would be killed.'[54]

A month after Himmler spoke to the Nazi elite in Posen, Hitler finally came out of the shadows and made a major speech at an event that was almost impossible for him to avoid – the twentieth anniversary of the Beer-Hall Putsch. He travelled to the Löwenbräukeller in Munich and addressed the party faithful on the afternoon of 8 November 1943, with the speech recorded and broadcast to the nation that evening.

We saw earlier how Hitler believed that 'the only stable emotion is hate',[55] and his speech certainly contained an excess of that, but he also linked it to the other primal emotion in the amygdala that we are familiar with – fear. He painted a picture of a Germany that had been under threat from the Bolsheviks for years. He ridiculed the idea that 'it might have been possible to appease the Bolshevik colossus,' saying that this was like 'chickens and geese' declaring 'that they no longer intend to attack the foxes, in the hope that the foxes will become vegetarians'.

He also employed a device that is often used by leaders who are fighting a losing war, known colloquially as the 'our boys didn't die in vain' argument,[56] or – in psychological terms – the 'sunk-cost fallacy'. It is the idea that just because there has previously been a large investment in a project, one should carry on investing even when new evidence suggests that there is little prospect of success.

'Every one of our brave soldiers who fought somewhere in Russia, and didn't return home, has the right to expect that others be as brave as he was,' said Hitler, demonstrating his commitment to the fallacy. 'He did not die so that others would betray what he fought for. Instead, he died so that by his sacrifice and the sacrifice of all his comrades and fellow Germans both on the front line and at home, the future of our homeland and the future of our nation [*Volk*] is secured.'[57]

In deploying the sunk-cost fallacy, Hitler combined a powerful emotional appeal with a false intellectual argument. Emotionally, who indeed wants to think that their loved ones have died for nothing? But his analysis lacked logic, since all these previous deaths couldn't influence Germany's future military prospects.

Nonetheless, psychological experiments have demonstrated how susceptible human beings can be to the sunk-cost fallacy.[58] Indeed, it is one of the most insidious of all cognitive biases. It's especially dangerous because in warfare it can lead to tens of thousands of people dying largely because tens of thousands have died before.

The SD found it hard to judge the effectiveness of Hitler's sunk-cost argument, as everyone they talked to knew that it was dangerous for them to respond in a way that might be considered defeatist. While one artisan in Lower Franconia gushed that 'It's remarkable what power the Führer has,' another SD report admitted that it was difficult to get an honest response because people were frightened 'of being brought to [a] reckoning' if they spoke out of turn.[59]

However, it is reasonable to conclude that – just as with Festinger's analysis of the cult that believed in spacemen – the Nazi core believers had their faith reinforced by Hitler's words, whereas the increasing number of those who were growing disillusioned with the regime were either unmoved by the speech or drifted still more into despair. And there was a lot to despair about. By the time that Hitler gave his speech in November 1943 the Italians had changed sides and were fighting with the Allies.

German paratroopers had managed to rescue the ousted Italian leader, Benito Mussolini, from imprisonment and Hitler had set him up as ruler of the 'Italian Social Republic', a puppet state in northern Italy on territory still occupied by the Germans. But the underlying truth was inescapable – the Italian elite had conspired to remove Mussolini when it was clear they were losing the war.

According to Goebbels, the psychological effect of his removal had caused Mussolini to construct an illusionary world. 'He is living a life of make-believe,' he wrote on 9 November, and 'surrounds himself with heroic nonsense that has no place in the world of reality'.[60] The irony of his words was evidently lost on Goebbels, since he could just as easily have been describing Hitler.

But even though the Nazi leadership were concerned by developments in Italy, it was more difficult for the Germans to act in the same way and remove Hitler. One reason was structural. Hitler, unlike Mussolini, was head of state, and there was no king above him who could conspire with others to destroy him. There was also a practical consideration which made Hitler more secure: it was hard to get close enough to arrest or kill him. Hitler spent most of his time at a military compound in East Prussia so the only people who could realistically remove him were those with access to his headquarters. That meant soldiers or others in the security forces, and they had all sworn an oath to be loyal to him.

Nonetheless, Hitler remained vulnerable, because many in the military elite operated within a belief structure that functioned independently of the Nazi regime. There existed a core of army officers – mostly of aristocratic birth – who thought Hitler was leading Germany to destruction and resolved to do something about it.

There is an immense popular mythology around the conspirators, a tendency to portray this story as one of heroic resisters resolutely opposed to Hitler for years, just waiting for their chance to assassinate him. But historical research demonstrates that the truth is less straightforward.[61]

Notably, army conspirators did not attempt to kill Hitler in the wake of the successes of 1940; it was only after the war turned against Germany that they decided to act. Nothing, we might usefully learn from this history, increases a political leader's risk of assassination by his generals more than military failure.

The ambiguous nature of the conspiracy against Hitler was represented in human form by Major General Henning von Tresckow, a senior commander with Army Group Centre. He and his fellow plotters appear to have been motivated to conspire against Hitler as much by their perception of his military incompetence as by the reports reaching them that the killing of the Jews had been extended from adult men to women and children.[62]

Psychologically, Tresckow and the other plotters benefited from their aristocratic origins. Their conviction that others of noble blood would respect a confidence was a fundamental part of their shared belief structure. For most of them, the Nazis had been useful tools – needed to smash communism within Germany, destroy democracy and revive a shared sense of national community. But now the balance had tipped and the downside of Nazism outweighed the upside. So they plotted together, in the knowledge that – aristocrat to aristocrat – their conversations were almost certainly secure.

Tresckow even felt confident enough to discuss the plan with a fellow aristocratic officer at Army Group Centre, Peter von der Groeben – not necessarily to recruit him to the cause, but to ask him to 'play devil's advocate' and raise any possible objection to the scheme. Tresckow told Groeben that even if the assassination were successful he was worried that people 'will forever say that a small group of reactionary aristocratic officers killed the victorious commander. We will be abused and vilified by the entire population.' On the other hand, 'there are a few of us who know how much personal evil there is behind it [that is, Hitler's regime] plus – and this is of equal importance – we can never win this war with him. No one will ever make peace with Hitler. And if we don't act, we will never be able to square it with our own conscience.' Groeben listened to Tresckow carefully and, while admitting he was 'probably' right, still refused to join the conspiracy.[63] But neither did he inform on Tresckow and reveal what he had been told. Aristocrat to aristocrat, their conversation remained confidential.

Hitler had to be removed. The plotters agreed on that. But intriguingly they did not try and kill him in the simplest way – by pulling out their pistols and shooting him in the head. Groeben confirmed that this would have been possible. 'Many people say, "Were you checked for weapons?" and the answer was "No." "So why didn't anybody shoot him?" I could have done it, any time. I had my briefcase with me, and of course I could have carried a pistol in there [to a meeting with Hitler]. And I was two steps away from him, I only had to draw and fire . . .'

Though it would have been possible for Groeben to shoot Hitler, he refused to countenance the idea. He thought that, as a mere colonel, it was not his 'mission to interfere with fate in this way'. Moreover, as he openly admitted, he was 'afraid. It would have been the end of me.'[64]

As discussed earlier, psychological research has demonstrated that it is hard for most people to shoot another person at close range.[65] That was certainly true for the conspirators, perhaps even more so given their oath and the army's tradition of loyalty to their supreme leader. Fabian von Schlabrendorff, who liaised between Tresckow and the other plotters in Berlin, was one of those who recognized the profound psychological difficulty of shooting Hitler. 'Even a hunter is gripped with feverish anticipation when the long-awaited object of his hunt finally appears within his sights,' he wrote. 'How much greater then is the turmoil in one's heart and mind when, after overcoming a multitude of obstacles, and with the knowledge that the odds are unfavourable, one pulls out a gun at the risk of one's life, fully aware that success or failure of the deed will decide the fate of millions!' Schlabrendorff revealed that 'a check on who would be willing to attempt an assassination in this way showed that even men whose courage was beyond doubt, and who had proved it innumerable times in combat, frankly admitted that they did not feel equal to the job.'[66]

That is the background to the first of a number of attempts on Hitler's life, starting in March 1943 when Hitler visited the headquarters of Army Group Centre. The conspirators subsequently claimed that the original plan had been to shoot Hitler, but that was changed when Field Marshal Kluge, the leader of the Army Group, withdrew his support from the plot. Why that prevented a lone officer from just aiming a bullet at Hitler's head during his visit is not clear. In any event, they came up with a new plan – one that was a good deal easier psychologically for the assassins. Tresckow placed a bomb in a package, saying it contained two bottles of liquor, and handed it to another officer who was travelling back with Hitler on a plane to the Führer's headquarters. This scheme also had the benefit, according to Schlabrendorff, of making Hitler's death look like an accident.[67] But the bomb failed to explode. What's astounding, given how much the plotters claimed to be acting out of honourable motives, is that in addition to Hitler they were prepared to kill innocent fellow officers travelling on the plane with him.

The plotters got another chance to kill Hitler just over a week later, when he was visiting an exhibition of captured Soviet weaponry in Berlin. A colleague of Tresckow's, an aristocrat called Rudolf-Christoph von Gersdorff, agreed to try and assassinate Hitler as he was touring the display. Gersdorff concocted an elaborate scheme whereby he would follow Hitler round the exhibition with a time bomb hidden under his clothes. But Hitler spent less time at the event than anticipated, leaving Gersdorff to hurry to the toilet and render his bomb harmless. Is it not remarkable, once again, that a hardened officer like Gersdorff, who was bravely prepared to sacrifice his own life to kill Hitler, was not prepared just to pull out a pistol and shoot Hitler in the face?[68]

Other potential attempts on Hitler's life were discussed among the conspirators in the autumn of 1943 and spring of 1944. One aristocrat volunteered to detonate a hand grenade close to Hitler, while another – one of the few who said he was prepared to take this step – said he would shoot Hitler at close quarters. But ultimately all this came to nothing.

The most famous attempt on Hitler's life was conducted by yet another aristocrat, Claus von Stauffenberg. He decided to plant a bomb close to Hitler at his military headquarters in East Prussia. By now – late July 1944 – the Nazi regime was dealing with two new crises. On 6 June, the Western Allies had launched D-Day, their amphibious invasion of northern France, and on 22 June Red Army soldiers had begun their own major offensive, Operation Bagration. In an operation which dwarfed D-Day in scale, Soviet forces smashed into units of Army Group Centre in one of the most devastating campaigns of the whole war.

Stauffenberg shared several characteristics with other resisters. He came from a noble family, one that traced its origins back to the thirteenth century; he had welcomed the Nazis' opposition to the Versailles treaty and their desire to build up the German Army; he had been delighted by the German victory over the Poles and still more thrilled by the defeat of the French; he was appalled by the mass killing of Jews and the increasing barbarity of the regime; and, above all, he recognized that Hitler was leading Germany to defeat.

After leaving a bomb in Hitler's conference room, Stauffenberg planned on hurrying back to Berlin to help orchestrate an uprising, one that depended on the assistance of General Fromm, head of the Reserve Army. But although the bomb exploded on 20 July, Stauffenberg succeeded in killing only three of his fellow officers and a stenographer. The one person he wanted to die – Adolf Hitler – escaped serious injury. His wounds were slight, and without his death or incapacitation the plotters had no hope of success.

Among Wehrmacht officers, there had never been universal acceptance that an attempt on Hitler's life was an acceptable way out of Germany's difficulties. When Gersdorff had suggested to Field Marshal Manstein that he participate in the conspiracy, Manstein had replied tersely, 'Prussian field marshals do not mutiny.'[69] And in the aftermath of the bomb's explosion many were outraged that their colleagues had plotted to kill their Commander-in-Chief. Karl Boehm-Tettelbach, a Luftwaffe officer who was present at Hitler's headquarters on 20 July and heard the bomb go off, was incensed by the assassination attempt.

'Nobody approached me,' he said in an interview after the war, 'because they knew that I wouldn't break my oath.' He was also angry that Stauffenberg had not been prepared to blow himself up in the attempt on Hitler, but had just planted the bomb and then returned to Berlin.[70]

Another Wehrmacht officer, Major Otto-Ernst Remer, who was instrumental in putting down the attempted coup in Berlin, shared that sentiment. He thought Stauffenberg was 'cowardly' and should have had the courage to 'use a pistol and shoot Hitler. This is what a real man would have done and I would have respected him.'[71]

Remer, Boehm-Tettelbach and others who criticized him believed that Stauffenberg's rush to the airport after planting the bomb destroyed his claim to be a hero. It didn't matter that he was subsequently caught and killed. He should have shot Hitler face to face or blown both of them up with a bomb and sacrificed himself in the process. Then he could have made a claim for heroic status.

This criticism of Stauffenberg would have made perfect sense to the anthropologist Ernest Becker. He wrote that 'man's tragic destiny' was to 'desperately justify himself as an object of primary value in the universe; he must stand out, be a hero . . .' It was vital, thought Becker, that we understand 'how natural it is for man to strive to be a hero'.[72] And, in the eyes of many of his fellow officers, Stauffenberg had botched his chance.

This sense that the plotters had acted in a reprehensible way – even that they were traitors – persisted after the war. When Gersdorff tried to join the newly created West German armed forces, the Bundeswehr, his application was rejected. Even with the war lost and Hitler long dead, the sense that Gersdorff and the other conspirators had 'betrayed' the honour of the officer corps still lingered.[73]

In the aftermath of the bomb attack, the SD reported a surge of anger among German civilians against the conspirators, and gratitude that Hitler had survived. The echoes of the 'stab in the back' – the lie that was central to the Nazis' belief structure – were strong. A study of letters from soldiers at the front also revealed their widespread disgust.[74] While censorship of the letters meant that soldiers were unlikely to voice support for the conspirators, there was no need to condemn them. So the broad revulsion at the assassination attempt appears genuine.

This wasn't the whole story, however. There were Germans who were less than ecstatic that Hitler had been spared. One police report

from southern Germany said that 'While the failure of the assassination attempt has unleashed enthusiasm among Party comrades and
those sections of the population who sympathize with the Party and
the National Socialist State, the other section of the population
refrains from any comment or opinion. The wish for a quick end to
the war is expressed generally.' Another frequent remark heard in the
same region was that if Hitler had been killed then 'the war might
have been over today.'[75] It was clear evidence of the growing split in
belief. In the wake of the assassination attempt, hard-core believers
found their faith in the regime reinforced while the less committed
simply wanted the war to end.

As for Hitler, he raged about the army officers who had conspired
against him and turned his fury on their entire social class. He told
Goebbels that the aristocracy were 'a cancerous growth on the German
people' and that 'some time later' it would be necessary to 'hold them to
account'. He admired Stalin for 'getting them off his back' and envied
'the wartime advantage this has given him'.[76]

But threats and anger did nothing to address the primary reason why
there had been an attempt on Hitler's life – which was that Germany
was heading towards catastrophe. The situation was so bad that Goebbels, who believed that it was dangerous for a propagandist to make
specific promises and then not deliver, gave a speech brimming with
false hope just six days after Stauffenberg's bomb had exploded. He
declared that Nazi advances in weaponry had 'not only caught up with
the enemy but outstripped them' and that 'recently, I saw some German
weapons, and looking at them not only made my heart flutter but made
it stop for a moment.'[77]

While it was true that the Nazi regime had started launching flying-
bomb attacks against Britain the previous month, there was little sign
that these were causing anything but minor damage to the Allied war
effort. The Germans had to take the existence of further, as yet unseen
'wonder weapons' on trust. And trust in Goebbels' words was in short
supply.

In private, even Goebbels was beginning to show signs of frustration
with the way things were going. Just before D-Day, he confided to his
diary that Hitler had told him that he was 'determined to strike' Britain
'a lethal blow if there is the slightest opportunity of doing so. At the
moment I'm rather puzzled by how he is actually going to do this, but

the Führer has so often made plans that at the time appeared absurd but he was then able to carry out.'[78]

This was the downside of trusting a man you believed always knew best. Having left major decisions to him for years, Goebbels had little choice but to keep trusting him, even when the walls were starting to tumble – and they were literally tumbling across Germany. The Allied bombing campaign had intensified in the first nine months of 1944, with nearly three times as many buildings destroyed or seriously damaged as in the same period the previous year. As a result around three and a half million people were without homes and had to be found new accommodation.[79]

It was a desperate situation that left many disillusioned, especially since the Nazi regime was increasingly unable to do anything to stop the bombing. In small acts of protest the use of the Hitler salute as a public greeting declined and pictures of the Führer were seen less often in private homes.[80] Propaganda which called for the *Volksgemeinschaft*, 'people's community', to become a *Schicksalsgemeinschaft*, a 'community of fate', did little to benefit those in need of a home or the means to cook a hot meal. But the bombing did not cause mass revolt, not just because people feared savage reprisal if they protested, but because civilians whose homes had been destroyed had to rely on the state for assistance and there was little point in attacking the institutions that were trying to save your life.[81] There was also the overarching concern that while the bombing was bad, the relentless march of the Red Army towards Germany might be worse.

Both Goebbels and Hitler knew this all too well – keeping the civilian population terrified of the approaching 'Bolshevik colossus' translated into a powerful reason to keep fighting. It was also a motivation for many German soldiers struggling to hold the Red Army back on the eastern front. Peter von der Groeben, for instance, was convinced that he and his comrades should persevere. 'One was a cog in the machine,' he said. 'It was our main task to try by military means to hold things up to some extent and to halt the collapse that was threatening in the east.'[82] He had an urgent interest in the fight. Groeben's family estate was in East Prussia, and the Red Army was getting closer every day.

The fears of Groeben and millions of other Germans appeared to be realized in October 1944 when the Red Army crossed into East Prussia and occupied the village of Nemmersdorf. After the Soviets had been beaten back – albeit temporarily – the Germans found that at least two women had been raped and more than two dozen villagers killed.[83]

Nazi propaganda exaggerated both the losses and the atrocities in an effort to demonstrate the bloodlust of their enemy. But while these stories certainly stoked fear in the German population, there were some who made a connection with the crimes their fellow country-men had committed in the east. One SD survey reported that a civilian in Stuttgart was heard to say, 'Have we not slaughtered Jews in their thousands?'[84]

It took tremendous courage to speak out like this. The SS, Gestapo and other security forces were ruthlessly enforcing 'loyalty' to the regime. Himmler, as Interior Minister, showed no mercy to fellow Germans who shirked the fight. But while terror increased, what was noticeably missing was the quality that the regime had claimed held all true Germans together – the *Volksgemeinschaft*.

As far back as 1941, a Nazi official in Upper Franconia had remarked that 'There can be no talk of a *Volksgemeinschaft*. Each thinks only of his own advantage.'[85] Now, four years later, that was truer than ever. In January 1945 one refugee fleeing from the Red Army described 'terrible scenes' at Pillau harbour, near Königsberg in East Prussia: 'At the harbour everyone was pushing towards the ships . . . Human beings became animals . . . The general confusion was now made even greater when completely disorganized military units streamed into the city and into houses, looted, intermingled with the refugees, and also pushed to get themselves onto the ships.' Some soldiers even 'put on women's clothing and thus attempted to get away on the ships'.[86]

In the last days of the regime the hard-line Gauleiter of East Prussia, Erich Koch, revealed his true character. He scurried away from his post, and when he reached the German port of Flensburg in the west he demanded that a U-boat take him to South America. His request was not heeded. But he was not alone in disobeying Hitler's order that Gauleiters set an example and fight to the last. Indeed, of forty-three serving Gauleiters only two died in the heroic way Hitler had demanded.[87]

Equally unheroic were the results of the 'Werwolf'[88] campaign. The Nazi regime had wanted Germans to rise up against the Allied occu-piers from behind the lines, using weapons stored in hidden supply dumps.[89] Germans were also supposed to cripple the Allied administra-tion of captured territory by refusing to collaborate. But there was no mass uprising, no concerted refusal to acknowledge the Allied occupation. Most people just felt a desire to survive.

Hitler despised such 'cowards' to the depths of his being. He expressed his own view on the way forward to Goebbels at the start of February 1945. 'The best thing to do is to burn one's bridges,' said Hitler. 'Not only professionally but also personally. The person who no longer cares whether or not he lives is usually the one who wins in the end.'[90]

It was a philosophy that both Goebbels and Göring had long admired. After talking to Göring in March 1943, Goebbels wrote in his diary: 'Göring realizes perfectly what is in store for all of us if we show any weakness in this war. He has no illusions about that. On the Jewish question, especially, we have taken a position from which there is no escape. That is all to the good. Experience shows that a movement and a people who have burned their bridges fight with much greater determination than those who can still retreat.'[91]

There is some psychological research that supports this position. One study concluded that when people feel they have no alternative, they tend to be mentally 'better off' than those who think they have options to change the restrictions around them.[92] Their focus, it seems, is clearer. It was an idea the eighteenth-century scholar Samuel Johnson famously understood. 'Depend upon it, Sir,' he wrote, 'when a man knows he is to be hanged in a fortnight, it concentrates his mind wonderfully.'[93]

This didn't mean that Hitler was averse to finding a way out of the war. But he faced three apparently insurmountable obstacles. The first was that he believed one should only negotiate from a position of strength – and Germany was growing weaker every day; the second was that the Allies had called for Germany's 'unconditional surrender' and they saw no reason to discuss terms with a country that was so obviously about to be defeated; and the third was that by March 1945 Hitler's tendency to construct alternative realities had reached epic proportions.

He even fantasized about doing a deal with the nation he most despised. 'A separate peace with the Soviet Union would not of course fulfil our 1941 goals,' wrote Goebbels on 12 March 1945, 'but the Führer hopes still to achieve a division of Poland, to be able to annex Hungary and Croatia to German sovereignty, and to gain freedom of operation against the West.' Goebbels found all this 'grand and convincing'. But he recognized there remained one problem. 'For the time being . . . there is no opportunity to achieve it.'[94]

Undoubtedly, Hitler was physically sick by this point in the war. He suffered from progressive coronary sclerosis, chronic stomach pains and – almost certainly – the early onset of Parkinson's disease. His health wasn't helped either by the various quack remedies prescribed to him by his less than competent personal doctor, Theodor Morell. But none of that was the fundamental reason for his behaviour in these final days.

Hitler had always been capable of imagining the world as he wanted it to be, rather than as it was, and he remained true to his own character and beliefs until his last breath. The shocking thing is not that he was like this, but that millions of people put their lives into the hands of such a man.

While Hitler may have been imagining a fictional world in which Germany could still acquire 'sovereignty' over Hungary and Croatia and secure 'freedom of operation' against the West, neither he nor Goebbels was plotting a way out that could save themselves. Both, by this point, understood that if Germany was beaten then they would have to commit suicide. Their bridges were well and truly burnt. But this wasn't a view shared by most other leading Nazis, many of whom sought to transition to a post-war life.

The key for these pragmatic Nazis was somehow to provide evidence to the victors that they had worked against the regime from the inside. Ideally, that they had saved the lives of the Nazis' greatest enemy – the Jews. That thought was almost certainly on Werner Best's mind as early as the autumn of 1943. Best was a committed Nazi, but he now saw his personal interests elsewhere.[95] While serving as the Reich's plenipotentiary in Denmark, he arranged for Danish Jews to be warned before they were due to be deported. By doing so he achieved two goals simultaneously. Since almost all the Jews fled across the narrow strait to neutral Sweden, he fulfilled the order from his Nazi superiors to make Denmark 'Jew-free', while at the same time he demonstrated to the Allies that he was anxious to save innocent lives. As Best was no doubt aware, this latter point would be useful leverage in any post-war trial. And so it proved. His Nazi past turned out to be no obstacle to a successful post-war business career.[96]

Albert Speer was another intelligent Nazi with an eye to the future. Notwithstanding his attendance at one of Himmler's Posen speeches, he found a Best-like way to provide a positive gloss to his reputation at the

2. Adolf Hitler visits German troops in Poland in autumn 1939. Much to the joy of
is soldiers and the Germans back home, the Wehrmacht defeated the Polish army in
ttle more than five weeks.

. The Nazi occupation of Poland was brutal, and atrocities were commonplace.
this extraordinary photograph, a group of Poles wait to be shot. Notice the bodies
f those already killed lying behind them.

34. General Johannes Blaskowitz, a leading Wehrmacht commander in Poland, protested vociferously about the atrocities committed by German security units in the wake of the invasion. But to little effect.

35. Georg Elser's resistance was more dramatic than Blakowitz's. In November 1939, he planted a bomb in a Munich Beer Hall in order to kill Hitler. The bomb exploded, but Hitler had left just before.

36. At a ceremony held on 19 July 1940, after the German victory in the west, Hitler promoted many of his leading Generals to the rank of Field Marshal. One of them basking in the glory, General – now Field Marshal – Wilhelm Keitel, later remarked: 'nothing convinces a soldier more than success'.

37. Many of the leading figures in the 'euthanasia' killing of selected disabled patients were young. Dr Horst Schumann, pictured here, was just thirty-three when he became director of the Grafeneck euthanasia centre. He later conducted horrendous medical experiments at Auschwitz.

38. Irmfried Eberl was younger still – only twenty-nine – when appointed to lead the team at the euthanasia unit at Brandenburg. He was a fanatical Nazi supporter, and later became commandant of the extermination camp at Treblinka.

39. Many of the killings during the war in the east were conducted by mobile killing squads. Here, a group of civilians are murdered on the edge of a pit.

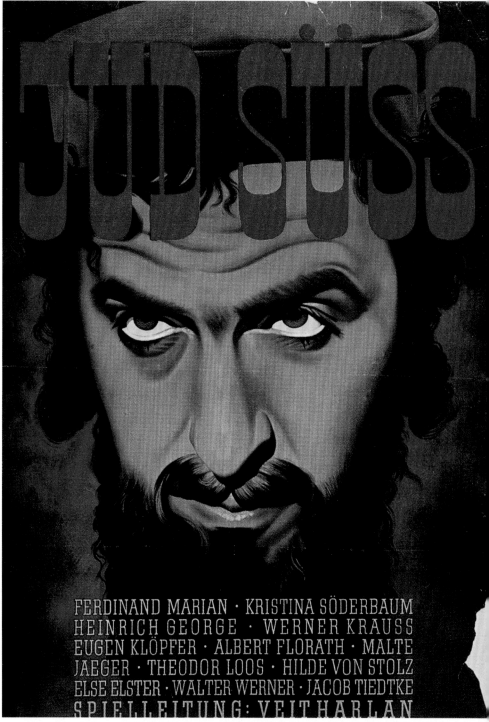

40. One of the most hateful pieces of Nazi propaganda ever made. *Jud Süss* (Jew Suss) was released in 1940, and purported to be a historical drama, but key elements were made up in order to make the story as anti-Semitic as possible. Himmler wanted everyone in the SS to watch it.

HANS ALBERS

IN DER HAUPTROLLE DES GROSSEN
JUBILÄUMS-FARBFILMS DER UFA:
V HLAVNÍ ÚLOZE JUBILEJNÍHO
BAREVNÉHO VELKOFILMU UFY:

MÜNCHHAUSEN

(DOBRODRUŽSTVÍ BARONA PRÁŠILA)

IN DEN WEITEREN ROLLEN: V DALŠÍCH ÚLOHÁCH:
BRIGITTE HORNEY · ILSE WERNER · F. MARIAN
H. SPEELMANS · KÄTHE HAACK · MARINA v. DITMAR · H. BRAUSEWETTER
SPIELLEITUNG
REŽIE · JOSEF von BAKY

Goebbels understood that it was also important to offer Germans distractions from the
[wa]r – like *Münchhausen*, a film released in 1943, which was a lavish piece of colour entertain-
[m]ent starring Hans Albers. It featured a sorcerer, a journey on a cannonball, sumptuous
[ba]nquets and topless young women bathing in a harem pool.

42. Clemens von Galen, the Bishop of Münster, who attacked the Nazis' policy of 'euthanasia' killings in a sermon he gave in Münster cathedral in August 1941. He spoke of the 'widespread suspicion, bordering on certainty' that the Nazis were killing 'innocent human beings'.

43. Hitler was furious about Galen's protest, but agreed with Goebbels that 'it would be best to defer the church problem' until 'after the war'.

44. A photo from 1944 catches Joseph Goebbels at a rare, unguarded moment. With the war going against the Germans, he is conferring with other leading Nazis. From left to right, Hermann Göring (back to camera), Goebbels, Heinrich Himmler (side on to camera) and Martin Bormann (wearing the Nazi armband).

45. In 1944, new Jewish arrivals at Auschwitz Birkenau await selection. Unbeknownst to them, they will shortly be sent either directly to the gas chambers or be allowed to live a little longer and likely worked to death.

46. A group of Nazi personnel from Auschwitz enjoy themselves. The existence of the gas chambers meant that most people who worked at Auschwitz were distanced from the killing – certainly more distanced than those who served in the killing squads in the Nazi occupied Soviet Union.

47. Two elderly German men in the rubble of a Berlin street in May 1945. This devastation was the ultimate consequence of Hitler's failed war of expansion.

48. A mass grave at Bergen-Belsen concentration camp in north Germany. It serves as a stark reminder of the horror of the Holocaust, a crime that will forever define the Nazi regime.

end of the war. During the final days of the conflict he took measures to hinder Hitler's order that German infrastructure should be destroyed. Like Best, he benefited from his actions – although not to the extent Best did. While Speer was spared the death penalty, he was still sentenced to twenty years in prison.

As the eastern front grew ever nearer to Berlin, Hitler started to turn against many Nazis previously famed for their loyalty. In March 1945 he humiliated the members of some of the most elite units in Germany. He ordered that soldiers of the 6th SS Panzer Army, commanded by Hitler's long-term colleague Sepp Dietrich,[97] remove their insignia denoting their pre-eminent status, because he thought they had failed in the defence of the Reich. This was obviously deeply humiliating for the Reichsführer SS, Heinrich Himmler.

The incident came at a time when Himmler was accelerating his own plans for life after the fall of the Third Reich. During the last months of the war, he negotiated with Count Folke Bernadotte of the Swedish Red Cross the release of several thousand Jews to Sweden. On 21 March he wrote a letter to Felix Kersten – who had acted as an intermediary in the deal – and claimed that he had always wanted to assist the Jews to emigrate and had only been prevented by the war. Now he was convinced that 'wisdom and rationality must rule' alongside 'the desire to help'.[98]

It was quite astonishing. Himmler, one of the leading architects of the Holocaust, responsible for the deaths of millions, thought that at the last minute he could turn himself into a saviour of the Jews. No wonder Hitler thought 'loyal Heinrich' had betrayed him at the end.

The actions of Best, Speer and many others like them are easy to understand. Self-interest in desperate situations is often the dominant human emotion. Astute as Best and Speer were, they likely calculated that their crimes could to some extent be offset by their later actions. But Himmler was different. How was it possible for him to imagine that he had any kind of future once Nazism was destroyed?

While we can't know the answer to that question for sure, we can make an informed guess. There had always been bemusement among leading Nazis that Britain and America hadn't recognized the danger to the 'civilized' world posed by Stalin's Soviet Union. Now there was hope that the Western Allies would soon split from Stalin. Perhaps a new war with the Soviets was likely? And who, Himmler must have thought, was better placed to help in that conflict than he was? Just before the war ended, he even asked Count Bernadotte to arrange for him to meet with General Dwight Eisenhower, the commander of Allied forces in Europe, so that the two of them could discuss a surrender of German forces in the west.[99] The idea of Himmler discussing anything with Eisenhower was ludicrous, but by now Himmler's self-delusion had reached almost Hitlerian levels.

Goebbels was more realistic – at least for short periods. On 22 March 1945 he told Hitler that 'our troops in the West are not fighting properly any more' and 'the people's morale, too, has deteriorated considerably, perhaps it has even reached vanishing point.'[100]

But a month later, in the crazed atmosphere of Hitler's bunker in Berlin, he was once more encouraging his leader's fantasies. As late as 25 April, with the Red Army having already encircled the German capital, the talk was still of doing deals with their enemies. 'If we successfully defend Berlin,' said Hitler, 'and there are signs of anti-Russian sentiment, then you will see that those people [among the Western Allies] who have the necessary vision will regain some courage in the face of this [Russian] colossus. These people might then say to themselves, if we work with Nazi Germany then perhaps we can stand up to this colossus.'[101]

It was perhaps the most significant example in twentieth-century history of cognitive dissonance – of dealing with the gap between the image of the world in one's own mind and the reality outside by choosing the former over the latter.

Inevitably, these daydreams came to nothing, and on 30 April 1945 Adolf Hitler put a gun to his head and committed suicide.[102] He had spent much of the time immediately preceding his death writing a testament in which he explained that he had done nothing wrong. Consistent to the last, he claimed that the Jews had been responsible for causing the Second World War and hinted that he was pleased that he had been able to instigate the Holocaust. He also demanded that the future German leadership should 'mercilessly' resist 'the world poisoner of all peoples, international Jewry'.[103]

The next day, 1 May, Goebbels and his wife killed themselves, having arranged for their six children to be murdered. Goebbels intended this to be a demonstration of his unswerving loyalty to Hitler and the Nazi regime. Just days before he had said that if 'the Führer were to suffer an honourable death in Berlin and Europe were to become Bolshevik, at the latest within five years the Führer would become a legend and Nazism a legendary movement, because he would have been immortalized by his final magnificent actions and all the human failings for which he is now criticized would be swept away at a stroke'.[104]

He was wrong. Just as mistaken was his judgement that murdering his own children would demonstrate that his family had stayed loyal to the end. Goebbels thought history would judge him heroic. Instead, he and his wife are remembered as two of the most heartless parents who have ever lived.

But at least Goebbels stayed with Hitler to the end. He was unusual. Most of the other senior Nazis didn't want to suffer the same fate as their Führer in Berlin. Several days before Hitler's suicide, Himmler had journeyed to Flensburg in the north-west of Germany and Göring south to Bavaria. Both places were safely out of reach of the advancing Red Army and in an area of the country that would soon be occupied by the Western Allies.

There was one question remaining. And Bernd Linn, an SS officer who fought in one of the last battles of the war, at Halbe, south of Berlin, expressed it on hearing of Hitler's death. 'That's over,' he said, 'finished.' Now, 'how could we build something new?'[105]

Postscript

The Nazis had expressed outrage at Germany's defeat at the end of the First World War. So the final irony of this history is that Germany's capitulation in 1945 was even more destructive than in 1918. The ruined cities, the territorial losses, the political changes, the nature of the occupation – all were transformative in ways the previous defeat had never been.

There was also a psychological dimension to this catastrophic loss – one which would influence the way many former Nazis came to think about themselves and the enemies they had been fighting.

That was partly because the immediate aftermath of the war was suffused with vengeance – especially on the Soviet side. For three days at the start of May 1945 Red Army soldiers marauded through the small town of Demmin in north-east Germany, setting fire to buildings and raping women. Waltraud Reski was eleven years old when she witnessed her mother being attacked. 'My sister, who is four years younger than me, and I, we always tried to shield our mother and screamed, but they only spared those women who were carrying a baby . . . I wanted to tear them away, but of course they had guns and they were waving them around and so on. This feeling of helplessness and everything, this cruelty, even today I am unable to find words for it.'

Her mother was one of many women in Demmin who were gang-raped: 'It's impossible to imagine what it is like to be raped ten or twenty times a day. So that one is hardly human any more . . . And my mother, she became a completely different person after this for the rest of her life . . . For me, it was as if all of a sudden I had to grow up. And I didn't feel like living. I saw everything in the blackest of clouds.'

Several hundred people decided that the only way of ending their suffering was to commit suicide, and many of them drowned in the nearby river. Reski's mother thought that she and her two daughters should kill themselves in the same way, so she 'grabbed' her children 'and wanted to run to the river'. Only the swift action of Reski's grand-mother managed to prevent their deaths.[1]

No one knows exactly how many people died in Demmin; estimates vary from seven hundred to over a thousand. This was almost certainly the worst mass suicide in German history. But even though events at Demmin were extreme, there were many other instances of the Red Army murdering and raping German civilians. The author of *A Woman in Berlin*[2] detailed her own experiences in the German capital in the early days of the Soviet occupation. As a group of Red Army soldiers threatened her, she was reduced to begging 'only one, please, please, only one'.[3]

Many of these rapists saw themselves as avenging the suffering the Germans had inflicted in the Soviet Union, and in a number of cases they forced husbands or fathers to watch as their wives or daughters were abused. A Soviet lieutenant in Zittau in south-east Germany asked local businessmen and their wives to a party, and then raped one of the women as the rest of his 'guests' looked on.[4]

This was about subjugation – not just the abuse of women but the destruction of Nazi men as the robust protectors of their families. 'Deep down we women are experiencing a kind of collective disappointment,' wrote the author of *A Woman in Berlin* as the war was about to end. 'The Nazi world – ruled by men, glorifying the strong man – is beginning to crumble, and with it the myth of "Man".'[5]

Many Germans felt that the atrocities perpetrated by the Red Army demonstrated that 'civilized' Europe had indeed been despoiled by 'barbaric hordes' from the east. One senior Nazi official, interviewed long after the war, described how his wife had been 'raped in front of the children by Russian soldiers'.[6] As far as he was concerned such actions proved that Hitler had been right all along about the nature of the Bolshevik threat.

There is no way of knowing precisely how many people were raped by the occupying forces. Estimates vary from 860,000 to about two million. The majority were assaulted by the Red Army, but a significant minority – perhaps 190,000 – also suffered at the hands of the other Allies, including the British, Americans and French.[7]

Many German women felt compelled to accept one 'protector' from among the invaders. They would have sex with him on condition that he kept others away. Plus the 'protector' might also provide much-needed extra rations. The author of *A Woman in Berlin* had sex with a major in the Red Army on these terms, and was troubled by the emotional and moral issues surrounding her conduct. 'By no means', she wrote, 'could it be said that the major is raping me. One cold word and he'd probably go his way and never come back.' Yet having been driven to this course of action by circumstance, and despite never freely giving her consent, she still asked herself 'whether I should now call myself a whore, since I am essentially living off my body, trading it for something to eat'.[8]

She and many thousands of other German women felt they had to radically alter their sexual mores in response to the desperate situation in which they now found themselves. In October 1945 the political scientist Gabriel Almond sought to explain the actions of some German women in the American-occupied area as motivated 'by the complete lack of entertainment, the hunger for chocolate, cigarettes, and so on, the lack of sexual satisfaction as a result of the absence of so many German men, and the complete demoralization that the defeat as such brought with it. It seems to be the same everywhere and goes further than the half-compulsory prostitution – in order to have something to eat – and in the coming winter will certainly spread.'[9]

The idea of 'sex for chocolates' trivializes the misery. Enlightened scholars have pointed out that the primary cause of the women's actions was not the desire for luxury goods but the need to obtain basic foodstuffs for themselves and their relatives.[10] We have to understand what happened as behaviour along a continuum. The action of a woman who accepted a 'protector' to avoid gang rape was different from that of a woman who was malnourished and had sex in order to gain extra food, or who willingly had a romantic relationship with an Allied soldier because she liked or even fell in love with him. But regardless of all those considerations, the painful reality was that though the war might have ended, the suffering of enormous numbers of German women had not.

Hunger – and the fear of starvation – played a key part in the behaviour and attitudes of Germans during this period. While the occupying forces did not deliberately seek to starve civilians, they didn't have a policy of caring that much for them either. The infamous Morgenthau Plan, which called for Germany to be deindustrialized, had not been adopted by the Allies but the thinking behind it lingered on.

General Lucius Clay, who administered the American Zone in Germany, even said in May 1945 that 'some cold and hunger will be necessary to make the German people realize the consequences of a war which they caused,' though he also believed that 'suffering should not extend to the point where it results in mass starvation and sickness.'[11] It was thus a confused attitude from the start, but one based on a retributive idea.

Two years later a Medical Board in the west of Germany claimed that Allied policy had meant that 'an entire people, once strong and healthy, has been weakened by hunger to the point of absolute incapacity and true disease'. A local politician in the Rhineland even made the spurious assertion in 1948 that in the three years since the war ended Germans 'have been forced to bear a level of hunger such as that known in no concentration camp in the world'.[12]

Inaccurate and offensive as this accusation was, it was indicative of the belief that in the aftermath of the war the Allies were punishing the Germans. The Nazis had always warned that the invaders sought to destroy Germany, which is why the original Morgenthau Plan had been such a propaganda gift for them.

The extent to which there was widespread hunger and malnutrition in Germany during these years is disputed, but what is certain is that the fear of starvation was very real. Many Germans remembered the Allied blockade after the First World War and the terrible suffering that had caused. So, not surprisingly, large numbers of them were now predisposed to believe the Nazi warning that having lost this new war an even worse fate now awaited them.

If the underlying philosophy of the Americans had been less than benevolent towards German civilians, towards captured enemy personnel it was positively punitive. 'Definitely I do not intend to go along with a ration that will cause prisoners to starve to death, or throw them into our hospitals,' said Major General Robert Littlejohn, the American Chief Quartermaster in Europe. 'Neither do I intend to be a party to a ration that will make the Germans fat.'[13] As a statement of American policy this turned out, at least as far as the *Rheinwiesenlager* – the 'Rhine meadows camps' – were concerned, to be only half true. No prisoner got fat, but many thousands did die. These camps contained almost two million German POWs and the conditions were dreadful, with prisoners forced to sleep in the open air. As many as 6,000 of them did not survive their imprisonment.

Conditions for those in Soviet captivity were often as bad, if not worse. John Noble, an American expatriate, was imprisoned by the

Soviets in the former Nazi concentration camp of Buchenwald. His family owned a factory in Dresden and had remained in Germany during the war. As foreigners they were immediately targeted by Stalin's secret police.

Over 7,000 prisoners died in Buchenwald under Soviet rule between 1945 and 1950, and Noble remembered the desperate measures inmates used to get food. 'In those barracks where people were literally dying,' he said, 'the guard would go through and touch the toe [of the prisoners lying in their bunks], and if it was still warm then he'd count [as someone to get the small daily ration of food] . . . So the prisoners tried to keep the toe [of a dead prisoner] warm . . . so that when the guard went through he thought: "He's still alive," so the food ration was there the next day.'[14]

The Soviets weren't the only ones to reuse Nazi concentration camps. The Americans imprisoned former SS and other leading Nazis in Dachau concentration camp outside Munich. This allowed Emil Klein, a committed Nazi who had taken part in the Beer-Hall Putsch, to tell the following anecdote when interviewed long after the war. 'I spent 30 years in Munich's business world,' he said, 'and many Jews came to see me wanting to sell me something. I had a big furniture business, and they had carpets or something. Some came and said: "Look, I was in a concentration camp." Do you know what I did? I said: "Me too." "What, you too? Where were you, then?" I say: "In Dachau." "Yes, I was in Dachau, too." Then I say: "When were you?" Then he says: "1943." I say: "I was there after '45." Then both of us laughed and shook hands. That's how life is, that's the game life plays.'[15]

This was an utterly disingenuous response. There is no equivalence between conditions in Dachau in 1943 under the Nazis and in 1945 under the Americans. Around 40,000 people died in Dachau at the hands of the Nazis and any Jew who was sent there in 1943 was fortunate to have survived. And though the post-war American regime in the camp was harsh, nothing like this occured. Nonetheless, Emil Klein's story is psychologically revealing. It was one of the many attempts by former Nazis to relativize the crimes of the regime.

Another was made by Rudolf Höss, commandant of Auschwitz, who wrote in his memoirs shortly before he was executed that his actions had been akin to those of a bomber pilot who had been ordered to destroy a town knowing that his bombs would kill 'principally women and children'.[16] Just as he had killed civilians in the gas chambers of Auschwitz, he argued, so Allied bomber pilots had killed civilians in the towns and cities of Germany.

Oskar Groening, a member of the SS garrison at Auschwitz, made the same comparison in an interview after the war. He claimed that the Allies were in no position to criticize the actions of the Nazis, since 'regardless of whether it was militarily necessary or not' they 'murdered women and children by throwing bombs of phosphorus on them'.[17]

Notwithstanding the troubling ethics of mass bombing, this is a false comparison for a host of reasons – not least that the bombing of German cities stopped the moment the war ended, whereas the Nazis' killing of civilians would have continued if Germany had won the war. Nor, of course, was there an Allied directive to exterminate all German women and children, as there was a Nazi directive to exterminate all Jewish women and children.

But this idea that the Allies were just as morally corrupt as the Nazis was a seductive one for many Germans – and not just former Nazis. Mathilde Wolff-Mönckeberg, a writer living in Hamburg, wrote that while she and her friends had striven 'with every nerve of our beings' for the 'downfall' of the Nazi regime,[18] they also condemned the hypocrisy of the Allies in 'proclaiming to the whole world that only Germany could have sunk so low in such abysmal cruelty and bestiality' while they conducted 'terror raids' and 'machine-gunned the defenceless population'. Her conclusion was simple: 'We are all the same, all equally guilty . . .'[19]

The convening of the International Military Tribunal at Nuremberg in November 1945 sought to demonstrate that this was a mistaken analysis, and to show the world that the Nazis were guilty of crimes that were not comparable with the actions of the Allies. Consequently, this was to be the first time that individuals would be charged with the offence of 'crimes against humanity'. It was an innovative approach to the question of ascribing blame in warfare and a landmark moment in the history of international law.

But the trials were fraught from the start with difficulties of definition and jurisdiction – so fraught that at a dinner at the Tehran conference in 1943 Stalin had proposed a much simpler solution to the problem. He said, possibly tongue in cheek, that after the war '50,000'

Germans – including leading 'technicians' and military officers – should be shot. Winston Churchill was outraged, and replied that he refused to 'sully my own and my country's honour by such infamy'. Roosevelt joked that he would compromise on '49,000' being killed.[20]

There was also the added complication that once the idea of physically liquidating leading Germans had been dropped in favour of a trial, the Soviets insisted on a judicial presence at the proceedings. But, as the world knew, during the 1930s Stalin had been instrumental in setting up the infamous Moscow show trials, where innocent defendants had been tortured into pleading guilty. Was that, some Germans wondered, the type of justice that would be handed out at Nuremberg?

However, even before the trial could start, a basic question had to be resolved – were any of the defendants mad? It turned out that the answer was straightforward. Allied psychologists examined the defendants and concluded that none of the twenty-one individuals to be tried in person 'as major war criminals' was insane. Even Julius Streicher, whose anti-Semitism reached stratospheric levels and who saw Jewish conspiracies everywhere, was judged mentally fit.

There was another issue that Allied psychologists wanted to consider. And though it didn't influence whether the defendants were able to stand trial, it was certainly a topic of immense public interest. Was there, as popular mythology suggested there might be, a Nazi personality type?

In an attempt to find out, each of the defendants – including leading Nazis such as Rudolf Hess, Hermann Göring and Albert Speer – were given a Rorschach test. They were told to examine various inkblots on paper and say what images and meaning they found within them. But while it was a relatively straightforward test to administer, it was anything but simple to interpret. And when added to the differing conclusions that various experts came to after interviewing the defendants, the consequence was a lack of clarity about what the psychological evidence from Nuremberg actually meant.

Two of the psychologists were completely at odds. One, Douglas Kelley, maintained that the Rorschach tests demonstrated that the Nuremberg defendants were not only 'essentially sane' but that 'such personalities . . . could be duplicated in any country of the world today.' Gustave Gilbert on the other hand believed that the psychological evidence showed how 'diseased elements of the German culture' were 'inflamed to epidemic proportions under the Nazi regime'. He even called an article he wrote based on what he had learnt 'The Mentality of SS Murderous Robots'.

In recent years, insofar as any consensus among experts has been reached, it is to give little credence to Gilbert's 'diseased' culture thesis and more to the belief that the defendants had disparate personalities. There was no unified Nazi 'type' and they were most certainly not 'robots'.[21]

The interviews the psychologists conducted with individual defendants at Nuremberg were a good deal more productive than the search for a unified personality type. Just like many other Germans, several of the defendants expressed contempt for the supposed 'hypocrisy' of the Allies. Göring pointed out that by 'grabbing' territory in the west of the United States from the indigenous population a hundred years before, the Americans had also engaged in 'aggressive warfare'. Ribbentrop, the Nazi Foreign Minister, agreed, and said, 'Haven't you heard about how the Americans slaughtered the Indians? Were they an inferior race too?'[22]

Hans Frank, the Nazi ruler of the General Government in Poland, deployed a similar argument. He said that while the Allies loudly claimed that '2,000 Jews a day' were murdered at Auschwitz, they appeared to have forgotten the '30,000 people who were killed in the bombing attacks on Hamburg in a few hours'.[23]

But Frank didn't succeed in relativizing the Holocaust. He admitted after the commandant of Auschwitz, Rudolf Höss, had given evidence that this was 'something that people will talk about for a thousand years'. Meanwhile Göring, having finally admitted that the extermination of the Jews had actually happened, tried to dissociate himself from the crime by saying that the murders at Auschwitz had occurred because Höss was a 'southern German' and a 'Prussian could never bring himself to do things like that'.[24] In expressing that view, he appeared to have forgotten that he had been born in Bavaria himself.

Ribbentrop voiced the hope that the Allies would decide that 'mistakes have been made on both sides' and 'that those of us here on trial are German patriots and that though we may have been misled and gone too far with Hitler, we did it in good faith and as German citizens'.[25] But the horror of the Holocaust, as revealed at Nuremberg through testimony and film, put paid to that delusion.

In discussion with a psychologist, several of the defendants tried to argue that it was mere happenstance that led to their Nazi careers. Göring said that he had been on his way to join the Freemasons in 1919 when he saw 'a pretty blonde pass by, and I picked her up'. As a result, he never went to the meeting and so didn't become a Freemason. But he claimed that if the blonde hadn't passed by and he had joined the Free-masons, he couldn't have subsequently become a Nazi as the movement was hostile to Freemasonry. Consequently, said Göring, 'you can't fathom your fate. It depends on such little things.'[26]

Hans Frank pointed to a similar decisive moment in his life – one that also involved a woman. He said he had a 'wonderful' girlfriend when he was young, but because of his 'stupidity' and a 'trick of fate' they didn't get married. However, if he had gone ahead and made a life with her, then 'I would not have become a Nazi' because she was opposed to the movement and he was so 'easily influenced, especially by a woman I love'.[27]

Essentially, these leading Nazis were struggling to understand how they had become the people they had. And they were doing their best to unpick the reasons why – when they had been so secure in the correct-ness of their worldview – they were now on trial for war crimes. But the psychological coping strategy they had chosen to employ was infant-ile. They claimed that, since life is essentially a matter of chance, they weren't to blame for what had happened to them. They were in the dock at Nuremberg because one of them fell for a pretty blonde and the other didn't marry his 'wonderful' girlfriend.

Neither of these arguments survives more than a moment's examin-ation. Göring was a committed nationalist in 1919 when he saw that blonde walk by, and he was already primed to become a revolutionary. It also seems to have slipped his mind that Hjalmar Schacht, Hitler's Minister of Economics, was a Freemason, and that didn't stop him becoming an influential member of the Nazi government. So, no, pick-ing up that blonde wasn't the turning point in his life he claimed.

Hans Frank's wistful speculation is even easier to refute. The reality was that he rejected his 'wonderful' girlfriend of his own volition. He made a choice that fitted with his worldview at the time. And that choice was to marry someone else and make a career as a Nazi.

Predictably, there was also a great deal of scapegoating among the defendants. Streicher stuck to his old script and insisted that 'World

Jewry controls this trial,' but most of the others understood that the traditional Nazi recourse of blaming the Jews was no longer product-ive.[28] A better way forward, they decided, was to scapegoat Nazis who weren't there – chiefly Heinrich Himmler. The Reichsführer SS was the ideal target: he had been in control of the security apparatus of the state and couldn't contradict them because he had committed suicide shortly after being captured. It was also possible to blame Himmler but still profess their faith in Hitler since the old ruse of 'if only the Führer knew' was still available for them to parrot if necessary. Ultimately, though, all this dissembling was of little avail. The evidence of the horrors perpetrated by the regime was overwhelming.

Even though the psychologists at Nuremberg weren't successful in agreeing on a 'personality type' that encompassed all the leading Nazis, what of the broader question: did this horror happen because of a 'German national character'? It's an issue that has generated an enor-mous amount of controversy over the years, and negotiating a calm journey through the thickets of this topic is not easy. But the starting point is obvious. The culture in which we are raised does have an enor-mous impact on who we are. Psychological research shows, for instance, that those living in an 'individualistic' culture like the United States tend to bring up their children in a different way to those living in a 'collectivist' culture like China.

The mistake is to generate racist conclusions from these studies. The Chinese don't have a 'collectivist' culture because these beliefs are racially inherent within them. One study proved, for example, that farmers from an area of China that produced wheat had similar 'indi-vidualistic' traits – such as a higher rate of divorce – to those in Western countries. To a large extent it was the cooperative nature of rice farm-ing that was driving the 'collectivist' culture elsewhere in China.[29]

The psychologist Professor Ervin Staub detected in Germany evi-dence of a 'strong respect for authority' that was 'deeply rooted', coupled with a 'monolithic' culture that 'stressed obedience, order, efficiency and loyalty to the group'.[30] But while it is true that there was an authori-tarian streak running through many German families and schools, together with a widespread belief in the superiority of German philoso-phy, music and writing, it is important not to overemphasize these factors. Plenty of Germans featured in this history didn't have a 'strong respect for authority', and 'monolithic' is not a word that comes to mind to describe German society in the immediate years after the First World War – which was a time of revolution and divisiveness. Similarly, there is little evidence that 'ordered' or 'efficient' are appropriate adjectives to use when describing the Nazi state. As many examples in this book demonstrate, while the Nazi propagandists wanted the world to think that the regime was ordered and efficient, the reality was, as the Nazi supporter Günter Lohse saw for himself, that 'behind the scenes' it was often 'total chaos'.[31] Moreover, a majority of Germans never even voted for the Nazis in a free election – Hitler's desire for a one-party Nazi state appealed only to a minority prior to 1933.

Nonetheless, the idea that these horrors happened because Germany was an 'authoritarian' society is still occasionally voiced in popular discourse. But as a single explanation it is insupportable. Leaving aside the fact that many of those who murdered Jews came from Lithuania, Ukraine, Romania and elsewhere, the motivation of the German perpetrators was complex, and while some came from strongly 'authoritarian' backgrounds, others didn't. People are multifaceted, influenced by family, by belief structure, by genetics, by friends, by education and so on. While the culture that surrounds us is important in our development, we remain individuals who are responsible for our choices, and different people's behaviour within the same culture can vary hugely. As Eugene Leviné, a German Jew who escaped the country in 1933, said in the context of his family's experience in Poland: 'Some of my family members were betrayed by Poles. Some of them were saved by Poles. So am I going to hate or love the Poles?'[32]

The truth is that the terrible crimes described in this book didn't so much happen 'because the Nazis were German' as because they were human beings. And although the genocide of the Holocaust is the worst example in history of a group being targeted for racist reasons, the fact is that racial injustice can happen anywhere. It certainly happened in America during the Second World War.

On 19 February 1942, just over two months after the Japanese attack on Pearl Harbor, President Franklin Roosevelt signed one of the most notorious Allied documents of the war – Executive Order 9066. This led to the internment of around 110,000 people of Japanese ancestry living in America, the majority of whom held American citizenship.

The assumption behind the government's decision to detain these innocent people was shocking. It was that they couldn't be trusted as a group – even if they held American citizenship and had family and businesses in America. As Lieutenant General John DeWitt, of the Western Defense Command, told a congressional committee in 1943, 'it makes no difference whether he is an American citizen, he is still a Japanese. American citizenship does not necessarily determine loyalty.'[33]

There was to be no individual assessment of culpability, no attempt to determine whether any individual was a Japanese 'spy' or not – just collective guilt based purely on race. Moreover, there was no evidence that those of Japanese descent in America were undermining the war effort. Even more incredibly, this lack of evidence didn't matter to DeWitt. Indeed, he twisted the reality to suit his prejudice in a masterly piece of double-think. 'The very fact that no sabotage has taken place to date', he said, 'is a disturbing and confirming indication that such action will be taken.'[34]

The prejudice and illogicality behind the policy didn't stop there. Ironically in Hawaii – the site of the Pearl Harbor attack and thus a place which Japanese forces had proved they could reach – the Japanese Americans were not interned in camps en masse. Since they made up more than a third of the people living on the islands, the local economy couldn't function without them.

Luckily, unlike Nazi Germany, America still possessed both a free press and the rule of law. At the end of 1944 the Supreme Court decided that it was illegal to detain an American citizen without due process. As a result, those who had been interned in camps were released. Just over forty years later, after an official inquiry had concluded that the detentions had been motivated by racism, President Reagan passed the Civil Liberties Act which offered both compensation to those affected and a long-overdue apology.

One scholar poses a key question about this travesty: 'what might have happened had Lieutenant General DeWitt governed the Western Defense Command with the kind of unrestrained authority possessed by the Nazi government?'[35] The reason why that is the right question to ask – even though it is one we can never answer – is that it reminds us that it was ultimately the political structures in America that held DeWitt back. It wasn't one individual hero, fighting against the odds, but the system.

★

Fortunately, the judges at Nuremberg didn't have to wrestle with these cultural and situational issues, they only had to decide whether the individuals in front of them had committed war crimes or not. And after due deliberation they found all but three of the defendants guilty.[36] However, by the time the verdicts were delivered in 1946, the focus of millions of Germans was more on adjusting to their post-Nazi existence than on the details of the trial.

It was a time when even the political geography of the country was unstable. In the aftermath of the defeat, Germany lost massive amounts of territory – about twice as much as had been taken away by the treaty of Versailles. Around twelve million Germans were displaced from their homes, and many suffered traumatically as they sought to find a new place to live. It is a history that is not as well known outside Germany as it should be.

Three years after the judgments at Nuremberg, what was left of Germany was split in two. The Soviet Zone in the east became a separate country and the other Allied zones of occupation became West Germany, with a new capital in the small city of Bonn on the River Rhine.

This is the background against which we should judge the results of the post-war survey of German attitudes conducted by the American Office of Military Government. In August 1947, 55 per cent of those questioned agreed with the proposition that National Socialism had been a 'good idea badly carried out'.[37] Given the reality of their lives in a broken land, and with the communists in control of much of eastern Europe, it is perhaps not surprising that a majority of the Germans questioned refused to reject Nazism outright – even though they knew of the crimes of the regime.

But life was about to get better, at least for the Germans living in the western part of the country. A combination of aid from the European Recovery Plan – also known as the Marshall Plan, after the American Secretary of State George Marshall – and an 'economic miracle', produced by currency and tax reforms, meant that the future for West Germany began to look brighter.[38]

In the light of all this upheaval, the appetite for 'punishing' the Nazis – at least 'ordinary' members of the party – was waning. While a third of former Nazis in the American Zone had been sacked from their jobs in the first two years after the war ended, the vast majority had been rehired by the end of 1947.[39] For the Western Allies the reasons behind this turnaround were clear. Not only would West Germany cease to function as a modern state if everyone who had supported the Nazis was removed, but the increasingly fractious relationship between the Western Allies and Stalin meant that it was in the West's political interests to strengthen the country.

This new attitude was symbolized by the way major industrialists were treated. Ferdinand Porsche, who had been accused of various crimes, was released in 1947. He was never prosecuted for the use of forced labour at his Volkswagen factory.[40] Alfried Krupp, whose vast industrial enterprise had provided the Nazis with armaments and who had been sentenced to twelve years in prison for 'crimes against humanity', was released early in 1951.[41]

Now, the Allies felt, was the time to 'put the past behind us' and the majority of Germans were glad to do just that. As millions had done before, they adapted to their new circumstances and changed their behaviour as the situation changed.

In the West Germany of the 1950s, many former Nazis shifted effortlessly into positions of responsibility and prestige. They had been ambitious individuals under Nazism and now they were ambitious individuals in this newly democratic land.

Take Konrad Meyer, for example. He joined the Nazi Party in 1932 and the SS the following year. A talented planning expert who specialized in agricultural science, he was one of the central figures in the creation of the notorious General Plan for the East – a monstrous and largely unfulfilled scheme that called for ethnic cleansing and genocide in the eastern territories.

He served three years in prison after the war and on his release resumed his studies, becoming a professor at the Technical University in Hanover in 1956. He had been involved in 'planning' under the Nazis and was now involved in 'planning' in post-war West Germany. Only this time his 'planning' didn't involve the death and displacement of millions of innocent people.

It was even possible for some of these former Nazis to look back with wistful longing at times gone by. Carl Rachor, who worked on another ruthless Nazi scheme, the Four-Year Plan, wrote in a letter in May 1955: 'My one and only wish is that succeeding generations might once again be entrusted with tasks such as those that we were privileged to fulfil with upright hearts, impassioned energy and painstaking labour.'[42]

In recent years there has been more of an attempt by prosecutors in the now unified Germany to hold selected members of the SS to account. However, it is too little too late. Out of the 6,500 SS who worked at Auschwitz between 1940 and 1945, fewer than 800 ever received any punishment.[43]

Interviewed fifty years after the end of the war, SS man Bernd Linn still felt able to say that he believed the Third Reich was a 'good time. Germany was on the up, otherwise Churchill wouldn't have wanted to fight us, would he? It's like that for every nation, if things are going well for a people, then they stick with it. And it was going well for us . . . What stood against us, against the Reich, was the whole world. So you defend yourself against it.' As for the idea that the Holocaust was a unique horror, he indignantly protested, 'No! Absolutely not! Let everyone wash their own dirty linen, then England will have enough to do, more than enough, the French too, the Dutch – look at all their colonies – they would do better to keep quiet.'[44]

Former Stormtrooper Wolfgang Teubert, interviewed around the same time, agreed that 'the positive side' of the Nazi regime 'outweighed the negative by far'. He maintained that 'the negative side partly came as a result of human shortcomings or crazy behaviour or things like that . . . Individual occurrences always happened, everywhere.' He also – without producing any evidence – claimed that 'probably' only '300,000 to 400,000' people died in the Holocaust.[45]

There was no telling these people they were wrong – demonstrably and factually wrong. The Nazi period had so impacted on them, they had devoted so much of their life to it, made so many sacrifices, that to acknowledge the truth about this history was to deny their very being.

But there is a bigger problem here than the noxious views of former Nazis. And it is that disturbing issue – discussed in the final section of this book – which is the reason this history is of such value to us today.

Twelve Warnings

Everything is fragile – often a great deal more fragile than we think. That is the central message that I have taken from my work.[1]

Time and again I met people who were shocked at how swiftly their world changed – from Germans devastated by the economic collapse of the early 1930s to Hungarian Jews who couldn't believe how quickly their lives had been shattered by the arrival of the Nazis; from Polish academics who arrived at a university meeting only to be arrested and taken to a concentration camp to German children who suddenly found their family home on fire and their mother brutalized in front of them. All these people and more taught me how fragile our lives and the institutions around us are.

It is especially concerning when combined with the knowledge that while the National Socialist German Workers' Party is thankfully no more, the essential values of Nazism – hatred, scapegoating, anti-Semitism, racism and violent nationalism – are still very much with us.

With that in mind, here are twelve warnings of how democracy can be corrupted that I take from a study of this terrible period. They all relate to the chapters bearing the same titles that form the rest of this book.

I offer them in support neither of the left nor of the right, but as someone who values democracy over dictatorship.

Spreading Conspiracy Theories

We all know that powerful figures can seek to hide the truth from us, and there are many examples in history where investigative journalists have uncovered genuine conspiracies. But this is very different from the kind of conspiracy theories peddled by the Nazis and other unscrupulous groups. Honest investigative journalists have no prior agenda and follow where the facts lead them. The Nazis, on the other hand, already held preconceived prejudices and twisted and bent reality to support them. Their 'conspiracy theories' were blind to the truth.

The most appalling instance of this, of course, was the conspiracy theory that helped underpin the Holocaust. 'We were convinced by our worldview that there was a great conspiracy of Jewishness against us,' said Oskar Groening, an SS man who worked at Auschwitz. 'And that was expressed in Auschwitz in the idea that said, "Here the Jews are being exterminated . . . what happened in the First World War – that the Jews put us into misery – must be avoided. The Jews are our enemies." So we exterminated nothing but enemies.'[2]

It is hard to credit, hearing these shocking anti-Semitic lies, but the Groening I met was an unexceptional man. After the war he had taken a job as a personnel officer in a glassworks and lived quietly with his wife. He was so 'normal' that he was rather boring to spend time with.[3] By far the most interesting thing about him was that he had once worked at Auschwitz.[4]

It is many years since Groening committed his crimes, but conspiracy theorists thrive today more than ever, helped by the fact that social media can be used to undermine previously trusted sources of news and information, and that it is often impossible for us to 'prove' basic facts about our own lives. Prove to me, for instance, that William the Conqueror and the Normans weren't extraterrestrials. Or that an invisible super-race doesn't control our every action. Or that human beings really landed on the moon.

Thirty years ago I experienced an even more shocking example of this kind of thinking. I met a fanatical former Nazi – a Belgian member of the SS – and heard him deny the Holocaust. My colleagues and I argued with him and told him of the vast amount of evidence proving the existence of the crime. There were even photographs of the dead at the concentration camps.

He looked at us contemptuously. 'And you really believe', he said, 'these pictures are true?'[5]

Using Them and Us

The ability to categorize swiftly is essential to our survival. We wouldn't exist if our ancestors hadn't been able to judge in an instant whether someone was a friend or foe. That's why the amygdala, which performs this brain function, is such a crucial part of our lives.

The problem is that this kind of rapid assessment can lead to immense prejudice. The temptation to lump groups together and say 'they're all the same' is strong. And even though another part of the brain can subsequently attempt to question the validity of that decision, the emotional power of the amygdala inputs first, whenever we feel threatened.

Would-be dictators exploit this. They try and amplify our tendency to divide the world into 'Them and Us' by pointing dramatically to a 'Them' – a group of easily identifiable people whom they can scapegoat.

There are enormous benefits for any dictator in trumpeting this kind of 'Them and Us' rhetoric. It not only creates intense emotional feelings among their supporters, but it reinforces a sense of 'Us-ness' linking the followers to the leader, and conveys the reassuring message that no matter what problems you face, you can always blame 'Them'.

Leading as a Hero

Theorists like Max Weber and Ernest Becker recognized how much personal heroism is a valuable component of leadership.[6] Adolf Hitler was aware of this truth as well: he benefited considerably from both his service as a soldier in the First World War and his seemingly 'heroic' show of defiance when on trial for high treason in 1924.

Similarly, many other dictators – from Napoleon Bonaparte to Benito Mussolini and from Fidel Castro to Marshal Tito – came to prominence in large part because they were perceived as heroes, even though in many cases the dictator's 'heroism' was either exaggerated or created for propaganda effect.

We saw in this history how Hitler was already aware that he would almost certainly receive a lenient sentence for high treason when he 'bravely' gave his defiant speeches in the courtroom. And while the image of Mussolini leading his Fascists in a March on Rome in 1922 became a vital part of the 'Duce' myth, the truth was very different – he had travelled to the Italian capital on a train dressed in a suit and bowler hat.[7] But that hardly fitted the actions of a hero.

The problem with trusting 'heroic leaders' is evident from this history. It is but a short step from considering a leader a hero to perceiving them as a quasi-parental figure who always knows best. As the social psychologist Erich Fromm pointed out in his *Escape from Freedom*, it can be seductive to hand over decision making to someone else – an individual you feel is better equipped to decide vital political and social questions.[8] But while it might be emotionally attractive to abrogate responsibility, it can also be extremely dangerous.

Corrupting Youth

Targeting people under the age of twenty-five takes advantage of the biological fact that the frontal cortex – the part of the brain that offers restraint and analytic judgement – is not yet fully formed. Consequently, adolescents are often the easiest people to mould into fanatics.

It wasn't just Hitler who intuitively understood this – other dictators have as well. In Cambodia many of Pol Pot's most zealous killers were under the age of twenty-five; in China Chairman Mao mobilized the students of the Red Guard to force through the catastrophe of the Cultural Revolution; and in the Soviet Union successive leaders placed great emphasis on the youths of the Komsomol.

Every dictator wants to ensure that children and adolescents are taught only their approved version of history. By such methods they create an incremental process of habituation to the 'new thinking'. If they keep it up for a generation or two, there will be few people left who ever knew any different.

I learnt that first hand when filming in Russia in the early 1990s, just after the fall of communism. I asked an intelligent woman in her twenties – a librarian – how she had reconciled the existence of the Nazi–Soviet pact of August 1939 with the anti-Nazi propaganda the Soviet Union had subsequently produced two years later about the 'Great Patriotic War' against Germany.

'I never had to have a view on that,' she said. 'Because it wasn't until last month that I heard the truth about the Nazi–Soviet pact.'

Conniving with the Elite

It's too often forgotten that dictators frequently do not seize control on their own, instead power is handed to them by others.

We saw earlier in this history how Hitler could not have become Chancellor of Germany without President Hindenburg's approval, and that Hindenburg first had to be convinced by those in the nationalist elite around him.

Other dictators, like Francisco Franco in Spain, were also helped in their rise to power by the backing of influential members of the elite. Franco benefited enormously from the support of senior figures in the Catholic church, who believed he was leading a crusade against the Republican opposition.[9]

During the Spanish Civil War, after Franco relieved the siege of the Alcázar of Toledo in September 1936, he received a personal telegram thanking him from the Primate of Spain, Cardinal Isidro Gomá y Tomás. In his reply, Franco acknowledged how much the approval of the Catholic elite meant to him: 'I could receive no better help than the blessing of Your Eminence.'[10]

Benito Mussolini gained even more direct backing from the elite in his quest for power. In October 1922, King Victor Emmanuel III decided to make him Prime Minister of Italy, with disastrous consequences for the country.

President Hindenburg, Cardinal Gomá y Tomás and King Victor Emmanuel. Three powerful members of an elite, each of whom was instrumental in the rise to prominence of a dictator.

Attacking Human Rights

This is a common goal of all dictators. You can't run an absolute dictatorship without eliminating the human rights of your population. No one must be allowed to question your judgement or to speak out against you.

One of the first steps is to extinguish the rule of law. And you may not have to wait until you have destroyed democracy to start trying. Even if you're just a would-be dictator who has been elected by a popular vote, it is still sometimes possible to cripple the legal system by altering the appointment procedure for judges and removing any judges that don't support the new regime.

Equally, you can't succeed as a dictator if journalists are able to publish criticism about you. So abolishing the free press is also high on the list of initial tasks.

The right to individual free speech is another early casualty of a dictator's rule, and longer term there is frequently an attempt made to penetrate the private lives of ordinary citizens. The use of children to denounce their parents is one aspect of this control, as are restrictions on sexual and reproductive rights.

However, once they have destroyed the human rights of their population, the mistake many dictators make with their propaganda is not to heed the advice of Joseph Goebbels – 'at all costs avoid being boring.'[11]

Goebbels understood how important it was to provide entertainment for the population. But he wasn't the first to grasp this truth. Roman emperors reached the same conclusion nearly 2,000 years before. They realized that gladiator fights – initially performed as tributes on the death of a person of nobility – could be extended into more lavish shows. The more the population of Rome liked what they saw, the more they thanked the person who paid for the entertainment.

Exploiting Faith

Hitler understood the immense power of faith. If your followers have complete faith in you then no amount of reasoned argument will convince them that they're wrong. For that reason, we should be sceptical of politicians who ask us to have 'faith' in their judgement.

That is why many dictators despise intellectuals. They fear scholars will challenge any of their beliefs that are faith-based. Hitler, for that reason, hated lawyers. He saw them as coldly questioning his actions and interfering on behalf of the weak. The only other profession Hitler despised as much were priests. That wasn't just because, like lawyers, they spoke out for the disadvantaged, but because they represented a rival faith-based belief system.[12]

Dictators frequently promise a transcendent reward – a future utopia – in exchange for their supporters' faith. Hitler offered a vision of the *Volksgemeinschaft*, while Stalin promised a communist paradise. It also helped in psychological terms, as we saw earlier, that such goals were always just out of reach.[13]

In offering their utopian visions, dictators often create a false version of the past as an imaginary reference point. 'Back then we were tremendous' is the pitch, 'and we can be so again.' The Nazis certainly did this.

The idea of the 'Third Reich' was to link the present to what were perceived as the past glories of the Holy Roman Empire and the Germany that Bismarck helped create.

Valuing Enemies

'The more enemies, the more honour,' said General Werner von Blomberg, German Minister of War in the 1930s.[14] It was a sentiment that his boss, Adolf Hitler, would have agreed with wholeheartedly.

Hitler revelled in enemies. He understood that one of the easiest ways to bond people together is to convince them who their enemies are. He created an atmosphere in which the population always felt there were dark forces ranged against them – both internally within Germany and externally in other countries. But Hitler was not alone: it's hard to think of a dictator who doesn't value enemies in much the same way.

Enemies aren't just useful for dictators because they're an easy way of bonding people together, they also help overcome complacency within the leadership group and keep the population dependent on the regime for protection. Stalin's paranoia was such that he placed enormous emphasis on the search for 'enemies of the people' – real or imagined – while Reinhard Heydrich announced in 1935 that it would take the Nazis 'years of bitter struggle finally to push back the enemy in all areas'.[15]

Shrewd dictators understand that the search for enemies must be never-ending. And if you don't have any enemies, then you need to create them.

Eliminating Resistance

While it is commonplace for dictators to eliminate the basic human rights of their subjects, it can be more challenging for them to target powerful groups like the church or the army. And it is from these groups that resistance often arises.

General Blaskowitz, who protested about the atrocities committed by the SS in Poland, straddled both groups. A committed Christian, he was also faithful to what he believed were the ideals of the military.[16]

Similarly, four years later, it was no coincidence that it was a group of army officers who were behind the plot to kill Hitler on 20 July 1944. And many of those conspirators – including the main protagonist, Claus von Stauffenberg – professed Christian beliefs.

For the reasons discussed earlier, while Hitler sought to eliminate resistance to his regime wherever he could, he didn't feel able to destroy all potential opposition within either the church or the army.[17] But Stalin took a different view. His regime targeted both the church and the military in ways Hitler never did. His purge of Red Army officers during the 1930s was savage. He didn't seem to care that many of the accused were innocent of any wrongdoing or that because of the purge he lost a number of his most talented generals.

Stalin, a keen student of history, was aware that Napoleon Bonaparte had successfully overturned the revolution that preceded him. Napoleon, a brilliant army officer, had proclaimed himself Emperor just twelve years after the monarchy had been overthrown. Stalin wanted, at all costs, to prevent another Napoleon doing the same thing to his revolution.

It is a common mistake to think that a mass movement of ordinary citizens can bring down a dictator. It can't, unless the army and security forces give them their support. So the astute dictator either corrupts these armed units with money and other benefits or, as Stalin did, keeps them in a constant state of anxiety about possible denunciation.

Escalating Racism

Feelings of 'Them and Us' exist in all societies, but often they aren't fuelled by racism. Soldiers, for instance, always experience emotions of 'Them and Us' when confronting their enemies, regardless of whether they consider their opponents 'racially inferior' or not. But, as Hitler knew, when combined with racism the 'Them and Us' dichotomy takes on a powerful new dimension. Hence German soldiers fighting on the eastern front in the Second World War behaved – almost always – in a more inhumane way than those fighting in the west.

Racism, as the Nazis demonstrated, is the toxic brew that can heighten 'Them and Us' feelings to murderous levels. It is a judgement that one of the wisest people I met in the course of my work agreed with unreservedly. He was Eugene Leviné, a German Jew who escaped to Britain just after Hitler came to power. 'There are always large numbers of people who are willing to persecute and hate,' he said, 'and if unemployment was a bit worse here [in the UK] and you advertised for a core of people to beat up or expel or possibly even kill either Asians, or Jews, or Irish, or even Welsh, and you offered them a going rate, of what, a thousand [pounds] a week, free uniform and accommodation, I don't think it would take you long to collect fifty thousand people. I'd get them together, I guarantee.'[18]

Killing at a Distance

A recurring theme of this history has been the psychological problems that people can experience if they are told to kill someone face to face. That difficulty, as we've seen, was a key reason why the Nazis developed more distanced methods of killing such as the gas chamber.

But it wasn't just the Nazis who understood the psychological benefits of killing at a distance. Many on the Allied side did as well. That is a truth I learnt twenty-five years ago when I interviewed Paul Montgomery, an American who flew bombing missions over Japan in the Second World War.

Even though he participated with his colleagues in the killing of thousands of civilians, he experienced no stress. 'I didn't have any regrets, to put it bluntly,' he told me. 'I was twenty-one years old that summer of the firebombing. And I really was wanting to get the war over and I wanted to go home. And if they told me to go bomb some cities, I went and bombed cities.'[19]

Distancing, once again, was primarily what allowed him and his flight crew to kill. 'It's not like going out and sticking a bayonet in somebody's belly, OK?' said Montgomery. 'You kill them from a distance . . . It's kind of like conducting a war through a video game.'[20]

While Montgomery insisted that he felt no racism towards the Japanese, he did admit that he felt 'hatred' towards them because he had 'lost some friends at Pearl Harbor'. So he was distanced from the people he was killing not just physically but emotionally as well.

It is a warning for the future, as warfare becomes more mechanized. Robots on the battlefield and other automated forms of attack can only help distance the human killers still further from those they destroy.

What a merciless dictator will do with such resources is terrifying to imagine.

Stoking Fear

While Hitler's hatred suffuses this history, he also understood the value of another closely linked emotion – fear. One of the most important reasons that Germans fought on as long as they did was fear of the approaching Red Army. Another was fear of being denounced to the Gestapo as a 'defeatist'.

Fear is one of the emotions that stems from the amygdala – which explains the immediate and often devastating power of the feeling – and is closely linked in the brain to aggression. That makes evolutionary sense. If you are walking on the savannah and you're suddenly confronted by a ferocious wild beast, then you have to be prepared to do something about it – instantly.

While we are unlikely to encounter an animal today that wants to devour us, dictators know that the same emotional reaction can be created via incendiary words. Such a tactic also plays into 'loss aversion', a cognitive bias we discussed earlier.[21] It follows that one of the most potent political statements of all is: 'Be frightened, they are coming for your homes and children.' It was a central part of Hitler's message to the German population in the final days of the war, and it will be a central part of many future dictators' rhetoric in years to come.

It's a long list, and we would do well to be vigilant. But this is not a counsel of despair – there is still cause for optimism. Adolf Hitler employed every one of the techniques listed above, but in the end – at enormous human cost – something tremendous happened.

The Nazis were defeated.

Acknowledgements

As I mentioned in the Introduction, I've been thinking about the issues I discuss in this book for more than thirty years. So, inevitably, there are an enormous number of people who have helped me along the way, from my colleagues in the various television production teams that I was privileged to lead, to the galaxy of academics I consulted, to the hundreds of people I met who lived through this history.

Over the years I have thanked all these people in my previous books, so I hope they will forgive me for not mentioning them all individually here. My collective thanks are no less genuine and heartfelt.

For this book, I first need to express an enormous debt of gratitude to Professor Sir Ian Kershaw, my close friend and mentor. Not only is he one of the greatest historians of the last hundred years, but he is also the kindest of men. Always supportive, he encouraged from the beginning my desire to see what insights psychology could offer this history. He also read this book in draft and his comments improved it enormously. The luckiest break of my intellectual life was meeting him. I can never repay all he has done for me.

The talented German historian Julia Pietsch once again did valuable work for me in German archives, and, of course, I thank the BBC for permission to quote from the various interviews conducted for the documentaries that I wrote and produced.

My good friend Baroness Stowell of Beeston, a former leader of the House of Lords, read the book before publication and gave me valuable insights from the perspective of a practising politician. Of course, the judgements and opinions expressed in this work remain mine alone.

I also thank Professor Victor Bailey, Distinguished Professor of Modern British History at the University of Kansas, for reading the book. And – as befits one of my former tutors at Oxford University – giving me his candid opinion. Fortunately, it was a positive one.

I'm grateful to Dr Caroline Dodds Pennock for a fascinating discussion about her work on Mesoamerican history and how these societies integrated violence into their culture during the postclassic period.

While this was not of immediate relevance to the history of the Nazis, it provided me with much food for thought.

I did a considerable amount of psychological research in preparation for writing this book and am grateful to members of the psychological community for the generous way they welcomed my enquiries. I want to give my special thanks to the academic psychologists and neuroscientists I interviewed for this project: Dr Lucy Foulkes and Professors Karen Douglas, Stephen Reicher, Robert Sapolsky, Jonathan Shedler and Essi Viding. Any errors in my interpretation of all this psychological work are, naturally, my responsibility not theirs.

Andrew Nurnberg, my literary agent for longer than I care to mention, gave wise advice as usual. This time he was supported by Michael Dean, who has increasingly taken over the practical side of agenting as Andrew steps back from the day-to-day running of the company he created.

At Viking Books my editor, Daniel Crewe, was an enormous help. The rest of his team, Emma Brown, Alex Mulholland, Anna Lambert and Olivia Mead, were also terrifically supportive. The book was meticulously copyedited by Peter James. I was fortunate to have the benefit of his expertise once again. In America, my publisher Clive Priddle at Public Affairs was a friend to this project and I'm grateful for all that he and his colleagues have contributed.

My wife, Helena, was – as always – full of valuable advice. I feel so guilty for burdening her, over the last more than thirty years, with knowledge of the terrible crimes committed by the Nazis. I can hardly think of a more touching demonstration of her love for me than her commitment to a subject she would never have chosen. What a wonderful person. I do not deserve her.

Our three children, Oliver, Camilla and Benedict, were also immensely encouraging. Now they are grown up I am the beneficiary of not just their love but their academic expertise. As luck would have it, both my sons have university degrees in Psychology and my daughter a degree in History. What a perfect combination for this project.

My last book was dedicated to my son Benedict and the one before that to my daughter Camilla. So now it's Oliver's turn, and I dedicate this work to him with a father's love.

Laurence Rees
London, August 2024

Notes

Abbreviations of Archives Cited

BAM	Bistumsarchiv Münster
BA-MA	Bundesarchiv-Militärarchiv Freiburg
BArch	Bundesarchiv
BayHStA	Bayerisches Hauptstaatsarchiv
BStU	Der Bundesbeauftragte für die Stasi-Unterlagen (now in Bundesarchiv)
DRA	Deutsches Rundfunkarchiv
GStA PK	Geheimes Staatsarchiv Preußischer Kulturbesitz
HHStAW	Hessisches Hauptstaatsarchiv Wiesbaden
IfZ	Institut für Zeitgeschichte
RGWA	Rossijski Gosudartstwenny Wojenny Archiw
StAL	Staatsarchiv Ludwigsburg
StAN	Staatsarchiv Nürnberg
ZStL	Zentrale Stelle der Landesjustizverwaltungen zur Aufklärung nationalsozialistischer Verbrechen

Prologue

1 Laurence Rees, *Auschwitz: The Nazis and the 'Final Solution'*, BBC Books, 2012, Kindle edition, p. 38.

2 Laurence Rees, *The Holocaust: A New History*, Viking, 2017, Kindle edition, p. 183.

3 Rees, *Auschwitz*, Kindle edition, p. 82.

4 For the reasons why I consider the Holocaust a crime of singular horror in the history of the human race, see Rees, *Holocaust*, Kindle edition, pp. 478–80.

Introduction

1 Declared a 'criminal organization' at the Nuremberg War Crimes Trial.
2 As I've written before, this kind of material needs to be treated with care and sensitivity. There are many potential pitfalls in dealing with oral history that you need to be trained to avoid. See Laurence Rees, *Their Darkest Hour*, Ebury Press, 2007, Kindle edition, pp. 7–8.
3 It wasn't just the fact that these witnesses to history were still alive that helped us, we also had two other lucky breaks. First, we met former Nazis when they felt old enough to speak freely – without worrying about the possible repercussions to their careers – but before they had started to endure the vicissitudes of their final years. And second, the fall of the Berlin Wall meant that many more people who had been unable to tell their stories before were now available to speak freely not just to me but to the production teams I was privileged to lead.
4 Karl Jaspers, *The Origin and Goal of History*, Routledge Classics, 2021, p. 167 (first published 1949).
5 Laurence Rees, *World War Two: Behind Closed Doors. Stalin, the Nazis and the West*, BBC Books, 2012, Kindle edition, pp. 220–25.
6 *The Stolen Child*, a film for BBC TV's *Timewatch*, produced by Catrine Clay, executive produced by Laurence Rees; first transmitted on BBC2, 10 February 1993. Also see Rees, *Their Darkest Hour*, Kindle edition, pp. 260–66.
7 Leda Cosmides and John Tooby, 'Evolutionary Psychology: A Primer', Center for Evolutionary Psychology, University of California, Santa Barbara, 1997, p. 11, https://www.cep.ucsb.edu/wp-content/uploads/2023/06/Evolutionary-Psychology-A-Primer-CosmidesTooby1993.pdf.
8 Walter Langer, *A Psychological Analysis of Adolf Hitler: His Life and Legend*, www.all-about-psychology.com, 2011, Kindle edition, p. 119.
9 Herbert Döhring, Karl Wilhelm Krause and Anna Plaim, *Living with Hitler: Accounts of Hitler's Household Staff*, Greenhill Books, 2018, Kindle edition, pp. 168–274. Also see the official website for the Kehlsteinhaus, https://www.kehlsteinhaus.de/english/.
10 James Waller, *Becoming Evil: How Ordinary People Commit Genocide and Mass Killing*, 2nd edn, Oxford University Press, 2007, pp. 64–9.
11 Robert Sapolsky, *Behave: The Biology of Humans at Our Best and Worse*, Vintage Digital, 2017, pp. 19–20.

12 Robert Sapolsky, 'Introduction to Human Behavioral Biology', Stanford University lecture, 2010, https://www.youtube.com/watch?v=NNnIG h9g6fA (from 8' 5" to 8' 14").

13 There have, of course, been attempts to penetrate Nazi mentalities before. But often they have either been an analysis of a single character, like Gitta Sereny's *Into That Darkness: From Mercy Killing to Mass Murder*, Pimlico, 1995 (first published 1974), an investigation into the mind of Franz Stangl, commandant of Treblinka extermination camp; or the story of groups of perpetrators as in Christopher Browning's *Ordinary Men: Reserve Police Battalion 101 and the Final Solution in Poland*, Harper Perennial, 2017 (first published 1992); or conceptual works such as Claudia Koonz's *The Nazi Conscience*, Harvard University Press, 2003; or in the form of biographical essays, like Joachim Fest's *The Face of the Third Reich*, Penguin, 1992 (first published 1970). It was reading Fest's book fifty years ago (!) that first piqued my interest in the question of why anyone would want to become a Nazi. But it's hard for me to think of any book on the market today that deals with this question head on within an overall history of the Nazis.

14 Goebbels address to the Officials and Directors of the Radio Corporation, Berlin, House of Broadcasting, 25 March 1933, https://ghdi.ghi-dc.org/ pdf/eng/English89_Exeter_new.pdf.

15 *Goebbels: Master of Propaganda*, BBC2, transmitted 12 November 1992, written and produced by Laurence Rees. Also see Laurence Rees, *Selling Politics*, BBC Books, 1992, p. 18.

Chapter 1: Spreading Conspiracy Theories

1 Anatol Lieven, *America Right or Wrong: An Anatomy of American Nationalism*, Oxford University Press, 2004, p. 23.

2 István Deák, *Weimar Germany's Left-Wing Intellectuals: A Political History of the Weltbühne and its Circle*, University of California Press, 1968, p. 66.

3 See, for instance, Christopher Clark, *Kaiser Wilhelm II: Profiles in Power*, Routledge, 2013, p. 239.

4 Hew Strachan, *The First World War*, vol. 1: *To Arms*, Oxford University Press, 2001, p. 123.

5 Previously unpublished testimony. (This form of words will be used to signify unpublished testimony gathered for various documentaries written and produced by Laurence Rees.)

6 Ernst Jünger, *Storm of Steel*, Penguin Classics, Kindle edition, 2016, p. 5.

7 Adolf Hitler, *Mein Kampf*, Houghton Mifflin, 1971, p. 161. We need to be extremely careful how we approach Hitler's words in *Mein Kampf*. Sections of the book, as we will see later in this work, are unreliable to the point of fantasy. This is one of the sections that is almost certainly accurate.

8 Margaret MacMillan, *The War That Ended Peace: How Europe Abandoned Peace for the First World War*, Profile Books, 2013, p. 575.

9 See the words of Professor Robert Citino, in conversation with Laurence Rees, at http://ww2history.com/experts/Robert_Citino/The_German_Army.

10 Ernst Röhm, *Die Geschichte eines Hochverräters*, Verlag Franz Eher Nachfolger, 1930 (first published 1928), p. 27.

11 Ibid., p. 28.

12 Ibid., p. 31.

13 Ian Sumner, *The First Battle of the Marne 1914: The French 'Miracle' Halts the Germans*, Osprey Publishing, 2012, Kindle edition, location 108.

14 Hew Strachan, *The First World War*, Simon & Schuster, 2003, p. 58.

15 These issues are discussed in *1914: The War Revolution*, a *Timewatch* film which first transmitted on BBC2 on 7 February 2003. The producer was Paul Bradshaw and the executive producer was Laurence Rees.

16 Eberhard Jäckel and Axel Kuhn (eds.), *Hitler. Sämtliche Aufzeichnungen 1905–1924*, Deutsche Verlags-Anstalt, 1980, pp. 64–9, quoted in Konrad Heiden, *The Fuehrer*, Robinson Publishing, 1999, pp. 70–72.

17 *Hitler's Table Talk 1941–1944*, Phoenix Press, 2000, night of 25–26 September 1941, p. 44.

18 Röhm, *Die Geschichte*, p. 34.

19 Lt Col. Dave Grossman, *On Killing: The Psychological Cost of Learning to Kill in War and Society*, Open Road Media, revised edition, 2014, Kindle edition, p. 38. Also see Roger J. Spiller, 'S. L. A. Marshall and the Ratio of Fire', *RUSI Journal*, vol. 133 (1988), pp. 63–71, for criticism of the survey conducted into the ratio of fire of American soldiers in the Second World War, and Robert Engen, 'Killing for Their Country: A New Look at "Killology"', *Canadian Military Journal*, 14 March 2023, for a broader analysis of Grossman's argument. Available online at: https://www.canada.ca/en/army/services/line-sight/articles/2023/03/killing-for-their-country-a-new-look-at-killology.html.

Also see Chapter 10 of this book, where it appears self-evident that many people found it hard to kill civilians at close quarters.

20 Grossman, *On Killing*, Kindle edition, pp. 66 and 198.

21 Randall L. Bytwerk, *Julius Streicher: Nazi Editor of the Notorious Anti-Semitic Newspaper Der Stürmer*, Cooper Square Press, 2001, p. 5.

22 Erich Maria Remarque, *All Quiet on the Western Front*, Vintage, 1996, Kindle edition, p. 6.

23 Ibid., p. 47.

24 Ibid., p. 201.

25 Ibid.

26 Jünger, *Storm*, Kindle edition, p. 99.

27 Ibid., pp. 99–100.

28 Hilton Tims, *Erich Maria Remarque: The Last Romantic*, Carroll & Graf, 2003, p. 2.

29 Ibid., p. 11.

30 See p. 102.

31 Jäckel and Kuhn (eds.), *Hitler. Sämtliche Aufzeichnungen*, pp. 70–72.

32 Author interview with Professor Sir Ian Kershaw.

33 Jay Winter, *Remembering War: The Great War between Memory and History in the Twentieth Century*, Yale University Press, 2006, p. 84.

34 Author interview with Professor Karen M. Douglas, University of Kent. Also see Karen M. Douglas, Robbie M. Sutton and Aleksandra Cichocka, 'The Psychology of Conspiracy Theories', *Current Directions in Psychological Science*, vol. 26, no. 6 (December 2017), pp. 538–42, and Karen M. Douglas and Robbie M. Sutton, 'What are Conspiracy Theories? A Definitional Approach to their Correlates, Consequences, and Communication', *Annual Review of Psychology*, vol. 74 (January 2023), pp. 271–98.

35 Robin Dunbar, *Grooming, Gossip and the Evolution of Language*, Faber & Faber, 2011, Kindle edition, p. 97.

36 Ibid., p. 8.

37 Rees, *Holocaust*, Kindle edition, pp. 27–8.

38 See pp. 44–7.

39 Rees, *Holocaust*, Kindle edition, p. 66. Eugene Leviné was the son of the revolutionary of almost the same name (Eugen without the final 'e') who was one of the leaders of the 1919 revolution in Munich.

40 See, for example, the stenographic report of the meeting of Reich Marshal Göring with the Reich Commissioners for the occupied territories and military commanders on the food situation, 6 August 1942. Léon Poliakov

and Josef Wulf, *Das Dritte Reich und seine Diener*, Ullstein, 1983, pp. 471ff. Also in document 170-USSR, in IMT, *Der Prozess gegen die Hauptkriegsverbrecher vor dem Internationalen Militärgerichtshof, Nürnberg, 14. November 1945–1. Oktober 1946*, vol. XXIX, Sekretariat des Gerichtshof 1949, pp. 385ff.

41 Borislav Chernev, *Twilight of Empire: The Brest-Litovsk Conference and the Remaking of East-Central Europe, 1917–1918*, University of Toronto Press, 2017, Kindle edition, p. 184.

42 Ibid., p. 22.

43 Robert Gerwarth, *November 1918: The German Revolution*, Oxford University Press, 2020, Kindle edition, pp. 50–52.

44 Vejas Gabriel Liulevicius, *War Land on the Eastern Front: Culture, National Identity and German Occupation in World War I*, Cambridge University Press, 2004, p. 249.

45 Previously unpublished testimony.

46 Gerwarth, *November 1918*, Kindle edition, pp. 58–9.

47 John Toland, *No Man's Land: 1918, The Last Year of the Great War*, University of Nebraska Press, 2002, pp. 259–60.

48 Ibid., p. 260.

49 David Murphy, 'The French Army in 1918', in Matthias Strohn (ed.), *1918: Winning the War, Losing the War*, Osprey Publishing, Kindle edition, 2018, p. 89.

50 Previously unpublished testimony.

51 Nick Lloyd, *Hundred Days: The End of the Great War*, Penguin, 2013, Kindle edition, pp. 59–60.

52 Edgar Feuchtwanger, *Imperial Germany 1850–1918*, Routledge, 2001, p. 193.

53 Alan Kramer, 'The Poisonous Myth: Democratic Germany's "Stab in the Back" Legend', *Irish Times*, 21 January 2019, https://www.irishtimes.com/culture/heritage/the-poisonous-myth-democratic-germany-s-stab-in-the-back-legend-1.3751185.

54 Laurence Rees, *The Nazis: A Warning from History*, BBC Books, 2012, Kindle edition, p. 15.

55 Stephan Malinowski, *Nazis and Nobles: The History of a Misalliance*, Oxford University Press, 2020, Kindle edition, p. 73.

56 Ibid., p. 77.

57 Klaus-Jürgen Müller, *General Ludwig Beck*, Harald Boldt Verlag, 1980, pp. 323–8, Beck's letter to his sister, Gertrude Beck, 28 November 1918, BArch, BA-MA N, 28/6.

58 Malinowski, *Nazis and Nobles*, Kindle edition, p. 80.

59 Previously unpublished testimony.

60 Jonathan Boff, *Winning and Losing on the Western Front*: *The British Third Army and the Defeat of Germany in 1918*, Cambridge University Press, 2012, p. 3.

61 *Stenographische Bericht über die öffentlichen Verhandlungen des 15. Untersuchungs-ausschusses der verfassunggebenden Nationalversammlung*, vol. 2, Norddeutschen Buchdruckerei, 1920, pp. 700–701, Hindenburg's testimony on 18 November 1919; see Anton Kaes, Martin Jay and Edward Dimendberg (eds.), *The Weimar Republic Sourcebook*, University of California Press, 1994, pp. 15–16.

62 *Berliner Tageblatt*, 20 November 1919, quoted in Anna von der Goltz, *Hindenburg: Power, Myth, and the Rise of the Nazis*, Oxford University Press, 2011, p. 66.

63 Author interview with Professor Karen M. Douglas.

64 Previously unpublished testimony.

65 Ernst H. Posse, *Die politischen Kampfbünde Deutschlands*, Junker und Dünnhaupt, 1931, pp. 46–7, quoted in Robert G. L. Waite, *Vanguard of Nazism: The Free Corps Movement in Postwar Germany 1918–1923*, Harvard University Press, 1952, p. 266.

66 Not quoted in Waite but in the original, Posse, *Die politischen Kampfbünde Deutschlands*, p. 46.

67 Röhm, *Die Geschichte*, pp. 79–81.

68 *Hitler's Table Talk*, 30 November 1941, evening, p. 138.

69 Rudolf von Sebottendorff, *Bevor Hitler kam. Urkundliches aus der Frühzeit der nationalsozialistischen Bewegung von Rudolf von Sebottendorff*, Deukula-Verlag Graffinger, 1933, pp. 57–60.

70 Lida Gustava Heymann with Anita Augspurg, *Erlebtes – Erschautes. Deutsche Frauen kämpfen für Freiheit, Recht und Frieden 1850–1940*, ed. Margrit Twellmann, Verlag Anton Hain, 1972, pp. 162, 164–7. Quoted in part, in a slightly different translation, in Gerwarth, *November 1918*, p. 9.

71 Michael Brenner, *In Hitler's Munich*, Princeton University Press, 2022, pp. 46–8.

72 Ibid., p. 48.

73 Thule Society admission documents, BArch, NS 26/865.

74 Allan Mitchell, *Revolution in Bavaria, 1918–1919: The Eisner Regime and the Soviet Republic*, Princeton University Press, 1965, p. 311.

75 Holger H. Herwig, *The Demon of Geopolitics: How Karl Haushofer 'Educated' Hitler and Hess*, Rowman & Littlefield, 2016, p. 62.

76 Previously unpublished testimony.

77 Previously unpublished testimony.

78 Eleanor Hancock, *Ernst Röhm: Hitler's SA Chief of Staff*, Palgrave Macmillan, 2008, p. 33.

79 Previously unpublished testimony.

80 Kaes, Jay and Dimendberg (eds.), *Weimar Republic Sourcebook*, pp. 9–12, first published as 'Ansprache des Reichsaußenministers Grafen Brockdorff-Rantzau bei Überreichung des Friedensvertrags-Entwurfs durch die Alliierten und Assoziierten Mächte', in Graf Brockdorff-Rantzau, *Dokumente*, Deutsche Verlagsgesellschaft für Politik und Geschichte, 1920, pp. 113ff.

81 Richard Hargreaves, *Blitzkrieg Unleashed: The German Invasion of Poland, 1939*, Stackpole Books, 2010, p. 18.

82 Ibid., p. 19.

83 Michael S. Neiberg, *The Treaty of Versailles*, Oxford University Press, 2019, Kindle edition, pp. 93–5.

84 Hitler, *Mein Kampf*, pp. 205–6.

Chapter 2: Using Them and Us

1 August Kubizek, *The Young Hitler I Knew*, Greenhill Books, 2006, pp. 157–9.

2 Hitler, *Mein Kampf*, pp. 56–62.

3 On Hitler's attitude to the Jews he knew personally in pre-war Vienna see in particular Brigitte Hamann, *Hitlers Wien: Lehrjahre eines Diktators*, Piper, 1996.

4 Karl Mayr (writing as 'A Former Officer of the Reichswehr'), 'I Was Hitler's Boss', *Current History*, vol. 1, no. 3 (November 1941), p. 193. Karl Mayr as a source needs to be treated with great care. He later became a fierce opponent of Hitler and died in a concentration camp. But this assessment chimes with the situation at the time.

5 Thomas Weber, *Becoming Hitler: The Making of a Nazi*, Oxford University Press, 2017, Kindle edition, p. 81. There are many and various theories about Hitler's behaviour during this period. Recognizing the significance of the Versailles treaty in Hitler's political development is certainly one of the most important. Also see Ian Kershaw, *Hitler: Hubris 1889–1936*, Penguin, 2001, Kindle edition, pp. 122–3.

6 Words of Hans Knoden, 24 August 1919, in Ernst Deuerlein, 'Hitlers Eintritt in die Politik und die Reichswehr', *Vierteljahrshefte für Zeitgeschichte*, vol. 7, no. 2 (1959), p. 200. Original text is in BayHStA, Abt. II, GrKdo 4, Bd 50/03.

7 Author interview with Professor Robert Sapolsky.

8 Ian Kershaw, *Hitler*, Routledge, 1991, p. 51.

9 Richard J. Evans, *The Coming of the Third Reich*, Allen Lane, 2003, p. 170.

10 BayHStA, Abt. IV, p. 3071.

11 Hitler, *Mein Kampf*, p. 220.

12 Ibid., p. 222.

13 Ibid., pp. 222–3.

14 Kershaw, *Hubris*, Kindle edition, p. 108.

15 BayHStA, Abt. IV, R W GrKdo, Bd 50/08. In English in J. Noakes and G. Pridham (eds.), *Nazism 1919–1945*, vol. 1: *The Rise to Power 1919–1934*, University of Exeter Press, 1991, pp. 12–14.

16 D. A. Jeremy Telman, 'Adolf Stoecker: Anti-Semite with a Christian Mission', *Jewish History*, vol. 9, no. 2 (Fall 1995), p. 95.

17 Hamann, *Hitlers Wien*. Also see Thomas Weber, *Hitler's First War*, Oxford University Press, 2010, p. 177, for an examination of Hitler's beliefs in the First World War.

18 Previously unpublished testimony.

19 Rees, *Holocaust*, Kindle edition, p. 38.

20 Previously unpublished testimony, and also see Laurence Rees, *The Dark Charisma of Adolf Hitler*, Ebury Press, 2012, Kindle edition, p. 114.

21 Himmler diary entry for 12 January 1922, in BArch, N 1126 141 K. Originals in Hoover Institution, Stanford University, Stanford, California.

22 Elke Fröhlich (ed.), *Die Tagebücher von Joseph Goebbels*, Teil I: *Aufzeichnungen 1923–1941*, vol. 1/1: *Oktober 1923–November 1925*, K. G. Saur, 2004, pp. 50–51, entry for 14 November 1923.

23 Ibid., pp. 116–17, entry for 31 March 1924.

24 Ibid., p. 312, entry for 8 June 1925.

25 A point Professor Christopher Browning made in an interview with the author. See Rees, *Dark Charisma*, Kindle edition, pp. 29–30.

26 Peter H. Merkl, *Political Violence under the Swastika*, Princeton University Press, 1975, p. 453.

27 Gordon Allport, *The Nature of Prejudice*, Perseus, 1954.

28 N. H. Baynes (ed.), *Speeches of Adolf Hitler: Representative Passages from the Early Speeches, 1922–1924, and Other Selections*, Howard Fertig, 2006, p. 15, Hitler speech of 12 April 1922.

29 Ibid., pp. 15–16.

30 Rees, *Dark Charisma*, Kindle edition, p. 31.

31 Previously unpublished testimony.

32 Joachim C. Fest, *Hitler*, Harcourt Brace Jovanovich, 1974, p. 133.

33 *Auf gut deutsch. Wochenschrift für Ordnung u. Recht*, ed. Dietrich Eckart, vol. 2, no. 30/34, Hoheneichen-Verlag, 1920, p. 392.

34 Though he once clarified what the content of one point meant: see p. 83.

35 *Goebbels' Diary*, entry for 8 April 1941, quoted in Rees, *Dark Charisma*, Kindle edition, p. 138.

36 *Hitler's Table Talk*, 13 December 1941, p. 144.

37 W. Breucker (Ludendorff's adjutant), *Die Tragik Ludendorffs*, Rauschenbusch, 1953, p. 107; also in English in J. C. R. Wright, *'Above Parties': The Political Attitudes of the German Protestant Church Leadership 1918–1933*, Oxford University Press, 1974, p. 78.

38 First published in *Völkischer Beobachter*, 22 April 1922.

39 Kurt G. W. Ludecke, *I Knew Hitler: The Story of a Nazi Who Escaped the Blood Purge*, Jarrolds, 1938, pp. 22–3.

40 Ibid., pp. 17 and 23.

41 See, for example, the testimony of Herbert Richter in Rees, *Dark Charisma*, Kindle edition, p. 37.

42 Hans Frank, *Im Angesicht des Galgens*, F. A. Beck Verlag, 1953, pp. 39–42.

43 Heiden, *The Fuehrer*, pp. 90–91.

44 *The Trial of German Major War Criminals: Proceedings of the International Military Tribunal . . .* (British edn), HMSO, 1947, part 9, p. 64.

45 Kershaw, *Hubris*, Kindle edition, p. 163.

46 Baynes (ed.), *Early Speeches*, p. 14, Hitler speech of 12 April 1922.

47 In English in Noakes and Pridham (eds.), *Nazism*, vol. 1, p. 16.

48 Baynes (ed.), *Early Speeches*, pp. 45–6, Hitler speech of 13 April 1923.

49 *Trial of the Major War Criminals*, vol. 12, p. 308, 26 April 1946, https://avalon.law.yale.edu/imt/04-26-46.asp.

50 Dennis E. Showalter, *Little Man, What Now? Der Stürmer in the Weimar Republic*, Archon Books, 1982, p. 24.

51 StAN, Polizeipräsidium Nürnberg-Fürth 541, doc. 187, copy of a judgment against Streicher, court of lay assessor at the district court in Schweinfurt, for an offence against religion, 5 September 1922.

52 Ludecke, *I Knew Hitler*, pp. 17–18.

53 Thomas D. Grant, *Stormtroopers and Crisis in the Nazi Movement: Activism, Ideology and Dissolution*, Routledge, 2004, Kindle edition, p. 33.

54 *Hitler's Table Talk*, 28–29 December 1941, p. 154.

55 Noakes and Pridham (eds.), *Nazism*, vol. 1, p. 23, Hitler memorandum of 7 January 1922.

56 Baynes (ed.), *Early Speeches*, pp. 40–41, Hitler speech of 28 July 1922.

57 See pp. 92–3.

58 Jeffrey S. Gaab, *Munich: Hofbräuhaus & History – Beer Culture, & Politics*, Peter Lang, 2006, p. 65.

59 Previously unpublished testimony.

60 Previously unpublished testimony.

61 Robert Gellately, *Hitler's True Believers: How Ordinary People Became Nazis*, Oxford University Press, 2020, Kindle edition, p. 44.

62 Christian Ingrao, *Believe and Destroy: Intellectuals in the SS War Machine*, Polity, 2015, Kindle edition, p. 15.

63 Previously unpublished testimony.

64 Previously unpublished testimony.

65 BArch, R 3001/12694, fols. 14–31. A part of the verdict is also printed in Lew Besymenski, *Die letzten Notizen von Martin Bormann. Ein Dokument und sein Verfasser*, Deutsche Verlags-Anstalt, 1974, pp. 296–306. And in Jochen von Lang with Claus Sibyll, *Der Sekretär. Martin Bormann: Der Mann, der Hitler beherrschte*, Deutsche Verlags-Anstalt, 1977, pp. 412–19.

66 *Vorwärts*, 26 June 1923, p. 1.

67 Rudolf Höss, *Commandant of Auschwitz*, Phoenix, 2001, pp. 43–5.

68 *Vossische Zeitung*, Morgenausgabe, 13 March 1924, p. 4.

69 Letter by Höss to H.H., 15 June 1924, quoted in Karin Orth, *Die Konzentrationslager-SS. Sozialstrukturelle Analysen und biographische Studien*, Wallstein Verlag, 2000, pp. 111–13.

70 Höss, *Commandant*, p. 45.

71 Martin Bormann, 'In den Kerkern der Republik: Der SA-Mann', *Völkischer Beobachter*, 10, 17 and 24 August 1929.

72 Höss, *Commandant*, p. 43.

Chapter 3: Leading as a Hero

1 Jäckel and Kuhn (eds.), *Hitler. Sämtliche Aufzeichnungen*, pp. 802–5. Also see Kershaw, *Hubris*, Kindle edn, p. 192.

2 Hancock, *Röhm*, p. 54.

3 Previously unpublished testimony of Emil Klein.

4 Hancock, *Röhm*, p. 59.

5 Heiden, *The Fuehrer*, p. 169.

6 Kershaw, *Hubris*, Kindle edition, p. 210.

7 Peter Longerich, *Heinrich Himmler*, Oxford University Press, 2012, Kindle edition, p. 69.

8 Ibid., pp. 68–9.

9 Hancock, *Röhm*, p. 68.

10 David King, *The Trial of Adolf Hitler: The Beer Hall Putsch and the Rise of Nazi Germany*, Macmillan, 2017, Kindle edition, location 1634. No one can be certain what happened to Ludendorff. It is possible he may even have stayed on the ground until told to stand by the police, although it is more likely that he did get up of his own accord and walk towards the enemy line.

11 Bytwerk, *Julius Streicher*, p. 18. Also Julius Streicher, *Kampf dem Weltfeind*, Stürmerverlag, 1938, pp. 24–5.

12 Kershaw, *Hubris*, Kindle edition, p. 211.

13 Jürgen Matthäus and Frank Bajohr (eds.), *The Political Diary of Alfred Rosenberg and the Onset of the Holocaust*, Rowman & Littlefield, 2015, Kindle edition, p. 29, entry for 5 June 1934.

14 King, *Trial of Adolf Hitler*, Kindle edition, location 1938. Hitler often threatened to kill himself if things went wrong and we can't know for sure how serious any attempt was. Professor Sir Ian Kershaw believes stories that Hitler had to be restrained from killing himself have 'no firm backing'. See Kershaw, *Hubris*, Kindle edition, p. 211.

15 King, *Trial of Adolf Hitler*, location 2068, quoting Otto Gritschneder, *Bewährungsfrist für den Terroristen Adolf H. Der Hitler-Putsch und die bayerische Justiz*, C. H. Beck, 1990, based on comments made by the then ninety-eight-year-old Alois Maria Ott.

16 Rees, *Nazis: A Warning from History*, Kindle edition, p. 28.

17 Albrecht Tyrell (ed.), *Führer befiehl . . . Selbstzeugnisse aus der 'Kampfzeit' der NSDAP. Dokumentation und Analyse*, Droste Verlag, 1969, pp. 281–3. Tyrell quotes extracts from *Der Hitler-Prozess vor dem Volksgericht in München*, Zweiter Teil, Knorr & Hirth, 1924, pp. 85–91. English translation in Noakes and Pridham (eds.), *Nazism*, vol. 1, p. 35.

18 Ella Rhodes, 'The Psychologist Guide to . . . Leadership', *Psychologist*, 9 May 2016, interview with Professor Alex Haslam, https://www.bps.org.uk/psychologist/psychologist-guide-leadership. Note that Professor Haslam was not talking specifically about Hitler and this connection is made by the author. See also S. Alexander Haslam, Stephen D. Reicher and Michael J. Platow, *The New Psychology of Leadership: Identity, Influence and Power*, Psychology Press, 2011, esp. ch. 3, pp. 41–76.

19 Tyrell (ed.), *Führer befiehl*, pp. 281–3; Noakes and Pridham (eds.), *Nazism*, vol. 1, p. 34.

20 Rees, *Dark Charisma*, Kindle edition, p. 56.

21 Professor Alex Haslam on the psychology of leadership, *Better Thinking*, Number 119, 2023, podcast with Nesh Nikolic, https://www.youtube.com/watch?v=2bXrVppV3GY (at 19' 25"). Again, note that Professor Haslam was not talking specifically about Hitler and the link is made by the author.

22 Tyrell (ed.), *Führer befiehl*, pp. 281–3; Noakes and Pridham (eds.), *Nazism*, vol. 1, p. 34.

23 Ernest Becker, *The Denial of Death*, Souvenir Press, 2011, Kindle edition, pp. 33–4.

24 Ian Kershaw, *The 'Hitler Myth': Image and Reality in the Third Reich*, Oxford University Press, 1987, p. 16, quoting Heinrich Class, *Wenn ich der Kaiser wär'*, Dieterich, 1914, p. 227.

25 Rees, *Dark Charisma*, Kindle edition, pp. 42–3.

26 Kubizek, *The Young Hitler I Knew*, pp. 83 and 185. Kubizek's recollections must be treated with care. For issues around his writing, and why he is, despite reservations, still an important source, see Kershaw, *Hubris*, Kindle edition, p. 20.

27 Allen Grabo and Mark van Vugt, 'Charismatic Leadership and the Evolution of Cooperation', *Evolution and Human Behavior*, vol. 37, issue 5 (September 2016), pp. 399–406, and Allen Grabo, Brian R. Spisak and Mark van Vugt, 'Charisma as Signal: An Evolutionary Perspective on Charismatic Leadership', *Leadership Quarterly*, vol. 28, issue 4 (August 2017), pp. 473–85.

28 Mark van Vugt and Allen E. Grabo, 'The Many Faces of Leadership: An Evolutionary-Psychology Approach', *Current Directions in Psychological Science*, vol. 24, no. 6 (December 2015), pp. 484–9. Also see B. R. Spisak, P. H. Dekker, M. Krüger and M. van Vugt, 'Warriors and Peacekeepers: Testing a Biosocial Implicit Leadership Hypothesis of Intergroup Relations Using Masculine and Feminine Faces', *PLOS One*, vol. 7, issue 1 (January 2012), https://journals.plos.org/plosone/article?id=10.1371/journal.pone.0030399.

29 Max Weber, *Essays in Sociology*, Routledge, 1998, p. 262.

30 King, *Trial of Adolf Hitler*, Kindle edition, location 3448–62.

31 Alexander Clifford, *Hindenburg, Ludendorff and Hitler: Germany's Generals and the Rise of the Nazis*, Pen & Sword, 2021, Kindle edition, pp. 95–6.

32 *New York Times*, 2 April 1924.

33 *The Times* (London), 2 April 1924.

34 See pp. 157–8.

35 Fröhlich (ed.), *Die Tagebücher von Joseph Goebbels*, Teil I, vol. 1/1, pp. 39–41, here p. 40, entry for 27 October 1923.

36 Ibid., pp. 76–7, here p. 77, entry for 21 January 1924.

37 For an analysis of how this contradiction was possible, see Rees, *Holocaust*, Kindle edition, pp. 60–61.

38 Fröhlich (ed.), *Die Tagebücher von Joseph Goebbels*, Teil I, vol. 1/1, pp. 160–61, here p. 161, entry for 4 July 1924.

39 Ibid., pp. 108–9, entry for 20 March 1924.

40 Longerich, *Himmler*, Kindle edition, p. 79.

41 Previously unpublished testimony.

42 Hancock, *Röhm*, pp. 71–3.

43 Ludecke, *I Knew Hitler*, pp. 217–18.

44 Ibid., p. 258.

45 Hancock, *Röhm*, pp. 80–81.

46 President Franklin Roosevelt was a master at understanding the eloquence of not replying. See Rees, *Behind Closed Doors*, Kindle edition, p. 191.

47 Adolf Hitler writing in the *Völkischer Beobachter*, 26 February 1925, p. 1. Clemens Vollnhals (ed.),. *Hitler: Reden, Schriften, Anordnungen. Februar 1925 bis Januar 1933*, Band I: *Die Wiedergründung der NSDAP, Februar 1925–Juni 1926*, K. G. Saur, 1992, pp. 1–4, here p. 2.

48 Peter D. Stachura, *Gregor Strasser and the Rise of Nazism*, Routledge, 2014, pp. 6–8.

49 Tyrell (ed.), *Führer befiehl*, pp. 281–3.

50 Fröhlich (ed.), *Die Tagebücher von Joseph Goebbels*, Teil I, vol. 1/1, pp. 315–16, here p. 315, entry for 15 June 1925.

51 Ibid., pp. 326–7, entry for 14 July 1925.

52 *Völkischer Beobachter*, 14 November 1925.

53 BArch, NS 26/896. The manuscript is also in BArch, NS 26/960. Salomon wrote this article under the pseudonym 'Frederick' and intended it 'only for the higher leaders of the NSDAP'. Also see Gellately, *Hitler's True Believers*, Kindle edition, pp. 73–5.

54 Kershaw, *Hubris*, Kindle edition, p. 301.

55 Elke Fröhlich (ed.), *Die Tagebücher von Joseph Goebbels*, Teil I: *Aufzeichnungen 1923–1941*, vol. 1/2: *Dezember 1925–Mai 1928*, K. G. Saur, 2005, entries for 15 February and 26 February 1926.

56 Ibid., entry for 13 April 1926.

57 Kershaw, *'Hitler Myth'*, p. 27. In the original German in Tyrell (ed.), *Führer befiehl*, p. 173.

Chapter 4: Corrupting Youth

1 Previously unpublished testimony.
2 Previously unpublished testimony.
3 Previously unpublished testimony.
4 Rees, *Their Darkest Hour*, Kindle edition, p. 35, and previously unpublished testimony.
5 Previously unpublished testimony.
6 Russel Lemmons, *Goebbels and Der Angriff*, University Press of Kentucky, 1994, ch. 1.
7 Peter Longerich, *Goebbels*, Bodley Head, 2015, Kindle edition, p. 123.
8 The sentence was finally commuted in July 1928 by an amnesty authorized by the Reichstag. See ibid., Kindle edition, p. 124.
9 'Was wollen wir im Reichstag?', *Der Angriff*, 30 April 1928, pp. 1f., quoted in Joseph Goebbels, *Der Angriff. Aufsätze aus der Kampfzeit*, Zentralverlag der NSDAP, 1935, pp. 71–3.
10 Elke Fröhlich (ed.), *Die Tagebücher von Joseph Goebbels*, Teil I: *Aufzeichnungen 1923–1941*, vol. 2/1: *Dezember 1929–Mai 1931*, K. G. Saur, 2005, pp. 316–17, here p. 316, entry for 3 January 1931.
11 'Propaganda und Politik. Das Referat des Berliner Gauleiters Dr. Goebbels am Freitag, 2. August 1929, nachmittags 5–6 Uhr', *Berliner Arbeiter-Zeitung*, 11 August 1929.
12 Previously unpublished testimony, and also Rees, *Nazis: A Warning from History*, Kindle edition, p. 36.
13 Larry Eugene Jones, *German Liberalism and the Dissolution of the Weimar Party System 1918–1933*, University of North Carolina Press, 1988, p. 350.
14 Previously unpublished testimony.
15 A snapshot of the membership taken on 1 January 1935 showed that 17 per cent of the members of the Nazi Party were under thirty, despite the overall German population containing less than 6 per cent in that age range. See Noakes and Pridham (eds.), *Nazism*, vol. 1, pp. 84–5, table of Nazi Party membership by age.
16 Ingrao, *Believe and Destroy*, Kindle edition, p. 25.
17 Previously unpublished testimony.

18 Jutta Rüdiger, leader in the late 1930s of the BDM, the Nazi youth movement for girls. Previously unpublished testimony.

19 Torsten Kupfer, *Generation und Radikalisierung. Die Mitglieder der NSDAP im Kreis Bernburg 1921–1945*, Historical Social Research, Transition (Online Supplement), No. 18, 2006, pp. 1–312, here pp. 74–109.

20 Previously unpublished testimony.

21 *Volkswacht*, May 1932, quoted in Kupfer, *Generation und Radikalisierung*, pp. 74–109.

22 Author interview with Professor Robert Sapolsky.

23 Baynes (ed.), *Early Speeches*, p. 40, Hitler speech of 28 July 1922.

24 *Völkischer Beobachter*, Bayernausgabe, 7 August 1929.

25 Fritz Fink, *Die Judenfrage im Unterricht*, Stürmerverlag, 1937, online in English at http://research.calvin.edu/german-propaganda-archive/fink.htm.

26 Jakob Graf, *Familienkunde und Rassenbiologie für Schüler*, J. F. Lehmanns, 1935, quoted in George L. Mosse (ed.), *Nazi Culture: Intellectual, Cultural and Social Life in the Third Reich*, University of Wisconsin Press, 1966, pp. 80–81.

27 Nico Voigtländer and Hans-Joachim Voth, 'Nazi Indoctrination and Anti-Semitic Beliefs in Germany', Proceedings of the National Academy of Sciences, vol. 112, no. 26 (June 2015), pp. 7931–6, https://www.ncbi.nlm.nih.gov/pmc/articles/PMC4491745/.

28 Previously unpublished testimony, and Rees, *Their Darkest Hour*, Kindle edition, p. 188.

29 Rees, *Their Darkest Hour*, Kindle edition, pp. 190–91.

30 Previously unpublished testimony.

31 Michael H. Kater, *Hitler Youth*, Harvard University Press, 2004, p. 106.

32 Ibid., p. 108.

33 Ibid., p. 81.

34 Previously unpublished testimony.

35 Previously unpublished testimony.

36 Kater, *Hitler Youth*, p. 15.

37 Eric A. Johnson and Karl-Heinz Reuband, *What We Knew: Terror, Mass Murder, and Everyday Life in Nazi Germany: An Oral History*, Basic Books, 2006, pp. 141–9, testimony of Hubert Lutz.

38 Report on the situation in Germany, No. 13, April 1935, in Bernd Stöver, *Berichte über die Lage in Deutschland. Die Meldungen der Gruppe Neu Beginnen aus dem Dritten Reich 1933–1936*, Verlag J. H. W. Dietz Nachfolger, 1996, pp. 427–72, here pp. 429–31.

39 J. Noakes and G. Pridham (eds.), *Nazism: 1919–1945*, vol. 2: *State, Economy and Society 1933–1939*, Exeter University Press, 2015, p. 227.

40 Previously unpublished testimony.

41 Arnold Talbot Wilson, *Walks and Talks Abroad: The Diary of a Member of Parliament in 1934–36*, Oxford University Press, 1939, p. 126, quoted in Julia Boyd, *Travellers in the Third Reich: The Rise of Fascism through the Eyes of Ordinary People*, Elliott & Thompson, 2017, Kindle edition, p. 171. Note, however, that when Wilson visited the Nazi concentration camp at Dachau his admiration for the regime somewhat dimmed. Even though he thought the inmates were adequately fed and housed, 'there was in the atmosphere of the camp', he wrote, 'something against which my soul revolted.' See Boyd, *Travellers*, p. 172.

42 Mary Fulbrook, *Bystander Society: Conformity and Complicity in Nazi Germany and the Holocaust*, Oxford University Press, 2023, Kindle edition, p. 109.

Chapter 5: Conniving with the Elite

1 *Die Nationalsozialistische Deutsche Arbeiterpartei. Referentendenkschrift*, Mai 1930, GStA PK, I. HA Rep. 84a, Nr. 3157, pp. 23–49, here pp. 44–7.

2 Elke Fröhlich (ed.), *Die Tagebücher von Joseph Goebbels*, Teil I: *Aufzeichnungen 1923–1941*, vol. 1/3: *Juni 1928–November 1929*, K. G. Saur, 2004, p. 287, entry for 21 July 1929.

3 *Völkischer Beobachter*, 16/17 June 1929.

4 *Völkischer Beobachter*, 14 August 1929.

5 *Völkischer Beobachter*, 1 April 1930.

6 *Vossische Zeitung*, Morgenausgabe, 6 December 1930, p. 5.

7 *Völkischer Beobachter*, 7/8 December 1930. Also quoted in Bärbel Schrader (ed.), *Der Fall Remarque. Im Westen nichts Neues. Eine Dokumentation*, Reclam-Verlag, 1992, pp. 134–5.

8 Fröhlich (ed.), *Die Tagebücher von Joseph Goebbels*, Teil I, vol. 2/1, p. 298, entry for 6 December 1930.

9 Ibid., p. 301, entry for 10 December 1930.

10 *Der Angriff*, 12 December 1930, pp. 1–2. Also quoted in Schrader (ed.), *Der Fall Remarque*, pp. 161–6.

11 Fröhlich (ed.), *Die Tagebücher von Joseph Goebbels*, Teil I, vol. 2/1, pp. 304–5, here p. 305, entry for 7 December 1930.

12 *Der Angriff,* 12 December 1930, pp. 1–2.

13 Sapolsky, *Behave,* Kindle edition, p. 52.

14 Ibid.

15 *Der Angriff,* 6 May 1931.

16 *Sozialistische Bildung,* May 1931, pp. 139–40.

17 *Der Angriff,* 7 May 1931.

18 Benjamin Carter Hett, *Crossing Hitler: The Man Who Put the Nazis on the Witness Stand,* Oxford University Press, 2008, Kindle edition, pp. 72–3.

19 Hancock, *Röhm,* p. 103.

20 *Völkischer Beobachter,* 6 November 1930.

21 Goebbels diary, 27 February 1931, in Longerich, *Goebbels,* Kindle edition, p. 179.

22 Reproduced as Doc. 54 in Constantin Goschler (ed.), *Hitler. Reden, Schriften, Anordnungen. Februar 1925 bis Januar 1933,* Band IV: *Von der Reichstagswahl bis zur Reichspräsidentenwahl, Oktober 1930–März 1932,* Teil 1: *Oktober 1930–Juni 1931,* K. G. Saur, 1994, p. 183. Goschler's source is BArch, Slg. Schumacher 403.

23 Longerich, *Himmler,* Kindle edition, pp. 112–13.

24 Previously unpublished testimony.

25 Nancy Dougherty, *The Man with the Iron Heart,* Welbeck, 2022, Kindle edition, p. 121.

26 Robert Gerwarth, *Hitler's Hangman: The Life of Heydrich,* Yale University Press, 2011, Kindle edition, pp. 105–6.

27 Ibid., p. 107.

28 Ibid., p. 95.

29 BArch NS 33/89, p. 41, Reichsführer SS (SS-HA/ZK./Az. B 17a), Berlin, 11 April 1938, regarding selection of candidates as SS leaders, mailing list V. Also see Tom Segev, *Soldiers of Evil: The Commandants of the Nazi Concentration Camps,* Diamond Books, 2000, p. 97. And Rees, *Holocaust,* Kindle edn, p. 26.

30 *Münchener Post,* 28/29 November 1931, p. 1.

31 Longerich, *Himmler,* Kindle edition, pp. 122–3.

32 *Vorwärts,* 26 November 1931, p. 1.

33 *Vossische Zeitung,* Morgenausgabe, 26 November 1931, p. 1.

34 Hermann Beck, *The Fateful Alliance: German Conservatives and Nazis in 1933: The Machtergreifung in a New Light,* Berghahn Books, 2008, pp. 78–80.

35 Professor Robert Sapolsky, 'Human Sexual Behaviour III and Aggression I', Stanford University lecture, May 2010, https://www.youtube.com/watch?v=JPYmarGO5jM (at 53' 44" to 57' 18").

36 Previously unpublished testimony.

37 Previously unpublished testimony, and Rees, *Nazis: A Warning from History*, Kindle edition, location 484–92.

38 Dougherty, *Iron Heart*, Kindle edition, p. 138.

39 Martin Kitchen, *The Third Reich: Charisma and Community*, Pearson Educational, 2008, pp. 234–5.

40 Dougherty, *Iron Heart*, Kindle edition, p. 138.

41 Ibid., p. 135.

42 Ibid., p. 33.

43 David de Jong, *Nazi Billionaires: The Dark History of Germany's Wealthiest Dynasties*, William Collins, 2022, Kindle edition, p. 34.

44 Longerich, *Goebbels*, Kindle edition, pp. 189 and 375.

45 Ibid., p. 198.

46 de Jong, *Nazi Billionaires*, Kindle edition, p. 36.

47 Timothy W. Ryback, *Takeover: Hitler's Final Rise to Power*, Headline, 2024, Kindle edition, p. 107.

48 Goltz, *Hindenburg*, p. 15.

49 Hans Otto Meissner and Harry Wilde, *Die Machtergreifung. Ein Bericht über die Technik des nationalsozialistischen Staatsstreichs*, J. G. Cotta, 1958, pp. 48, 49 and 273, quoted in Eugene Davidson, *The Unmaking of Adolf Hitler*, University of Missouri Press, 1996, p. 458.

50 Dorothy Thompson, *I Saw Hitler!*, Farrar & Rinehart, 1932, pp. 13–34.

51 Goltz, *Hindenburg*, p. 141.

52 Ibid., pp. 140–41.

53 Longerich, *Goebbels*, Kindle edition, p. 211.

54 *Vorwärts*, 27 February 1932; Goltz, *Hindenburg*, p. 165.

55 Hancock, *Röhm*, p. 114.

56 Elke Fröhlich (ed.), *Die Tagebücher von Joseph Goebbels*, Teil I: *Aufzeichnungen 1923–1941*, vol. 2/2: *Juni 1931–September 1932*, K. G. Saur, 2004, pp. 235–6, here p. 235, entry for 7 March 1932.

57 Helmut Klotz (ed.), *Der Fall Röhm*, pp. 8–11, in BArch, N 1150/115, Nachlass Walter Luetgebrune, pp. 524–43, here pp. 533–6.

58 Ibid., pp. 16–17, in BArch, N 1150/115, Nachlass Walter Luetgebrune, pp. 541–2.

59 Ibid., p. 7, in BArch, N 1150/115, Nachlass Walter Luetgebrune, p. 532.

60 Fröhlich (ed.), *Die Tagebücher von Joseph Goebbels*, Teil I, vol. 2/2, p. 244, entry for 17 March 1932. Once in power the Nazis would persecute those who committed homosexual acts. Himmler had a particular hatred for

homosexuals, and thousands were sent to concentration camps, where many perished. See Rees, *Holocaust*, Kindle edition, pp. 154–6.

61 Hancock, *Röhm*, p. 115.

62 See p. 115.

63 Franz von Papen, *Memoirs*, André Deutsch, 1952, pp. 162–3. In German in Franz von Papen, *Der Wahrheit eine Gasse*, Paul List Verlag, 1952, p. 195.

64 See pp. 72–3.

65 Kershaw, *Hubris*, Kindle edition, p. 368.

66 See Daniel Kahneman and Amos Tversky, 'Prospect Theory: An Analysis of Decision Under Risk', *Econometrica*, vol. 47, no. 2 (March 1979), pp. 263–91, and Daniel Kahneman, *Thinking, Fast and Slow*, Farrar, Straus & Giroux, 2013. Also see Kazuhisa Nagaya, 'Why and Under What Circumstances Does Loss Aversion Emerge?', *Japanese Psychological Research*, vol. 65, issue 4 (October 2023), pp. 379–98.

67 *Nazis: A Warning from History*, BBC TV, episode 1: 'Helped into Power', written and produced by Laurence Rees; first transmitted on BBC2, 10 September 1997.

68 Otto Meissner, 'Aufzeichnung über die Besprechung des Herrn Reichspräsidenten mit Adolf Hitler am 13. August 1932 nachmittags 4.15', quoted in Walther Hubatsch, *Hindenburg und der Staat. Aus den Papieren des Generalfeldmarschalls und Reichspräsidenten von 1878 bis 1934*, Musterschmidt, 1966, p. 338. In English in Noakes and Pridham (eds.), *Nazism*, vol. 1, p. 104.

69 Roderick Stackelberg, *Hitler's Germany: Origins, Interpretations, Legacies*, Routledge, 2014, p. 99.

70 Kershaw, *Hubris*, Kindle edition, p. 395.

71 Hinrich Lohse, 'Der Fall Strasser', held in Forschungsstelle für die Geschichte des Nationalsozialismus in Hamburg; in English in Noakes and Pridham (eds.), *Nazism*, vol. 1, p. 111.

72 Ibid.; in English in Noakes and Pridham (eds.), *Nazism*, vol. 1, p. 113.

73 Gerwarth, *Hitler's Hangman*, Kindle edition, p. 62.

74 Eberhard Jäckel, *Hitler in History*, Brandeis University Press, 1984, p. 15.

75 Previously unpublished testimony of Karl Boehm-Tettelbach.

76 There is a huge psychological literature on groupthink. Irving L. Janis, *Groupthink*, Houghton Mifflin (Academic), 1982, is a good place to start, and among the myriad scientific papers on the subject is David Ahlstrom and Linda C. Wang, 'Groupthink and France's Defeat in the 1940 Campaign', *Journal of Management History*, vol. 15, no. 2 (2009), pp. 159–77.

77 Kershaw, *Hubris*, Kindle edition, p. 421.

78 *Documents on British Foreign Policy, 1919–1939*, vol. 3, HMSO, 1960, pp. 197–201; also in Kaes, Jay and Dimendberg (eds), *Weimar Republic Sourcebook*, pp. 80–84.

Chapter 6: Attacking Human Rights

1 Previously unpublished testimony.
2 Previously unpublished testimony.
3 Kershaw, *Hubris*, Kindle edition, p. 432.
4 Previously unpublished testimony. Also see Papen, *Memoirs*, p. 264.
5 Andreas Wirsching, '"Man kann nur Boden germanisieren". Eine neue Quelle zu Hitlers Rede vor den Spitzen der Reichswehr am 3. Februar 1933', *Vierteljahrshefte für Zeitgeschichte*, vol. 49, no. 3 (2001), pp. 517–50, here pp. 522–4.
6 Ibid., pp. 545–8. Another of the senior officers present, Lieutenant General Liebmann, thought that Hitler gave two options for the future – one was the task of gaining more 'export opportunities', the other was 'conquest of new living space in the east and its ruthless Germanization'. This latter option, Hitler said, was 'probably better'.
7 Rees, *Their Darkest Hour*, Kindle edition, pp. 199–204, and previously unpublished testimony.
8 Hitler's press conference for foreign correspondents, 3 February 1933, https://www.theguardian.com/world/2017/feb/03/hitler-adolf-interview-archive-1933.
9 Max Domarus (ed.), *Hitler. Reden und Proklamationen 1932–1945. Kommentiert von einem deutschen Zeitgenossen*, Band 1: *Triumph, Erster Halbband 1932–1934*, R. Löwit, 1973, p. 192, Hitler speech of 1 February 1933.
10 Papen, *Memoirs*, p. 264.
11 *Trials of War Criminals before the Nuernberg Military Tribunals . . .*, vol. VI: 'The Flick Case', United States Government Printing Office, 1952, p. 44.
12 Georg von Schnitzler on Hitler's Appeal to Leading German Industrialists on 20 February 1933 (Affidavit, 10 November 1945), in United States Chief Counsel for the Prosecution of Axis Criminality, *Nazi Conspiracy and Aggression*, vol. VII, United States Government Printing Office, 1946, Document 439-EC, https://ghdi.ghi-dc.org/docpage.cfm?docpage_id=2259.
13 *Trials of War Criminals*, vol. VI, p. 44.
14 de Jong, *Nazi Billionaires*, Kindle edition, p. 4.

15 Elke Fröhlich (ed.), *Die Tagebücher von Joseph Goebbels*, Teil I: *Aufzeichnungen 1923–1941*, vol. 2/3: *Oktober 1932–März 1934*, K. G. Saur, 2006, p. 137, entry for 28 February 1933.

16 Rudolf Diels, *Lucifer ante portas. Zwischen Severing und Heydrich*, Inter-verlag, 1949, p. 143.

17 J. A. S. Grenville, *The Jews and Germans of Hamburg: The Destruction of a Civilization 1790–1945*, Routledge, 2012, pp. 60–62. Solmitz's journal entries have an intriguing dimension to them, because her husband had converted from Judaism to Christianity. This meant, in the eyes of the Nazis, that he was still a Jew and vulnerable to persecution.

18 Richard Hofstadter, 'The Paranoid Style in American Politics', *Harper's Magazine*, November 1964, https://harpers.org/archive/1964/11/the-para noid-style-in-american-politics/.

19 The first sign of this was the *Brown Book of the Reichstag Fire and Hitler Terror*, first published in Paris six months after the fire.

20 There is a vast literature on this subject. See, for instance, Hans Mommsen, 'Der Reichstagsbrand und seine politischen Folgen', *Vierteljahrshefte für Zeitgeschichte*, vol. 12, no. 4 (1964), pp. 351–413, and Kershaw, *Hubris*, Kindle edition, pp. 456–61. Also see Benjamin Carter Hett, *Burning the Reichstag: An Investigation into the Third Reich's Enduring Mystery*, Oxford University Press, 2014, and Uwe Soukup, *Die Brandstiftung. Mythos Reichstagsbrand – Was in der Nacht geschah, in der die Demokratie unterging*, Heyne, 2023.

21 Patrick Leman and Marco Cinnirella, 'A Major Event Has a Major Cause: Evidence for the Role of Heuristics in Reasoning about Conspiracy The-ories', *Social Psychological Review*, vol. 9, no. 2 (October 2007), pp. 18–28.

22 Bernard V. Burke, *Ambassador Frederic Sackett and the Collapse of the Weimar Republic 1930–1933: The United States and Hitler's Rise to Power*, Cambridge University Press, 1994, p. 287.

23 Previously unpublished testimony.

24 Nikolaus Wachsmann, *KL: A History of the Nazi Concentration Camps*, Little, Brown, 2015, p. 30.

25 Rees, *Their Darkest Hour*, Kindle edition, pp. 36–8.

26 Wachsmann, *KL*, pp. 29–31.

27 Victor Klemperer, *I Shall Bear Witness: The Diaries of Victor Klemperer 1933–1945*, Phoenix, 2003, p. 8, entry for 17 March 1933.

28 Goltz, *Hindenburg*, pp. 171–3.

29 Carolyn Birdsall, *Nazi Soundscapes: Sound, Technology and Urban Space in Germany 1933–1945*, Amsterdam University Press, 2012, p. 53.

30 Erich Ebermayer, *Denn heute gehört uns Deutschland . . . Persönliches und politisches Tagebuch. Von der Machtergreifung bis zum 31. Dezember 1935*, Paul Zsolnay Verlag, 1959, p. 46, entry for 21 March 1933.

31 *Völkischer Beobachter*, 22 March 1933.

32 Domarus (ed.), *Hitler. Reden und Proklamationen*, vol. 1, pp. 232–3, Hitler speech of 23 March 1933.

33 Otto Wels speech, 23 March 1933, in *Verhandlungen des Reichstags, VIII. Wahlperiode 1933*, Druck und Verlag der Reichsdruckerei, 1934, p. 33, Hitler speech of 23 March 1933; also in Domarus (ed.), *Hitler. Reden und Proklamationen*, vol. 1, p. 240.

34 *Verhandlungen des Reichstags, VIII. Wahlperiode 1933*, pp. 35–6, Hitler speech of 23 March 1933; also in Domarus (ed.), *Hitler. Reden und Proklamationen*, vol. 1, pp. 244–6.

35 *Münchner Neueste Nachrichten*, 13 March 1933, quoted in Longerich, *Himmler*, p. 149.

36 Robert Gellately, *The Gestapo and German Society*, Oxford University Press, 1991, pp. 55–6.

37 Jonathan Petropoulos, *The Faustian Bargain: The Art World in Nazi Germany*, Oxford University Press, 2000, pp. 21–2.

38 Ebermayer, *Denn heute gehört uns Deutschland*, pp. 69–71, here p. 70, entry for 30 April 1933.

39 'Deutschland-Bericht der Sopade [Social Democratic Party of Germany]', 3rd year, no. 2 (February 1936), in *Deutschland-Berichte der Sozialdemokratischen Partei Deutschlands (Sopade) 1934–1940. Dritter Jahrgang, 1936*, Verlag Petra Nettelbeck/Zweitausendeins, 1980, pp. 151–278, here p. 157.

40 R. F. Baumeister and M. R. Leary, 'The Need to Belong: Desire for Interpersonal Attachments as a Fundamental Human Motivation', *Psychological Bulletin*, vol. 117, no. 3 (1995), pp. 497–529. Once again, there is a great deal of literature on this fundamental topic. See, for instance, M. Carvallo and S. Gabriel, 'No Man Is an Island: The Need to Belong and Dismissing Avoidant Attachment Style', *Personality and Social Psychology Bulletin*, vol. 32, no. 5 (2006), pp. 697–709.

41 Rees, *Nazis: A Warning from History*, Kindle edition, p. 66.

42 *Völkischer Beobachter*, 29 March 1933.

43 Rees, *Holocaust*, Kindle edition, p. 83.

44 Previously unpublished testimony.

45 Previously unpublished testimony.

46 Sir Horace Rumbold to Sir John Simon, 26 April 1933, C 3990/319/18, pp. 4–9, accessible via https://www.patriciarobertsmiller.com/2020/12/07/horace-rumbolds-april-1933-memo-about-hitler/.

47 Moritz Föllmer, *Culture in the Third Reich*, Oxford University Press, 2020, p. 37.

48 Ibid., pp. 37–8. Hirschfeld, doubly vulnerable as both Jewish and gay, managed to leave Germany, dying in exile in Paris in 1935.

49 Ebermayer, *Denn heute gehört uns Deutschland*, pp. 77–80, here pp. 78–9, entry for 10 May 1933; pp. 82–4, here pp. 83–4, entry for 14 May 1933.

50 de Jong, *Nazi Billionaires*, Kindle edition, pp. 62–3.

51 Hans-Adolf Jacobsen and Werner Jochmann (eds.), *Ausgewählte Dokumente zur Geschichte des Nationalsozialismus 1933–1945*, Verlag Neue Gesellschaft, 1961, vol. 2, statement by Adolf Hitler before the Reich governors [Reichsstatthalter] on 6 July 1933 on the conclusion of the revolution. In English in Noakes and Pridham (eds.), *Nazism*, vol. 1, pp. 170–71.

52 Jacobsen and Jochmann (eds.), *Ausgewählte Dokumente zur Geschichte des Nationalsozialismus*, vol. 2; first published in the NSDAP's *Nationalsozialistische Monatshefte*, 4 June 1933.

53 Hancock, *Röhm*, p. 132.

54 Ibid., p. 144. Blomberg is the only source for this, so it is possible he was over-egging Röhm's views in order to exaggerate the threat from the Stormtroopers.

55 Klaus-Jürgen Müller (with Ernst Willi Hansen), *Armee und Drittes Reich 1933–1939. Darstellung und Dokumentation*, Ferdinand Schöningh, 1987, p. 195.

56 Jürgen Förster, 'Complicity or Entanglement? Wehrmacht, War and Holocaust', in Michael Berenbaum and Abraham J. Peck (eds.), *The Holocaust and History: The Known, the Unknown, the Disputed and the Reexamined*, Indiana University Press, 2002, p. 268.

57 Hancock, *Röhm*, p. 149.

58 Kurt Gossweiler, *Die Röhm-Affäre. Hintergründe – Zusammenhänge – Auswirkungen*, Pahl-Rugenstein, 1983, p. 68.

59 Jacobsen and Jochmann (eds.), *Dokumente zur Geschichte des Nationalsozialismus*, vol. 2. In English in Noakes and Pridham, *Nazism*, vol. 1, pp. 174–6.

60 Adam Tooze, *The Wages of Destruction: The Making and Breaking of the Nazi Economy*, Penguin, 2007, p. 67.

61 Wachsmann, *KL*, p. 58.

62 Christopher Dillon, *Dachau and the SS: A Schooling in Violence*, Oxford University Press, 2015, p. 52.

63 Wachsmann, *KL*, p. 83. Eicke shot Röhm with the help of his SS colleague Michael Lippert.

64 Dillon, *Dachau*, p. 88.

65 Office of United States Chief of Counsel for Prosecution of Axis Criminality, Nazi Conspiracy and Aggression, United States Government Printing Office, 1946, vol. VII, Deposition of Kate Eva Hoerlin (Dr Schmid's wife), 7 July 1945, pp. 883–8.

66 Howard M. Sachar, *The Assassination of Europe 1918–1942: A Political History*, University of Toronto Press, 2015, pp. 175–6.

67 Hancock, *Röhm*, pp. 162–3.

68 *Völkischer Beobachter*, 3 July 1934.

69 *Völkischer Beobachter*, 1 July 1934, Hitler order to the new Chief of Staff of the Stormtroopers, Viktor Lutze.

70 Previously unpublished testimony.

71 Domarus (ed.), *Hitler. Reden und Proklamationen*, vol. 1, p. 421, speech of 13 July 1934.

72 Ibid., pp. 425–6.

73 Tracy B. Strong, 'Carl Schmitt: Political Theology and the Concept of the Political', in Catherine H. Zuckert (ed.), *Political Philosophy in the Twentieth Century: Authors and Arguments*, Cambridge University Press, 2011, p. 42.

74 Kershaw, *'Hitler Myth'*, p. 87.

75 DRA, Nr. C 1117 (at 77' 50"), Goebbels speech of 25 March 1933 to the Radio Corporation, Berlin.

Chapter 7: Exploiting Faith

1 Uriel Tal, *'Political Faith' of Nazism Prior to the Holocaust*, Tel Aviv University, Faculty of Humanities, 1978, p. 30.

2 Hitler, *Mein Kampf*, ch. 6, p. 180.

3 Rees, *Holocaust*, Kindle edition, p. 109.

4 Rees, *Dark Charisma*, Kindle edition, p. 128.

5 Ibid. In years to come, however, there were officers who were prepared to set aside their oath and act against Hitler. See pp. 301–6.

6 See p. 284.

7 Hitler, *Mein Kampf*, ch. 6, pp. 180–81.

8 Rees, *Selling Politics*, p. 81.

9 'Die zukünftige Arbeit und Gestaltung des deutschen Rundfunks. Ansprache Goebbels an die Intendanten und Direktoren der Rundfunk-gesellschaften, Berlin, Haus des Rundfunks', 25 March 1933, in Helmut Heiber (ed.), *Goebbels Reden*, vol. 1: *1932–1939*, Droste Verlag, 1971, p. 94.

10 Initially, Goebbels praised an early political film, *Hitlerjunge Quex* (Hitler Youth Quex), released in September 1933. The film is about a Hitler Youth who is killed by communists and has a vision of Nazi flags 'fluttering before us' as he dies. See Eric Rentschler, *The Ministry of Illusion: Nazi Cinema and its Afterlife*, Harvard University Press, 2002, pp. 55–6. But he subsequently realized that works like this were just too heavy-handed.

11 Interview with Wilfred von Oven, in BBC film *Goebbels: Master of Propaganda*, written and produced by Laurence Rees.

12 *Völkischer Beobachter*, 1 February 1934.

13 Interview with Arthur Maria Rabenalt, in *Goebbels: Master of Propaganda*.

14 Ibid., explaining the purpose of the entertainment films.

15 Goebbels diary entry for 1 March 1942, quoted in David Welch, *The Third Reich: Politics and Propaganda*, Routledge, 1993, Kindle edition, p. 56.

16 Goebbels address to the press, 'On the Establishment of a Reich Ministry for Popular Enlightenment and Propaganda', 15 March 1933, *German History in Documents and Images*, https://ghdi.ghi-dc.org/sub_document.cfm?document_id=1579.

17 Kenneth O'Reilly, *Asphalt: A History*, University of Nebraska Press, 2021, p. 109.

18 For an analysis of 'in' and 'out' groups in relation to hate, see Roy F. Baumeister and David A. Butz, 'Roots of Hate, Violence, and Evil', in Robert J. Sternberg (ed.), *The Psychology of Hate*, American Psychological Association, 2013, Kindle edition, pp. 120–21.

19 Rees, *Selling Politics*, pp. 20–21. According to Fritz Hippler, a Nazi film-maker who worked closely with him, Goebbels believed that 'the real primary forces of men are moved by the unconscious . . . On these primary sources the moving picture works in a particularly intensive manner, and this medium he therefore wanted to use in a particularly pointed way.' It turned out that this assessment was correct in respect of anti-Semitic drama films. In 1940 *Jud Süss* (Jew Süss) was released to great acclaim in Germany. This was a historical drama about a Jew who served the Duke of Württemberg in the eighteenth century. Key elements in the story were made up – such as Süss' rape of an 'Aryan' maiden – and the

drama twisted other facts wherever Goebbels thought it necessary. This loathsome piece of work demonstrated the power of anti-Semitic propaganda when presented as entertainment drama rather than through didactic documentary. Himmler thought the film so valuable that he ordered everyone in the SS to watch it. See David Welch, *Propaganda and the German Cinema 1933–1945*, Oxford University Press, 1983, pp. 284–92.

20 See pp. 93–5.

21 Rees, *Holocaust*, Kindle edition, p. 90.

22 G. M. Gilbert, *Nuremberg Diary*, Da Capo Press, 1995, p. 9.

23 Significantly, however, those opposition politicians sent to the camps who were Jewish were often treated worst of all. For instance, Max Abraham – doubly hated because he was both a Jew and a Social Democrat politician – was arrested in June 1933. He and three other Jews were forced to hit each other with truncheons for the amusement of the Stormtroopers, and then imprisoned in Papenburg concentration camp where Abraham was ordered by SS guards to conduct a Jewish 'service' in a manure pit. When he refused to cooperate he was beaten so badly that he was lucky to survive. See Rees, *Holocaust*, Kindle edition, pp. 95–7.

24 Höss, *Commandant*, p. 71.

25 W. Langhoff, *Die Moorsoldaten*, Verlag Neuer Weg, 2014, Kindle edition, pp. 284–9.

26 Ibid., pp. 290–93.

27 Michel Reynaud and Sylvie Graffard, *The Jehovah's Witnesses and the Nazis: Persecution, Deportation, and Murder 1933–1945*, Cooper Square Press, 2001, pp. 89–90.

28 Höss, *Commandant*, pp. 88–9.

29 Ibid., p. 91.

30 Longerich, *Himmler*, Kindle edition, pp. 217–19.

31 See, for example, 'Psychologist on Why Funerals Are Fundamental to Processing Grief', National Public Radio, 14 December 2020, https://www.npr.org/sections/coronavirus-live-updates/2020/12/14/946402101/psychologist-on-why-funerals-are-fundamental-to-processing-grief.

32 Der Reichsführer SS, *Vorschläge für die Abhaltung einer Totenfeier*, SS-Hauptamt, [1942]. Also see Longerich, *Himmler*, pp. 292–3.

33 BArch, NS 19/4003, fols. 190–228, The Reichsführer SS's speech on the occasion of the lieutenant-generals' [Gruppenführer] meeting on 8 November 1936 in Dachau, here fols. 197–200.

34 Der Reichsführer SS, *Vorschläge für die Abhaltung einer Totenfeier*.

35 BArch, R 9361 III/514455, SS-Führerpersonalakten, Joseph Altrogge, quoted in part in Segev, *Soldiers of Evil*, p. 98.

36 Segev, *Soldiers of Evil*, p. 99, interview with Johannes Hassebroek.

37 Hilary Earl, *The Nuremberg SS-Einsatzgruppen Trial 1945–1958: Atrocity, Law, and History*, Cambridge University Press, 2009, pp. 62–3. On a number of occasions Reinhard Höhn acted as the intermediary between students he believed were useful for the SD and their first contact with Reinhard Heydrich. See Michael Wildt, *An Uncompromising Generation: The Nazi Leadership of the Reich Security Main Office*, University of Wisconsin Press, 2009, p. 96.

38 Ingrao, *Believe and Destroy*, Kindle edition, pp. 66–7. Ohlendorf's plea to the American Tribunal on 13 February 1948 has to be interpreted carefully, but these sections appear credible.

39 Hitler, *Mein Kampf*, pp. 338–9.

40 Mosse (ed.), *Nazi Culture*, pp. 64–5.

41 Götz Aly and Susanne Heim, *Architects of Annihilation*, Weidenfeld & Nicolson, 2015, Kindle edition, p. 58.

42 Wildt, *An Uncompromising Generation*, p. 77.

43 Sir Nevile Henderson, *Failure of a Mission: Berlin 1937–1939*, Hodder & Stoughton, 1940, p. 80.

44 Hermann Burte, *Sieben Reden von Burte*, Hünenburg-Verlag, 1943, p. 20.

45 Previously unpublished testimony.

46 BArch Berlin NS 10/550, Wiedemann to Bormann, 5 June 1935.

47 Previously unpublished testimony.

48 Rees, *Nazis: A Warning from History*, Kindle edition, pp. 86–7.

49 James M. Diehl, 'Victors or Victims? Disabled Veterans in the Third Reich', *Journal of Modern History*, vol. 59, no. 4 (1987), pp. 720–21.

50 Karl Binding and Alfred Hoche, *Die Freigabe der Vernichtung lebensunwerten Lebens. Ihr Maß und ihre Form*, Felix Meiner Verlag, 1920, p. 43.

51 Ibid., pp. 49–54.

52 Michael Burleigh, *Death and Deliverance: 'Euthanasia' in Germany 1900–1945*, Pan Books, 2002, pp. 43–4.

53 Ibid., pp. 44–5.

54 Tom L. Beauchamp and LeRoy Walters (eds.), *Contemporary Issues in Bioethics*, Wadsworth Publishing, 1999, p. 538.

55 Omar S. Haque, Julian De Freitas, Ivana Viani, Bradley Niederschulte and Harold J. Bursztajn, 'Why Did So Many German Doctors Join the Nazi

Party Early?', *International Journal of Law and Psychiatry*, vol. 35, nos. 5–6 (2012), pp. 473–9.

56 Robert Jay Lifton, *Witness to an Extreme Century*, Free Press, 2011, p. 278.

57 Karl Brandt, Hitler's own doctor, gave testimony to this effect at the Nuremberg Doctors' Trial in 1947: see United States Military Tribunal Nuremberg, Case I (Medical Case), *Transcript of Proceedings*, p. 2482.

58 Rees, *Dark Charisma*, Kindle edition, p. 181.

59 Burleigh, *Death and Deliverance*, p. 47.

60 Welch, *Propaganda and the German Cinema*, pp. 122–3.

61 Max Domarus (ed.), *Hitler. Reden und Proklamationen 1932–1945. Kommentiert von einem deutschen Zeitgenossen*, Band I: *Triumph, Zweiter Halbband 1935–1938*, R. Löwit, 1973, p. 790, Hitler speech of 14 March 1936.

62 Henderson, *Failure of a Mission*, p. 73.

63 RGWA Fond 1355, Opis 1, Delo 19, Blatt 171; Henrik Eberle (ed.), *Briefe an Hitler*, Lübbe, 2007, pp. 217–18.

64 RGWA Fond 1355, Opis 2, Delo 8, Blatt 405; Eberle (ed.), *Briefe*, pp. 99–100.

65 RGWA Fond 1355, Opis 1, Delo 13, Blatt 120; Eberle (ed.), *Briefe*, pp. 159–60.

66 RGWA Fond 1355, Opis 1, Delo 30, Blatt 44; Eberle (ed.), *Briefe*, pp. 246–7.

67 RGWA Fond 1355, Opis 1, Delo 14, Blatt 341–4; Eberle (ed.), *Briefe*, p. 143.

68 Reinhard Heydrich, *Wandlungen unseres Kampfes*, Eher [c. 1936].

69 Philipp Rupprecht, *Der Giftpilz*, Der Stürmer, 1938. See https://perspectives.ushmm.org/item/pages-from-the-antisemitic-childrens-book-the-poisonous-mushroom.

70 J. T. Cacioppo and G. G. Berntson, 'The Affect System: Architecture and Operating Characteristics', *Current Directions in Psychological Science*, vol. 8, no. 5 (October 1999), pp. 133–7; A. Vaish, T. Grossmann and A. Woodward, 'Not All Emotions Are Created Equal: The Negativity Bias in Social-Emotional Development', *Psychological Bulletin*, vol. 134, no. 3 (2008), pp. 383–403; G. J. Norman, C. J. Norris, J. Gollan, T. A. Ito, L. C. Hawkley, J. T. Larsen, J. T. Cacioppo and G. G. Berntson, 'Current Emotion Research in Psychophysiology: The Neurobiology of Evaluative Bivalence', *Emotion Review*, vol. 3, issue 3 (2011), pp. 349–59. See https://positivepsychology.com/3-steps-negativity-bias/.

71 Dmitri Volkogonov, *Stalin: Triumph and Tragedy*, Weidenfeld & Nicolson, 1991, p. 279. Beria's words were reported to Volkogonov by A. A. Yepishev.

72 Rees, *Nazis: A Warning from History*, Kindle edition, p. 59.

73 Detlef Schmiechen-Ackermann, 'Der "Blockwart". Die unteren Parteifunktionäre im nationalsozialistischen Terror- und Überwachungsapparat', *Vierteljahrshefte für Zeitgeschichte*, vol. 48, no. 4 (2000), pp. 575–602.

74 Gellately, *The Gestapo and German Society*.

75 Johnson and Reuband, *What We Knew*, p. 344.

76 Richard J. Evans, 'Coercion and Consent in Nazi Germany', Raleigh Lecture on History, *Proceedings of the British Academy*, vol. 151 (2007), https://www.thebritishacademy.ac.uk/documents/2036/pba151p053.pdf.

77 Johnson and Reuband, *What We Knew*, p. 145.

78 *Life* magazine, 6 August 1945, p. 8.

79 Previously unpublished testimony.

80 Report on the situation in Germany, No. 15, June 1935, in Stöver, *Berichte über die Lage in Deutschland*, pp. 518–56, here p. 529.

81 Goebbels diary entry, 7 September 1937, quoted in de Jong, *Nazi Billionaires*, Kindle edition, p. 102. Also see de Jong, *Nazi Billionaires*, pp. 69–70.

82 While the 'people's car' never became the totem for the *Volksgemeinschaft* that Hitler had wanted, the name of the vehicle and its creator live on. Volkswagen subsequently became a world-famous car company, and Dr Porsche founded a luxury car firm that continues to produce some of the world's most envied vehicles. But how many people today know that Porsche was a member of both the Nazi Party and the SS, or that Adolf Hitler laid the cornerstone for the Volkswagen factory at Wolfsburg in 1938?

83 BArch, R 58/567, fols. 84–5, 88, Preußische Geheime Staatspolizei, Staatspolizeistelle für den Landespolizeibezirk Berlin, Januar 1936.

84 BArch, R 58/3044a, fols. 104–8, Preußische Geheime Staatspolizei, Staatspolizeistelle für den Landespolizeibezirk Berlin, 6. März 1936, Übersicht über die Ereignisse im Monat Februar 1936.

85 As Professor Sir Ian Kershaw puts it, 'Most of those Berliners angered at their economic plight supported, probably enthusiastically, Hitler's coup [in ordering troops to enter the Rhineland].' See Ian Kershaw, '*Volksgemeinschaft*: Potential and Limitations of the Concept', in Martina Steber and Bernhard Gotto (eds.), *Visions of Community in Nazi Germany: Social Engineering and Private Lives*, Oxford University Press, 2014, Kindle edition, p. 38.

86 Curt Elwenspoek, *Der rechte Brief zur rechten Zeit. Eine Fibel des schriftlichen Verkehrs für jedermann*, Hesse & Becker Verlag, 1936, pp. 53–4. Also see Steber and Gotto (eds.), *Visions of Community in Nazi Germany*, p. v.

87 Sapolsky, *Behave*, Kindle edition, pp. 87–90.

88 Dr Tal Ben-Shahar, *Happier: Learn the Secrets to Daily Joy and Lasting Fulfill-ment*, McGraw-Hill, 2007, pp. 3–5. Also see E. A. Locke and G. P. Latham, 'Building a Practically Useful Theory of Goal Setting and Task Motivation: A 35-Year Odyssey', *American Psychologist*, vol. 57, no. 9 (2002), pp. 705–17. And for a discussion on the relevant phenomenon known as 'Post-Olympic Blues' see K. Howells and M. Lucassen, 'Post-Olympic Blues – The Diminution of Celebrity in Olympic Athletes', *Psychology of Sport and Exer-cise*, vol. 37 (2018), pp. 67–78.

Chapter 8: Valuing Enemies

1 Simon Heffer (ed.), *Henry 'Chips' Channon: The Diaries*, vol. 1: *1918–1938*, Cornerstone Digital, 2021, Kindle edition, pp. 557–8, entry for 6 August 1936.

2 Ibid., p. 569, entry for 16 August 1936.

3 Arnd Krüger, 'United States of America: The Crucial Battle', in Arnd Krüger and William Murray (eds.), *The Nazi Olympics: Sport, Politics, and Appeasement in the 1930s*, University of Illinois Press, 2003, p. 52.

4 Maurice Roche, *Mega-events and Modernity: Olympics and Expos in the Growth of Global Culture*, Routledge, 2000, p. 118.

5 G. S. Messersmith, Vienna, to James Clement Dunn, US State Depart-ment, Washington, DC, 4 December 1935, George S. Messersmith Papers in the University of Delaware Library, https://udspace.udel.edu/items/67007956-a463-4d57-a594-5be8d4b509e7.

6 G. S. Messersmith, Berlin, to William Phillips, Undersecretary of State, Washington, DC, 26 June 1933, George S. Messersmith Papers in the University of Delaware Library, http://udspace.udel.edu/handle/19716/6176.

7 G. S. Messersmith, Vienna, to James Clement Dunn, US State Depart-ment, 4 December 1935.

8 Rudi Ball, an ice hockey player and a German of Jewish origin, took part in the Winter Olympics. Like Helene Mayer, he had been living outside Germany before the Games.

9 Susan D. Bachrach, *The Nazi Olympics: Berlin 1936*, United States Holocaust Memorial Council, 2000, pp. 101–3.

10 Allen Guttmann, *The Olympics: A History of the Modern Games*, University of Illinois Press, 2002, p. 68.

11 Bachrach, *Nazi Olympics*, pp. 92–6. Also see Ian Kershaw, *Hitler: Nemesis 1936–1945*, Penguin, 2001, p. 7.

12 Bachrach, *Nazi Olympics*, p. 68.

13 James Q. Whitman, *Hitler's American Model: The United States and the Making of Nazi Race Law*, Princeton University Press, 2018, p. 3.

14 Ibid., p. 1.

15 Krüger, 'United States of America: The Crucial Battle', p. 50.

16 Guttmann, *The Olympics*, p. 66.

17 Klemperer, *I Shall Bear Witness*, Kindle edition, p. 307, entry for 13 August 1936.

18 Heffer (ed.), *Channon: The Diaries*, vol. 1, pp. 566–7, Kindle edition, entry for 13 August 1936.

19 Ibid., p. 567, entry for 13 August 1936.

20 Ibid., p. 560, entry for 8 August 1936.

21 Guttmann, *The Olympics*, p. 70.

22 Leni Riefenstahl, *Olympia – Festival of Nations*, 1936 (at 36' 37").

23 'Aufzeichnung ohne Unterschrift' (August 1936), in *Akten zur deutschen auswärtigen Politik 1918–1945*, Serie C: 1933–1937, *Das Dritte Reich: Die ersten Jahre*, vol. V/2: *26. Mai bis 31. Oktober 1936*, Vandenhoeck & Ruprecht, 1977, Dokumentnummer 490, pp. 793–801.

24 George Orwell, Review of *Mein Kampf*, *New English Weekly*, 21 March 1940.

25 Professor Adam Tooze in conversation with the author; see http://ww2history.com/experts/Adam_Tooze/Hitler_and_rearmament.

26 *Documents on German Foreign Policy 1918–1945*, United States Government Printing Office, 1949–83, Series C (1933–1937), vol. V, Document Number 490, pp. 853–62.

27 Tooze, *Wages of Destruction*, pp. 198–9.

28 International Military Tribunal (IMT), *Der Prozess gegen die Hauptkriegsverbrecher vor dem Internationalen Militärgerichtshofs, Nürnberg, 14. November 1945–1. Oktober 1946*, vol. XXXVI, Sekretariat der Gerichtshof, 1949, pp. 489ff.

29 Elke Fröhlich (ed.), *Die Tagebücher von Joseph Goebbels*, Teil I: *Aufzeichnungen 1923–1941*, vol. 3/2: *März 1936–Februar 1937*, K. G. Saur, 2001, pp. 388–90, here p. 389, entry for 23 February 1937.

30 Hermann Göring, *Aufbau einer Nation*, E. S. Mittler & Sohn, 1934, pp. 51–2.

31 Leon Goldensohn, *The Nuremberg Interviews: Conversations with the Defendants and Witnesses*, ed. Robert Gellately, Pimlico, 2007, Kindle edition, p. 110.

32 See p. 83.

33 Elke Fröhlich (ed.), *Die Tagebücher von Joseph Goebbels*, Teil I: *Aufzeichnungen 1923–1941*, vol. 6: *August 1938–Juni 1939*, K. G. Saur, 1998, pp. 245–6, here p. 246, entry for 1 February 1939.

34 See p. 70.

35 *Trial of the Major War Criminals before the International Military Tribunal, Nuremberg* vol. IX, The International Military Tribunal, 1947, pp. 418–19, Hermann Göring's testimony, 18 March 1946, https://avalon.law.yale.edu/imt/03-18-46.asp#Goering5.

36 Ian Kershaw, 'The "Hitler Myth": Image and Reality in the Third Reich', in David F. Crew (ed.), *Nazism and German Society 1933–1945*, Routledge, 1994, p. 202.

37 Elke Fröhlich (ed.), *Die Tagebücher von Joseph Goebbels*, Teil I: *Aufzeichnungen 1923–1941*, vol. 4: *März–November 1937*, K. G. Saur, 2000, p. 214, entry for 10 July 1937.

38 Blomberg was Minister of Defence until May 1935, when his title changed to Minister of War.

39 Rees, *Nazis: A Warning from History*, Kindle edition, p. 52, interview with Karl Boehm-Tettelbach.

40 *Documents on German Foreign Policy*, Series D (1937–1945), vol. I, pp. 29–39, minutes of the conference in the Reich Chancellery, Berlin, held on 5 November 1937.

41 See pp. 129–31.

42 BA-MA N 28/4, quoted in Müller, *General Ludwig Beck*, pp. 498–501, Beck document of 12 November 1937. It is not clear whether Beck wrote this for himself or to show to others.

43 *Trial of the Major War Criminals*, vol. 12, 25 April 1946, Morning Session, testimony of Hans Bernd Gisevius, p. 196, https://avalon.law.yale.edu/imt/04-25-46.asp.

44 Fritsch's court martial would subsequently reveal the perfidy of the Gestapo. Not only was he innocent – it was a case of mistaken identity – but the Gestapo had known the truth beforehand. Even though Himmler's and Heydrich's reputations were damaged by the affair, by the time the truth emerged it was too late to give Fritsch his old job back. See Davidson, *The Unmaking of Adolf Hitler*, p. 186.

45 Gerwarth, *Hitler's Hangman*, Kindle edition, pp. 116–18.

46 BA-MA N 81/2 und OKW 898, quoted in Müller, *General Ludwig Beck*, pp. 477–85.

47 Edgar Röhricht, *Pflicht und Gewissen. Erinnerungen eines deutschen Generals 1932 bis 1944*, Kohlhammer, 1965, pp. 119ff.

48 Nicholas Reynolds, *Treason Was No Crime*, William Kimber, 1976, p. 138.

49 Essi Viding, *Psychopathy: A Very Short Introduction*, Oxford University Press, 2019, Kindle edition, p. 70.

50 Peter Hoffmann, *The History of the German Resistance 1933–1945*, McGill-Queen's University Press, 1996, p. 46.

51 Goldensohn, *The Nuremberg Interviews*, Kindle edition, pp. 165–6.

52 Ibid., p. 160.

53 Kurt von Schuschnigg, *Austrian Requiem*, Victor Gollancz, 1947, p. 23.

54 Kershaw, *Nemesis*, p. 66.

55 Norman A. Graebner and Edward M. Bennett, *The Versailles Treaty and its Legacy: The Failure of the Wilsonian Vision*, Cambridge University Press, 2011, p. 150; Robert Boyce, *The Great Interwar Crisis and the Collapse of Globalization*, Palgrave Macmillan, 2009, p. 436.

56 Previously unpublished testimony.

57 *Wiener Neueste Nachrichten*, 17 March 1938, p. 3.

58 Reinhard Heydrich to Gauleiter Josef Bürckel, 17 March 1938, in Dokumentationsarchiv des österreichischen Widerstandes (ed.), '*Anschluß' 1938. Eine Dokumentation*, Österreichischer Bundesverlag, 1988, p. 440.

59 Rees, *Nazis: A Warning from History*, Kindle edition, p. 102.

60 Susan T. Fiske and Federica Durante, 'Stereotype Content across Cultures: Variations on a Few Themes', in Michael J. Gelfand, Chi-yue Chiu and Ying-yi Hong (eds.), *Handbook of Advances in Culture and Psychology*, vol. 6, Oxford University Press, 2016, pp. 209–47. Also see interview with Professor Fiske at https://www.youtube.com/watch?v=pAg8RNb8zS8.

61 Author interview with Professor Robert Sapolsky.

62 Peter Longerich, *Holocaust: The Nazi Persecution and Murder of the Jews*, Oxford University Press, 2010, Kindle edition, p. 106.

63 *San Francisco Examiner*, 12 March 1938.

64 Sapolsky, *Behave*, Kindle edition, p. 754.

65 Papen, *Memoirs*, pp. 430–38.

66 Goldensohn, *The Nuremberg Interviews*, Kindle edition, p. 166.

67 Rafael Medoff, *America and the Holocaust: A Documentary History*, University of Nebraska Press, 2022, p. 71.

68 *Völkischer Beobachter*, Wiener Ausgabe, 27 March 1938.

69 Irving Abella and Harold Troper, ' "The Line Must Be Drawn Somewhere": Canada and Jewish Refugees, 1933–9', in Michael R. Marrus

(ed.), *The Nazi Holocaust*, Part 8: *Bystanders to the Holocaust, Volume 1*, Meckler, 1989, p. 239. National Archives, Washington, DC, State Department Records, Memorandum on Refugees, 1938, files 900-1/2: 840–48.

70 *Documents on German Foreign Policy*, Series D, vol. V, Document Number 640, Circular of the State Secretary, 8 July 1938, pp. 894–5.

71 Debórah Dwork and Robert Jan van Pelt, *Flight from the Reich: Refugee Jews 1933–1946*, W. W. Norton, 2009, p. 99, Roger Makins, Memorandum 25 March 1938, PRO FO 371/2231.

72 Rees, *Holocaust*, Kindle edition, pp. 163–4.

73 Domarus (ed.), *Hitler. Reden und Proklamationen*, vol. 1, p. 899, Hitler speech of 12 September 1938.

74 Jillian Jordan, Roseanna Sommers and David Rand, 'The Real Problem with Hypocrisy', *New York Times*, 13 January 2017. Also see Jillian Jordan, Roseanna Sommers, Paul Bloom and David Rand, 'Why Do We Hate Hypocrites? Evidence for a Theory of False Signaling', *Psychological Science*, vol. 28, no. 3 (March 2017), pp. 356–68.

75 'Juden, was nun?', *Das Schwarze Korps*, 24 November 1938, p. 1.

76 Domarus (ed.), *Hitler. Reden und Proklamationen*, vol. 1, p. 899, Hitler speech of 12 September 1938.

77 BArch, RW 4/31, Amtliches Tagebuch vom Chef des Wehrmacht-Führungsstabes, Abt. Landesverteidigung Oberst Jodl für die Zeit vom 4.1.1937–24.8.1939, p. 48.

78 Leonidas E. Hill (ed.), *Die Weizsäcker-Papiere 1933–1950*, Propyläen Verlag, 1974, p. 145, entry for 9 October 1938.

79 BArch, RW 19/41, p. 56, Wehrwirtschaftsinspektion VII (Munich), Wirtschaftsbericht August 1938, 9.9.1938.

80 Hill (ed.), *Die Weizsäcker-Papiere*, p. 145, entry for 9 October 1938.

81 'Rede Hitlers vor der deutsche Presse (10. November 1938)', *Vierteljahrshefte für Zeitgeschichte*, vol. 6, no. 2 (1958), pp. 175–91.

82 Elke Fröhlich (ed.), *Die Tagebücher von Joseph Goebbels*, Teil I: *Aufzeichnungen 1923–1941*, vol. 9: *Dezember 1940–Juli 1941*, K. G. Saur, 1998, pp. 425–7, here p. 426, entry for 5 July 1941.

83 'Rede Hitlers vor der deutsche Presse (10. November 1938)', pp. 175–91.

84 Walter H. Pehle (ed.), *November 1938: From 'Reichskristallnacht' to Genocide*, Berg, 1991, p. 41; see https://www.jewishvirtuallibrary.org/reactions-to-kristallnacht.

85 Ruth Levitt (ed.), *Pogrom – November 1938: Testimonies from 'Kristallnacht'*, Souvenir Press/The Wiener Library for the Study of the Holocaust and Genocide, 2015, report B.66, p. 87.

86 Testimony of Rudi Bamber, in Rees, *Nazi: A Warning from History*, Kindle edition, p. 72.

87 Fröhlich (ed.), *Die Tagebücher von Joseph Goebbels*, Teil I, vol. 6, p. 180, entry for 10 November 1938.

88 Jürgen Matthäus and Mark Roseman (eds.), *Jewish Responses to Persecution 1933–1946*, vol. 1: *1933–1938*, AltaMira Press, 2010, document 12-2, pp. 345–7, letter from Josef Broniatowski, Częstochowa (Poland), no date (most likely early November 1938).

89 Hitler's Secret Speech to military commanders, 10 February 1939, available online at: https://ghdi.ghi-dc.org/sub_document.cfm?document_id=1543.

90 *Documents on German Foreign Policy*, Series D, vol. VII, pp. 200–204, Hitler conference, 22 August 1939.

91 Previously unpublished testimony.

Chapter 9: Eliminating Resistance

1 Memorandum Brief of the Prosecution, Crimes against Peace: Counts one and four; Planning, Preparing, Initiating and Waging Wars of Aggression and Invasions, the Common Plan or Conspiracy, 26 August 1948, Records of the United States Nuremberg War Crimes Trials Interrogations, 1946–1949, 898, Roll 58, 30.

2 Elisabeth Wagner (ed.), *Der Generalquartiermeister. Briefe und Tagebuchaufzeichnungen des Generalquartiermeisters des Heeres General der Artillerie Eduard Wagner*, Günter Olzog Verlag, 1963, p. 103.

3 Jürgen Matthäus, Jochen Böhler and Klaus-Michael Mallmann (eds.), *War, Pacification, and Mass Murder, 1939: The Einsatzgruppen in Poland*, Rowman & Littlefield, 2014, Kindle edition, pp. 13–15.

4 'The Myth of "The Bloody Sunday of Bydgoszcz" Dispelled', Polish Institute of National Remembrance, https://1september39.com/39e/articles/2332,The-Myth-of-quotThe-Bloody-Sunday-of-Bydgoszcz-Dispelled.html.

5 *The Nuremberg Trials*, vol. 9, DigiCat, 2022, p. 954, 22 March 1946, Morning Session. Also see Hermann Göring's testimony at p. 730.

6 Melita Maschmann, *Account Rendered: A Dossier on My Former Self*, Plunkett Lake Press, 2013, Kindle edition, p. 76.

7 Hargreaves, *Blitzkrieg Unleashed*, p. 236.

8 Peter Fritzsche, *Life and Death in the Third Reich*, Belknap Press of Harvard University Press, 2008, Kindle edition, location 1803–7.

9 Neil C. Renic, *Asymmetric Killing: Risk Avoidance, Just War, and the Warrior Ethos*, Oxford University Press, 2020, p. 125.

10 Gerhard Wolf, *Ideology and the Rationality of Domination: Nazi Germanization Policies in Poland*, Indiana University Press, 2020, p. 56.

11 Matthäus, Böhler and Mallmann (eds.), *War, Pacification, and Mass Murder*, Kindle edition, p. 54, Report by Helmuth Bischoff, commander of Einsatzkommando 1/IV, 8 September 1939.

12 Wildt, *An Uncompromising Generation*, p. 224.

13 Ibid., p. 225.

14 Ibid., p. 236.

15 Matthäus, Böhler and Mallmann (eds.), *War, Pacification, and Mass Murder*, Kindle edition, p. 59, Interrogation of 'Bruno G', former member of Einsatzkommando 2/IV, concerning reprisals in Bromberg, 1 December 1964.

16 Aly and Heim, *Architects of Annihilation*, Kindle edition, p. 64.

17 Ibid., p. 127.

18 See the discussion of research by Professor Susan Fiske and her colleagues, pp. 197–8.

19 Jacob Sloan (ed.), *Notes from the Warsaw Ghetto, from the Journal of Emanuel Ringelblum*, iBooks, Kindle edition, 2006, p. 19, entry for 12 February 1940.

20 Ibid., p. 17, entry for 7 February 1940.

21 Gerwarth, *Hitler's Hangman*, Kindle edition, p. 135.

22 Matthäus, Böhler and Mallmann (eds.), *War, Pacification, and Mass Murder*, Kindle edition, pp. 140–41, Interrogation of Fritz Liebl, member of Einsatzkommando 3/I by SS and Police investigators, December 1939.

23 BArch, R 9361-III/529347, SSO-file Alfred Hasselberg.

24 Ibid.

25 See pp. 242–7.

26 Matthäus, Böhler and Mallmann (eds.), *War, Pacification, and Mass Murder*, Kindle edition, p. 141.

27 Lina Heydrich, *Leben mit einem Kriegsverbrecher*, Verlag W. Ludwig, 1976, p. 119.

28 See p. 243.

29 Matthäus, Böhler and Mallmann (eds.), *War, Pacification, and Mass Murder*, Kindle edition, p. 70, Testimony by Josef Lemke about German atrocities in Wejherowo in late 1939; date of interview 10 February 1971.

30 See pp. 295–6.

31 Alexander B. Rossino, *Hitler Strikes Poland: Blitzkrieg, Ideology, and Atrocity*, University Press of Kansas, 2003, pp. 68–9.

32 IMT, *Der Prozess gegen die Hauptkriegsverbrecher vor dem Internationalen Militär-gerichtshof*, vol. XXXV, Sekretariat der Gerichtshof, 1949, pp. 87–91, here pp. 89–90, Document 419-D, Report of the Army District Command XXI (Poznań) to the Commander of the Reserve Army from 23 November 1939.

33 Hildegard von Kotze (ed.), *Heeresadjutant bei Hitler 1938–1943. Aufzeichnungen des Majors Engel*, Deutsche Verlags-Anstalt, 1974, pp. 67f.

34 Brief von Wilhelm Ritter von Leeb an Franz Halder vom 19.12.1939, Durchschlag des maschinenschriftlichen Entwurfs im Nachlass Ritter v. Leebs; Entwurf, im Original handschriftlicher Vermerk: 'ab durch Kurier am 20.12.39. Becker, Mjr'. See Georg Meyer (ed.), *Generalfeldmarschall Wilhelm Ritter von Leeb. Tagebuchaufzeichnungen und Lagebeurteilungen aus zwei Weltkriegen*, Deutsche Verlags-Anstalt, 1976, pp. 473–4.

35 BArch, RH 53-23/23, fols. 11–28, The Commander-in-Chief East [Ober-befehlshaber Ost], 6 February 1940, notes for a meeting with the Commander-in-Chief of the Armed Forces on 15 February in Spala (Nurem-berg document NO-3011).

36 Heinrich Nolte, 'Landesverrat oder Hochverrat? Als Adjutant bei Halder, Oktober 1939 bis Juni 1940', *Kampftruppen*, vol. 5 (1969), pp. 120–22, here p. 122.

37 Elke Fröhlich (ed.), *Die Tagebücher von Joseph Goebbels*, Teil I: *Aufzeichnungen 1923–1941*, vol. 7: *Juli 1939–März 1940*, K. G. Saur, 1998, pp. 177–9, here p. 177, entry for 2 November 1939.

38 Author interview with Professor Essi Viding.

39 Richard Giziowski, *The Enigma of General Blaskowitz*, Leo Cooper, 1997, pp. 15–24.

40 Abschrift Aussage Huppenkothen der 20. Juli 1944, IfZ Munich, ZS 249 (Huppenkothen), p. 158, Walter Huppenkothen's post-war testimony. Also see Hans-Adolf Jacobsen, *Fall Gelb. Der Kampf um den deutschen Operations-plan zur Westoffensive 1940*, Franz Steiner Verlag, 1957, p. 10.

41 *Kriegstagebuch des Oberkommandos der Wehrmacht (Wehrmachtführungsstab)*, vol. I: *1. August 1940–31. Dezember 1941*, Bernard & Graefe Verlag, 1965, p. 950. On General Warlimont's command this page of the war diary had been replaced by a moderated text in order not to upset Hitler. The ori-ginal page was carefully preserved.

42 Ernest R. May, *Strange Victory: Hitler's Conquest of France*, Hill & Wang, 2015, p. 285, Report from 15 December 1939.

43 John Vincent (ed.), *The Crawford Papers: The Journals of David Lindsay, Twenty-seventh Earl of Crawford and Tenth Earl of Balcarres, 1871–1940, during the Years 1892 to 1940*, Manchester University Press, 1984, p. 602, entry for 25 August 1939.

44 Charles Burdick and Hans-Adolf Jacobsen (eds.), *The Halder War Diary 1939–1942*, Greenhill Books, 1988, p. 72, entry for 14 October 1939.

45 Kershaw, *Nemesis*, p. 268.

46 General Wilhelm Ritter von Leeb called the proposed attack on western Europe 'mad'. See Meyer (ed.), *Leeb. Tagebuchaufzeichnungen und Lagebeurteilungen*, pp. 187–8, entry for 9 October 1939.

47 Letter written by Walther Nehring, a general of the armoured corps, to Geyr von Schweppenburg, a fellow general, on 26 October 1967, about whether his (Nehring's) armoured regiment would have acted against Hitler; document in IfZ Munich, ED 91/16.

48 Monatsbericht der Gendarmerie-Station Waischenfeld, 26.11.1939, in Martin Broszat, Elke Fröhlich and Falk Wiesemann (eds.), *Bayern in der NS-Zeit*, vol. 1, Oldenbourg, 1977, p. 135.

49 Aus deutschen Urkunden 1935–1945, Imperial War Museum Department of Documents, pp. 174–5. Also see Longerich, *Himmler*, Kindle edition, pp. 461–5.

50 BArch, NS 7/221, fol. 3.

51 Ibid.

52 Previously unpublished testimony.

53 Ernst Klee, Willi Dressen and Volker Riess (eds.), *'The Good Old Days': The Holocaust as Seen by its Perpetrators and Bystanders*, Konecky & Konecky, 1991, p. 70, Report of Dr August Becker on 5 June 1942 to SS Obersturmbannführer Rauff about the number killed in three gas vans between December 1941 and June 1942.

54 Maria Otero Rossi, 'Euphémismes et crimes de masse: Psychanalyse et mise en sens avec l'Histoire', *Recherches en Psychanalyse*, vol. 19, no. 1 (2015), pp. 68–76, https://shs.cairn.info/revue-recherches-en-psychanalyse1-2015-1-page-68.?lang=fr.

55 Albert Bandura, *Moral Disengagement: How People Do Harm and Live with Themselves*, Worth Publishers, 2016, p. 53.

56 Previously unpublished testimony.

57 Heinrich Himmler, 'Rede vor Gauleitern und anderen Parteifunktionären am 29.2.1940', quoted in Bradley F. Smith and Agnes F. Peterson (eds.), *Heinrich Himmler. Geheimreden 1933 bis 1945 und andere Ansprachen*, Propyläen Verlag, 1974, pp. 115–44.

58 Alfred Konieczny and Herbert Szurgacz (eds.), *Praca przymusowa polaków pod panowaniem hitlerowskim 1939–1945* (= Documenta Occupationis, vol. X), Instytut Zachodni, 1976, pp. 118–21, doc. II-9, Guidelines of the Reichsführer SS on the special treatment of the Polish civilian workers and prisoners of war employed in the Reich.

59 See p. 171.

60 Burleigh, *Death and Deliverance*, p. 108. Burleigh notes, on the same page, that though Hölzel managed to avoid the appointment, it wasn't before he had 'inducted several nurses into a task which included a built-in number of fatalities'.

61 See p. 246.

62 C. F. Rüter et al. (eds.), *Justiz und NS-Verbrechen. Sammlung deutscher Strafurteile wegen nationalsozialistischer Tötungsverbrechen 1945–1966*, vol. XXVI, Amsterdam University Press/K. G. Saur, 2001, pp. 555–83, here pp. 558–9. Also quoted in Ernst Klee, *Euthanasie im NS-Staat. Die 'Vernichtung lebensunwerten Lebens'*, S. Fischer Verlag, 1983, pp. 84–5.

63 See pp. 15–16. Also Grossman, *On Killing*, Kindle edition, pp. 150–51.

64 Ibid., p. 151.

65 Burleigh, *Death and Deliverance*, p. 140.

66 Karsten Linne (ed.), *Der Nürnberger Ärzteprozeß 1946/47. Wortprotokolle, Anklage- und Verteidigungsmaterial, Quellen zum Umfeld*, Mikrofiche-Edition/K. G. Saur, 1999, fols. 2687–8, transcript of Hans Heinrich Lammers' testimony, Nuremberg Medical Case, 7 February 1947.

67 Walter Kohl, *'Ich fühle mich nicht schuldig'. Georg Renno, Euthanasiearzt*, Paul Zsolnay Verlag, 2000, p. 320.

68 BArch, B 162/3170, fol. 167, testimony of Werner Dubois, 18 September 1961.

69 BArch, B 162/4428 (AR-Z 251/59, vol. 4), fols. 703–4, statement of Werner Dubois, 7 September 1961.

70 Michael Grabher, *Irmfried Eberl. 'Euthanasie'-Arzt und Kommandant von Treblinka*, Peter Lang, 2006, p. 17; original in HHStAW 631a, No. 1633.

71 Frank Hirschinger, *'Zur Ausmerzung freigegeben'. Halle und die Landesheilanstalt Altscherbitz 1933–1945*, Böhlau Verlag, 2001, p. 110; original in BStU, MfS ZUV 45 (Untersuchungsvorgang Otto Hebold), vol. 5, p. 18.

72 Christopher Browning, *The Origins of the Final Solution: The Evolution of Nazi Jewish Policy, September 1939–March 1942*, Cornerstone Digital, 2014, Kindle edition, pp. 186–9.

73 Patrick Montague, *Chełmno and the Holocaust: The History of Hitler's First Death Camp*, I. B. Tauris, 2012, pp. 21–8.

74 Note that many others later claimed a hand in the planning. Also that another factor in the change in plan was the knowledge that the original plan had likely fallen into the hands of the Allies. See Andrew Roberts, *The Storm of War, a New History of the Second World War*, Penguin, 2009, Kindle edition, pp. 48–9.

75 Rees, *Dark Charisma*, Kindle edition, p. 262; author interview with Professor Adam Tooze.

76 Winston Churchill, *The Second World War*, vol. II: *Their Finest Hour*, Penguin, 2005, p. 38.

77 Halder, *War Diary*, p. 103, entry for 25 February 1940; p.106, entry for 17 March 1940.

78 Predictably, in a country without basic human rights, these demonstrations were ordered and controlled by the regime. But that does not mean that the joy of large numbers of those who participated was not genuine – as testimony confirms.

Chapter 10: Escalating Racism

1 Hitler, *Mein Kampf*, pp. 660–61.

2 Halder, *War Diary*, p. 346, entry for 30 March 1941.

3 Erhard Moritz (ed.), *Fall Barbarossa. Dokumente zur Vorbereitung der faschistischen Wehrmacht auf die Aggression gegen die Sowjetunion*, Deutscher Militärverlag, 1970, pp. 258–9.

4 Hans-Heinrich Wilhelm, *Rassenpolitik und Kriegführung. Sicherheitspolizei und Wehrmacht in Polen und in der Sowjetunion 1939–1942*, R. Rothe, 1991, pp. 133–40, here pp. 133–4, 138–9, Colonel General Georg von Küchler, notes for a speech to his divisional commanders on 25 April 1941; original in BArch, RH 20-18/71, AOK 18/Ia Nr. 406/41, g.Kdos.

5 Gerd R. Ueberschär and Wolfram Wette (eds.), *Der deutsche Überfall auf die Sowjetunion. 'Unternehmen Barbarossa' 1941*, Fischer Taschenbuch Verlag, 2011, pp. 262–3; original in BA-MA, RW 39/20.

6 See pp. 38–9.

7 *Trial of the Major War Criminals*, vol. 4, p. 482 (statement of Erich von dem Bach-Zelewski, 7 January 1946), https://avalon.law.yale.edu/imt/01-07-46. asp. Bach-Zelewski wrongly dates the meeting to earlier in 1941, but Himmler's desk diary confirms that the meeting was in June, just prior to the invasion. See Peter Witte et al. (eds.), *Der Dienstkalender Heinrich*

Himmlers 1941/42, Hans Christians Verlag, 1999, pp. 171–2. See also Longerich, *Holocaust*, Kindle edition p. 181.

8 Aly and Heim, *Architects of Annihilation*, Kindle edition, p. 239.

9 Heinz Höhne, *The Order of the Death's Head: The Story of Hitler's SS*, Penguin, 2000, p. 356. Helmut Langerbein, *Hitler's Death Squads: The Logic of Mass Murder*, Texas A&M University Press, 2004, p. 28.

10 Longerich, *Himmler*, Kindle edition, p. 521.

11 Wildt, *An Uncompromising Generation*, p. 273. These young members of the Security Police returned to their base in Berlin for the new term which started in November 1941, after several months in the killing fields. There was also probably a view taken – see ibid., p. 287 – that they should be returned earlier than planned so that they could avoid suffering psychological damage.

12 Langerbein, *Hitler's Death Squads*, p. 28.

13 Zygmunt Bauman, *Modernity and the Holocaust*, Polity Press, 2007, Kindle edition, p. 70.

14 Browning, *Origins of the Final Solution*, Kindle edition, pp. 309–10.

15 Ute Hoffmann and Dietmar Schulze, '. . . *wird heute in eine andere Anstalt verlegt'. Nationalsozialistische Zwangssterilisation und 'Euthanasie' in der Landes-Heil- und Pflegeanstalt Bernburg – eine Dokumentation*, Regierungspräsidium Dessau, 1997, p. 111.

16 See p. 276.

17 Rees, *Nazis: A Warning from History*, Kindle edition, pp. 295–6.

18 Rees, *Holocaust*, Kindle edition, pp. 245–6.

19 Testimony of Otto Ohlendorf, *Trial of the Major War Criminals*, vol. 4, p. 320, 3 January 1946, Morning Session, https://avalon.law.yale.edu/imt/01-03-46.asp.

20 Waller, *Becoming Evil*, pp. 108–13.

21 See, for example, Langerbein, *Hitler's Death Squads*, pp. 8–9, 153 and 180. Also see Browning, *Ordinary Men*, Kindle edition, pp. 171–4.

22 Waller, *Becoming Evil*, p. 113. Also see Stanley Milgram, *Obedience to Authority: An Experimental View*, Harper Perennial, 2017.

23 Author interview with Professor Robert Sapolsky.

24 Lecture by Professor Stephen Reicher on Milgram to the British Psychological Association annual conference, 2018, https://www.youtube.com/watch?v=RFOI6FJQBXY.

25 Ervin Staub, *The Roots of Evil: The Origin of Genocide and Other Group Violence*, Cambridge University Press, 1989, Kindle edition, p. 79.

26 Erich Fromm, *Escape from Freedom*, Open Road, 2013, Kindle edition. First published in 1941, the book also contains an interesting – though dated – analysis of the 'Psychology of Nazism', pp. 204–37.

27 BArch, NS 19/4010. Also reproduced in Smith and Peterson (eds.), *Heinrich Himmler. Geheimreden*, pp. 162–83, here pp. 169–70, speech of 6 October 1943. He also gave another speech at Posen two days earlier.

28 Browning, *Origins of the Final Solution*, Kindle edition, pp. 281–2.

29 Robert D. Hare, Elizabeth León-Mayer, Joanna Rocuant Salinas, Jorge Folino and Craig S. Neumann, 'Psychopathy and Crimes against Humanity: A Conceptual and Empirical Examination of Human Rights Violators', *Journal of Criminal Justice*, vol. 81 (2022).

30 See 'Sexual Sadism Disorder', *Psychology Today*, https://www.psycho logytoday.com/gb/conditions/sexual-sadism-disorder. Also see George R. Brown, 'Sexual Sadism Disorder', in MSD Manual, Professional Version, July 2023, https://www.msdmanuals.com/professional/psychiatric-disorders/paraphilias-and-paraphilic-disorders/sexual-sadism-disorder. And J. Reich, 'Prevalence and Characteristics of Sadistic Personality Disorder in an Outpatient Veterans Population', *Psychiatry Research*, vol. 48, no. 3 (1993), pp. 267–76, https://pubmed.ncbi.nlm.nih.gov/8272448/. This gives an 8.1 per cent prevalence of sadistic personality traits and disorders among a group of veterans selected from a psychiatric outpatients' clinic.

31 Klee, Dressen and Riess (eds.), *'The Good Old Days'*, p. 179.

32 Ingrao, *Believe and Destroy*, Kindle edition, p. 159.

33 Langerbein, *Hitler's Death Squads*, pp. 67–70.

34 Longerich, *Himmler*, Kindle edition, p. 309, speech of 4 October 1943.

35 Klee, Dressen and Riess (eds.), *'The Good Old Days'*, p. 97.

36 Ben Shalit, *The Psychology of Conflict and Combat*, Praeger, 1988, p. 48, quoting Miron and Goldstein's research in 1979.

37 Christopher Browning, *Nazi Policy, Jewish Workers, German Killers*, Cambridge University Press, 2000, pp. 151–2.

38 Browning, *Ordinary Men*, Kindle edition, p. 83.

39 Previously unpublished testimony, and Rees, *Their Darkest Hour*, Kindle edition, p. 22.

40 Klee, Dressen and Riess (eds.), *'The Good Old Days'*, p. 76.

41 H. Tajfel, M. G. Billig, R. P. Bundy and C. Flament, 'Social categorization and intergroup behavior', *European Journal of Social Psychology*, vol. 1, issue 2, April/June 1971, pp. 149–178. For an analysis of Tajfel's work, see

Dominic Abrams, *Social Identifications: A Social Psychology of Intergroup Relations and Group Processes*, Routledge, 1998.

42 See pp. 6–7.

43 Laurence Rees, *Horror in the East: The Brutal Struggle in Asia and the Pacific in WWII*, BBC Books, 2011, Kindle edition, p. 29.

44 Ibid., p. 30.

45 Ibid., p. 44.

46 Ibid., p. 169.

47 Waller, *Becoming Evil*, pp. 38–9.

48 Browning, *Ordinary Men*, Kindle edition, p. 56. Browning's *Ordinary Men*, along with Daniel Jonah Goldhagen's *Hitler's Willing Executioners: Ordinary Germans and the Holocaust*, Knopf, 1996, were both published in the 1990s and prompted much debate. Goldhagen's book was heavily criticized by many historians for a host of reasons. See, for example, the views of the distinguished German historian Eberhard Jäckel: 'Einfach ein schlechtes Buch' ('Simply a bad book'), *Die Zeit*, 17 May 1996.

49 Browning, *Ordinary Men*, Kindle edition, pp. 61–2.

50 Earl, *The Nuremberg SS-Einsatzgruppen Trial*, p. 206.

51 Langerbein, *Hitler's Death Squads*, p. 146.

52 Author interview with Professor Essi Viding.

53 Höss, *Commandant*, p. 148.

54 Klee, Dressen and Riess (eds.), *'The Good Old Days'*, p. 62, statement of teleprinter engineer Kiebach, Einsatzgruppe C.

55 Ibid., p. 111, statement of SS Obersturmführer August Häfner, Sonderkommando 4a.

56 *Trials of War Criminals before the Nuernberg Military Tribunals . . .*, vol. IV: *'The Einsatzgruppen Case' . . .*, United States Government Printing Office, 1950, p. 491. In German in Kazimierz Leszczyński (ed.), *Fall 9. Das Urteil im SS-Einsatzgruppenprozeß, gefällt am 10. April 1948 in Nürnberg vom Militärgerichtshof II der Vereinigten Staaten von Amerika*, Rütten & Loening, 1963, pp. 122–3.

57 Previously unpublished testimony.

58 Wildt, *An Uncompromising Generation*, pp. 286–7.

59 Ibid., p. 289.

60 Rees, *Their Darkest Hour*, Kindle edition, pp. 70–71.

61 *Trials of War Criminals before the Nuremberg Military Tribunals*, vol. IV, p. 491.

62 Author interview with Professor Essi Viding.

63 Previously unpublished testimony, and Rees, *Nazis: A Warning from History*, Kindle edition, pp. 215–16.

64 Ibid.

65 Longerich, *Himmler*, Kindle edition, pp. 345–6.

66 Christian Ingrao, *The SS Dirlewanger Brigade: The History of the Black Hunters*, Skyhorse Publishing, 2011, Kindle edition, p. 26, Situation Report 15/10/1943 written by Kube's staff after his assassination the previous month, but also, in part, quoting Kube's words.

67 Rees, *Behind Closed Doors*, Kindle edition, pp. 290–91.

68 Previously unpublished testimony.

69 Longerich, *Himmler*, Kindle edition, p. 346.

70 See pp. 255–6.

71 https://www.yadvashem.org/odot_pdf/Microsoft%20Word%20-%20 6236.pdf.

72 But note that even though the death camps of Auschwitz, Treblinka, Sobibór, Bełżec and Majdanek were all killing people via gas chambers by 1942, the shootings did not stop but carried on in parallel. In fact during Operation Harvest Festival on 3 and 4 November 1943 an incredible 42,000 Jews were shot, primarily at Majdanek but also elsewhere. See https://encyclopedia.ushmm.org/content/en/timeline-event/holocaust/1942-1945/operation-harvest-festival.

73 Witte et al. (eds.), *Der Dienstkalender Heinrich Himmlers 1941/42*, p. 195.

74 'Leben eines SS-Generals. Aus den Nürnberger Geständnissen des Generals der Waffen-SS Erich von dem Bach-Zelewski', *Aufbau*, vol. XII, no. 34 (23 August 1946), p. 2.

75 Browning, *Ordinary Men*, Kindle edition, p. 24.

76 'Leben eines SS-Generals', p. 2; and recollection of former SS General Karl Wolff, *The World at War*, Thames Television, 27 March 1974, quoted in Martin Gilbert, *The Holocaust: The Jewish Tragedy*, Collins, 1986, p. 19.

77 Rees, *Holocaust*, Kindle edition, p. 258.

Chapter 11: Killing at a Distance

1 See pp. 321–2.

2 See p. 240. Of course, in the Milgram experiment, as previously discussed, although the subjects thought they were delivering electric shocks this was only an illusion. No one was hurt during the experiment.

3 Rees, *Holocaust*, Kindle edition, p. 247.

4 Wachsmann, *KL*, pp. 262–7.

5 Ibid., pp. 270–74.

6 Testimony of Dr Albert Widmann, 1960, StAL, EL317III, Bü53.

7 Testimony of Wilhelm Jaschke, Vilsbiburg, 5 April 1960, BArch, 202, AR-Z 152/159; partly in Rees, *Holocaust*, Kindle edition, p. 260.

8 Testimony of Dr Albert Widmann, 1960, StAL, EL317III, Bü53.

9 Ibid.

10 Ibid.

11 Widmann's idea of what was 'legitimate', however, stretched as far as creating poison bullets in early 1944 in direct contravention of international treaty. Experiments on condemned prisoners later that year demonstrated that the bullets Widmann had invented caused an extremely painful death. Thankfully they were never used in combat. See Wildt, *An Uncompromising Generation*, p. 187.

12 Testimony of Dr Albert Widmann, 1960, StAL, EL317III, Bü53. Widmann was sentenced to six years and six months in prison.

13 Segev, *Soldiers of Evil*, pp. 175–9. Fritzsch and his wife split up during the war and Fritzsch almost certainly died in the Battle for Berlin.

14 Rees, *Selling Politics*, p. 24.

15 See p. 104.

16 Rees, *Auschwitz*, Kindle edition, p. 89.

17 Höss, *Commandant*, p. 147.

18 See, for example, the testimony of Sonderkommandos Dario Gabbai and Morris Venezia about the horror of this killing method: Rees, *Auschwitz*, Kindle edition, pp. 289–90.

19 Peter Löffler (ed.), *Bischof Clemens August Graf von Galen. Akten, Briefe und Predigten 1933–1946*, vol. 2: *1939–1946*, Matthias-Grünewald-Verlag, 1988, pp. 876–8; original in BAM, Fremde Provenienzen, A 8, Niederschrift der Predigt des Bischofs von Münster, Sonntag, den 3. August 1941, in der St. Lambertikirche in Münster.

20 Kershaw, *'Hitler Myth'*, p. 178.

21 Ibid.

22 Note, however, that Galen's sermon was likely one of a number of factors in that decision. See David Cesarani, *Final Solution: The Fate of the Jews 1933–1949*, Macmillan, 2016, p. 284.

23 Beth A. Griech-Polelle, *Bishop von Galen: German Catholicism and National Socialism*, Yale University Press, 2002, Kindle edition, pp. 20, 30 and 132–4.

24 Elke Fröhlich (ed.), *Die Tagebücher von Joseph Goebbels*, Teil II: *Diktate 1941–1945*, vol. 1: *Juli–September 1941*, K. G. Saur, 1996, pp. 251–5, here p. 254, entry for 18 August 1941.

25 There was one famous German demonstration protesting against the deportation of the Jews. This was held outside the Jewish community building on Rosenstrasse in Berlin between 27 February and 6 March 1943. But this was not a case of ordinary Germans protesting at the removal of Jewish families out of principle. It was a protest by the non-Jewish German wives of Jewish men who had been confined in the building prior to deportation. See https://encyclopedia.ushmm.org/content/en/article/the-rosenstrasse-demonstration-1943.

26 Thus echoing Hitler's words. Griech-Polelle, *Bishop von Galen*, Kindle edition, p. 107.

27 Ibid., pp. 62–3.

28 See pp. 218–19.

29 Domarus (ed.), *Hitler. Reden und Proklamationen*, vol. 2, pp. 1762–3, Hitler speech of 3 October 1941.

30 *Preussische Zeitung*, vol. 11, no. 281 (10 October 1941), p. 1.

31 Elke Fröhlich (ed.), *Die Tagebücher von Joseph Goebbels*, Teil II: *Diktate 1941–1945*, vol. 2: *Oktober–Dezember 1941*, K. G. Saur, 1996, pp. 84–90, here pp. 87, 89–90, entry for 10 October 1941.

32 Elke Fröhlich (ed.), *Die Tagebücher von Joseph Goebbels*, Teil II: *Diktate 1941–1945*, vol. 3: *Januar–März 1942*, K. G. Saur, 1994, pp. 87–93, here p. 93, entry for 11 January 1942.

33 Ibid., pp. 208–13, here p. 213, entry for 29 January 1942.

34 Rees, *Selling Politics*, p. 83.

35 Laurence Rees, *Hitler and Stalin: The Tyrants and the Second World War*, Viking, 2020, Kindle edition, p. 159.

36 Baynes (ed.), *Early Speeches*, p. 29, Hitler speech of 28 July 1922 (first published in *Völkischer Beobachter*, 16 August 1922).

37 Domarus (ed.), *Hitler. Reden und Proklamationen*, vol. 2, pp. 1794–8, Hitler speech of 11 December 1941.

38 Author interview with Professor Karen M. Douglas.

39 Max Domarus (ed.), *Hitler: Speeches and Proclamations 1932–1945*, vol. 3: *1939–1940*, Bolchazy-Carducci, 1997, pp. 1447–9, Hitler speech of 30 January 1939.

40 Fröhlich (ed.), *Die Tagebücher von Joseph Goebbels*, Teil II, vol. 2, pp. 498–9, entry for 13 December 1941.

41 J. L. Freedman and S. C. Fraser, 'Compliance without Pressure: The Foot-in-the-Door Technique', *Journal of Personality and Social Psychology*, vol. 4, no. 2 (1966), pp. 195–202.

42 Aly and Heim, *Architects of Annihilation*, Kindle edition, p. 192.

43 Ervin Staub, 'The Psychology of Bystanders, Perpetrators, and Heroic Helpers', in Leonard S. Newman and Ralph Erber (eds.), *Understanding Genocide: The Social Psychology of the Holocaust*, Oxford University Press, 2002, Kindle edition, p. 12.

44 Montague, *Chełmno and the Holocaust*, pp. 34 and 40.

45 Ibid., p. 32.

46 Rees, *Auschwitz*, Kindle edition, p. 114, testimony of Zofia Szałek.

47 Testimony of Kurt Moebius, interrogated 8 November 1961, p. 6, 2 ZStL 203 AR-Z 69/59 Bd3.

48 Höss, *Commandant*, p. 206.

49 *KL Auschwitz Seen by the SS*, Auschwitz-Birkenau State Museum, 1998, p. 105, testimony of Pery Broad.

50 Höss, *Commandant*, pp. 230–31.

51 Although the vast majority of those killed in the death camps in the General Government were Jews, Sinti and Roma were also murdered there, as were non-Jewish Poles.

52 Sereny, *Into That Darkness*, p. 54.

53 BArch, R 9361-III/63391, personal SS file of Lorenz Hackenholt, fol. 2, handwritten CV.

54 BArch, B 162/4428 (AR-Z 251/59, vol. 4), fols. 703–4, statement of Werner Dubois, 7 September 1961, and BArch, B 162/3170, fol. 167, testimony of Werner Dubois, 18 September 1961.

55 BArch, B 162/3170, fol. 167, testimony of Werner Dubois, 18 September 1961.

56 BArch, R 9361-III/516134, SSO file Dr August Becker, Disziplinar-Sache Dr Becker, August / Hackenholt, Lorenz, wegen Tätlicher Beleidigung.

57 Yitzhak Arad, *Belzec, Sobibor, Treblinka: The Operation Reinhard Death Camps*, Indiana University Press, 1999, pp. 70–71.

58 BArch, B 162/3171, fol. 69, 77 (pp. 1511 and 1519 of AR-Z 252/59), interrogation of Karl Alfred Schluch, 10 November 1961.

59 BArch, B 162/3171, fol. 85 (p. 1527 of AR-Z 252/59), interrogation of Ernst Willy Grossmann, 9 November 1961.

60 BArch, B 162/3171, fol. 27 (p. 1469 of AR-Z 252/59), interrogation of Robert Jührs, 11 October 1961.

61 Michael S. Bryant, *Eyewitness to Genocide: The Operation Reinhard Death Camp Trials, 1955–1966*, University of Tennessee Press, 2014, p. 47.

62 Rees, *Holocaust*, Kindle edition, p. 340.

63 There were three distinct camps that are normally collectively referred to as 'Auschwitz': the original main camp by the Sola river, the large new camp at Auschwitz Birkenau just over a mile away to the north-west, and Auschwitz Monowitz, three miles east of Birkenau.

64 Michael Jones, *After Hitler: The Last Days of the Second World War in Europe*, John Murray, 2015, p. 195; article by Boris Polevoy, *Pravda*, 2 February 1945.

65 *KL Auschwitz*, pp. 129–30.

66 The vast majority of those sent to Sobibór and the other Reinhard camps were murdered shortly after arrival. A mere handful were occasionally selected to work in the camp – performing tasks like cleaning the camp or sorting the belongings of those who were killed. Toivi Blatt, a Polish Jew, was one of those selected for this work.

67 Rees, *Auschwitz*, Kindle edition, location 3862–77.

68 There is a vast literature on confirmation bias. See for instance Rüdiger F. Pohl (ed.), *Cognitive Illusions: Intriguing Phenomena in Thinking, Judgment and Memory*, Routledge, 2017.

69 Rees, *Nazis: A Warning from History*, Kindle edition, pp. 286–7. Like Toivi Blatt, Samuel Willenberg was one of the few Jews selected on arrival at an Operation Reinhard camp to work, and so he wasn't killed immediately. Also like Toivi Blatt, Willenberg survived the war only because he took part in a breakout from his camp – Willenberg from Treblinka in August 1943 and Blatt from Sobibór in October 1943.

70 There was, for a brief period, a 'family camp' in Auschwitz that held around 18,000 men, women and children deported from the ghetto camp of Theresienstadt in Czechoslovakia between September 1943 and July 1944. The Nazis planned to use these Jews for propaganda purposes. The vast majority of children and old people who arrived at Auschwitz were sent to the gas chamber on arrival. See Rees, *Auschwitz*, Kindle edition, p. 237.

71 Rees, *Holocaust*, Kindle edition, pp. 371–2.

72 Jadwiga Bezwińska and Danuta Czech (eds.), *Amidst a Nightmare of Crime: Manuscripts of Prisoners in Crematorium Squads Found at Auschwitz*, Howard

Fertig, 1992, p. 56, deposition of Alter Feinsilber (also known as Stanisław Jankowski).

73 Arad, *Belzec, Sobibor, Treblinka*, p. 87.

74 BArch, B 162/21871, fols. 317–25, Franz Suchomel, 'Christian Wirth genannt "Christian der Grausame" oder "Stuka"', p. 6.

75 Earl W. Kintner (ed.), *Trial of Alfons Klein, Adolf Wahlmann, Heinrich Ruoff, Karl Willig, Adolf Merkle, Irmgard Huber, and Philipp Blum (The Hadamar Trial)*, William Hodge, 1949, p. 91.

76 BArch, B 162/21871, fols. 317–25, Suchomel, 'Christian Wirth genannt "Christian der Grausame" oder "Stuka"', pp. 1, 6.

77 Only with the arrival of hundreds of thousands of Hungarian Jews from May to July 1944 was the killing capacity of Auschwitz stretched, but even then the gas chambers could cope with the demand; it was the crematoria that struggled. So pits were dug and bodies burnt in the open air.

78 See the Auschwitz Museum calculations at https://www.auschwitz.org/en/history/auschwitz-and-shoah/gas-chambers/. The limitation on the killing capacity at Auschwitz Birkenau tended to be the Nazis' ability to dispose of the bodies. As the Auschwitz Museum states: 'According to calculations made by the Zentralbauleitung on June 28, 1943, the crematoria could burn 4,416 corpses per day – 1,440 each in crematoria II and III, and 768 each in crematoria IV and V. This meant that the crematoria could burn over 1.6 million corpses per year. Prisoners assigned to do the burning stated that the daily capacity of the four crematoria in Birkenau was higher – about 8 thousand corpses.'

79 Rees, *Their Darkest Hour*, Kindle edition, p. 27, testimony of Oskar Groening.

80 Jill Stephenson, *Women in Nazi Germany*, Routledge, 2013, Kindle edition, p. 42.

81 United States Holocaust Memorial Museum, *12 Years That Shook the World*, Erin Harper and Dr Patricia Heberer Rice discuss Pauline Kneissler, https://www.ushmm.org/learn/podcasts-and-audio/12-years-that-shook-the-world/convinced. Kneissler gave these lethal injections at a mental hospital in the period after the euthanasia gassing centres had stopped their work.

82 Wendy Lower, *Hitler's Furies: German Women in the Nazi Killing Fields*, Vintage Digital, 2013, Kindle edition, p. 154.

83 Ibid., pp. 132–3 (Erna Petri). Also see pp. 137–8 (Gertrude Segel).

84 Elissa Mailänder, *Female SS Guards and Workaday Violence: The Majdanek Concentration Camp 1942–1944*, Michigan State University Press, 2015, pp. 68–9.

85 Margarete Buber-Neumann, *Under Two Dictators: Prisoner of Stalin and Hitler*, Vintage Digital, 2013, Kindle edition, pp. 231–2.

86 Craig Haney, Curtis Banks and Philip Zimbardo, 'A Study of Prisoners and Guards in a Simulated Prison', *Naval Research Reviews*, vol. 26 (September 1973), pp. 1–17.

87 See, for instance, Richard A. Griggs, 'Coverage of the Stanford Prison Experiment in Introductory Psychology Textbooks', *Teaching of Psychology*, vol. 41, issue 3 (July 2014), pp. 195–203. See also Stephen Reicher and S. Alexander Haslam, 'Rethinking the Psychology of Tyranny: The BBC Prison Study', *British Journal of Social Psychology*, vol. 45, issue 1 (2006), pp. 1–40.

88 Mailänder, *Female SS Guards*, p. 92.

89 Ibid., p. 219.

90 Ibid., pp. 242 and 237.

91 Klee, Dressen and Riess (eds.), '*The Good Old Days*', pp. 291–2.

92 Mailänder, *Female SS Guards*, p. 265.

93 Renate Wiggershaus, *Frauen unterm Nationalsozialismus*, Peter Hammer Verlag, 1984, p. 96, as quoted in Stephenson, *Women in Nazi Germany*, Kindle edition, pp. 112–13.

94 Bauman, *Modernity and the Holocaust*, Kindle edition, p. 167.

Chapter 12: Stoking Fear

1 Previously unpublished testimony.

2 Previously unpublished testimony.

3 Robert Scott Kellner (ed.), *My Opposition: The Diary of Friedrich Kellner – A German against the Third Reich*, Cambridge University Press, 2018, p. 268, entry for 7 August 1943.

4 Domarus (ed.), *Hitler. Reden und Proklamationen*, vol. 2, pp. 1975–6, Göring speech, Reich Ministry of Aviation, 30 January 1943.

5 Leon Festinger, Henry W. Riecken and Stanley Schachter, *When Prophecy Fails: A Social and Psychological Study of a Modern Group that Predicted the Destruction of the World*, Wilder Publications, 2014, Kindle edition, p. 3.

6 Ibid.

7 Ibid., p. 4.

8 As with all these classic studies, there is a huge literature debating the merits of the work. See, for instance, Camille Morvan with Alexander J.

O'Connor, *An Analysis of Leon Festinger's A Theory of Cognitive Dissonance*, Routledge, 2017, and Fernando Bermejo-Rubio, 'The Process of Jesus' Deification and Cognitive Dissonance Theory', *Numen*, vol. 64, no. 2/3 (2017), pp. 119–52.

9 Ulrich Herbert, 'Echoes of the *Volksgemeinschaft*', in Steber and Gotto (eds.), *Visions of Community in Nazi Germany*, Kindle edition, p. 62, SD report from 3 September 1942.

10 'Nun, Volk, steh auf, und Sturm brich los! Rede im Berliner Sportpalast', the written version of Goebbels' speech of 18 February 1943, reprinted in Joseph Goebbels, *Der steile Aufstieg. Reden und Aufsätze aus den Jahren 1942/43*, Zentralverlag der NSDAP, Verlag Franz Eher Nachfolger, 1944, pp. 167–204. See https://research.calvin.edu/german-propaganda-archive/goeb36.htm.

11 Domarus (ed.), *Hitler. Reden und Proklamationen*, vol. 2, p. 1985, from the Führer's Headquarters, 3 February 1943.

12 Anthony Eden, statement in House of Commons, 17 December 1942, https://api.parliament.uk/historic-hansard/commons/1942/dec/17/united-nations-declaration#S5CV0385P0_19421217_HOC_280.

13 Minutes of Goebbels' propaganda conference, 12 December 1942, quoted in Peter Longerich, *'Davon haben wir nichts gewusst!' Die Deutschen und die Judenverfolgung 1933–1945*, Siedler Verlag, 2006, p. 257.

14 Ibid., p. 259.

15 Fröhlich (ed.), *Die Tagebücher von Joseph Goebbels*, Teil II, vol. 3, pp. 401–8, here p. 408, entry for 3 March 1942.

16 Elke Fröhlich (ed.), *Die Tagebücher von Joseph Goebbels*, Teil II: *Diktate 1941–1945*, vol. 4: *April–Juni 1942*, K. G. Saur, 1995, pp. 179–90, here p. 183, entry for 27 April 1942.

17 Interview in *Goebbels: Master of Propaganda*, BBC TV 1992, written and produced by Laurence Rees.

18 Katyn was one of several murder sites for these people taken from occupied Poland. Other locations included Kalinin and Kharkiv prisons.

19 Elke Fröhlich (ed.), *Die Tagebücher von Joseph Goebbels*, Teil II: *Diktate 1941–1945*, vol. 8: *April–Juni 1943*, K. G. Saur, 1993, p. 115, entry for 17 April 1943.

20 See pp. 38–9.

21 Rees, *Holocaust*, Kindle edition, p. 364.

22 Lars Svendsen, *A Philosophy of Evil*, Dalkey Archive Press, 2010, p. 160. Original Stangl quote in Sereny, *Into That Darkness*, pp. 232–3.

23 See pp. 240–41. Also Waller, *Becoming Evil*, pp. 216–17, where he also discusses the Stangl quote.

24 *Touched by Auschwitz*, BBC TV, written and produced by Laurence Rees; first transmitted on BBC2, 27 January 2015.

25 Rees, *Auschwitz*, Kindle edition, pp. 360–61.

26 There was also an uprising by Sonderkommandos at Auschwitz in October 1944, although this was crushed by the SS. The most famous of several escapes from the camp was by Rudolf Vrba and Alfred Wetzler in 1944. See Rees, *Auschwitz*, Kindle edition, pp. 305–6.

27 David Stahel, *Operation Barbarossa and Germany's Defeat in the East*, Cambridge University Press, 2009, p. 73.

28 'Vom Wesen der Krise', *Das Reich*, 30 May 1943, reprinted in Goebbels, *Der steile Aufstieg*, p. 283.

29 Domarus (ed.), *Hitler. Reden und Proklamationen*, vol. 2, p. 1970, Hitler's New Year proclamation on 1 January 1943.

30 Ibid.

31 Ibid., p. 1989, Hitler's proclamation to soldiers of Army Group South, 19 February 1943.

32 Hugh Gibson (ed.), *The Ciano Diaries*, Simon Publications, 2001, p. 569, entry for 11 January 1943. The Germans did construct two types of flying bomb: the V1 first launched against the Allies in June 1944 and the V2 first launched against the Allies in September 1944. While both were new types of weapon, and responsible for several thousand deaths, neither was a miraculous war-changing invention.

33 Weber, *Essays*, p. 248.

34 Gibson (ed.), *The Ciano Diaries*, p. 583, entry for 23 December 1943.

35 Longerich, *Goebbels*, Kindle edition, p. 711, diary 30 October 1943.

36 Uriel Tal, *Religion, Politics and Ideology in the Third Reich: Selected Essays*, Routledge, 2004, p. 28.

37 Mary Ann Frese Witt, *The Search for Modern Tragedy: Aesthetic Fascism in Italy and France*, Cornell University Press, 2001, p. 95. Mussolini wrote this in 1912.

38 Elke Fröhlich (ed.), *Die Tagebücher von Joseph Goebbels*, Teil II: *Diktate 1941–1945*, vol. 9: *Juli–September 1943*, K. G. Saur, 1993, p. 169, entry for 27 July 1943.

39 Ibid., p. 160, entry for 25 July 1943.

40 Longerich, *Himmler*, Kindle edition, pp. 486–7.

41 Elke Fröhlich (ed.), *Die Tagebücher von Joseph Goebbels*, Teil II: *Diktate 1941–1945*, vol. 10: *Oktober–Dezember 1943*, K. G. Saur, 1994, pp. 276–80, here p. 279, entry for 12 November 1943.

42 *Trial of the Major War Criminals before the International Military Tribunal*, vol. XXIX: *Documents and Other Material in Evidence*, The International Military Tribunal, 1948, Numbers 1850-PS to 2233-PS, Document 1919-PS, pp. 110–73, here pp. 145–6, 164, 170, Himmler Posen speech, 4 October 1943.

43 Ibid.

44 Toivi Blatt testimony in *Auschwitz: The Nazis and the 'Final Solution'*, BBC TV, episode 4: 'Corruption', written and produced by Laurence Rees; first broadcast on BBC2, 1 February 2005.

45 Rees, *Auschwitz*, Kindle edition, p. 225.

46 Linda Breder testimony in *Auschwitz: The Nazis and the 'Final Solution'*, episode 4, 'Corruption'.

47 See the testimony of Konrad Morgen in Frankfurt-am-Main on 8 March 1962, and at the Auschwitz trial in Frankfurt, in Hermann Langbein, *Der Auschwitz-Prozess. Eine Dokumentation*, Neue Kritik, 1995, pp. 143–5.

48 Rees, *Auschwitz*, Kindle edition, pp. 245–7.

49 Himmler Posen speech, 4 October 1943.

50 Himmler Posen speech, 6 October 1943, in Smith and Peterson (eds.), *Heinrich Himmler. Geheimreden*, pp. 169–70.

51 Rees, *Auschwitz*, Kindle edition, p. 172.

52 Smith and Peterson (eds.), *Heinrich Himmler. Geheimreden*, p. 170.

53 Richard Holmes (ed.), *The World at War: The Landmark Oral History*, Ebury Press, 2007, p. 327.

54 Timothy P. Jackson, *Mordecai Would Not Bow Down: Anti-Semitism, the Holocaust, and Christian Supersessionism*, Oxford University Press, 2021, p. 62.

55 See p. 39.

56 See Yuval Noah Harari, *Homo Deus: A Brief History of Tomorrow*, Vintage, 2016, Kindle edition, pp. 349–53, for a discussion about 'Our Boys Didn't Die in Vain'.

57 Domarus (ed.), *Hitler. Reden und Proklamationen*, vol. 2, pp. 2051, 2054, Hitler speech of 8 November 1943.

58 See, for instance, Hal R. Arkes and Catherine Blumer, 'The Psychology of Sunk Cost', *Organizational Behavior and Human Decision Processes*, vol. 35, issue 1 (1985), pp. 124–40, https://www.sciencedirect.com/science/article/abs/pii/0749597885900494; and David Ronayne, Daniel Sgroi and Anthony

Tuckwell, 'Evaluating the Sunk Cost Effect', IZA Institute of Labor Economics, 2021, IZA DP no. 14257, https://docs.iza.org/dp14257.pdf.

59 Kershaw, *'Hitler Myth'*, p. 212.

60 Fröhlich (ed.), *Die Tagebücher von Joseph Goebbels*, Teil II, vol. 10, pp. 257–64, here p. 263, entry for 9 November 1943.

61 Malinowski, *Nazis and Nobles*, Kindle edition, pp. 260–64.

62 Johannes Hürter, 'Auf dem Weg zur Militäropposition. Tresckow, Gersdorff, der Vernichtungskrieg und der Judenmord. Neue Dokumente über das Verhältnis der Heeresgruppe Mitte zur Einsatzgruppe B im Jahr 1941', *Vierteljahrshefte für Zeitgeschichte*, vol. 52, no. 3 (2004), pp. 527–62, here pp. 552–8.

63 Previously unpublished testimony.

64 Rees, *Dark Charisma*, Kindle edition, pp. 382–3.

65 See pp. 15–16.

66 Fabian von Schlabrendorff, *The Secret War against Hitler*, Westview Press, 1994, pp. 268–9. Georg von Boeselager was one of those who admitted that he wasn't able to shoot Hitler in cold blood (see ibid., p. 269). There were also rumours that Hitler wore a bullet-proof vest. But even if, as the rumours also attested, he had a bullet-proof hat on his head, a shot in his face would still almost certainly have proved fatal. (See Kershaw, *Nemesis*, pp. 660–61.)

67 Schlabrendorff, *The Secret War against Hitler*, p. 231.

68 After the war, Gersdorff presented himself as the archetypal German hero – someone who didn't immediately recognize the barbaric nature of the 'war of extermination' in the east. But Gersdorff knew what the Einsatzgruppen were doing. See Hürter, 'Auf dem Weg zur Militäropposition', pp. 527–62.

69 Norman J. W. Goda, 'Black Marks: Hitler's Bribery of His Senior Officers during World War II', in Emmanuel Kreike and William Chester Jordan (eds.), *Corrupt Histories*, University of Rochester Press, 2004, p. 124.

70 Rees, *Their Darkest Hour*, Kindle edition, pp. 229–30.

71 Holmes (ed.), *The World at War*, p. 419.

72 Becker, *The Denial of Death*, Kindle edition, p. 25. Also see pp. 70–72.

73 Don Allen Gregory, *After Valkyrie: Military and Civilian Consequences of the Attempt to Assassinate Hitler*, McFarland, 2019, p. 178.

74 Kershaw, *'Hitler Myth'*, pp. 217–18.

75 Ibid., p. 217.

76 Elke Fröhlich (ed.), *Die Tagebücher von Joseph Goebbels*, Teil II: *Diktate 1941–1945*, vol. 13: *Juli–September 1944*, K. G. Saur, 1995, pp. 201–17, here p. 214, entry for 3 August 1944.

77 Helmut Heiber (ed.), *Goebbels-Reden*, vol. 2: *1939–1945*, Droste Verlag, 1972, pp. 356–7, Goebbels speech, broadcast 26 July 1944.

78 Longerich, *Goebbels*, Kindle edition, p. 733, Goebbels diary for 6 June 1944, referencing a conversation he had with Hitler the day before, 5 June.

79 Richard Overy, *The Bombing War: Europe 1939–1945*, Penguin, 2014, Kindle edition, p. 470.

80 Kershaw, '*Volksgemeinschaft*: Potential and Limitations of the Concept', p. 40.

81 Overy, *Bombing War*, Kindle edition, pp. 478–85.

82 Previously unpublished testimony.

83 Ian Kershaw, *The End: The Defiance and Destruction of Hitler's Germany 1944–1945*, Allen Lane, 2011, p. 113.

84 Ibid., pp. 114–18.

85 Kershaw, '*Volksgemeinschaft*: Potential and Limitations of the Concept', p. 40.

86 Ibid.; Richard Bessel, 'The End of the *Volksgemeinschaft*', in Steber and Gotto (eds.), *Visions of Community in Nazi Germany*, Kindle edition, p. 291.

87 Kershaw, *The End*, p. 319.

88 'Werewolf' in English.

89 Frederick Taylor, *Exorcising Hitler: The Occupation and Denazification of Germany*, Bloomsbury, 2011, Kindle edition, pp. 58–67.

90 Longerich, *Goebbels*, Kindle edition, p. 775, Goebbels diary for 6 February 1945.

91 Louis P. Lochner (ed.), *The Goebbels Diaries*, Hamish Hamilton, 1948, p. 200, entry for 2 March 1943.

92 Kristin Laurin, Aaron C. Kay and Gavan J. Fitzsimons, 'Reactance versus Rationalization: Divergent Responses to Policies that Constrain Freedom', *Psychological Science*, vol. 23, no. 2 (February 2012), pp. 205–9, https://www.researchgate.net/publication/221744497_Reactance_Versus_Rationalization_Divergent_Responses_to_Policies_That_Constrain_Freedom. Also see Association for Psychological Science, 'People Rationalize Situations They're Stuck with, but Rebel when They Think There's an Out', 1 November 2011, https://www.psychologicalscience.org/news/releases/people-rationalize-situations-theyre-stuck-with-but-rebel-when-they-think-theres-an-out.html.

93 James Boswell, *The Life of Samuel Johnson, LL. D.*, J. Richardson, 1823, vol 3, p. 171.

94 Elke Fröhlich (ed.), *Die Tagebücher von Joseph Goebbels*, Teil II: *Diktate 1941–1945*, vol. 15: *Januar–April 1945*, K. G. Saur, 1995, pp. 475–88, here p. 486, entry for 12 March 1945.

95 See pp. 110–11.
96 Prosecutors were aware of Werner Best's history with the Nazi Party. But though he was initially sentenced to death by Danish authorities, he was released from prison in 1951. In the early 1970s he was charged again but declared medically unfit to stand trial. He still lived many more years, dying in 1989. See Ingrao, *Believe and Destroy*, Kindle edition, pp. 238–40.
97 Sepp Dietrich features on the cover of this book.
98 Felix Kersten, *Totenkopf und Treue. Heinrich Himmler ohne Uniform. Aus den Tagebuchblättern des finnischen Medizinalrats Felix Kersten*, Robert Mölich Verlag, 1952, pp. 358–9, Himmler's letter of 21 March 1945.
99 Longerich, *Himmler*, Kindle edition, p. 728.
100 Fröhlich (ed.), *Die Tagebücher von Joseph Goebbels*, Teil II, vol. 15, pp. 559–74, here p. 568, entry for 22 March 1945.
101 '". . . warum dann überhaupt noch leben!" Hitlers letzte Lagebesprechungen am 23., 25. und 27. April 1945', *Der Spiegel*, 10 January 1966, pp. 37–8.
102 Kershaw, *Nemesis*, pp. 1037–8 note 156 for a detailed examination of the evidence about the method of Hitler's suicide.
103 Domarus (ed.), *Hitler. Reden und Proklamationen*, vol. 2, pp. 2236–7, 2239, Hitler's Political Testament, 29 April 1945.
104 '". . . warum dann überhaupt noch leben!"', *Der Spiegel*.
105 Previously unpublished testimony.

Postscript

1 Previously unpublished testimony, and Rees, *Their Darkest Hour*, Kindle edition, pp. 249–54.
2 After her death, and the republication of her book, the author was revealed as a German journalist called Marta Hillers, who was thirty-three when the Red Army arrived in Berlin in 1945.
3 Anonymous, *A Woman in Berlin*, Virago, 2011, Kindle edition, p. 76.
4 Norman M. Naimark, *The Russians in Germany: A History of the Soviet Zone of Occupation, 1945–1949*, Harvard University Press, 1995, p. 93.
5 Anonymous, *A Woman in Berlin*, Kindle edition, p. 61.
6 Previously unpublished testimony from an interview with Dr Fritz Arlt.
7 Miriam Gebhardt, *Crimes Unspoken: The Rape of German Women at the End of the Second World War*, Polity, 2017, Kindle edition, pp. 2 and 19.

Gebhardt's own figure of 860,000 includes both women and men who were raped. Women comprise the greater proportion.

8 Anonymous, *A Woman in Berlin*, Kindle edition, p. 140.

9 Naimark, *The Russians in Germany*, pp. 121–2.

10 Hsu-Ming Teo, 'The Continuum of Sexual Violence in Occupied Germany, 1945–49', *Women's History Review*, vol. 5, no. 2 (1996), pp. 191–218, quoting Ute Frevert, *Women in German History: From Bourgeois Emancipation to Sexual Liberation*, Berg, 1989, p. 258.

11 Kaete O'Connell, 'The Taste of Defeat: Food, Peace and Power in US-Occupied Germany', in Heather Merle Benbow and Heather R. Perry (eds.), *Food, Culture and Identity in Germany's Century of War*, Palgrave Macmillan, 2019, p. 211.

12 Alice Weinreb, '"For the Hungry Have No Past nor Do They Belong to a Political Party": Debates over German Hunger after World War II', *Central European History*, vol. 45, no. 1 (2012), pp. 50–78.

13 Rolf-Dieter Müller, (ed.), *Der Zusammenbruch des Deutschen Reiches 1945. Die Folgen des Zweiten Weltkrieges*, Deutsche Verlags-Anstalt, 2008, p. 420.

14 Rees, *Behind Closed Doors*, Kindle edition, p. 385.

15 Previously unpublished testimony.

16 Höss, *Commandant*, p. 165.

17 Rees, *Auschwitz*, Kindle edition, pp. 365–6.

18 Mathilde Wolff-Mönckeberg, *On the Other Side: Letters to My Children from Germany 1940–46*, Persephone Books, 2016, p. 131, dated 1 May 1945. Separated from her children, Wolff-Mönckeberg wrote letters to them during the war, and in the immediate aftermath, that circumstances prevented her from sending.

19 Ibid., p. 140, dated 17 May 1945.

20 Winston S. Churchill, *The Second World War*, vol. V: *Closing the Ring*, Penguin, 2005, pp. 329–30.

21 Waller, *Becoming Evil*, pp. 59–70 and 77.

22 Gilbert, *Nuremberg Diary*, pp. 43 (Göring) and 152 (Ribbentrop).

23 Ibid., p. 265.

24 Ibid., p. 266. Note that the quotes 'southern German' and a 'Prussian could never bring himself to do things like that' attributed to Göring were Gilbert's recollection of what Göring said, rather than direct quotes from him.

25 Goldensohn, *The Nuremberg Interviews*, Kindle edition, p. 188.

26 Gilbert, *Nuremberg Diary*, pp. 15–16.

27 Goldensohn, *The Nuremberg Interviews*, Kindle edition, pp. 30–32.

28 Gilbert, *Nuremberg Diary*, p. 388.

29 Thomas Talhelm, Xuemin Zhang and Shigehiro Oishi, 'Moving Chairs in Starbucks: Observational Studies Find Rice-Wheat Cultural Differences in Daily Life in China', *Science Advances*, vol. 4, issue 4 (2018), https://www.science.org/doi/10.1126/sciadv.aap8469. Also see Sapolsky, *Behave*, pp. 560–62.

30 Ervin Staub, 'The Psychology of Bystanders, Perpetrators, and Heroic Helpers', in Leonard S. Newman and Ralph Erber (eds.), *Understanding Genocide: The Social Psychology of the Holocaust*, Oxford University Press, 2002, Kindle edition, p. 16. The notion that there exists a particular 'authoritarian personality' was popularized shortly after the war by the publication of *The Authoritarian Personality* by Theodor Adorno and his colleagues Else Frenkel-Brunswik, Daniel Levinson and Nevitt Sanford (Harper & Brothers, 1950). The book was subsequently criticized for a number of reasons, including methodological issues. See, for instance, Waller, *Becoming Evil*, p. 85. Waller concludes that 'the original hypotheses about the psychodynamics of the authoritarian personality have yet to be validated.'

31 Rees, *Nazis: A Warning from History*, Kindle edition, p. 46.

32 Previously unpublished testimony. Also see Kurt Lewin, *Resolving Social Conflicts and Field Theory in Social Science*, ed. Gertrud Weiss Lewin, American Psychological Association, 1997 (first published 1948), Kindle edition. Much of the psychological literature on national character now seems quaintly dated. The pioneering social psychologist Kurt Lewin – a German who emigrated to America in 1933 – thought he saw clear differences between Americans and Germans in psychological terms. In his *Resolving Social Conflicts* he wrote at p. 21: 'In America, two scientists or politicians may emerge from a hard theoretical or political fight and yet be on cordial terms with each other. In Germany, for most persons, a political or even a scientific disagreement seems to be inseparable from moral disapproval. The congratulations that the defeated candidate for the presidency sends to the elected, after a hard battle, would sound rather strange in Germany.'

While those sentiments might possibly have been true when Lewin wrote them – although they read like the broadest of generalizations – they are certainly not true today. Not only did the 'defeated candidate for the presidency' in America in 2020 not congratulate the winner, but, having lost the election, he attempted to destroy the whole democratic process. It is hard to imagine anything similar happening in contemporary Germany. It is a reminder, once again, of the danger of thinking of 'national character' as either universal or fixed.

33 Testimony of Lt General DeWitt before a subcommittee of the House Naval Affairs Committee, 13 April 1943. Also see Gen. John L. DeWitt Personal Papers, United States National Archives Identifier 7432140, https://text-message.blogs.archives.gov/2013/11/22/a-slaps-a-slap-general-john-l-dewitt-and-four-little-words/.

34 Erika Lee, *The Making of Asian America*, Simon & Schuster, 2015, p. 217.

35 George R. Mastroianni, *Of Mind and Murder: Toward a More Comprehensive Psychology of the Holocaust*, Oxford University Press, 2019, Kindle edition, p. 362.

36 This refers only to the 'Trial of the Major War Criminals before the International Military Tribunal' at Nuremberg.

37 Mastroianni, *Of Mind and Murder*, Kindle edition, p. 326.

38 David R. Henderson, 'German Economic Miracle', *Econlib*, https://www.econlib.org/library/Enc/GermanEconomicMiracle.html.

39 Taylor, *Exorcising Hitler*, Kindle edition, p. 364.

40 de Jong, *Nazi Billionaires*, Kindle edition, p. 224. Also see Ofer Aderet, 'Details of Porsche's Nazi Ties Spoil Centennial Bash', *Haaretz*, 11 October 2009, https://www.haaretz.com/israel-news/culture/2009-10-11/ty-article/details-of-porsches-nazi-ties-spoil-centennial-bash/0000017f-e0c9-d75c-a7ff-fccd387c0000.

41 de Jong, *Nazi Billionaires*, Kindle edition, pp. 234 and 236.

42 Aly and Heim, *Architects of Annihilation*, Kindle edition, p. 28.

43 Aleksander Lasik, 'The Apprehension and Punishment of the Auschwitz Concentration Camp Staff', in *Auschwitz 1940–1945: Central Issues in the History of the Camp*, vol. V, Auschwitz–Birkenau State Museum, 2000, pp. 99–119.

44 Previously unpublished testimony.

45 Previously unpublished testimony.

Twelve Warnings

1 Rees, *Their Darkest Hour*, Kindle edition, p. 260.

2 Ibid., pp. 24–30, here p. 26.

3 At first sight you might think this is an example of what Hannah Arendt famously called 'the banality of evil' – a phrase she used in her book *Eichmann in Jerusalem: A Report on the Banality of Evil*, Penguin Classics, 2006 (first published 1963). But while I had the same experience as her on meeting former Nazis who had committed terrible acts, and felt they didn't conform to the

caricature killers of our imagination, I have a problem with the word 'banal' in this context. Evil, to my mind, is never banal; and nor was the Nazi belief system that underpinned the actions of perpetrators like Eichmann or Groening, no matter how ordinary they seemed as personalities after the war.

4 Educated in Germany in the 1930s, after leaving school Groening worked in a bank, but coming as he did from a family of German nationalists he volunteered to join the SS shortly after the war broke out. After he was posted to Auschwitz, his banking experience came in useful when he worked in the economic section at the camp, counting the money stolen from the murdered Jews. Several years after I met him, and nearly seventy years after the end of the war, the German authorities decided to prosecute him. He was finally convicted in 2015 of being an accessory to mass murder and sentenced to four years in jail. But he died in March 2018 at the age of ninety-six before entering prison.

5 Rees, *Their Darkest Hour*, Kindle edition, p. 167.

6 See pp. 70–72.

7 Ian Kershaw, *Personality and Power: Builders and Destroyers of Modern Europe*, Allen Lane, 2022, pp. 60–61.

8 See p. 241.

9 Kershaw, *Personality and Power*, p. 245.

10 Paul Preston, *Franco*, Harper Perennial, 2012, Kindle edition, p. 271.

11 See p. 155.

12 *Hitler's Table Talk*, 19 January 1942, p. 227. He explained here that while he was against duelling in general he was 'inclined' to 'permit' it 'between priests and between lawyers'.

13 See pp. 179–80.

14 Geoffrey P. Megargee, *Inside Hitler's High Command*, University Press of Kansas, 2000, p. 20.

15 See p. 174.

16 See pp. 218–19.

17 See pp. 128–9, 220, 261.

18 Previously unpublished testimony.

19 It is important to note that in moral terms, as I've written elsewhere, I don't believe there is an equivalence – as many Nazis claimed – between the Allied bombing campaigns and the Holocaust. See Rees, *Auschwitz*, Kindle edition, pp. 365–7. And this book pp. 319–20.

20 Rees, *Their Darkest Hour*, Kindle edition, pp. 13–18.

21 See p. 121.

Index

Abel, Theodore 44
Abraham, Max 369n23
adolescence 92–3
All Quiet on the Western Front (Remarque)
   17, 102–4
Allies 24–5, 286, 320, 322
  bombing of Germany 287, 291, 294,
    297, 307
  see also Versailles, treaty of
Allport, Gordon 45
Almond, Gabriel 317
Altrogge, Joseph 162–3
American Olympic Committee 181
amygdala 38, 332–3, 340
animal experiments 240
anti-Semitism 52
  BDM (Bund Deutscher Mädel) 97
  census (1916) 19–20
  confusing approaches to 41–4
  films 157
  in Germany 19–20
  Goebbels 43, 76, 103–4
  Himmler 43
  Hitler *see* Hitler, Adolf: Jews
  Klein 42–3
  media 157–8
  Nazis 93–4, 184
  Streicher 52, 157–8
  see also Jews
Aplerbeck mental hospital 171–2
appeasement 4
Arco auf Valley, Count Anton von 31
Ardennes Forest 232–3
armed forces *see* German Army
artillery 16
asylums 168, 171–2
Aufseherinnen (overseers) 279–80, 281
Augspurg, Anita 31
Auschwitz 57, 160, 254, 257–9, 273, 391n70

Block 11 259
  code 14f13 scheme 259–60
  doctors 278
  Fritzsch's experiment 259
  gas experiments 259–60
  theft from Jews 296
Auschwitz Birkenau 270, 273
  fake shower deception 274–5, 289–90
  modernity 273
  permanence 273
  supervision 278
Auschwitz Museum 392n78
Austria
  Germany invasion (First World War)
    arrests and imprisonment 196
    'Aryanization' process 198
    opposition to 196
    violence and looting 197
    welcome of 196
  incorporation into the Reich 198–9
  Jews
    deportations of 198, 200
    humiliation of 197–8
    targeting of 196–7, 197–8
    theft from 198, 200
  referendum (1938) 196
  threatened by Hitler 194–5
  welcome for Hitler 198–9

Babi Yar killings 252
Bach-Zelewski, Erich von dem 252–3
Backe, Herbert 236
Baillet-Latour, Count Henri de 184
Bamber, Rudy 143
Bamberg conference 82–4
Bandura, Professor Albert 225–6
Bauer, Gustav 35
Bauman, Professor Zygmunt 237, 282
Bavaria 29–30, 31

BDM (Bund Deutscher Mädel) 95
  anti-Semitism 97
  education 95
  ideological training 96
  pregnancies 97
  sex appeal of Hitler 96
  sexual encounters 96–7
  Volksgemeinschaft 95
Beck, József 206–7
Beck, Ludwig 26, 27, 190
  difficulties facing 193
  Hitler and agreement with broader
      policies 193, 203–4
    concerns about war plans 191
    failure to confront 193–4
  mentality 192–3
  Prussian military tradition 194
  viewed as a relic 193
Becker, Ernest 71, 305, 333
Beer-Hall Putsch 64–72, 73, 74, 77,
    80, 205
Bełżec death camp 269–72, 273,
    277–8
Beria, Lavrenti 175–6
Berlin Olympic Games (1936) 181–3
  celebrated success of 184–5
  hypocrisy 184
  lavish hospitality 184
  Olympic training courses for
      Jews 182
  politicization of 182, 184
  removal of anti-Semitic signs 184
Bernadotte, Count Folke 311–12
Best, Werner 55, 110–11, 209, 310, 311
biased thinking 45
Binding, Professor Karl 168, 169
Birenbaum, Halina 289
Bischoff, Helmuth 211, 212
Bismarck, Otto von 71
Black Thursday 89–90
Blaskowitz, General Johannes
  attack on Poland 209
  cataloguing and circulation of
      atrocities 216–17, 219
  Christianity 218, 337
  damage to career 218
  despised by Nazis 218
  education 218–19
  environmental influences 218–19
  genetic predisposition 218
  limited resistance 218–19, 221
  memo of complaint to Hitler 216
  worldview 220
Blatt, Toivi 274–5, 296
Blobel, Paul 247–8, 249
Blomberg, Werner von 125, 129, 130–31,
    147, 148, 150, 190, 337
  concerns about Hitler's war
      plans 191
  marriage 191, 193
  removal from office 191, 193
  scandal 191–2
Blumentritt, General 235
Boehm-Tettelbach, Karl 155, 304–5
Bolsheviks 21, 22, 287–8, 299
Bolshevism 38, 81, 110
  Hitler *see* Hitler, Adolf: Bolshevism
  Jews and 21, 32, 74
Bonaparte, Napoleon 16, 333, 338
Börgermoor concentration camp 159
Bormann, Martin 7, 48, 57, 261
  accessory to murder 58
  background 57
  imprisonment 58, 59
  reaction to conviction 59
Bouhler, Philipp 228
Braemer, Major General 215
brain, the 38, 92–3, 332–3, 334, 340
  Them and Us thinking 38–9, 104
  undeveloped 92–3
Brandenburg euthanasia centre 231
Brauchitsch, General Walther von 194,
    216, 219
  fearful of attacking western
      Europe 222
  loyalty to the army 223
  meeting with Hitler 222–3
Braun, Otto 121
Braunsteiner, Hermine 281
Brecht, Bertolt 146
Breder, Linda 296
Brest-Litovsk, treaty of 22

Britain
    military strength 221–2
    repelling Germany 221–2
    support from America 234
    see also Allies
Broad, Pery 274
Brockdorff-Rantzau, Count Ulrich
    von 35
Brown House 106
Browning, Christopher 246
Brückner, Hermine 281
Brundage, Avery 181–2, 184, 184–5
Brüning, Heinrich 114, 115, 119
Buber-Neumann, Margarete 279–80
Buchenwald concentration camp 255,
    277, 319
Buchner, Adolf 248–50
Buddha 5
Bumke, Professor Oswald 169
Bund Deutscher Mädel *see* BDM (Bund
    Deutscher Mädel)
Bundeswehr 305
Bürckel, Josef 148, 197
Bürgerbräukeller 77, 219, 220
Burte, Hermann 165–6

Castro, Fidel 333
Catholic church 173–4, 261–2
    removal of crucifixes 260–61
Central Powers
    armistice with Russia 21
    peace treaty with Russia 22
    peace treaty with Ukraine 21–2
    strikes 21
Centre Party 140
Chamberlain, Neville 195, 203
Channon, Sir Henry 'Chips' 181, 184
charismatic leadership 72, 292
Chełmno death camp 267–9
China 324
Christianity 47–8, 132, 140, 173–4
Churchill, Winston 3, 4, 222, 233, 321
Ciano, Count 292
Class, Heinrich 71
Clay, General Lucius 317–18
cognitive biases 7, 121, 278, 289, 299–300

cognitive dissonance 284, 292, 312
collectivist cultures 324
communism/communists 55, 86, 92, 96,
    131, 133
    accused of burning the Reichstag
        134–5, 136
    anti-democracy 122
    denied permission to hold
        demonstrations 86
    denied police protection 86
    fear of uprising 135
    general elections (1932) 122
    meetings in the Reichstag 134
    violent confrontations with
        Stormtroopers 121
    see also Bolsheviks; Bolshevism
Communist Party 31–2, 134, 138
concentration camps 137–8, 144, 149, 205
    breaking wills 159–60
    Christmas carol 159
    conversion to National Socialism 159
    euphemisms 225
    execution chambers 254–5
    Jehovah's Witnesses 159–61
    methods of murder 254–5
    murder of commissars 254
    political opponents of the Nazis 158
    re-education of inmates 158
    reuse of 319
    secrecy of 276
    SS brutality 158–9, 160
    see also Auschwitz; death camps; gas
        chambers; *individual concentration
        camps*
confirmation bias 94, 275
conspiracy theories 11–36
    communist uprisings 135–6
    German Army defeat 27–8
    Holocaust 11, 332
    inconsistencies in believers 265
    Jews
        and Bolshevism 21, 32, 74
        control of America 102, 265
        control of world finance 43
        plotting global power 43, 143
        and traitors 30

Jews – *cont'd.*
  language and 19
  loss of First World War 11, 13, 24
  plot to kill Hitler 219–20
  Reichstag fire 134–6
  scapegoating 19, 20
  secrets 19
  spread of 331–2
Conze, Werner 164
Cosmides, Professor Leda 6
Coubertin, Baron Pierre de 184
Cuno, Wilhelm 56
Czechoslovakia 202–3, 207

Dachau concentration camp 196, 254, 258, 319
Dall'Armi, Max von 149
Danzig 207
Darré, Walther 188
Das Reich 291
Das Schwarze Korps 201
Dawes Plan 74–5
death camps 271
  secrecy of 276
  see also Auschwitz; concentration camps; killing centres; *individual death camps*
Demmin 315–16
Der Angriff (The Attack) 87, 103
  apology 104
  duping of 104
  'Night at the Front' article 104
Der ewige Jude (The Eternal Jew) 157, 258
Der Fall Röhm (booklet) 118
Der Giftpilz (The Poisonous Mushroom) 175
Der Hitlerjunge Quex (Hitler Youth Quex) 368n10
Der Stürmer (newspaper) 158
Deutsche Werkgemeinschaft 50, 53
Deutscher Kampfbund (German Combat League) 62
Deutscher Volkswille (newspaper) 53
Deuxième Bureau 221–2
DeWitt, Lieutenant General John 326
Dickel, Professor Otto 50–51, 52, 53

dictators/dictatorship 63, 334
  conniving with elites 334–5
  corrupting youth 334
  destruction of human rights 127, 152, 335–6
  fear of intellectuals 336
  Hitler *see* Hitler, Adolf: dictatorship
  perception as heroes 333–4
  promise of future utopia 336–7
  Them and Us thinking 332–3
  value of enemies 337
  see also Mussolini, Benito; Stalin, Joseph
Die Deutschen Heldensagen (The Sagas of German Heroes) 71
Die Freigabe der Vernichtung lebensunwerten Lebens (Allowing the Destruction of Worthless Life) 168–9
Diels, Rudolf 134
Dietrich, Otto 263–4
Dietrich, Sepp 311
Dirlewanger, Oskar 250–52
disabled people
  euthanasia 227–31
  gassing experiment 256–7
  killed by explosives 256
  medically sanctioned killings 168–9, 171–2
  Opfer der Vergangenheit (Victims of the Past) 172–3
  propaganda against 171–3
  sterilization 169–70
  veterans of First World War 168
  visits to asylums 171–2
  vulnerability to mistreatment 168
dopamine 180
Douglas, Professor Karen M. 19, 28, 265
Drake, Francis 165
Drexler, Anton 39, 41, 50–51, 51, 52
Dubois, Werner 230–31
Duesterberg, Theodor 117
Dühring, Eugen 41
Dunbar, Professor Robin 19
Dziekanka psychiatric hospital 232

Eagle's Nest 7
Eberl, Dr Irmfried 231, 237, 276
Ebermayer, Erich 140, 142, 143, 146
Ebert, Friedrich 27, 29, 35
Eckart, Dietrich 47, 53
Eglfing-Haar mental hospital 228
Ehlert, Herta 281
Eichmann, Adolf 198, 266, 289
Eicke, Theodor 148–9, 160–61
Einsatzgruppe A 237, 238
Einsatzgruppe B 252–3
Einsatzgruppen 209–10, 211, 212, 215,
    241, 273
  atrocities 234
  background of leaders 236–7
  members 237
  motivation 236–7
  murder of Jews 236–7, 252–3
  psychopaths 242
Einsatzkommandos 231, 247, 249
Eisenhower, General Dwight 312
Eisner, Kurt 29, 30–31
Elser, Georg 219–20, 223
enemies, valuing 181, 186–7, 337
escapism 287
eugenics 169–70
euphemisms 225–6, 228–9
European Recovery Plan 327
euthanasia
  child euthanasia scheme 228
  diffusion of responsibility 228
  of the disabled 227–31
  euphemistic language 228–9
  experts 270–71
  mentality of perpetrators 228, 229–30
  methods of 229
  see also gas chambers; killing,
      action of
Évian conference (1938) 199–201
  cynicism 200
  excluded countries 200
  exclusion of Palestine discussion 200
  hypocrisy 201–2
  limited value of 201
evolutionary psychology 6
Executive Order 9066 325–6

faith 161, 164, 179, 283
  exploiting 336–7
  Hitler's view 154–5, 292–3, 336–7
  Mussolini's view 293
  reason and 155
fake shower deception 229–30, 274–5,
    289–90
Falkenhorst, Colonel General 235
fear 212, 235–6, 249–50, 283–313, 340
Felder, Josef 127
Feldherrnhalle war memorial 65
Festinger, Professor Leon 284, 290, 296
First Reich 28
First World War
  artillery 14, 15–16, 25
  Austria *see* Austria
  battles 13–14, 23–4
  Central Powers/Russian peace
      treaties 21–2
  conspiracy theories 11, 13, 24
  deaths 13, 14
  Fourteen Points peace proposal 34
  Germany *see* German Army: First
      World War; Germany: First
      World War
  Ludendorff offensive 23–4
  missing soldiers 16
  modern weaponry 13–14
  revolution in warfare 14–15
  snipers 211
  trench warfare 14, 17
Fiske, Professor Susan 197–8
Flossenbürg concentration camp 254
Foch, Ferdinand 24–5
foot-in-the-door technique 266
France
  defeat 233
  military intelligence 221–2
  military strength 221–2
  panic of Bulson 233
  repelling Germany 221–2
Franco, Francisco 335
François-Poncet, André 148
Frank, Hans 49, 218, 269, 322, 323
Franz, Kurt 281
Frederick the Great 13

Freemasons 323
Freikorps 28, 29, 32, 33, 58, 62
Freisler, Roland 183
French Army 13
Frentz, Walter 253
Freud, Sigmund 146
Fritsch, General Werner von 190, 194
  concerns about Hitler's war plans 191
  exoneration 199
  removal from office 191
  scandal 192–3
Fritsch, Theodor 52
Fritzsch, Karl 257–8, 259
Fromm, Erich 241, 334
Fromm, General Friedrich 304
frontal cortex 92–3, 334
Frontbann 77
Frontgemeinschaft 46–7
Frontiers, Battle of the 13, 14

Galen, Clemens von 260–61, 262
gas chambers 255–6, 256–7, 260, 270–71, 271–2
  Bełżec 269–72, 273, 277–8
  Chełmno 267–9
  criticisms of 260
  experiments 256–7, 259
  fit and unfit for work 275
  psychological benefits for killers 229–30
gas vans 231–2, 252, 256, 267–8, 268–9
Gauleiters 227, 308
Gemlich, Adolf 41
German Army
  Army Group Centre 303, 304
  cooperation with Einsatzgruppen 215
  First World War
    deaths and casualties 24
    difficulties 14
    propaganda 25
    returning as heroes 27
    'stab in the back' lie 27–8
    successes 13–14, 24
  Hitler
    conspiracy against 301–6
    oath of allegiance to 154–5

    restoring to greatness 130
    support for 147–8
    support from 128–30, 132
    preeminence over Stormtroopers 147, 149
    war weariness 284–5
German Labour Front 177
German people
  concept of 128
  Germanness 12
  lack of desire for war 203
  moaning 178, 179
  support for Hitler 179
  togetherness 11–12
German Sixth Army 285
German Workers' Party 37, 39, 40
  Christianity and 47–8
  Hitler
    ridicules 40
    seventh member claim 39, 40
    unveiling of party programme 40, 42, 47–8
  renamed Nazi Party *see* Nazi Party
  socialism and 45
  Volksgemeinschaft 44–5
German youth
  education 93–5
  encouraged to join Hitler Youth 95
  superiority of German people 94–5
  see also Hitler Youth
Germany 232
  anti-transport strike 123
  authoritarianism 324–5
  deportation of Jews 267
  deportation of Polish Jews 206
  destruction of rule of law 152
  economic crisis 31, 63–4, 89–90, 92, 101
  economic recovery 74–5, 126
  emergency legislation 114
  existential threat 221
  First World War 21–4
    anti-Semitism 19–20
    armistice 25–6
    army *see* German Army
    bread rationing 18

census (1916) 19–20
dishonest media coverage of
 14, 27
humiliation of ruling classes 26–7
Jewish scapegoating 18–19, 20
mutinies 26
optimism 11–14, 24
protests 23, 26
shortages of food and supplies 35
surrender 25–7
treaty *see* Versailles, treaty of
foreign occupation of the Ruhr 55–6
government *see* Reichstag
hyperinflation 56, 63–4
importance of heroes 71
independence of states 12
industry 157
Kapp Putsch (1920) 63
May Day celebrations 62
nation of victims 165
National Assembly elections (1919) 29
pan-German movement 41
post-Second World War
 displacement from homes 327
 division 327
 leniency towards industrialists 328
 life after 327
 Marshall Plan 327
 rehiring of Nazis 327–8
potential attack by Poland 124
Prussian Interior Ministry 101
Reichsmark 69
Rentenmark 69
revolution
 Bavarian republic 29–30, 31, 32
 Beer-Hall Putsch 64–9, 64–72, 73,
  74, 77, 80, 205
 fear of 27
 Jewish scapegoating 30, 32
 killing of hostages 32–3
 Räterepublik in Munich 31–2
 riots 28, 29
 suppression of 29
Second World War
 Allied bombing of 287, 291, 294,
  297, 307

capitulation 315
claims of Allied corruption 320
concerns of army commanders
 221–2, 232, 233
death sentences to defeatists 294–5
declaration of war on America
 264–5
delays to invasions 232
firebombing of Hamburg 291
German POWs 318–19
heading towards catastrophe 306
Hitler *see* Hitler, Adolf: Second
 World War
hunger and starvation 317–18
invasion of Austria *see* Austria
invasion of Czechoslovakia 207
invasion of France *see* France
invasion of Poland *see* Poland
invasion of the Soviet Union *see*
 Soviet Union 234
Manstein's plan 232–3
mass suicides 315
Morgenthau Plan 317–18
plans to invade western Europe
 221–2, 232
protectors 316–17
public awareness of propaganda
 and reality 286
rape of women 315–17
Red Army invasion 307–8
'Werwolf' campaign 308–9
Spanish flu epidemic 31
unemployment 85, 90
unification 12, 20, 28–9, 41
universities 91
Weimar constitution
 Article 48 114, 115
 section 175 105–6, 118
Young Plan (1929) 89–90
Gersdorff, Rudolf-Christoph von 303,
 304, 305, 397n68
Gestapo 142, 176, 198
Gilbert, Gustave 321–2
Glaeser, Ernst 11
Globocnik, Odilo 269–70, 276–7
Gnade, Lieutenant 244

Goebbels, Joseph
  African film 88
  anti-parliamentary stance 87
  anti-Semitism 43, 76, 103–4
  appointed Minister for Popular
    Entertainment and
    Propaganda 145
  beliefs 75–6, 81, 87–8, 88–9
  burning bridges approach 309
  categorizing Poles 218
  concerns about psychological
    setback 263
  criticizes Dietrich 263–4
  criticizes German government 88
  defamation case 116
  destroying enemy's morale 287
  disability 75
  disapproval of lying 264
  elected Reichstag deputy 87–8
  emotional and intellectual conflict
    80–81
  girlfriend Else 43
  Hitler and 76, 83, 203
    on Hitler's speech 80–81
    love of 188–9
    trust in 306–7
  hypocrisy of 104
  imprisonment 87
  individual and public opinion 88
  influence of 8–9
  instilling fear 285
  Jewish filth slur 104
  justification of Kristallnacht 205–6
  large industry 157
  maligning enemies 87
  marriage to Quandt 113
  mentality 75
  Mussolini's departure 293
  Mussolini's make-believe life 300
  Nazism 76
  objects to Röhm's homosexuality
    106, 118, 119
  propaganda 18, 89, 104
    anti-Semitic films 157
    athletes 183
    atrocity propaganda campaign 286
    boring news 156–7
    cheerful topics 286–7
    control of press 145–6
    dangers of priests to children 174
    entertainment films 156
    false hope 306
    glosses over difficulties 291
    Hindenburg's endorsement of
      Hitler 139–40
    importance of 155, 156
    managing hatred 157
    mistake 285
    moving pictures 368–9n19
    political films 155–6
    primitive German public 263–4
    savageness of Bolsheviks 287–8
    simplicity and repetition 263–4
    'Total War' speech 285, 287
    whataboutism 286
  protest against Remarque's
    film 102–4
  public appeal for warm clothing 263
  risk of alienating Catholic
    soldiers 261
  socialism 80
  suicide 312–13
  target for opponents 106
Gomá y Tomás, Cardinal Isidro 335
Göring, Hermann 16, 123, 165
  acceptance of Hitler's plans 188
  accuses Allies of hypocrisy 322
  admits extermination of Jews 322
  Beer-Hall Putsch 67, 77
  connecting with Hitler 50
  deaths at Stalingrad 283
  disconnect in Nazi psyche 283–4
  fate argument 323
  hospitalization 67
  Leadership Principle 189
  meeting Hitler 50
  meeting of richest businessmen 133
  Nuremberg trials 188, 189, 210, 321,
    322, 323
  Reichstag fire 134–5
  Stormtroopers 77, 137
  support for Hitler 152

Grafeneck euthanasia centre 231
Greater German People's
    Community 74
Greiser, Arthur 267, 268
Grodziec ghetto 267–8
Groeben, Peter von der 302, 307
Groener, General Wilhelm 26, 115
Groening, Oskar 298, 320, 332, 403n4
Gross-Rosen concentration camp 254
Grossman, Dave 15–16
Grossmann, Willy 272
Grynszpan, Herschel 205, 206
Guderian, Heinz 35
Gulags 3
Günther, Professor Hans 164

Hackenholt, Lorenz 271–2
    Hackenholt Foundation 272
Hähnel, Bruno 43, 46, 171–2
Halder, General Franz 216, 217
    diary entry 222, 233
    fearful of attacking western Europe
        222, 223
    loyalty to Hitler 222
    loyalty to the army 223
Halifax, Lord 195
Hammerstein-Equord, Kurt von 129–31
Hanfstaengl, Putzi 68
Hartheim euthanasia centre 231
Hartl, Albert 174
Haslam, Professor Alex 70, 355n21
Hassebroek, Johannes 163
Hasselberg, Alfred 214–15
Heiden, Konrad 49
Heimsoth, Dr 118
Held, Heinrich, Minister-President of
        Bavaria 77, 141
Henderson, Sir Nevile 165, 173, 195, 200
Heredity and Racial Biology for Students
        (book) 94
heroism 333–4
    Hitler 70–71, 333
    leadership and 333
    personal heroism 72, 333
Hess, Rudolf 16, 83, 171
    Nuremberg trials 321

Heydrich, Reinhard 209, 337
    announcement of Final Solution
        272–3
    career 108
    command of Einsatzgruppen 209
    command of SD 109
    court of honour 108
    death 273
    discharged from the navy 108
    exposing 'perverted' priests 174
    family life 107–8
    head of police 142
    Jews
        assimilated 175
        hidden threat of 175
        Zionists 174–5
    joins Nazi Party 108–9
    Lina von Osten,
        engagement to 108
        letter to 214–15
        marriage to 113
    political activism 109
    Reinhard camps *see* Reinhard camps
    Transformations of Our Struggle (book)
        174
    view of politics 108
    violence of Nazis in Austria 197
Heymann, Lida Gustava 31
Hielscher, Margot 9
Hillers, Marta 316–17
Himmler, Heinrich 4–5, 269
    anti-Semitism 43
    appointed Minister of the Interior
        294
    appointed Reichsführer SS 107, 149
    appointment of Globocnik 270
    Beer-Hall Putsch 65–6
    benefits of living in poverty 297
    character and personality 76–7, 295–8
        hypocrisy and self-interest 311
        influenced by physical appearance
            109
        positivity 270
        second chances 109
        self-delusion 312
    chief of German police 141

Himmler, Heinrich – *cont'd.*
  decent behaviour 215
  ethnic cleansing operations 224–5
  fictional mental world 296–7
  fight against Bolshevism 110
  flees Germany 313
  funerals and deaths 161–3
  grandiose plans 110
  hatred of atheism 161
  hatred of Christianity 161
  Hitler's humiliation of 311
  ignores Dirlewanger's brutality 251–2
  Jews
    extermination of 267–8, 295
    justification of murders 295
    killing children 298
    reveals murders 295
  Nazism 76–7
  order to kill Polish insurgents 211
  planning for post-war life 311–12
  platitudes 224
  Posen speeches 294–6, 296–7, 299
  preparation for murder of Russians
      236
  procreation order 224
  protective custody 141
  racial fanaticism 227
  relationship with Heydrich 109
  relocation of ethnic Germans 225
  rescues Eicke 148–9
  rituals and ceremonies 161–2
  speech to killing squads 253
  SS
    belief system for 160–61, 161–3
    command of 107
    decency of 295–6, 297–8
    elite recruits 107–8, 110
    pride in 295, 297–8
  suicide 324
  superiority of Nordic blood 227
  vision of Greater Germanic
      Reich 294
  warped concept of decency 243, 250
  widening of killing policy 241–2
Hindenburg, President Paul von 101
  advisers 115
  appoints Papen as Chancellor 119–20
  approval of Young Plan 90
  death of 153, 154
  deflects blame 25, 27–8
  dislike of Nazis 116
  dismisses Brüning 119
  emergency decrees 114
  groupthink of allies 126
  'Hero of Tannenberg' 27, 28, 114
  Hitler
    appoints as Chancellor 125,
        126, 335
    control of as Chancellor 126
    endorsement of 139–40
    rejects Chancellorship bid 122–3
    view of 115, 116
  justifies executions 150–51
  libel action against Goebbels 116
  presses Kaiser for armistice 25
  responsibility for political crisis
      114–15
  stands for Presidential re-election
      116–17, 119
  support for new regime 132–3
Hingst, August 276
Hippler, Fritz 258
Hirschfeld, Magnus 146
Hitler, Adolf 6, 7, 17, 202
  anger at aristocracy 306
  anger at Brauchitsch 222–3
  anger at Drexler's merger proposal
      50–51
  anti-democracy 122, 133
  appeal to German youth 93
  appeal to power groups 132–3
  appointed Commander-in-Chief 192
  attempts on life 219–20, 222–3, 301–6
  Austrian homecoming 198–9
  basks in success of Olympics 185
  Beer-Hall Putsch 64–5, 67–9
    depression 68
    guilty of high treason 73
    imprisonment 68, 74
    release from prison 77
    sentenced to fortress
        imprisonment 74

trial 69–71, 72
beliefs
  anti-Semitism *see* Hitler, Adolf:
    Jews
  brute force 145
  classes 46
  on human nature 79
  National Socialism 45–6
  pan-Germanism 40–41
  positive Christianity 48
  role of women 112–13
  stupidity of the masses 155
  Volksgemeinschaft 44–8
benefits of Röhm's death 149
big business 133
Bolshevism
  commitment to annihilate
    Marxism 129
  hatred of 82, 132, 167, 185–6, 187
  lectures soldiers about 38
breach of the peace 69
burning bridges approach 309
Chancellor
  appointment as 100, 125, 126,
    127–8
  bid for 122–3, 124–5
  radio broadcast to German people
    131–2
character and personality
  belief in own genius 166–7
  bloated egotism 207
  certainty of thought 185–6, 189
  impulsiveness 61
  leadership qualities 70, 82–3, 189,
    292–3
  prizes loyalty 109, 177
Christianity 132, 140, 173
commitment to rearmament 157
competing pressures 64
confidential briefing to journalists
  204–5
control of capitalism and socialism 265
cooperation with right-wing
  groups 62
deal with Stalin 207–8
dictatorship 51, 127, 152, 192, 292–3

diplomatic strategy 195
either/or actions and arguments 51
enemies
  elimination of 149–50
  removal of 191–2
  value of 181, 186–7, 337
euthanasia order 229, 230
expansion of living space 129, 131,
  187, 191
faith 154, 155, 336–7
  emotion 154
  German's loss of 292–3
fictional past 37
German nation 12–13
German Workers' Party *see* German
  Workers' Party
hatred of cowardice 308–9
hero status 61, 70–72
illness 309–10
importance of army to 37
Jews 143
  accuses of plotting 143
  versus Aryans 51
  blames for Germany's problems
    41–2, 74, 143
  categorizes as a race 41, 42
  control of America 102, 265
  control of Bolsheviks 38, 42, 74
  death penalty for economic
    sabotage 187–8
  Gemlich letter 41, 42, 44
  hatred of 41, 74, 122, 143
  parasitic race 258–9
  prophecy 265–6
  removal of 42
  justifies executions 150–51
  leeching off Hindenburg 131–2,
    132–3, 139–40
  letters from followers 173
  Ludendorff and 63
  meeting with Hammerstein-Equord
    129–31
Mein Kampf 36, 39, 40, 41, 74, 129, 131,
  154, 164, 173, 346n7
misfit reputation 37
misjudgements of 115–16

Hitler, Adolf – *cont'd.*
  murder of disabled people 171
  Nazi Party *see* Nazi Party: Hitler
  offers hope to followers 49
  opposition to Versailles treaty 36
  people's car 178
  plan to conquer the east 129–30
  popularity 152
  Presidential election campaign 117–19
  proclaimed Head of State 154
  propagation of lies and myths 39–40, 41
  public support for 176
  purification of foreign influence 18–19
  racism 164
  re-entering the Rhineland 178–9
  recruitment of socialist soldiers 30
  rejection of homosexuality 119
  rhetorical skills 38, 40, 48–9, 52, 72, 186
  Second World War
    absence from public view 291–2, 293–4
    cognitive dissonance 312
    deception 204
    designs on Austria 194–5, 195–6
    fantasizing about wonder weapons 292
    fictional world 309–10
    grasping at straws 292
    hatred of Czechoslovakia 202
    key positions for trusted allies 294
    loss of prestige 203
    meeting to outline plans for war (1937) 190–91
    memo outlining inevitability of war 185–8
    plans to invade western Europe 221–2, 232
    rearmament expenditure 185, 187
    self-pity 292
    success by any means 187
    threat of America 264–5
    threat of the Soviet Union 234–5
    two-front war 234
    vulnerability 301
  speeches
    anti-Semitism 38
    Beer-Hall trial 70
    commitment to *Volksgemeinschaft* 131–2
    defeating communism 187
    eliminating the weakest 93
    exporting Jews 199
    false dichotomies 51
    international hypocrisy over Jews 201–2
    killings of enemies 151
    National Socialism 45–6
    power of 49–50
    psychological sequencing 206
    struggle and action 54
    sunk-cost fallacy, Löwenbräukeller, 1943 299–300
    winning at all costs 187
  sterilization law 169–70
  suicide 312
  supremacy of army over Stormtroopers 147–8
  Them and Us thinking 48, 51, 186–7
  using democracy 77
  value of radical thinking 167
  view of Poland 206–7
  wartime experiences 15
Hitler Youth
  appeal of Nazi Party 86–7, 91–2, 193
  appeal of Nazis' commitment to violence 92
  bonding 98
  growth of 91
  intimidation of teachers 98
  militarism of 99
  praised by prominent Englishmen 99–100
  pressure to conform 98
  psyche 99
  radicalization of 100
  undeveloped critical faculties 92–3
  violence 97–8
Hoche, Professor Alfred 168–9

Hofbräuhaus beer hall 40
Hoffmann, Johannes 32
Hofstadter, Professor Richard 135–6
Höhn, Professor Reinhard 163
Holocaust 42, 95, 127, 165, 167, 171, 325
    Allies' collective statement 286
    conspiracy theory 11, 332
    development of 262, 266–7, 272
    euphemism 225
    excuses by perpetrators 229, 286, 312,
        322, 329
    factories of murder 267
    incremental decision making 266
    mentality of perpetrators 230
    'special treatment' 225
    start of 272–3
Hölzel, Dr Friedrich 228
Höppner, Rolf-Heinz 266–7
Horn, Wolfgang 248–9
Höss, Rudolf 16, 57, 160, 247, 296
    imprisonment 58, 59
    justification of executions 319–20
    memoirs 58, 59
    murder of Kadow 57–8
    Nuremberg trials 322
    pleased with gas experiment 259
    reaction to conviction 59
    Them and Us thinking 60
    view of Globocnik 270
House of Romanov 20
Hugenberg, Alfred 23–4, 126
human rights 127, 152, 335–6
    dictators and 127
    elimination of 135
    'For the Protection of People and
        State' decree 137
hunter gatherers 6
hypocrisy 201–2

IG Farben 133
in-group 157, 162, 261–2
individualistic cultures 324
Ingolstadt demonstration 23
International Military Tribunal *see*
    Nuremberg trials
iron law of inequality 82

Israel 289
Italy 293, 300
    Italian Social Republic 300

Jagemann, Franz 97–8, 225, 226
Japan 264
Jaschke, Wilhelm 256
Jaspers, Karl 3
Jehovah's Witnesses 159–61
Jerusalem 5
Jesus 5
Jewish Question 41, 52, 93–4, 286
    fast-acting means of murder 267,
        268–9
    'Final Solution' 225, 266, 272–3
    gas vans 231–2, 252, 256, 267–8, 268–9
    radical solutions to 266–7
Jews 3
    in Austria *see* Austria: Jews
    categorized as a race 42
    conspiracy theories against *see*
        conspiracy theories: Jews
    dog attacks 281
    exclusion from *Volksgemeinschaft* 45
    Heydrich's categorization 174–5
    Himmler *see* Himmler, Heinrich:
        Jews
    Hitler *see* Hitler, Adolf: Jews
    murders
        by the Einsatzgruppen 236–7,
            252–3
        in Lithuania 238
        by the Romanian Army 238
        in Ukraine 238, 252
    Nazi Party *see* Nazi Party: Jews
    passivity of, accusation 288–9
    in Poland *see* Poland: Jews
    resistance 288, 290
    restrictions and restraints 20
    scapegoating of 18–19, 20, 30, 44
    shops and businesses boycotted 143,
        144
    in the Soviet Union *see* Soviet Union:
        Jews
    subject to attacks 143, 144
    theft from 198, 200, 226, 244–5, 296

Jews – *cont'd.*
    urban stereotyping of 20
    violence against 205–6
    see also anti-Semitism; Auschwitz;
        concentration camps; death
        camps; gas chambers; Holocaust
Jodl, General 202, 203, 290
Johnson, Samuel 309
Jud Süss (Jew Süss) 157, 368–9n19
Jührs, Robert 272
Jünger, Ernst 12, 17–18, 26
'just world' hypothesis 240–41, 278, 289

Kadow, Walther 57–8
Kahr, Gustav von 63, 64–5, 69
Kaina, Erwin 277
Kaiser *see* Wilhelm II, Kaiser
Karmi, Aharon 288
Katyn, forest of 287–8
Keitel, General Wilhelm 194, 199
Kelley, Douglas 321
Kellner, Friedrich 283
Kersten, Felix 311
Kielmansegg, Johann Adolf Graf von
        151, 154
killing, action of
    carbon monoxide poisoning 256–7
    at close range 16, 229, 255, 302, 339
    dehumanizing victims 243
    at a distance 15–16, 229, 339–40
    by explosives 256
    eye contact 244
    fake shower deception 229–30, 274–5,
        289–90
    gassing 255–6, 256–7
    insecticides 258–9
    lethal injection 254
    methods of 254–7, 267–9
    power of the group 245
    shared responsibility 16, 228, 229–30
    working to death 254
    see also euthanasia; Nazi killing
        squads
killing centres 230–31, 260
    see also death camps
Klein, Emil 12, 33, 283

on annexing Austria 196
anti-Semitism 42–3
Beer-Hall Putsch 65
on famine and inflation 56
Hitler's trial 70
joins Stormtroopers 55
on life in a concentration camp 319
organizing Hitler Youth 99
Volksgemeinschaft 46
Klemperer, Victor 139, 184
Klotz, Helmut 118
Kluge, Field Marshal 303
Kneissler, Pauline 279
Koch, Erich 48, 308
Konekamp, Eduard 213
Kowalczyk, August 259
Krantz, Erna 95
Kristallnacht 205–6
Kroll Opera House 140
Krupp 23, 157
Krupp, Alfried 328
Kube, Wilhelm 251
Küchler, Colonel General 235
Kursk, Battle of 291

Lächert, Hildegard 281
Landau, Felix 243
Landsberg prison 74, 77
Lange, Herbert 231–2
Langer, Walter 7
language 19
League of German Girls *see* BDM
        (Bund Deutscher Mädel)
Lechfeld military camp 38, 39
Leeb, General Wilhelm Ritter von 216
Lenin, Vladimir 21, 22, 81
    see also Bolsheviks; Bolshevism
Leviné, Eugene 20, 32, 127, 325, 339
Lewin, Kurt 401n32
Ley, Robert 177
Liebknecht, Karl 28, 29
Liebl, Fritz 214
Linn, Bernd 56, 107, 196, 207–8, 248,
        313, 329
Lipp, Dr Franz 32
Lippert, Michael 148

Lithuania 238
Littlejohn, Major General Robert 318
Łódź ghetto 213, 267
Lohengrin 186
Lohse, Dr Günter 128, 145, 166, 167, 325
Lonauer, Dr Rudolf 231
lone killers 219–20
loss aversion 121, 340
Lossow, General Otto von 62, 63, 120
    Beer-Hall Putsch 64–5, 69
    judgement of Hitler 72–3
Lubbe, Marinus van der 134, 136
Lüdecke, Kurt 52, 53, 78, 113
    cherry diet regime 53
    conversion to Nazism 49
    recollection of Hitler's speech 48–9
Ludendorff, General 25, 48, 62–3, 64,
        354n10
    acquitted of charges 73
    Beer-Hall Putsch 66
    Hitler and 63
    house arrest 66
    Ludendorff offensive 23–4
Luitpold gymnasium 32, 33
Lutz, Hubert 176
Luxemburg, Rosa 28, 29
Luxenburger, Professor Hans 169

Magill, Franz 242
Majdanek death camp 279, 281
Malitz, Bruno 181–2
Mann, Golo 22
Manstein, General Erich von 232, 304
Mao, Chairman 334
'March Violets' 142
Marne, First Battle of the 14
Marshall Plan 327
Marx, Karl 21
Marxism 45–6
Maschmann, Melita 210
Matthaei, Captain Fritz 24
Mattner, Walter 242
Mauthausen concentration camp 196,
        255
Mayer, Helene 182
Mayr, Captain Karl 37–8, 350n4

medical profession 167–8
    corruption of Hippocratic ideals 167
    economic self-interest 171
    future opportunities 171
    joining the SS 171
    members of Nazi Party 170–71
    sterilization 169–70
Mein Kampf (Hitler) 36, 39, 40, 41, 74,
        129, 131, 154, 164, 173, 346n7
Meinecke, Friedrich 11
Meinhold, Helmut 212
Meissner, Otto 115, 122
mental illness *see* disabled people
Merkl, Peter 44
Messersmith, George 181, 182
Metzner, Alfred 242
Meyer, Konrad 328
Milestone, Lewis 102
Milgram, Stanley 238–9
    Milgram experiment 239–40, 254
Minsk 252–3, 255
Moebius, Kurt 269
Moll, Otto 275
Moniz, Egas 7
Montgomery, Paul 339
Morell, Theodor 310
Morgen, Konrad 296
Morgenthau Plan 317–18
Mozart Hall 102
Müller, Heinrich 142
Münchener Post (newspaper) 106, 109
Münchhausen (film) 287
Münster 261, 262
Murr, Wilhelm 138
Mussolini, Benito 64, 87, 293, 300, 333, 335

National Socialism 45–6, 147, 171, 176,
        327
    see also Nazi Party
National Socialist German Students'
        Association 112
National Socialist German Workers'
        Party *see* Nazi Party
Nazi killing squads
    absolved of individual
        responsibility 243

Nazi killing squads – *cont'd.*
  'acting under orders' defence 246–7
  authority figure 241
  concentration camps 254
  drunkenness 244
  human mine detectors 251
  inability to accept responsibility 249
  Jewish women and children
      241–2, 243
  justification for actions 248–50
  mentalities of 238–40, 241, 243, 253
  murder of commissars 235, 254
  psychological damage 247–8, 252–3,
      255
  rape and pillage 251
  recruitment of poachers 252
  refusals 246–7
  sadists 242, 250, 251, 258
  systemic method 238
  theft 244–5
  see also killing, action of; SS
      (Schutzstaffel)
Nazi Party
  attacking Mozart Hall 102
  attacks on Catholic church 174
  banning of 74–5
  Beer-Hall Putsch 64–9
  'block wardens' 176
  book burning 146
  Christianity and 173–4
  comparison with Soviet Union
      oppression 176
  corruption 179
  Darwinian struggle for
      supremacy 166
  decision making without
      consequences 268
  dichotomy of consent 179
  dynamism 167
  educational propaganda 93–5
  financial disarray 125
  financial support from big business
      133–4
  Four-Year Plan 328
  fractured decision making 263
  General Plan for the East 328

Gold Party Badge 40
government
  general election (1928) 84
  general election (1933) 138–9
  general elections (1932) 121–2, 123
  participation in 124
  Thuringia electoral success
      (1929) 90
growing popularity of 101
Hitler
  appointed chairman 51–2
  balancing competing interests 144
  Bamberg conference 82–4
  broad concepts 50
  dictatorial powers 51–2
  humiliation of members 311
  nominates Rosenberg as successor
      67–8
  party of struggle and action 54
  provokes communists 55
  re-forming of 77–8
  rejection of socialism 82–3
  rejects land expropriation proposal
      82–3
  resignation from 51
  Us-ness 78
imprisonment of opponents 137–8
infighting 54, 166
intellectuals 163–6
Jews
  anti-Semitism 93–4, 184
  banned from sporting
      organizations 181–2
  shops and businesses boycotted
      143, 144–5
  targeting of 144
killing squads *see* Nazi killing
      squads
Kristallnacht 205–6
lifting of ban 77
members/membership 55, 85, 89, 91
  changes in allegiances 142
  doctors 170, 237
  'March Violets' 142
  mentalities of 4, 6, 8, 11
  opportunists 142

Index 421

reasons for joining 44
witnessing carnage of First World
  War 16
Nazism
  animal imagery 258
  appeal to young Germans 196
  Christianity and 47–8
  conspiracy theories see conspiracy
    theories
  eyewitness accounts 3–4, 5–6,
    344n3
  horrors of 5–6
  medicine and gardening 237
  purpose of 74, 102
  paramilitaries see Stormtroopers
  plans to combat communist uprising
    110–11
  police protection 86
  propaganda 101, 145
  protection rackets 146
  pseudo-Darwinian philosophy 88,
    91, 93–4
  Reichskonkordat 173–4
  rejection of Weimar Republic 56
  respect for British people 165–6
  revolution 103, 105
    Beer-Hall Putsch 64–9
    trial of army officers 105
  role of women 278–9
  socialism 80
  structural confusion 167
  swastika 55
  targeting the working class 177
  transcendent purpose 136
  transition to post-war life 310–11
  unachievable targets 268
  violence 54, 111
  Volksgemeinschaft 44–5
  women voters 111
  young members see Hitler Youth
  see also Einsatzgruppen; German
    Workers' Party; SS
    (Schutzstaffel)
Nazi personality type 7, 345n13
  German national character 324–5
  Goebbels 75, 76

Himmler 76–7, 109, 295–8
Hitler see Hitler: character and
  personality
psychological coping strategy 323
Rorschach test 321–2
unified personality type 7, 321, 322
Nazi–Soviet pact (1939) 207–8, 334
The Nazis: A Warning from History
  (documentary and book) 3
Nebe, Arthur 236, 255, 256, 257, 271
negative bias 175
Neithardt, Judge Georg 69, 73
Neu Beginnen (New Beginning) 99,
  177–8
Night of the Long Knives 149–50, 151
NKVD 287
Noble, John 318–19
Nollendorfplatz 103
Nolte, Heinrich 217
Nordic race 164, 174, 227
Noske, Gustav 29
Nuremberg rallies 93, 97, 201
Nuremberg trials 158, 189, 191, 194, 199,
  210, 238, 243
  Allied psychologists 321
  crimes against humanity offence 320
  defendants
    acting under orders defence 246–7,
      249, 257
    claiming innocence 230, 298–9
    disparate personalities 322
    Frank 322, 323
    Göring 322, 323
    Höss 322
    insanity test 321
    Nazi personality type see Nazi
      personality type
    Ribbentrop 322
    scapegoating among 323–4
    Streicher 323
  difficulties of definition and
    jurisdiction 320–21
  guilty verdicts 327
  labelled as show trials 261
  Rorschach test 321
  Stalin's murderous proposal 320–21

obedience experiment 239–40
Oberlindober, Hanns 168
Ohlendorf, Otto 163–4, 165, 236–7, 238
Olympia (film) 185
*On Killing: The Psychological Cost of
    Learning to Kill in War and Society*
    (Grossman) 15–16
Operation Bagration 304
Operation Harvest Festival 387n72
Operation Reinhard camps *see*
    Reinhard camps
Opfer der Vergangenheit (Victims of the
    Past) 172–3
Oppenheim family 31
Organization for German Students
    (Deutsche Studentenschaft) 146
Orwell, George 186
Osten, Lina von (later Heydrich) 108
  intelligence 114
  marriage to Heydrich 113
Ott, Alois Maria 68
Ott, Lieutenant Colonel Eugen 124
out-group 157
Oven, Wilfred von 155, 264
Owens, Jesse 182–3

Palestine 200–201
Papen, Franz von 119–20, 199
  anti-democratic credentials 121
  appointed Chancellor 119–20
  contempt for 120–21
  criticizes the Stormtroopers 148
  downfall of 124
  judgement of Hitler 120
  lacking legitimacy 120, 121
  motion of no confidence 123
  reverses ban on Stormtroopers 121
Pearl Harbor 264, 325–6
People's Court 183
personal heroism 72, 333
personality *see* Nazi personality type
Petzel, General Walter 215–16
Pfaller, Alois 23, 32, 86
  beaten unconscious 138
  flees to the Soviet Union 138
  on Nazi Party's electoral success 90–91

on unemployment 90
Pfannmüller, Dr Hermann 228
Pillau harbour 308
Pinochet, Augusto 242
Pokorny, Lieutenant Colonel 22
Pol Pot 334
Poland 4–5, 124, 206
  Nazi atrocities 209–10, 214–17, 235–6
  'Bloody Sunday of Bromberg' 210–11
  deportations of Poles 224–5, 226
  destruction of leadership class 213–14
  enemy propaganda 216
  ethnic cleansing 224–5, 226
  euthanasia of the disabled 227–31
  Nazi execution squads 214, 215, 216
  fear and revenge 212
  gassing experiments 231–2
  General Government 269, 270
  Germanization of 227, 268, 269
  intellectual approach 212–13
  investigation into excessive brutality
    214–15
  Jews
    blame on 212
    ghettoization of 213
    humiliation of 215–16, 217
    persecution and murder of 212,
      213, 214–16, 216–17, 225
    population of 213
    uprising 288–9
  justification for indiscriminate
    reprisals 212
  justification for invasion 209
  killing of ethnic Germans 210–11
  Operation Tannenberg 213–14
  partisan threat 211
  primitive and civilized peoples 212
  special security units 209–10
  support from Britain and France 207
  Them and Us thinking 226–7
  threat from Hitler 207
  uprising by freedom fighters 251
Polevoy, Boris 273
police force (German) 141–2
Polish Army 211
Porsche, Dr Ferdinand 178, 328

Potsdam 139
prisons 137–8
proportionality bias 136
Prussia 13
Prussian Secret State Police 178, 179
psychological research
  charismatic leadership 72
  cognitive biases 7
  collectivist cultures 324
  dehumanizing victims 243
  history 8
  Hitler's immediate success 38
  inconsistencies in conspiracy
    believers 265
  individualistic cultures 324
  'need to belong' 143
  pressure of group dynamic 245
  scapegoating 19, 28
  susceptibility of young people to
    Nazism 92
psychology 6–7
psychopaths 242

Quandt, Günther 146
Quandt, Harold 113
Quandt, Magda
  appearance 113
  intelligence 114
  marriage to Goebbels 113

Rabenalt, Arthur Maria 156, 287
Rachor, Carl 328
racial defilement 94
racism
  in America 183
  in Germany 164, 183, 339–40
  Hitler 164
  in Poland 209–26
  scholarly confirmation 164
  in the Soviet Union 234–5, 237–8
  SS (Schutzstaffel) 164
Radio Moscow 285
Rath, Ernst vom 205, 206
Ravensbrück concentration camp
  279–80, 281
Reagan, Ronald 326
Red Army 235, 236, 285

approach towards Germany 307–8
German reassessment of 290–91
murder and rape 315–17
Operation Bagration 304
vengeance 315–16
refugees 200
Reichenau, Colonel Walther von 129,
  130–31
Reichsflagge 62
Reichskriegsflagge group 65–6
Reichsnährstand 188
Reichstag 87, 114
  burning of 134–5, 136
  dissolution (1932) 123
  Enabling Act 140–41, 143
  fire decree 137
  general election (1924) 77–8
  general election (1928) 84
  general election (1930) 115
  general election (1933) 138–9
  general elections (1932) 121–2, 123
  Law Concerning the Head of State of
    the German Reich (1934) 154
  Law for the Prevention of
    Hereditarily Diseased Offspring
    169–70, 171
  Law for the Restoration of the
    Professional Civil Service 141
  motion of no confidence 123
Reichswehr 115, 124
  distrust of Stormtroopers 128–9
  Hitler's assurances to 130
  Hitler's vision 129–30
Reinhard camps 273, 275, 276
  see also Bełżec death camp; Sobibór
    death camp; Treblinka death
    camp
Remarque, Erich Maria 16–17, 18,
  102–4, 146
Remer, Major Otto-Ernst 305
Renno, Dr Georg 230
Reserve Police Battalion 244
resistance 218–19
  alternative belief system 261–2
  elimination of 209, 211, 337–8
  genetic component 218

resistance – *cont'd.*
  Jews 288, 290
  psychological reality 220
  psychology of 215
Reski, Waltraud 315
Reynaud, Paul 233
Rheinwiesenlager 'Rhine Meadow
    camps' 318
Ribbentrop, Joachim von 167, 200, 322
Richter, Herbert 24, 25
Riefenstahl, Leni 185
Ringelblum, Emanuel 213
Röhm, Ernst 13, 14, 61, 77
  appalled at revolution 29–30
  appointed Chief of Staff of the
      Stormtroopers 105
  armed insurrection 62
  arrest 148
  Beer-Hall Putsch 65–6
  cleansing of Munich 33
  contentious article 147
  creation of Frontbann 77
  disfigurement 15
  execution of 148, 149
  fighting with Rosenberg 118–19
  homecoming 105
  homosexuality 105–6, 118, 151
  illness 148
  imprisonment 66
  membership of right-wing groups 61
  opposition to section 175 118
  probation 73
  relationship with Hitler 78, 79
  resignation from Frontbann 78
  resignation from Stormtroopers 78
  scandal 118–19
  supremacy of Stormtroopers over
      army 147–8
  wartime experiences 15
Romanian Army 238
Rommel, Lieutenant Colonel Erwin 99
Roosevelt, President Franklin D. 264,
    265, 321, 325
  convenes international conference
      199–200
  hypocrisy 201

Rorschach test 321–2
Rosenberg, Alfred 67–8, 74, 79, 81,
    118–19
Rossi, Maria Otero 225
Rüdiger, Jutta
  appeal of national socialism 111–12
  impressed by Hitler's speech 112
  indoctrinating German girls 95–6
  inspired by Hitler 96
  leader of the BDM 95, 112
  on motherhood 112
  on racial segregation 97
  on setbacks 283
Rumbold, Sir Horace 127, 145
Russia
  armistice with Germany 21
  Brest-Litovsk treaty 22
  civil war 20–21
  Provisional Government 20–21
  see also Soviet Union
Russian Revolution 21–2, 81
Rzgów ghetto 267–8

Sachsenhausen concentration camp 160,
    254–5
Sackett, Frederic 137
sadism 242, 250, 251, 258
St Petersburg 20
Salomon, Franz Pfeffer von 81–2
Sapolsky, Professor Robert 38, 92, 93,
    104, 180, 198, 240
Schacht, Hjalmar 133, 323
Scheidemann, Philipp 35
Schenk, Mathias 251
Schicksalsgemeinschaft 'community of
    fate' 307
Schlabrendorff, Fabian von 302–3
Schlageter, Albert 58
Schleicher, General Kurt von 115, 129
  appointed Chancellor 124
  conspires with Nazis 124
  execution of 150
  objects to Papen 124
Schluch, Karl 271–2
Schmidt, Charlotte 194
Schmidt, Otto 192

Schmitt, Professor Carl 152
Schmundt, Major Rudolf 193
Schroeder, Manfred von 131
Schultz, Erwin 248
Schumann, Dr Horst 231
Schuschnigg, Kurt 194–5, 196
Schutzstaffel (Protection Squad) *see* SS
SD (Sicherheitsdienst) 109, 163, 176, 300
Sebottendorff, Rudolf von 30, 31
Second Reich 28–9
Second World War
    America *see* United States of America
        (USA)
    Austria *see* Austria
    Czechoslovakia 202, 203, 207
    D-Day 304
    France *see* France
    Germany *see* Germany: Second
        World War
    Hitler *see* Hitler: Second World War
    Poland *see* Poland
Seibert, Willi 247
Seisser, Colonel Hans von 63
    Beer-Hall Putsch 64–5, 69
self-determination 34
Shakespeare, William 165–6
Sicherheitsdienst (Security Service) *see*
    SD (Sicherheitsdienst)
Six, Franz 163, 164, 165
6th SS Panzer Army 311
Slavic states 164, 165
Smoleń, Kazimierz 254
Sobibór death camp 271, 273, 274–5,
    277–8, 290
Social Democratic Party (SPD) 29, 32,
    110, 117, 140–41, 152
social psychology 238–9
socialism 45, 80
Solmitz, Luise 135, 364n17
Sonderkommando 275–6
Sonnenstein euthanasia centre 259–60
Soviet Union 81, 234
    German invasion (Second World
        War) 234
        atrocities 234, 235, 237–8, 251
        Battle of Kursk 291

Battle of Stalingrad 283–4, 285
dead bodies at Katyn 287–8
deadlock 263
Dietrich's message of victory
    263–4
killing squads *see* Nazi killing
    squads
Operation Typhoon 262
partisan threat 248–50
racism 234–6, 237–8
Red Army counter-attack 264
Russians perceived as animals
    235–6
victory at Kiev 262
war of extermination 234–5
Jews
    murder of 236, 238, 243, 244, 249
    murder of women and children
        241–2, 243, 248, 250
    theft from 244–5
Komsomol 334
terror and purges 175–6
women fighters 279
see also Russia
Spanish Civil War 335
Sparta 93
Spaun, Fridolin von 26–7, 28, 34
Speer, Albert 298–9, 310–11, 321
SS (Schutzstaffel) 106–7
    army officers' objections 215–16
    atrocities against civilians 215–16, 226
    Auschwitz 278
    boasting of killings 215
    concentration camps 158–9, 160,
        254–5
    distinction from Stormtroopers 107
    elite recruits 163–4
    execution squads 214, 215
    fight against Bolshevism 110
    Himmler *see* Himmler, Heinrich: SS
    motto 107
    murders in error 150
    Operation Reinhard camps 276
    punishment 329
    racism 164
    recruitment of doctors 171

SS (Schutzstaffel) – *cont'd.*
  selection for gas chambers 275
  sexual relations
    with 'ethnically alien population'
      294, 297
    with wives of conscripted soldiers
      224
  theft 226, 296
  varying behaviours of 275–6
Stadelheim prison 149
Stalin, Joseph 4, 189–90, 207–8, 220, 337
  Moscow show trials 321
  Nuremberg trials proposal 320–21
  purges 175, 176, 190, 338
Stalingrad, Battle of 283–4, 285
Stanford prison experiment 280
Stangl, Franz 270, 276–7, 288–9
Staub, Professor Ervin 267, 324
Stauffenberg, Claus von 304, 305, 338
Stennes, Walter 106
sterilization 169–70
Sterneckerbräu beer hall 37
Stolen Child, The (film) 4–5
Storm of Steel (Jünger) 17
Stormtroopers 49, 54, 65, 86, 121, 261
  abuses 146–7
  arrest of leaders 148
  auxiliary police 137
  banning of 77
  criticisms of 148
  disrupting opponents' meetings 54
  enforcing boycott of Jewish shops
    144–5
  expansion of 147
  growing power of 147
  homosexuality 151
  importance to Hitler 106
  parades 128
  potential liability 106
  provoking opponents 54–5
  purge against 149–50
  unpopularity of 148
Strasser, Gregor 124, 150
  Beer-Hall Putsch 80
  First World War 80
  resigns from Nazi Party 124, 125

  reworking the Nazi programme
    82–3
  socialism 80
Streckenbach, Bruno 237, 248
Streicher, Julius 16, 52–3, 79, 157–8
  anti-Semitism 52–3, 157–8
  in awe of Hitler 52, 53
  Beer-Hall Putsch 66–7
  character of 53–4
  cherry diet regime 53
  debts 53
  'Jewish Murder Plot' article 158
  joins Nazi Party 53
  Nuremberg trials 323
  propaganda newspaper 53
  theories 53
Strength through Joy (Kraft durch
    Freude) 177–8
Stresemann, Gustav 63
Stülpnagel, General 221
Suchomel, Franz 277
Sudetenland 202, 203
Suggestions on How to Conduct a Funeral
    (booklet) 161–2
Sulzbach, Herbert 24
sunk-cost fallacy 299–300

Tannenberg, First Battle of 213–14
Tavor, Moshe 289
Teubert, Wolfgang 85, 137
  boycott of Jewish shops 144–5
  disrupting political meetings 85–6
  fighting communists 92
  justification of Nazism 329
  Strength through Joy 177
  superficial anti-Semitism 85
  Volksgemeinschaft 85
Teutonic Order 214
Teutons 161
Thälmann, Ernst 117
Them and Us 60, 104
  asylums 172
  dichotomizing 38–9
  dictators 333
  ethnic cleansing 226
  Germans and Poles 209–10

Hitler 48, 51, 186–7
Höss 60
Poland 226–7
psychological power of 135
rapid assessment 332–3
Russians 235–6
soldiers 338
Them-ness 258, 333
Us-ness 70, 78, 189, 333
Volksgemeinschaft 45–6, 48, 55
Thiepval monument 16
Third Reich
golden era 3, 9
idea of 28–9
Thompson, Dorothy 115–16
Thule Society 30, 31, 67
time and place 4–5
Tito, Marshal 333
Tooby, Professor John 6
Tooze, Professor Adam 187
Transformations of Our Struggle
(Heydrich) 174
Treblinka death camp 237, 271, 273, 275,
276, 277, 288–9
clean-up operation 277
destruction of 277–8
implosion of 276
rotting bodies 276–7
Tresckow, Major General Henning von
301–2, 303
Triumph of the Will (documentary) 68
Trotsky, Leon 21
Tsar 20–21

Ukraine 21–2, 238, 252, 262
United States of America (USA) 22–3
American Office of Military
Government 327
Civil Liberties Act 326
land grab 322
racial discrimination 183
Second World War
apology to Japanese interns 326
entry into 264–5
Executive Order 9066 325–6
internment 325–6

stock market crash (1929) 89–90
University of Tübingen 91

Varanasi 5
Venezia, Morris 275–6
Versailles, treaty of 33–6
alterations to 195
German anger 34–6, 49–50
loss of territory 34, 209
reparations 34, 55, 89, 126
unfairness of 195
war guilt clause 34–5
Victor Emmanuel III, King 335
Viding, Professor Essi 194, 218, 220,
247, 249
völkisch movement 20, 77–8
Völkischer Beobachter (newspaper) 59, 67,
79, 102–3, 105, 143, 210
Volksgemeinschaft 'people's community'
76, 80, 143, 156, 178
anti-Semitism and 44
concept of 44–5, 46, 47, 95
existence in the mind 179
fading of 308
Frontgemeinschaft and 46–7
in-group of Germans 157, 162, 261–2
Hitler 47–8, 122, 132, 147, 336
hope of German people 44
indoctrination of German girls 95
journey towards 180
misunderstandings of 45–6
out-group of Jews 157
psychological power 180
statement of intention 179
Teubert 85–6
Them and Us 45–6, 48, 55
unfulfilled promises 178
vagaries of 179
value to Nazis 46
Volkswagen 178
Vorwärts (newspaper) 110, 117
Vossische Zeitung (newspaper) 102, 110

Waffen SS 3
Wagner, Adolf 260
Wagner, Dr Gerhard 170, 172

Wagner, Eduard 209
Wagner, Richard 71, 186
Wall Street Crash (1929) 89–90
Wandervogel 91
warnings 3–4
Warsaw ghetto 213, 288–9
Wason, Peter 275
Watson, John 7
Weber, Max 72, 292, 333
Wehrmacht 196, 211, 248, 262–3, 263
Weimar Republic 56
Weiss, Dr Bernhard 87
Weiss, Martin 243
Weizmann, Chaim 199
Weizsäcker, Ernst von 203
Wels, Otto 140–41
Wessing, August 262
Westarp, Countess Heila von 32
Weygand, Maxime 25
whataboutism 286
Widmann, Dr Albert 229, 255–6, 257, 271, 387n11
Wiedemann, Fritz 167
Wilhelm II, Kaiser 26–7
    abdication 26–7
    flees Germany 26–7
    German nationalism 12
    refuses to fight 26–7
Willenberg, Samuel 275
Wilson, President Woodrow 33–4
Wilson, Sir Arnold 99–100, 359n41
Wilson, Woodrow 34–5

Winterton, Lord 200
Wirth, Christian 270–71, 276–7
Wolff-Mönckeberg, Mathilde 320
Wolff, Theodor 28
A Woman in Berlin (Hillers) 316
women
    Aufseherinnen (overseers) 279–80, 281
    crimes in occupied territories 279
    cruelty and brutality 281–2
    disparities of violence perpetrated 281
    nurses administering euthanasia 279
    role of 278–9
    transformation of 280
    uniforms 280
    work 279
workers 177
World War I *see* First World War
World War II *see* Second World War

Yale University 239–40
Young, Owen 89
Young Plan (1929) 89–90
youth
    brain development 85, 92–3, 334
    corrupting 85–100, 334
    see also Hitler Youth

Zelionka, Petras 244
Zimbardo, Philip 280
Zöberlein, Hans 102
Zuckmayer, Carl 18
Zyklon B 258, 259, 274, 281